Changing Parties

Changing Parties

An Anthropology of British Political Party Conferences

Florence Faucher-King

First published 2005 by
PALGRAVE MACMILLAN
Houndmills, Basingstoke, Hampshire RG21 6XS and
175 Fifth Avenue, New York, N.Y. 10010
Companies and representatives throughout the world

PALGRAVE MACMILLAN is the global academic imprint of the Palgrave Macmillan division of St. Martin's Press, LLC and of Palgrave Macmillan Ltd. Macmillan® is a registered trademark in the United States, United Kingdom and other countries. Palgrave is a registered trademark in the European Union and other countries.

ISBN-13: 978–1–4039–0462–1 hardback
ISBN-10: 1–4039–0462–6 hardback

This book is printed on paper suitable for recycling and made from fully managed and sustained forest sources.

A catalogue record for this book is available from the British Library.

Library of Congress Cataloging-in-Publication Data
Faucher-King, Florence.
   Changing parties : an anthropology of British political party conferences / Florence Faucher-King.
      p.   cm.
   Includes bibliographical references and index.
   ISBN 1–4039–0462–6 (cloth)
   1. Political parties—Great Britain—Congresses.   2. Great Britain—Politics and government—Congresses.   I. Title.
   JN1117 F38 2005
   306.2′ 6′ 0941—dc22   2005048057

10   9   8   7   6   5   4   3   2   1
14   13   12   11   10   09   08   07   06   05

Printed and bound in Great Britain by
Antony Rowe Ltd, Chippenham and Eastbourne

To Rich and Lila

Contents

Glossary and List of Abbreviations or Acronyms

BNFL	British Nuclear Fuel
Board	Supreme decision-making body (Conservative party)
CAC	Conference Arrangement Committee (Labour party)
CLP	Constituency Labour Party
Composite	Policy documents composited from different motions that were debated by the Labour Conference prior to the adoption of Partnership in Power in 1997
CPC	Conservative Policy Centre
CPF	Conservative Policy Forum
FPC	Federal Policy Committee (Liberal Democrats)
FCC	Federal Conference Committee (Liberal Democrats)
GMC	General Management Committee of a Constituency Labour party (Labour party)
GPEx	Green Party Executive
IPPR	Institute for Public Policy Research (think tank)
JPC	Joint Policy Committee (Labour party)
MfSS	Manifesto for a Sustainable Society (Green Party)
NGO	Non-Governmental Organisation
NEC	National Executive Committee (Labour party)
NPF	National Policy Forum (Labour party)
NU	National Union of Conservative Associations
OMOV	One member one vote
OWOW	"Other Ways of Working", Green Party working group
PLP	Parliamentary Labour Party
PolCom	Policy Committee (Green Party)
PPC	Prospective Parliamentary Candidate
Quangos	Quasi autonomous non-governmental organisations
RSPB	Royal Society for the Protection of Birds
SOC	Standing Orders Committee (Green Party)
TU	Trade Union
WWF	World Wildlife Fund, now called The Global Conservation Organisation

Acknowledgments

The research in this book could not have been undertaken without the assistance of numerous people and organisations. I would like to thank the Conservative Party, the Green Party, the Labour Party and the Liberal Democrats for granting me access to their conferences and to other meetings. I am indebted to many party activists and staff who welcomed me and shared their views and experiences with me and to the journalists, lobbyists and campaigners who spoke to me and answered my queries. They cannot all be named but I would like to thank them all and especially Arlene Ryan, Chris Poole, Penny McCormack and Don Smith who opened doors for me. I also want to thank Jon Sopel, George Pascoe-Watson and Ivan Rudd. Special thanks to Willie Sullivan and John Taylor for long conversations and their friendship. A special mention should be made of Mike Woodin, a friend and admirable politician, whose untimely death is a great loss not only to friends and family but also to politics in general. This research was made possible by the support of Saint Peter's College, the Maison Française at Oxford, the Politics Department of Stirling University and the CEVIPOF at Sciences Po, Paris. The Robert Schumann and Jean Jaurès Foundations contributed some additional funds. Gavin Williams and Vernon Bogdanor provided precious support when I was trying to define my project and "infiltrate" British parties. Finally, I would like to thank the following friends and colleagues: Stephen Ingle was of great support as Head of Department, colleague and friend. He also had the patience to read through earlier drafts and provided extremely valuable comments. Paul Whiteley encouraged me from the very start on this long exploration of British parties and even considered possibilities of a joint research project. I am sorry we never made it to the Young Conservatives Ball! He provided insightful reading of very rough drafts of this book. I thank Florence Haegel, Nicolas Sauger and Ariane Chebel d'Appollonia for their helpful suggestions on various drafts. Nina Eliasoph, whose own work was an important step in the development of my argument, has offered valuable remarks on several chapters. Special thanks to Eric Shaw for his extremely helpful suggestions on the final draft and at very short notice.

Thanks to my parents for their infallible support throughout and particularly in the last couple of years of this project. Finally, special thanks to Rich without whom this book would not be the same. He relentlessly encouraged me to find my own voice and provided innumerable insightful comments in discussions and detailed reading of drafts. Thank you for your love, for making me laugh and for your support through tough times. Any errors are of course my responsibility alone.

1

An Anthropological Approach to "Conventional Politics"

When I arrived in Britain in the mid-1990s, I was struck by the peculiarity of British political party conferences. These annual gatherings are familiar to any observer of British politics. For over a century, they have temporarily diverted attention away from Westminster and towards the seaside resorts of Britain. Every autumn, media attention is focused for about a month on internal party politics. British party conferences do not have the *gravitas* of party congresses in continental Europe where the emphasis is on crucial strategy decisions and executive renewal.[1] Nevertheless, they attract thousands of participants and are considered sufficiently important that all parties are prepared to divest substantial sums to hold such meetings in full media glare. It is virtually impossible to conceive of political life in Britain without thinking of party political life. One can argue that annual conferences contribute to reinforcing the central position of political parties because they highlight their extra-parliamentary existence and allow these organisations to address voters beyond the confines of specific electoral campaigns.

Conferences are taken for granted as a feature of British political life, which is perhaps why they are, at the same time, dismissed as internal affairs with little importance for the polity as a whole. This attitude has become so entrenched that observers of the British political scene have become oblivious to what remains one of the most intense periods of activity in the political year. This relative lack of interest is reflected in the few works that have been dedicated to them. There are two academic exceptions: Lewis Minkin published an exhaustive study of the Labour conference in 1978, and in 1989 Richard Kelly produced a study of the Conservative conference "system". Both focused on a single party. This project is different: I am interested in what these *apparently* archaic and arcane events reveal about particular ways of

1

thinking about politics and practising it. Rather than concentrate on a single organisation, I compare the three main parliamentary parties with the much smaller and politically marginal Green Party. Beyond the idiosyncrasies of individual parties (some of which I intend to show reveal specific "group styles"), conferences can also help us understand British modes of dealing with politics: they are windows into the transformations undergone by British parties and by British society since the 1990s. Conferences play a central role in the life of each party and are therefore crucial in any process of change. They adopt reforms; they effect, and reflect, change. I wish to invite the reader on a *détour* (Balandier, 1985) to the enchanted and un-chartered territories of off-season British seaside resorts.

Where there has been a strong impulse to demonstrate the hard scientific dimension of the discipline, political science has developed models imported from economics. Partly as a consequence of this, the concept of culture remains controversial within the field. Some have argued that "the analysis of group values or customs such as those associated with the term culture [is] irrelevant to political inquiry" and "symbolic displays and rhetorical practices are epiphenomenal" (Przeworski quoted by Wedeen, 2002: 714) or that culture is the "fallback to explain apparently irrational behaviour" (Kuper, 1999: 10). When culture is considered relevant, the concept is predominantly approached and operationalised in two ways. First, following Weber and Parsons, culture is said to be linked to "deeply held" values that shape action because they provide the ends towards which these actions are oriented. This allows a survey-based approach to culture-as-(relatively-fixed)-values that makes cross-national comparisons possible (Almond and Verba, 1963; Inglehart, 1990). Here, culture is given an explanatory role in comparative politics whilst numbers and regressions provide the impression that results are "objective", that is consistent with scientific standards. Such an approach misses the complexity of contexts of interactions and tends to reduce culture to cognitive items that can be more easily made explicit. Second, interpretativist approaches reject or at least wish to supplement such standards of verification in favour of plausibility and largely build from Geertz's concept of culture as symbolic action, emphasising the need for a "thick-description" of events and social contexts (Geertz, 1993; Scott, 2003; Welch, 1993), with a strong focus upon the underlying "meaning" of such actions. The danger with this latter approach lies in overlooking the processes by which ongoing practices and systems of meaning are constantly changing and thus in taking culture as a coherent body or homogeneous system of meanings. Indeed, many "political scientists (...) think of culture as connoting fixed group traits" (Wedeen, 2002: 716). Such a conceptualisation of culture has been of little explanatory power and misses the diversity and the constant evolution of understandings, experiences, practices and interpretations within a group. Indeed, as Richard King puts it,

> cultures are not homogeneous and static entities or essences (...); rather they are historically evolving processes, which are distorted if they are reified. In so far as a culture persists, it is constantly subject to revisions, reinterpretations and transformations of one kind or another (King, 1999: 79).

I believe political science can learn from recent work in sociology and anthropology which takes culture as consisting of symbols and practices that help people create meanings for themselves. This move does not imply that there is an intrinsic, hidden structure of meaning that can be decoded by the outside observer.[2] The processes through which meanings are constructed involve experiences and interactions, and their effects. People are informed by conventions (Berger and Lückmann, 1984) but they also improvise, adapt and interpret them (de Certeau, 1990; Goffman, 1990).

It is not possible to study human societies in the same manner as we study the natural world precisely because, as Max Weber put it, man is suspended in webs of signification he has himself spun. Indeed, a narrow instrumentally rational reading of political behaviours misses the fact that human behaviour is multi-layered, culturally mediated and not admissible to a purely rationalist explanation in all instances. Moreover, it relies on the implicit idea that there is a universal underlying means/ends schema that governs actions and that culture shapes behaviours by defining what people want (Swidler, 1986: 274). It is more fruitful to see culture as a repertoire of prefabricated chains of actions (rather than individual acts) that can be strategically used according to circumstances. "People developing new strategies of action depend on cultural models to learn styles of self, relationships, co-operation, authority and so forth" (Swidler, 1986: 279) but on the other hand, there are often gaps between explicit norms and actual practices because culture does not impose a single unified pattern of action. Individuals and groups are "reluctant to abandon familiar strategies of action". Thus, they tend to construct their strategies from limited repertoires and appear to "cling to cultural values".[3]

Party conferences are not the place where collective beliefs are enacted but rather where some British political repertoires of action are elaborated and transmitted. Comparing these group styles points to the competing repertoires and ideologies articulated and promoted by different political parties. The resilience of the conference season reflects an attachment to political strategies revolving around parties in a representative democracy that is structured by the predominant role of Parliament. However, the weight of the executive in a dominant one-party-government has dramatically increased under the premiership of Margaret Thatcher and then with Tony Blair. Since 1997, Labour has imposed tight discipline upon a huge majority in the House of Commons as well as its grassroots. Moreover, policy networks have opened up new spaces for public debate beyond Westminster. Conferences provide the framework in which new practices of political deliberation and communication can emerge. "When people are learning new ways of organising individual and collective action, practising unfamiliar habits until they become familiar, then doctrine, symbol and ritual directly shape action" (Swidler, 1986: 278). In other words, it is in periods of change that culture plays its most important role because it provides a form of traditional support and justification that is both resilient and flexible.

To gain a proper understanding of how British political parties have changed, one must consider broader trends within British society. Deference has been eroded through social mobility and the decline of class-based politics.[4] The Thatcher revolution facilitated the development of a new kind of entrepreneurial individualism, challenging traditional hierarchies and communities. Information technologies and mass media culture have contributed to a further individualisation through mass-marketing techniques. "Private enterprise" has become the dominant model for making sense of collectivities and social organisations. Individuals are seen as consumers and treated as such in all sectors of life from education to politics. From private businesses to universities, social services and local government (Le Galès, 2004; Newman, 2001; Power, 1999), the same approach to management applies, with its obsession with audits and standards. Like every other major organisation in modern Britain, political parties require a written framework document and a paper trail to establish a "benchmark" for accountability (Sklair, 2001). This cultural shift is exhibited in changing attitudes to authority, legitimacy and the self and reflects a move towards a highly rationalised and entrepreneurial conception of the human being (Rose, 1999). If party members have become stakeholders[5] and citizens are now to be treated as consumers, then it is hardly surprising if their loyalty to political organisations is as limited as their loyalty to brands and outlets. How can one mobilise them for the public good (Hirschmann, 2002)?

The politics of rituals

If many political scientists are sceptical about how useful the concept of culture might be for understanding modern political practices, even more neglect the insights to be gained from anthropology.[6] In particular, it can be interesting to consider the symbolic dimensions of politics that sometimes escape the modern westerner's gaze precisely because of the tendency to become preoccupied with instrumental actions. Western cultural prejudices tend to associate rituals with far away, "primitive" groups while developed societies are seen as modern, rational and "disenchanted". However, "there can be no politics without symbols, nor without accompanying rites" (Kertzer, 1988: 181) and this also is true of modern societies. Political analysts sometimes seem to fear that talking about rituals might divert attention away from the "real world" of secularised societies or from the study of power[7] – as if power could be abstracted from its social embeddedness (Foucault, 1984) or as if rituals were not thoroughly infused with, and constitutive of, power relationships (Bell, 1992: 215; Bourdieu, 2001; Wedeen, 1998). Belief in the inherent rationality of mainstream western politics is so powerful that most political anthropologists search for an "Other" (Badie and Sadoun, 1996) or focus on the "margins", such as David Kertzer on the Italian Communists (1996), Marc Abélès (1989) on politics in rural France (Abélès, 1989) or myself (1999a) on the Greens. Few have followed the example of Abélès in studying mainstream political institutions such as the French *Assemblée Nationale* and the *European Parliament* (Abélès, 1999, 1992 respectively).

In this book, I propose to analyse mainstream parties partly in an attempt to demonstrate that the exoticism of non-instrumental and ritual practices is everywhere amongst us. My aim is to "exoticise" modern western polities and denaturalise the world that we would otherwise take for granted. I have turned my attention to Britain because as a native of France its political culture is both familiar and unfamiliar to me. This has allowed me to raise questions that might remain unformulated by a "native". The political culture of modern Britain, however, is sufficiently akin to my own background to gain an appreciation of subtle cultural differences and different group styles within each organisation. It is indeed easier to see "strangeness" in the everyday political practices of "others":

> The famous anthropological absorption with the (to us) exotic (...) is, thus, essentially a device for displacing the dulling sense of familiarity with which the mysteriousness of our own ability to relate perceptively to one another is concealed from us. (...) Understanding a people's culture exposes their normalness without reducing their particularity (Geertz, 1993: 14).

Of course, this *détour* calls for a *retour* to one's own political culture and context with new questions and a fresher look at a world that for this reason can no longer be taken for granted. Sadly, there is not enough space to offer comparative reflections or a cross-national dimension to my analysis of British political parties. The breadth of such analysis would inevitably be to the detriment of its depth.[8]

Debates in anthropology about what constitutes ritual have been complex and contested (Bell, 1992, 1997). For the purpose of this analysis, I will take ritual to denote behaviour that is repeated, rule-bound, referring to ongoing traditions or otherwise invoking a reference point that transcends the narrow framework of a choosing and acting individual. It is executed with a sense of itself as a performance – as an event that is on display. Rituals have generally come to be understood as referring mainly to non-instrumental forms of action that have a clearly communicative dimension related to the use of symbols (Asad, 1993: 60; Bell, 1992: 25). There are a number of practices enacted at conference that can be analysed through the lens of ritual studies. With their repetitiveness, their set speeches and rules, their well-defined roles and decorum, British party conferences are more than mere customs or ephemeral performances of seaside gladiatorial jousting. Conferences are all the time being actively reinvented and transformed, associated with new symbols and new phases of representative government.

Like the question of which came first the chicken or the egg, the anteriority of myth or ritual has long been discussed. The dominant view – that myths are the source and inspiration of ritual behaviour – privileges the cognitive and belief-oriented aspects of human beings and implies that myths and symbols always pre-exist cultural performance. In contrast to this Geertzian approach, I will take the position (following in the tradition of anthropologists such as Robertson Smith, Talal Asad, Pierre Bourdieu and Catherine Bell) that embodied practices are constitutive elements in the performative production and re-production of a set of internalised values. Ritual acts may have conscious or explicitly cognitive dimensions to them but what gives them their "affective" power lies in the fact that they operate at a largely "unconscious", embodied and performative level. Values and ideology are often taken as the cement, the *raison d'être* of political parties. However, studies of party activism have shown that activists ignore the details of political and economic theories that form the ideological basis of their party and only the most sophisticated amongst them can maintain consistency between such an ideology and the needs of their organisation (Barnes, 1968; Faucher, 1999a: 39). Values are the outcome of interactions between individuals and relate to rituals in so far as these collective and performative events help connect us with identities larger than ourselves (Elias, 2001).

Rituals "construct and inscribe power relationships" (Bell, 1997: 83) and are thus also interesting for what they do, rather than solely for what they mean. Too much effort has been put on the search for an abstract and overarching notion of ritual, argues Catherine Bell, whilst research should focus instead on what people do and how they do it in specific contexts (Bell, 1997: 82). According to Catherine Bell, ritual is

> part of a historical process in which past patterns are reproduced but also reinterpreted and transformed. In this sense, ritual is frequently depicted as a central arena for cultural mediation, the means by which various combinations of structure and history, past and present, meanings and needs, are brought together in terms of each other (Bell, 1997: 83).

In his studies of ritual in modern Italian politics, David Kertzer suggests that ritual "discourages critical thinking" (1988: 85) because it plays a major role in conferring legitimacy through the "naturalisation" of ways of behaving. "Through ritual, as through culture more generally, we not only make sense of the world around us, but we are also led to believe that the order we see is not of our own (cultural) making, but rather an order that belongs to the external world itself" (Kertzer, 1988: 85). It is therefore not surprising if observers of the British political scene are oblivious to the idiosyncratic nature of the British conference season. Lukes further argues that ritual helps "define as authoritative certain ways of seeing society: it serves to specify what in society is of special significance, it draws people's attention to certain forms of relationship and activity – and, at the same time therefore, it deflects their attention from other forms, since every way of seeing is also a way of not seeing". Rituals in this view encourage the "internalisation of particular political paradigms" (Lukes, 1975: 302). They silence dissent and contribute to maintaining the *status quo*.

In a political context, the strategic use of such practices is all the more important as they can also subvert established hierarchies and patterns of action (Dirks, 1992; Turner, 1989a). Thus, beyond rituals themselves, we need to look at the "objectification" of a practice (Bell, 1992: 211) that contributes to giving a performance the aura of tradition. Through this process, new values are incorporated and legitimated. It is an effective strategy to impose a particular interpretation of events and although rituals are often seen as slowing down change, they can also be used to manage change. "Each ritual event is a patterned activity to be sure, but it is also invented anew as it happens. (...) The authenticity of the event [is] inscribed in its performance, not in some time and custom sanctioned version of the ritual" (Dirks, 1992: 237). Moreover, meanings change with repetition either through forgetting or elaboration – one forgets wider associations and develops new ones – or because the event has an effect upon networks of meaning and thus changes the system to which it belongs (Goody, 1977). Paradoxically, its very conservatism makes ritual a potent force for political change.

Written rules and interviews with party officials and politicians[9] only unveil what the party is prepared to say about itself. Party elites rarely spontaneously acknowledge the strategic uses of rules. To really understand how parties work, one also needs to look at the practices through which values are constructed and shared by party members. Since 1993, I have observed the various changes undergone by British party conferences in terms of organisation, stage-management and policy-making. Despite their denigration of rituals, party officials actively work on ritualisation – the "invention of tradition"[10] to legitimate new practices and ideologies. Over the years, the "masters of rituals" have strategically adapted the symbols used and changed the official interpretation that can be drawn from such performances. The combination of various methods ranging from observation and interviews on the one hand and work on original documents and secondary sources on the other is necessary to analyse the rules, rituals and routines[11] which define, within a party, what can be done and who the legitimate actors are. These methods not only trace the changes but they also highlight actors' interpretations of their practices.

Ironically, given Kertzer's point that rituals "naturalise" certain practices, labelling an action a "ritual" in our modern secularised setting has the reverse effect of denaturalising it.[12] This is because to call a performance a ritual today is to highlight the culturally constructed nature of the action and to associate it with pre-modern modes of behaviour. It also annihilates some of its "magical" effect on participants and viewers. Such a move also denies such actions legitimacy because it calls into questions their instrumentality or effectiveness. Hence, using the word "ritual" in a modern context to describe an action already predisposes one to see it as an artificial attempt to confer legitimacy and produce social cohesion. This partly explains the reaction of party officials to questions about the importance of opening and closing ceremonies or merit awards. They describe conference rituals as "quaint practices" indulged in "to please the activists" (see Chapter 3). It is indeed difficult to admit publicly in contemporary Britain where everything has to be "modernised", the survival of practices that appear "non-rational". On the other hand, Francois Mitterrand ironically described the Congress of the Socialist Party as *la Pâque des socialistes, chaque fois ils rescucitent* (the Socialists' Easter, each time they resurrect). Applied to a party attached to the secular ideal of *laïcité* to the point of being occasionally anti-religious,[13] such a comparison is above all mischievous. This candour about rituals, however, is the exception rather than the norm in France but it draws attention to the importance of ritual practices for even the most "secular" party organisation.[14] If one follows the work of Mary Douglas, it comes as no surprise that the acknowledgement of the prominence of rituals in politics is made by a politician trained by Jesuits. However, in sharp contrast, the wholesale denigration of ritual by British party elites itself reflects a Protestant culture immersed in a vigorous anti-ritualist tradition (Douglas, 1976: 61). It also reflects the dominant "modernist" and "reformist" spirit that has dominated British political life since the 1980s. Douglas argues that man is a "ritual animal" and "social rituals create a reality which would be nothing without them (...) it is impossible to have social relations without symbolic acts" (Douglas, 1976: 62). As she points out, historically and culturally, the denigration of rituals in a British context is linked to Protestant attempts to denigrate Catholic rituals. Interestingly, the politics of labelling and the negative connotations associated with "ritual" also convince party organisers to place them at less prominent moments in the timetable.

Modernist sensibilities not withstanding, I agree with scholars such as Douglas and Kertzer in arguing that rituals retain an important role in contemporary political life. Rituals indeed are crucial in modern liberal democracies, as in all other societies, precisely because they confer (and sometimes even challenge) legitimacy. Political life without rituals is a politics divested of its social legitimacy.

The conference season

Party conferences corresponded to a particular phase in British politics: they formed an integral part of the political cycle based on parliamentary domination where parties were paramount. The centre of gravity of British politics in the 1990s however has shifted away from Parliament and parties as policy networks have become more dense and complex. The gladiatorial face-to-face sparring between the Government and Her Majesty's Loyal Opposition (be it at Prime Minister's Question Time or indirectly through conference debates) is seen as too conflictual. As Janet Newman points out "governance has become the defining narrative of British government at the start of the new century" (2001: 11). This challenges the notion of Britain as a unitary state with a strong executive and emphasises the role of local, regional and national political elites in forging coalitions with private businesses, voluntary associations and other agents in order to mobilise resources and enhance the chances of orienting policies towards negotiated goals.[15]

Because they refer to symbols and practices that are no longer seen as predominant in contemporary British political life, conferences are generally dismissed as vestigial. Moreover, their declining reputation today is partly linked to the banalisation of political images caused partly by over-exposure in the media-saturated 1990s and the adoption of marketing techniques. The professionalisation of their production has bred scepticism regarding their spontaneity and thus their authenticity. Audiences are not only *blasé* but increasingly more sophisticated in their judgements, whether this is linked to rising levels of education, cognitive mobilisation or greater political awareness (Inglehart, 1990). TV audiences are less loyal[16] and more likely to switch channels at the mention of politics, especially when politics seems to be reduced to rival teams of managers for public resources (Pattie *et al.*, 2004).

"Politics is no longer associated with a remote figure of power" but has become personalised (Balandier, 1992: 111) with political personnel being given a "celebrity" dimension. Images and sound bites create heroic figures capable of capturing the imagination. Since the 1970s, a "democracy of the public" has replaced party democracy (Manin, 1996: 279) and personalities have surpassed party affiliation and programmes as a crucial aspect of electoral presentation. Communication technologies play a role all the more important as there is no independent demand on the electoral market (Schumpeter, 1942). Politicians articulate their offer in a competitive and unpredictable environment. The outcome is an executive/electorate relationship that is both more direct and more dependent upon images. Politicians now engage in direct political debate with the electorate, increasingly bypassing Parliament. Whilst the press, a "cold" medium, favours ideologies and battles of ideas, and radio privileges orators and speeches, television thrives on images rather than oratory skills. These images are all the more potent because they convey a sense of immediacy and transparency (Balandier, 1992: 117–118) which obscures the process of mediation taking place (see Chapter 6).

Compared to other European countries,[17] Britain has a long and venerable tradition of parliamentary politics so much so that in 1991 about three-fifths of Britons associated government with parties and Parliament (Merelman, 1991: 23). With over 100 years of precedent, conferences are an integral element of British democracy: for a month every year, the main political organisations hold their national gatherings by the seaside. Thanks to the considerable attention that they receive, conferences act as reminders of the existence of political parties, whilst at the same time, taking them temporarily outside of Westminster. They are an opportunity for parties to address the electorate outside an electoral campaign[18] and for politicians to be seen meeting "real people". The conference city, be it Brighton, Blackpool or Bournemouth, becomes for a few days a microcosm of the nation and a symbol of the "accessibility" and representative function of politicians in a democracy. Photo opportunities are organised for instance at local schools or at the racetrack. Thus, politicians are presented as "in touch" with the common citizen, mixing with "ordinary" people.

The "conference season"[19] marks the end of the summer recess and the beginning of the new parliamentary year. It draws attention to the inner workings of political parties and also restores the political structure after the interruptions of the "silly season".[20] It is a calendar ritual[21] that is inextricably linked in its timing and significance to the new session of Parliament with its wigs and robes, the MPs' procession led by Black Rod to the House of Lords and the Queen's speech.[22] Party conferences create a double sense of community as they clearly demarcate partisan groups from each other and also place party opposition within the larger framework of national institutions.[23] By taking part in this national ritual, parties reaffirm the supremacy of Parliament in the polity,[24] and acknowledge a certain "pecking order". In the age of television (and now webcams), voters can watch their gladiators perform from home or in the office. The leader's conference speech provides an occasion to demonstrate his/her might and charisma. The conference season actualises the political map, frames ideological debates and clarifies the positions of the competing teams. It legitimises political organisations and the ways in which social and political conflicts are mediated, displaced or relocated in Westminster. It offers a stage for a public but pacific expression of competing ideologies. It reminds citizens of what constitutes a "proper" way to behave in politics. It celebrates political commitment and political activity. For parties it is an annual rite of renewal. In its ritualised conferment of legitimacy on political elites, it highlights the sacred dimension of politics.[25]

Following the anthropologist Victor Turner (1989a), it is illuminating to analyse the conference season as a liminal period or a threshold between ordinary life and the beginning of parliamentary season. Power (like the Polynesian *manu*) at this time appears strangely close thanks to Cabinet ministers, their Shadows and parliamentarians, whose presence gives the event an extraordinary and intensified dimension. Indeed, for a long time, Conservative politicians were only guests at the National Union Conference. Politicians were, however, the main attraction and the culmination of the week was of course the leader's speech. The parties have always been aware of this attraction and now actively promote the presence of the great and the powerful, as an incentive for members (and the media) to attend the conference. Moreover, traditional hierarchies are somehow blurred for the participants who are able to mix with the political elite of the country and are in a position to ask questions, and even challenge them on occasion. Party conferences are usually held in coastal towns, as if to symbolise the farthest reaches of the nation on the edge of the political mainland. To stretch the analogy, one can see here an attempt to demonstrate how politics reaches out to the electorate beyond the confines of Westminster.[26] Furthermore the seaside context enhances the out-of-time, out-of-place character of conferences[27] and has also added a Bacchanalian and festive spirit to such occasions (see Chapter 3). These resorts not only offer accommodation facilities but they are also relatively attractive for a week's holiday[28] – though increasingly less so now. In the 1990s, the three main parties decided to get together to exert effective pressure on conference centres and service providers, such as telecom companies who wire up the facilities for the party and the media. "We share experiences", explain organisers for the three main parties. Not only does a representative of the other parties always attend conferences but organisers also use the opportunity to explore the facilities to be provided for the following year. The presence of such observers, often seen as outrageous by the rank-and-file, also allows parties to copy each other in terms of session format or stage management.

Party cultures

Angelo Panebianco (1988) has offered one of the most interesting models for the study of parties, taking into account the influence of their origins on future developments. We can thus contrast parties according to their genetic (parliamentary or civil society) types.

Parties originating within Parliament have tended to become cadre-parties, then electoral-professional parties. They place democratic legitimacy in their parliamentarians, anointed by universal suffrage. Cadre-parties appeared in Britain in the 1830s[29] when parliamentarians created external organisations because successive reforms of the electoral system made it crucial for sitting MPs to gather the support of newly registered voters.[30] The Liberals and the Conservatives developed into elite-centred parties (Wolinetz, 2002: 143), with the leadership holding tight rein over policy-making and strategy.[31] The Liberals created the precursor of a political party in Birmingham in the late 19th century (Ostrogorski, 1979), and the Conservatives soon followed this example. But these remained isolated groups until the foundation of the National Union of Conservative Associations (NU) in 1867. The extra-parliamentary wing of the Liberal party was founded ten years later. In this context, the party conference served primarily as a means to mobilise supporters. In both the Liberal and the Conservative cases, the role of the membership in political decision-making was no more than an afterthought. In fact, the political and voluntary organisations were kept separate. The parliamentary party retained considerable autonomy in formulating policies with little or no influence from the membership. The Liberal Democrats were founded in the context of a much smaller and weaker parliamentary representation and therefore have tended to treat their members with greater consideration.[32]

Parties emanating from civil society consider that the source of their legitimacy rests within the party itself, that is its members (Seiler, 2003: 316). Members are essential resources for mass parties because they provide free labour, in particular at election time. They also bring funds through fees and donations. Compared to the previous generation of parties, these organisations shifted power from parliamentary office to the party on the ground.[33] They granted their grassroots more influence over leadership and policies, mainly through the election of a congress of delegates. The objective was to prevent the emergence of an oligarchy removed from the preoccupations of the movement (Michels, 1962). The Labour party is the archetypal example of such an organisation. It was founded at a 1900 conference of trade unions and socialist societies to promote working-class representation and interests. The constitution sought to ensure that the annual conference remained the sovereign decision-making body where policies were debated and adopted, officials elected and held accountable. More than 70 years later and in a very different political context, the Green Party also emerged from civil society and espoused a similar model of organisation.[34] If the democratic nature of internal procedures were not at first an absolute priority, the Green Party adopted the "new politics" agenda and form of organisation in the 1980s (Faucher, 1999a; Kitschelt, 1990). They have developed structures devoted to participative democracy, creating numerous obstacles to the emergence of anything more than a purely functional leadership.

A second dimension, proximity to state power, is important to understand the evolution of British parties. For most of its history, the Westminster model has been characterised by a two-party system, largely enforced thanks to the "first-past-the-post" electoral system. Indeed, plurality severely restricts access to Parliament – and to a lesser degree to local government. It creates a majoritarian bias for the allocation of seats that strongly disadvantages smaller organisations (Faucher, 2000) and means that only two parties can seriously consider governmental office. Another consequence is the predominance of single-party government. In the 1920s, the struggle between the Liberal and the Labour party ended with the latter becoming the second main player alongside the Conservatives. The situation remained unchanged until the 1970s, when centre politics regained some visibility. Fourteen Liberal MPs were elected in 1974. New parties were created such as the Greens but also the short-lived Social Democratic Party (SDP). Heir to the Liberals and the SDP, the Liberal Democrats have expanded their parliamentary representation to 46 in 1997, 52 in 2001 and 62 MPs in 2005. On the other hand, the Greens claim one Lord but have yet to send their first MP to Westminster.[35] This dimension, which encompasses both the probability of exercising governmental responsibilities but also the desire to attain such a goal, has important consequences on parties. It affects attitudes to (and practice of) the internal organisation. Removed from power with hardly any chance of attaining it under the current system, the Greens have focused their attention on policies and participative democracy at the expense of electoral efficacy. One can argue that their limited resources and their radicalism have contributed to maintaining their marginal status (Faucher, 1999a) but it is more important here to highlight how executive power has been a factor influencing the evolution of party organisations regarding the role attributed to members in policy-making or leadership accountability. The position of parties relative to government evolves and so do their organisation and practice of politics.

Conferences were first "invented" when parliamentarians were trying to organise their supporters at the time of enfranchisement. The first Tory conference was held in 1867. In the following years, the event only attracted a handful of participants (7 including the officers at the second conference in Birmingham and 36 in 1869) until the National Union decided to mark the occasion with a banquet in 1872 at which Disraeli gave a speech (Bulmer-Thomas, 1965: 112). The foundation of the Labour party in 1900 transformed the symbolism and the role of the annual conference. Because it allowed representatives from the membership to deliberate policies and decisions,[36] it linked the event to the question of intra-party democracy.

British political parties' annual gatherings were originally semi-private affairs. These national gatherings play different roles in each organisation but they share a number of functions, from developing policy options and legitimising policy choices, to publicising party activities, building party cohesion, social integration and sharing campaigning experiences. These functions vary according to party culture but have also changed under the influence of the wider cultural, institutional and political environment. Today, the model for party democracy is not the conference of delegates but deliberative democracy through a multiplication of open forums (Chapter 8) or direct democracy through the ballots (Chapter 9). Maurice Duverger (1964) was optimistic when he announced that the mass party model would contaminate other parties. Nevertheless, they have often been the implicit reference for those looking at party organisations. Through the recent "emphasis upon 'democratisation', modernisers within [the Labour and the Conservative] parties have achieved a degree of organisational symmetry in their respective parties unthinkable less than a decade before" (Judge, 1999: 95). As a consequence, party conferences offer an interesting prism through which changes in British political parties can be compared.[37]

The Conservatives

The Conservative conference has always been conceived as a rally of the faithful, an opportunity for volunteers to meet up with like-minded individuals from around the country in order to socialise and exchange experiences and ideas. The meeting was organised by the NU, a body legally autonomous from both the professional (Central Office) and the political (the Conservative Parliamentary group) "wings" of a "notional"

Conservative Party. In the early days, most MPs did not bother to attend: the gathering had no power and their presence was almost a superfluous expense. The first political debate was held in 1876 and the question of members' influence remained meaningless until the adoption of a unitary constitution in 1998.

Conservatives believe in democracy by consent, in which voters are given a power to control rather than initiate (Beer, 1982: 96). It is a "government of the people, for the people but not by them".[38] Voters can choose between alternative teams but the government, once in office, have a right to govern and should not be bound by a mandate. Between elections, voters are expected to be passive. In the classic Tory approach, the role of the party is to help the diffusion of Conservative values and ideals through the country and not the production of party policies. It is a model based on deference and trust in the elite's legitimacy to lead. Such an understanding of society is mirrored in the party organisation: members have a limited role, the leadership is free to adapt its policies according to what it perceives is the best option for the party and the country. From the end of the 19th century to the Thatcher period, the primary objective of the Conservative party has been the conquest and retention of power.[39] Efficiency in electoral competition implied a quick decision-making process, focused around the personality of the leader and grounded in a culture of deference and a belief in the right of elites to govern. Helped by an indeterminate number of unaccountable committees that he was able to consult without having to follow their advice, the Conservative leader enjoyed great autonomy. His power was thus only hindered by the necessity to preserve the support of his followers. In many ways, his supremacy became unchallenged from the day of his nomination so long as he remained successful. The Conservative leader appoints all senior officials and representatives as well as the *Front Bench* team (McKenzie, 1964: 55–56). He determines policy orientations (Beer, 1982: 246; McKenzie, 1964: 62–65). Networks, committees and informal rules limit the autonomy of the leader since he still has to abide by accepted norms of conduct and therefore to know the party and its hierarchs (Norton and Aughey, 1981: 258–259).

The Labour party

The originality of the Labour Party has lain in the centrality of conference. The Labour movement followed a model of delegatory democracy in which the annual conference acted as the sovereign body of the organisation. The various components of this indirect organisation sent delegates to the yearly meeting. Each constituent kept its identity and autonomy but most visibly contributed to the collective endeavour at conference. Here was the place where policies and strategies were debated and adopted, where executive officers were elected and their actions monitored. With the 1906 constitution, the parliamentary party was called to present a report on its efforts to implement the instructions of the conference. The "parliamentary party report" contributed to focusing attention on conference as the moment of accountability for the party leadership.

The exhaustive research conducted by Minkin (1980) has shown how the conference played a crucial role in the complex organisation of the Labour party and in particular in the subtle interplay of powers between the constituent members (trade unions, socialist societies and constituency parties) as well as between various committees and groups (the National Executive and its sub-committees, the parliamentary party and various other groups acting as liaison between others). Often backed by the big unions, the National Executive Committee (NEC) long dominated proceedings. However, the balance of power began to shift in the 1980s as the leadership proceeded to "modernise" the party. Beyond the Policy Review (Shaw, 1994; Taylor, 1997), the organisation itself was reformed. Power was centralised with the leadership establishing a firmer control over the party and over the organisation of the sovereign conference. However, the most important transformations were introduced only after the Labour party returned to power in 1997.

The Labour Co-ordinating Committee produced a report in 1996 that clearly showed the direction of future changes, giving the blueprint of a "Project" to modernise the organisation of the Labour party. Not only did the document set the tone of the reforms but also suggested a step-by-step transformation of ways of working that would turn the still chaotic, committee-driven party, dominated by unions and activists, into an efficient massive organisation. Under Blair's leadership, Labour has become modelled on private business and treats its members as stakeholders. For a party that began its life as an organisation of socialist, trade unionists and working-class activists, this has been a remarkable transformation, and one that would have been unthinkable without Margaret Thatcher's "revolution" in British politics in the 1980s.

The Liberal Democrats

The National Liberal Federation was founded at a conference in 1877 attended by delegates from 95 local associations. Chamberlain was elected President (Cook, 2002: 14) but it took about ten years for the

Federation to grow in influence and move its base to London. Behind a façade of representation, the Liberal Federation had a centralised organisation that made the Conservatives' National Union look amateurish.[40] Although the Liberal party was created by politicians and exercised governmental power in turns until the 1930s, its conferences played a more important role than is the case for the Conservatives.[41] Disappointments on the electoral scene contributed to make the conference an important occasion to boost the morale of supporters. In 1970, the Party Assembly attracted 900 delegates to Brighton, 600 fewer than 4 years before. Turmoil in the two-party system in the 1970–80s revived the organisation.

Today's party is the product of the merger between the Liberals and the SDP, a secession from Labour founded in 1981[42] that had demonstrated an early awareness of the importance of communication. To attract media attention, the SDP organised its first conference on a train going from Perth to Bradford and London. The "rolling conference" saved expensive and long journeys whilst those who chose to travel on board the conference train enjoyed the conviviality, the singing and the drinking. It also made for "good television, far better than the usual pictures of bored-looking delegates in seaside conference halls": journalists liked the innovation. "The symbolism of the whole occasion worked: the chartered train and the new party were both on the move" (Crewe and King, 1995: 141). The novelty soon faded out: in 1982, the train broke down and the journalists were bored (Crewe and King, 1995: 162). As the party failed to live up to its ambition, it looked into strategic partnerships.

Ideological proximity and electoral self-interest led to the constitution of an Alliance between the old Liberal party and the SDP. Despite coming less than one point behind Labour in the 1983 general election, the new British political centre only won 23 MPs.[43] The Liberal/SDP merger first happened on the ground as several constituency associations joined forces in 1987 (Cook, 2002: 188) but the proposal encountered considerable resistance. David Owen's supporters within the SDP considered that the Liberals were both "weak and unreliable" on many issues. Nevertheless, a few months (and several conferences) later, the merger was ratified in 1989.

The Social and Liberal Democrats tried to reconcile in their structure the centralised, hierarchical tendencies of the SDP with the decentralised, pluralistic thrust of the Liberals. The first two years were tough: their finances were in trouble, the membership stagnant and they came fourth, behind the Greens, in the 1989 European elections. In 1990, the

Blackpool conference adopted a less complicated name, clarified its policies, and chose an emblem. Conferences have provided the Liberal Democrats with opportunities to construct a distinctive identity in a political system that has difficulties conceiving of the possibility of an alternative to a strictly dichotomous opposition. Liberal Democrats contrast what they claim are democratic procedures that give members a real say on policy-making to what happens in the Labour and Conservative parties. They are suspicious of the idea of discipline and mandates and praise their ability to address in conferences controversial issues that are carefully avoided by the bigger parties. Although conferences' decisions become party policy, the Liberal Democrat electoral manifesto has often left out some of the most controversial and radical policies.

The Green Party

Analysis of British party political life is often limited to the two main organisations or extended to include a third national party, the Liberal Democrats. Such focus on parliamentary parties becomes increasingly problematic when we consider the growing importance of extra-parliamentary politics. Although the electoral system has successfully kept potential competitors at bay, small parties have relentlessly attempted to enter the field, demonstrating the strength of political mobilisation outside the traditional borders of conventional Westminster politics. Despite the odds, the oldest European Green Party has consistently presented candidates at general elections in order to force mainstream parties to pay attention to its ecological agenda. Conferences focus the attention of outside observers and it is difficult to imagine today a British political party without an annual conference. To be sure, the first decision of a new organisation is to hold an annual gathering with the hope that it will place them on the political map.[44] The Greens have held regular meetings since 1974. In 1977, the conference adopted a constitution. The following year, the party approved an electoral strategy, breaking away from the tradition of environmental associations. The party has voluntarily maintained a relatively weak structure, limiting the role of the national organisation to the co-ordination of initiatives from below. The conference has thus been the only place where a common organisational culture could develop. Moreover, delegates concentrate decision-making powers: they elect members of national committees, control the work of the party executive, adopt policies and debate strategy options. An inclusive conference is the corner stone to the participative democracy that the Greens aspire to because it creates the conditions of a face-to-face and responsible community. The Greens argue that, unlike in mainstream parties, all motions adopted at conference become party policy and are included in the *Manifesto for a Sustainable Society* (MfSS). Their claims to be "truly" democratic are largely ignored by parliamentary parties because they can be dismissed as an "irrelevant" electoral threat. Although recent successes under proportional representation confirm the role played by "first-past-the-post" in excluding them from national political visibility, their practices have contributed to limit the effectiveness of their organisation in a political environment increasingly dominated by the media and by the personalisation of politics.

"Modernising" political parties?

During the years I have followed them (1994–2003), British parties grew obsessed with change, partly because of the successes of New Labour. Not only have its opponents endeavoured to emulate its example and, as a consequence, adopted some of its rhetoric and innovations but the New Labour government has also contributed to the transformation of the institutional, legal, cultural and political environment in which all parties evolve.

In his first conference speech as Labour leader, Tony Blair declared that "parties that do not change die, and this party is a living movement, not a historical monument". Since 1994, Blair has relentlessly pushed Labour into a new kind of permanent revolution guided by a quasi-evangelical vision of change for its own sake.[45] Labour has made "modernisation"[46] its *motto*: it was marketed as "new" and artificially contrasted with "old" Labour. "Old Labour" became a scapegoat charged with all the evils (incompetence, division, bureaucracy, lack of democracy) from which the party wished to distance itself. Self-labelled modernisers considered that a reform of the organisation was an electoral necessity, if only to convince voters that the party had reformed and was indeed different from its earlier unelectable incarnation. Because it merges teleological undertones,[47] the idea of ineluctable progress and positive connotations of technological developments, modernisation is a powerful rhetorical tool. It is marvellously ambiguous. Tony Blair has many times expressed a vision of change that combines fatalism and voluntarism and denies any other alternative:

> The issue is: do we shape [change] or does it shape us? Do we master it, or do we let it overwhelm us? That's the sole key to politics in the

modern world: how to manage change. Resist it: futile; let it happen: dangerous. So – the third way – manage it.[48]

There are many ways in which parties can change: policies are redrafted and strategies are adapted.[49] New leaders play a determining role (Wilson, 1994) because they establish their authority thanks to symbolic and practical decisions that strengthen the position of their teams or of their ideas. Both Tony Blair and William Hague marked the beginning of their leadership with symbolic and organisational reforms (respectively in 1994 and 1997), with variable success. Beyond the evolution of rules, practices are adapted. The culture of the organisation is also ultimately affected. Change cannot be imposed from above and is always met with some resistance because organisations are Conservative and actors strategic (Crozier and Friedberg, 1981). The conversion of the Conservative party to a unitary organisation with formal procedures for the consultation of members in 1998 was too abrupt to affect practices and the disappointing consequences of the 2001 leadership election contributed to entrench established modes of conduct. In 1992, the new Green Party constitution was the result of a coup. The disputes that ensued led to resignations, to a secession and, ultimately, to the progressive repealing of the most contentious clauses. To avoid failure, it is thus necessary to "convince" members to embrace new rules or practices. A slow, step-by-step process often avoids upfront conflicts and is most effective when the reform is preceded by a phase of "consultation". This can even be conducted by party elites to lead to the desired conclusion. Tom Sawyer, the former Labour General Secretary, candidly explains how new policy-making procedures were presented as "dictated by circumstances", experimented on and then institutionalised. "When it's done, it's done, nobody thinks about it."[50] The Conservatives followed the same approach in 2000 – with far less "consultation", admitted in substance by Chris Poole.

These structural reforms also had symbolic implications. In the case of Labour, much more than the Conservatives, they have contributed to changing the image of the party for members and voters. "Conference is not only the place where politics takes place symbolically, as necessary celebration, ritual renewal and so on, but is often the site of political change itself" (Gaffney, 1991: 13). Political initiatives are announced; symbolic events leave a mark on the party's identity as demonstrated by Kinnock's attack on the Militant Tendency in 1985 or the re-branding of the Labour party in 1995. Conference actualises changes in party structure and symbols, whether new procedures need to be endorsed or because it is a decisive nexus for the diffusion of new ideas, interpretations and practices. Moreover, the omnipresence of the media means that they have become a crucial element in any public relations strategy because the image projected affects not only members' perceptions but also those of the wider public, including opponents and journalists. Change of image, however, is not enough if it does not appear consistent with the "reality" of the party. New Labour's modernisers were convinced that the culture of the party had to change because, like a business, the members (staff) who promote (sell) the organisation and its policies (products) have to share the values of the company to be properly convincing as "ambassadors in the community". Conferences, then, are windows through which the outside observer can follow the processes of change.

Structure of the book

In this book, I attempt to trace how British annual party conferences have changed at the turn of the Millennium and what it tells us about change in party organisations and symbolic practices. Conferences are probably the best place to observe the evolutions of the relationships between the grassroots and the elites and the transformation of each party's modes of interaction. In Chapter 2, I explore individual motivations to attend conference and show that although approaches that focus upon instrumental rationality are helpful, they are insufficient in explaining why participants invest so much in these apparently archaic and "quaint" events. I suggest instead that we take into account other approaches to activism and consider participation in terms of expressive, rather than outcome-oriented action. In this light, we can understand conference attendance as an affirmation of group-identity. In Chapter 3, I go on to analyse ways in which the conference has a central role to play in the construction of party identity, applying the insights of "new social movement" approaches to mainstream organisations. Not only does the annual conference contribute to the "imagined community" of each party, it also structures and frames what members do and what they think they have in common. This is explored in terms of each party's specific group styles. These styles emerge progressively over time and thereby provide an element of stability to political parties. At the same time, a group's styles evolve, reflecting changes as well as acting upon them. Chapter 4 focuses on the legitimisation of leadership and the construction of hierarchies through the ritualisation of a number of conference practices. Party organisers endeavour to give the leader's speech a particular atmosphere of enthusiasm and solemnity that creates the impression of charisma, with the hope of turning the show into an event of national importance that justifies media attention. The most important environmental factor for the transformation of politics in the late 20th century has been the expansion of electronic media and competition between media outlets. In Britain, political parties and the media have developed complex relationships, characterised by mutual accusations and mistrust as well as interdependency. In Chapter 5, the preparation of conference is examined. Over recent years, party leaderships have asserted tighter control over the conference agenda and timetable in order to ensure the promotion of favourable issues and coverage. This development has only been possible because grassroots' input on the intra-party political agenda has been further limited whilst the conference preparatory phase has lost some of its integrative function. In order to better control both party image and news agenda, party elites have perfected the stage management of conference. Media attention and each political party's increased concerns about its public image have also had an impact on the role party members are accorded in policy-making. It is therefore important to examine the elaboration of the conference agenda and the directing of conference debates. Chapter 6 discusses the impact of news media on recent transformations of conferences, looking at the influence their inquisitive and critical presence has had upon the management of conferences by party elites. The means invented by parties to maintain control over their image are contrasted with journalists' efforts to avoid being instrumentalised by partisan propaganda.

In Chapter 7, I consider plenary session debates not in terms of the content of policy formation but as performances and highlight how the presence of the media has contributed to self-discipline amongst delegates and representatives in a collective attempt to produce a desired impression of professionalism and competence. Whilst conferences seem to be increasingly dominated by the objectives of party leaderships, thereby challenging the idea that conferences are the primary locus of intra-party democracy, democratic procedures are taken for granted within western liberal regimes and there has been a growing academic and public debate about the nature of representative government. Societal demands for greater democratic participation and governmental responsiveness have coincided with a spiral of demobilisation that has particularly affected mainstream political parties. One of their responses to a perceived challenge to their legitimacy has been the introduction of organisational reforms that emphasise deliberative democracy as a means to reconnect politicians with the grassroots. Chapter 8 analyses how the multiplication of small-group discussions affects the patterns of vertical communication within parties and critically examines the claim that conference seminars and policy forums make party leaderships more responsive to their members' preoccupations. The challenge for parties is to convince their members that promises of wider consultation are matched with genuine influence upon party orientations. Conference votes have been potent symbols of intra-party democracy. They seem to confer decision-making powers to delegates and representatives. They also contribute to the legitimisation of the organisation through a symbolic acceptance of societal norms.

Chapter 9 examines the evolutions of voting practices and the consequences on party boundaries and identities of another set of organisational reforms introduced at the same time. Following a movement that simultaneously happened in continental Europe, British political parties have adopted procedures inspired by an individualist model of democracy. All have granted their members new individual rights to vote for the selection of candidates, leaders and internal officers. Members have been balloted on draft manifestos and party organisation and supporters are also increasingly consulted. What are the implications of the introduction of "direct democracy" procedures on activism since it is clear that party leaderships have also intended to use such reforms to bypass activists? Finally, Chapter 10 explores the significance of the exponential growth of the political and commercial conference fringe. Similar to what has happened at the Edinburgh Festival, the fringe has become an event in itself, almost overtaking the official scene. This development reflects not only a reaction against increasing restrictions imposed upon debates in the main hall by public relations considerations but also a fundamental transformation of the relationship between political parties and civil society. It highlights in particular a shift away from traditional Westminster-centred politics to a multi-levelled model of governance (Wilson, 2004: 10–11). Moreover, the opaque interaction between business interests and politics raises the important question of funding for political parties.

2
Why Do People Attend Conferences?

Political parties are said to be in crisis: voters are less loyal and members more difficult to recruit and to mobilise (Whiteley and Seyd, 2002). However, they seem to encounter fewer difficulties in attracting members to their regular national gatherings. British party conferences are amongst the biggest political meetings of the Western world.[1] In the early 1990s, Labour and the Conservatives claimed up to 6000 participants. As the 1997 general election drew closer, the anticipated change of government made conferences more attractive: the Conservatives dispatched more than 11,000 passes[2] in 1996, nearly twice as many as Labour.[3] Attendance figures are increasingly viewed as a testimony of the popularity of the party and efforts are made to attract visitors, whether members or not. The number of passes issued has turned into an arms race with all parties competing. In 2002, the Liberal Democrats claimed to have delivered 4500 passes[4] and Labour 25,000.[5] Beyond delegates and representatives, conference attracts many other participants from local party apparatchiks, would-be politicians and local councillors, MPs, lobbyists and diplomats, cause group activists and journalists. The party in government has the advantage because it can claim to be closest to the corridors of power. Lobbyists, businesses and interest groups are all eager to be informed of future policy orientations as well as to make useful contacts. The media send large crews because what happens is likely to be news. The conference crowd creates a beehive effect that gives the impression of a vibrant policy community. The Labour party makes sure most visitors turn up for the Prime Minister's speech on the Tuesday by issuing day passes. In 2002 for instance, large groups of school children were roaming the Winter Gardens (Blackpool) before settling in at the Opera house to watch the speech on a giant screen. The Conservative party's crisis has recently translated into quiet and relatively "empty" conferences. Organisers are discreet about figures but it is clear that the audience has shrunk: the number of seats has been reduced in the conference auditorium and some were even available to latecomers during debates. The change is all the more striking as the Conservatives used to fill the hall, sitting on the stairways, listening with impressive attention to discussions and speeches. To compensate for a drop in applications for a conference pass, the Conservatives have opened their conference to all party members with the creation of two-day and business passes at reduced prices.

The paradox of conference participation

Until 1965, participation in collective action was largely taken for granted. Despite low levels of mobilisation, scholars endeavoured to explain why people did not participate rather than the opposite. In an important book, Mancur Olson argued that what had to be questioned were not the motives of those who did not mobilise but those of the few who actually did (Olson, 1965). The economist argued that an instrumentally rational actor – *homo economicus* – weighs the costs and benefits of his actions before making any decision.[6] Such an individual is unlikely to mobilise for the provision of collective goods and would instead wait until others' actions have obtained it. He would then benefit from the outcome without having to bear any of the costs incurred in getting it. On this view, it is "rational" to behave so because one individual's contribution is unlikely to make much difference (Barry, 1970: 32). When individuals adopt "free-riding" strategies, political parties find it difficult to recruit members. Like other voluntary organisations working for the production of collective goods, they need to provide selective incentives to attract supporters.

Conference participation beckons similar questions and it is not always easy to find volunteers to go to conference. It is often seen as an archaic practice that compares poorly with the new leisure activities on offer in modern British society. It is also an expensive hobby for all but the Labour delegates and those supported by their organisations or employers.[7] Conferences last up to a week and many people cannot afford to take several days off.[8] Registration fees can be high, even with early booking discounts.[9] Transport, accommodation and food add to the bill. Industrious participants at the three main conferences can attempt to survive with the light buffets provided by fringe meeting organisers although lunching and dining of such sandwiches can be a tough experience, which only the most desperate participants can sustain. These costs discriminate against those poor in time or money. Pensioners and the middle-classes are over represented. Such disenfranchisement is bemoaned by the Liberal Democrats who cannot afford to attend as often as they would like. Nevertheless, only parties with extra-parliamentary origins are officially wary of means-testing democratic participation and only Labour systematically sponsors its delegates through their local party, their union or socialist society. The position of the Greens is ambiguous because the financial situation of the party makes such subsidies simply unimaginable.[10]

Liberal Democrats Conference 2002, Brighton

Despite being a fully elected representative, Ann only has a day pass and only attends when conference is in the South. An MP concurs: he has only been coming to conference since his election to Westminster. Before that he could not afford it.

Green Party Conference 1994, Hastings

Debbie is flattered to have been chosen as her local group's representative to the Green Conference though she thought her party colleagues had been mischievous in electing her whilst she had fallen asleep during the meeting. A gardener for London public parks, she has taken a week off and can hardly afford the expenses involved but was keen nevertheless to play her part in the democratic process.

The cost of conference participation does not deter everybody as all parties boast growing attendance figures.[11] The evaluation of cost and benefits is both subjective and objective: a self-employed therapist will lose some of his income, a single-parent may find it difficult to arrange child-care, a businessman may be overworked. On the other hand, the first may be looking for a new career in politics, the second may be keen to meet up with new people and the third might reasonably expect to meet with colleagues from their sector. Costs may be considered too high for a holiday in Blackpool in early October when more people can afford and might prefer a week in Ibiza but for those with political ambition attendance represents a long-term investment more cost-effective than university education. The selection of delegates/representatives is the object of a special meeting and often of a ballot.[12]

Approaches derived from a rational choice perspective assume that individuals are primarily self-interested. The solution to the paradox of collective action thereby is seen in the allocation of incentives as a reward for participation. Indeed, research has not only demonstrated the role of such rewards in the mobilisation of party activists (Seyd and Whiteley, 1992; Whiteley and Seyd, 2002; Whiteley *et al.*, 1994) but has also shown the importance of other incentives. Collective incentives are based on the provision of collective goods and whether the organisation is perceived as an effective vehicle for achieving them (Whiteley and Seyd, 2002: 52–53). The idea that conferences are important policy-making bodies is a key to the attachment felt by Labour, Green and Liberal Democrat activists to their organisation and one of the first responses offered by many activists to explain their presence at conference. It justifies their feeling of personal efficacy and their confidence in democratic institutions. It gives a rationale for participation in these costly and time-consuming events. Policy-making is deeply embedded in Labour's conference because the groups that form Labour hold their own annual conferences with a policy-making function. However, there has been a clear difference in the motives of delegates for attending argues Matthew Taylor, former Assistant General Secretary: "trade unions' delegates used to come for a week of paid holidays by the seaside,[13] constituency delegates are much more serious, they want to listen to debate, to work". The former are often in groups, sometimes chaperoned by their officials. The latter are sometimes isolated and all the more anxious about fulfilling their responsibility.

Labour Conference 1997, Bournemouth

Pamela is concerned about having to report on debates and to account for her votes to her constituency party. She conscientiously attends all sessions. Others, more experienced with the conference process, though as dedicated to its policy-making role, focus their efforts on the preparation of the agenda (Chapter 5) and the negotiations that help secure the outcome of votes (Chapter 9).

If participation in policy-making was one of the reasons to attend conference, it is of little surprise that the "value" of attendance has been reassessed in the Labour party. Despite the official claim that conference has retained its pivotal role in policy-making, experienced activists know that its decision-making powers have been eroded.

Although "members are marginally more inclined to think that the leadership pays attention to them under Blair than under Kinnock" (Seyd and Whiteley, 2001: 86), there is a general feeling that organisational reform has stripped conference of its influence. As a consequence, some local Labour parties decided to use their limited financial resources to fund local government elections rather than subsidise conference delegates. Such decisions show the attachment to a particular model of party conference but also the ways in which groups will balance the costs of participation with its outcome. In 2000, 200 labour constituency parties did not bother to send a delegation (Fielding, 2003: 136). Officials are well aware of what appears to have become an enduring problem despite claims that "nearly all" parties now send a delegation. Liberal Democrats enjoy conference deliberations and their contribution to the elaboration of party policy but they also praise the self-discipline that leads their fellow members to avoid bringing up contentious issues as the general election approaches.

Policy-making, though, is only one of the possible motivations for participants – one would otherwise have to ponder the self-delusion of party members. Most have more realistic expectations. Selective incentives can be subdivided into process (such as taking part in policy debates or mixing with like-minded people), and outcome (such as the prospect of being elected as a councillor). In politics, people may stand for the public good and they also compete for prizes that are in short supply, such as honour, power or wealth (Bailey, 1969). Some of them are up for grabs at conference; some can only be enjoyed through conference participation or can be attained because of resources gathered at conference. New acquaintances are made and old ones are reactivated. These contacts are crucial for anybody wishing to build a network, exchange services and favours. This is true in all parties, whatever their attitudes to hierarchies, democracy, leadership and personalisation of power.

Honour and fame

Because the conference is the main scene for interactions within the party, it plays an important role in the distribution of honours and social gratifications. Hierarchies are very important for Conservatives and a number of them coexist. Owing to its parliamentary origin, the Conservative party has preserved a clear distinction between the voluntary and political wings of the organisation, each with its own system of mobilisation and rewards.[14] The value of each reward varies according to the social position of the contender: if a factory worker or a primary teacher may be proud of being a Constituency secretary, a successful businessman who has a "Personal Assistant" may find the title not very appealing. In the Conservative party, anybody who is somebody is Chairman of something (or Deputy Chairman). These innumerable chairmanships[15] bestow on the holder influence as well as public recognition.

It is important for parties to rotate the highest honorary positions – usually linked to the voluntary organisation – so that many can be rewarded. Mandates are usually short and only renewable a limited number of times. However, the glow of the position remains after the end of the mandate[16] and stepping down does not necessarily involve losing all influence as networks persist and new positions are created.[17] Moreover, British governmental parties have other ways of rewarding deserving supporters. Spoils include honours (such as peerages or Order of the British Empires (OBEs)), places on "quasi autonomous non-governmental organisations" (*quangos*) and private company boards, jobs in think tanks and charities.[18] Many businessmen, for instance, choose to stay out of parliamentary politics and rise through the National Union (now the Convention). They enjoy considerable influence in the corridors of power through formal and informal committees, networks and social clubs. Such informal influence is an incentive that contributes to explaining dedication to the party. In a party that places high value on merit and distinction, it is important to show differences in status. The annual conference is used by the party to show gratitude to benefactors of all kinds through symbolic rewards. Traditionally, the great and the good would sit on the platform throughout the conference week. Nowadays, sitting on stage is strictly limited but about 700 platform passes were issued by the National Union in 1996 to senior volunteer members, ministers and guests.[19] Moreover, 900 permutations were planned for the occupation of the few stage seats in order to allow many to have a short span on the platform. "Most people do as they are told," explains Chris Poole, "but they also need to be chaperoned and entertained." Indeed, they are treated as special guests. What makes these perks valuable is primarily the public recognition that accompanies them. Senior volunteers of the party have privileged access to politicians throughout the year and more than one occasion to drink champagne and socialise. Conference, however, allows them to enjoy these benefits in full view of everybody else. They can feel that they belong to the elite. These are legitimising acts (Barker, 2001) because the whole party participates in them.

Conferences provide political parties with other opportunities to honour valued members. Exceptional fundraisers, hardworking local secretaries or record breaking veterans who have been members for over 50 years receive a medal, a hug from the leader, loud cheers from the conference. Conservative Conference Chairmen receive a silver bell at the end of the week while their wives are given a bunch of flowers. These ceremonies are important for those who are thus publicly thanked and glow in their 15 minutes of fame. Many activists approach power and politicians with a sense of awe. The body language is telling in face-to-face interactions be it in the main hall or on the fringe. Celebrities are increasingly invited to conferences and are greeted with excitement rather than reverence. Some are prepared to pay expensive fees[20] to attend special dinners and feel cheated if the expected guests do not turn up. "We were told there would be a celebrity on every dinner table – we did not have one on ours but Rick Wakeman came to talk to us later", one complains, "[and] at the Pavilion disco there were no celebrity acts as there were at the last conference." Talking to or just seeing ministers or even senior politicians close up makes the day of many ordinary activists, particularly conference novices.[21] Of the representatives to the 1986 Conservative conference, 70 per cent gave it as a reason to attend (Kelly, 1989: 157). Such encounters bestow a fleeting sense that one belongs to the country's elite even when this is little more than rubbing shoulders. Conference allows a temporary blurring of social boundaries.

Labour Conference 1995, Brighton

The Women's reception is a good occasion to meet delegates. Julie seizes the opportunity to introduce me (and herself!) to the party celebrities wandering past us with their drink. Suddenly Blair arrives. By chance, we stand in his way and Julie steps in to introduce me once more. After a few minutes, Clare Short rescues him from our corner to push him towards more "sisters" before his short speech. The conference officially starts tomorrow but Julie is more than delighted to have already met so many people she considers heroic figures and had only seen on TV before.

Gathering resources

Power is not something that one can hold and possess. It is the ability to "conduct conducts" or the ability to influence the choices of actions of another person by influencing what are the possible alternative futures (Foucault, 1984). It is exercised through networks of relationships and is linked to knowledge of rules, ways of behaving and other actors – allies, competitors and opponents. Power is about anticipating the reactions and actions of others or framing one's arguments to modify the ways in which alternatives are conceived.[22] Networks of acquaintances and friendships are created and/or reactivated at conference.[23] Local councillors are particularly active at conference, which they attend as representatives, delegates or visitors. They attend not only to meet national politicians but also increasingly to connect with other actors involved in local politics, from charities to businesses. They learn about recycling, water supplies or the protection of natural habitats and they find resources for later use in their capacity as councillor or party activist. Aspiring politicians and those who want to further their career within the internal apparatus use conference as an opportunity to be noticed. For them, conference is a week-long marathon: they go from fringe meetings to private receptions. In Labour, MPs and ministers who get invited to more than they would care to attend often give out their invitation cards to delegates from their constituency. "Personal" invites are collected, sought for and swapped.[24] The quality of other potential guests largely determines attendance.[25] The strategy is the same in all parties.

Green Party Spring Conference 1993, Wolverhampton

At the lunch and coffee breaks, John Norris meets as many people as he can, going from table to table sometimes, greeting all those he knows, introducing himself to others. By the end of conference, he virtually knows everybody and has ensured he no longer is an anonymous candidate when he stands for internal office. Indeed, he is elected Chair of the Executive Committee.

"Most of the work is on the edges" rather than in the main hall, explains a Labour delegate. Hanging around the main hotel bars, one can efficiently network whilst spying on who engages in similar activities. Discussions on these occasions are often superficial because those involved are on the look out for other people they want to talk to. A Liberal Democrat local councillor with parliamentary ambition comes for the training sessions where she learns how to deal with the media and how to respond to interviews. "Conference is important for those who want to do something in the party" adds another who edits the Green Liberal Democrats' magazine. Indeed, conference is an important place for the socialisation of activists. Novices discover formal and pragmatic rules for "political manipulation, its own language of political wisdom and political action". The "appropriate language and the rules of the game [have to be learnt] before [one] can play effectively" (Bailey, 1969: 6).

Labour Conference 2002, Blackpool

The Conference is about networking and scheming. The best place for this is undoubtedly the bar of the Imperial Hotel. Tuesday evening a small group decides to have a drink there (a Minister's policy adviser, a former member of the NEC, a former member of an NPF policy commission – and a French observer). Beyond the security scanning, the hotel is packed and navigation through the crowd takes a little while. The day has been eventful, so activists and observers are thirsty. The bars are full and private parties spill out in the corridors. Ministers and journalists can be seen rushing between a fringe meeting and a reception. Bill Clinton is guest of honour at a fundraising dinner. We settle in a corner but a young woman, who works for a trade union and wants to join the discussion, convinces us to sit at a more strategic table. She wants to be able to observe who is with whom, who comes and goes, who talks to whom and for how long. Do they look like they are friends? A couple of other acquaintances join us a little later.

The ability to influence decisions and other people's conduct is often institutionalised in positions and roles. Obtaining these positions is an arduous and highly competitive process in most organisations. The competition is all the more severe as more is at stake and the organisation is closer to governmental power. Thus, in a small and extra-parliamentary party such as the Greens, promotions can be quick.[26] Reputations are made at the conference, as speaking from the rostrum grants immediate if often short-lived fame. Constituency officers are present and it is thus an occasion to shine, explains Ann Widdecombe: "you are displaying yourself, they see performances and at some point they will be looking for candidates, so that can be helpful although you are not going to sway it just like that unless you have a very big impact like Hague". In Labour, those speaking on behalf of the NEC endeavour to be given a good topic and a good time slot to address the conference.[27] These interventions are occasions to raise their profile and a good speech at the right time improves recognition levels amongst party members.

As one admits candidly, it saves trips to constituencies to meet the grassroots.[28]

In pre-electoral year, such as 1996 and 2000, conferences are arenas where prospective candidates attempt to catch the attention of the media and to appear on the local radio or TV news. "In 1996", recalls Ruth Kelly, "there were great expectations and prospective candidates were under a lot of pressure. I tried to speak but I wasn't called. I also put a press release on crime in my constituency with the help of the Candidate Resource Centre." I met Stephen at a private reception in 2000. He wanted to be selected as a parliamentary candidate and was at the conference with his wife. They had worked out a strategy to maximise his chances. They were mingling on their own but she would discreetly call him if she met someone important. Ruth Bagnall was a local Labour councillor and a relentless activist. She worked part time and devoted most of her time to politics. In 2003, she was keen to be selected as a candidate and believed that years of effort were about to come to fruition. She explained that conference was an exciting and exhausting experience: she worked hard to be called to the rostrum; she spoke at seminars and networked arduously on the fringe.

Elections and selections

Until recently, the role of congresses in continental Europe was to adopt a strategy, select the national executive and the leadership.[29] By contrast, the most important political positions are not at stake at British conferences (Punnett, 1992). Since the 1980s, all parties have progressively adopted new selection procedures and leaders are elected by the membership.[30] Leaders are thus not accountable at conference even if their performance is crucial to establish and confirm legitimacy (Chapter 4). Formal challenges are rare.[31] Nevertheless, a number of key positions are at stake within each organisation. The Labour conference elects the General Secretary,[32] the Treasurer, members of the Conference Arrangement Committee (CAC) and of the National Constitutional Committee, two auditors and the majority of members of the executive (NEC).[33] Liberal Democrat conference representatives elect just over half of the members of federal committees[34] by postal ballot after conference. The Greens elect members of their executive committee by postal ballot, except when there are fewer than two candidates. Then, the vote is held at conference.[35] The Conference of the NU was primarily a debating forum with no constitutional influence on either policies or on politicians, nor the forum for the election of its officers.[36]

Power also exists through the resistance it fosters. In the Green and Labour parties, *rapports de force* are expressed through elections. Factions count their support in votes. At the height of the internal Labour wars in the 1980s, the annual conference played a decisive role as the main arena where battles were fought. Many activists complain that journalists are too keen to find division but most also enjoy the jousting that goes on at conference. They select which fringe meetings and plenary debates to attend because there might be a *frisson*. They themselves want to assess a politician's performance or measure the support he receives from the audience. Even though they do not always catch the headlines, internal elections often capture the atten-tion of the activists.[37] These ballots reveal the strength of groups and show internal fault lines. This is particularly striking in the case of Labour where the constituency section of the NEC has often been a battlefield between the right and left.[38] "The NEC elections are riveting", argues Diana Jeuda, because "they do not necessarily deliver what the leadership wants and therefore are quite useful; they diffuse some anger". Indeed, the leadership can be publicly humiliated. In 1997, Peter Mandelson failed to be elected. As the party machine and the leadership became more organised, they have pushed their opponents to do the same. Slates of candidates face counter slates. Non-aligned activists also think about setting up their network of support to promote their interests. The outcomes have been varied because manoeuvres are increasingly complicated. In 1998, the Left coalition Grassroots Alliance won four of the six constituency seats on the NEC against candidates supported by the "party machine".[39] Paradoxically, their success was probably enhanced, rather than hindered, by the expensive campaign fought by Members First's candidates. To prevent the reproduction of such bad publicity during conference, ballots are now held in the spring and the results announced several months before the conference.[40]

Constituency representatives on the National Policy Forum (NPF) are elected by conference delegates at regional meetings on the eve of conference. These positions are increasingly sought after and competition has increased. "One can get really involved in these games. I enjoy the NPF immensely." This is an opinion widely shared: the meetings "are a lot of fun" and it is a "pity the majority of party members are excluded". Successful candidates are usually well connected. A former member explains for instance how important it is to foster good relationships with the constituency secretary who is informed of vacancies, receives the adequate forms and has access to names and addresses of members to canvass. Moreover, links with activists from other constituencies are necessary because it is a regional ballot. Finally, friendships or acquaintances from all over the country are helpful as they know potential voters and can speak favourably of a candidate in exchange for similar favour, now or in the future. Candidates supported by the leadership benefit from covert support for their individual campaign. A delegate recalls how he was elected to the NPF in 1998:

> For years I had been making a deal with several constituencies [for internal elections] and I had spoken about [my wish] to be on the slate. Some guy I had met at a previous conference rang me to tell me they needed to know what was happening in [my region]. I explained to him what we did (...) so he rang me again and told me I was on the slate.

He obtained a list of delegates to canvass. He "delivered" the votes for his region and the slate won all the seats.

Labour Conference 2002, Blackpool

Around a drink at the Imperial Hotel, two activists discuss the results of the NPF elections to be announced the following day with mixed feelings. After some time away from the forum, Willie is eager to get back where the action is but he is sceptical regarding his chances. He has been outspoken and thinks he is now out of favour. Friends reported that they had received phone calls or letters "rubbishing" him. Diana is optimistic about her own case because she is "from the acceptable left" and is relatively well known amongst delegates. Her gloss on this is that "I am loyal but I am completely free thinking. Number 10 kept me because they thought it is important that we have a range of views".

Conformism is the best route to a successful career, particularly in disciplined parties such as the three major British ones. Because there are few enviable positions, the "gates" are carefully controlled. "If you are known to be taking a position which is not aligned with the leadership, it is likely that there will be a sanction. There is a 'machine' that goes into action that will rubbish you within the party and stop you, block you from any position (...) people who are ambitious tow the line", explains a Scottish activist.[41] Moreover, the *Excalibur* database developed for the 1997 general election campaign has been used to "keep tabs on its own more outspoken, dissenting MPs" (Bale, 2000: 284), sending reports to constituency parties to use the threat of de-selection. Similar ruthless practices are used against members or even journalists who are seen as potential threats. Considerable efforts have been devoted by New Labour to assess who might provide reliable support or is likely to cause trouble. Teams of officers listen to speeches at regional and national conferences and record voting patterns. In this sense as well knowledge is power! Those who can claim to know what is best for the organisation (because of their awareness of the political sphere and its evolutions) can impose discipline upon others. If activists are, at least in part, motivated by the prospect of a political career, then it is not surprising that they adopt the strategies most likely to increase their chances of being selected.[42] Most of those with ambition take such constraints into account. Cohesion is the norm in British parties and dissent the exception, even at times of growing restlessness: "the leadership is powerful and lots of people want to be associated with it".

Aspiration makes activists more manageable and predictable (Carty, 2004), so it is often easier to assert oneself or to resist pressure from an elected position. Resistance in institutional positions is an option that is only open to those with sufficient resources (such as famous MPs of the Labour Left or powerful trade union figures) or with little ambition to go further. However organised and strategic the leadership is, resistance remains a possibility. For instance, the independence of the CAC was, through the 1960s, preserved because some of its members chose systematically to stand against the alleged pressures of the NEC prior to the official opening of conference (Minkin, 1980: 136). The "party machine is not as powerful as they think they are", argues a former New Labour staff member, reflecting on their inability to prevent the elections of "independents".

Bonding with friends

Instrumental motives partly explain conference participation but do not give us the full picture. One only needs to consider the sheer enthusiasm of many regular participants who have attended conference, sometimes for over 30 or 40 years in one capacity or another, some of whom describe themselves as "conference junkies". The very comparison with drug addiction underlines how even activists fail to provide a purely rational, instrumental explanation for their enduring participation.

Sociability is one of the attractions of the conferences most mentioned by activists from all parties, but especially by those from seldom active local groups (such as many Green or Labour groups in safe Conservative seats). The justifications given by party activists to explain their behaviours are stereotypical variations on a limited number of themes. They do not demonstrate self-reflexivity but an ability to provide a discursive interpretation of one's conduct that echoes arguments commonly expressed within the organisation (Faucher, 1999a: 152–153; see Eliasoph, 1998). The party conference also attracts heterogeneous groups of representatives that converge to the seaside without really mixing. There are, in all parties, participants with few connections or little ambition. They stay amongst themselves and do not get invited to the reception, nor do they dare to go to the bar at the main hotels. They rub shoulders with others but their exchanges remain restricted by invisible social boundaries. If some Tories take the opportunity to attend cocktail parties, fundraising dinners and black tie events, others simply go out for dinner before retiring to their hotel. Although conference usually involves meeting new people, the experience of most representatives and delegates revolves around a small group of friends and acquaintances from one's local party. Conference is an extra-ordinary setting for ordinary encounters. Labour delegations hang out together and usually have at least one formal restaurant meal together, usually graced by the presence of the MP, if there is one. Oxford Greens, who belong to one of the most active and successful local parties, sit at the same table in the hall and often stick together through the week. Thus, conference is also an opportunity to socialise with people one regularly meets. Why go so far and spend so much money if that is the case?

Conference attendance allows members to meet up with like-minded types and have "conversations" that refresh the implicit nature of their worldview because they "take place against the background of a world that is silently taken for granted" (Berger and Lückmann, 1984: 172). The assumption of shared worldviews is an important social lubricant: in such contexts "one does not need to justify beliefs and actions", explains Jenny Jones, then Green Party Executive Chair. Participation is thus crucial to reinforce their sense of identity. "[What] is keeping me in the Green Party [are] the wonderful people you can't find anywhere else (. . .) people who are really alive, people who are really thinking and people whose values are the same as yours. That's so important. The Green Party is like a second community to me," enthuses Alex Begg. The group gives meaning to their actions and the world they live in. In many ways, conferences are comparable to churches where people go to meet fellow believers. Back in their town, many Green activists only face criticism and irony. It is thus necessary for them to regularly rejuvenate their trust in their own worldview and their political commitment. Without reaffirming interactions, it is difficult to carry on seeing life through tinted glasses. "You come [to conference] for the excitement, for the opportunities to discuss, you cherish opportunities to knock ideas around, you know you go home having grown spiritually, intellectually, emotionally" explains a Green. Another concurs "I've never come so close to people really talking deeply about things they really believed in fundamentally. I liked the fact that people were just as interested in listening to me as they were in having me hear what they'd got to say."

As the media had relentlessly announced their demise since their surprised successes of June 1989, in the early 1990s, Greens found conferences particularly helpful in raising spirits. It made them feel less isolated. It motivated them to keep electoral campaigning.[43] It reminded them of the existence and the solidarity of the Green community, refreshed for the doubters what it means to be Green. Thus, conference attendance becomes like an annual "fix" and some book their time long in advance. Similar feelings are expressed in other parties by activists who admit how their own self-identity is bound up with the collective. A Labour activist explains "I don't think I can conceive of leaving [the party], it is a bit like your born family, you think different things quite often, it is incredibly sociable." Within mainstream society, politically minded individuals are increasingly seen as unusual, writes Jeremy Paxman (2003: 144). Party members are in the minority and they need comfort. A former member of the Labour NEC admits:

I came initially as a visitor for years and occasionally as a delegate, then from the 1980s onwards as part of a union delegation. Then with the NEC. It was hard work, part of it desperately stressful but it was such a privileged thing to do.

When they cannot be selected as delegates/representatives, such activists come as visitors. They hang around fringe meetings, the bars and exhibitions. "It's such a powerful place." Activists are often enthusiastic about the conference because it gives them the feeling that they are part of something bigger than themselves.

Belonging and identity

Motivations for action are often assessed by means of surveys. By definition, those who respond to questionnaires do so within a framework that has been set by the social scientist. What is important to realise however is that this contributes to a naturalisation of the idiom of instrumental rationality. Eliasoph (1998) shows for instance how individualism has become the only common language of politics in the US, to such an extent that activists re-frame their public interventions to fit within the narrow parameters of civic life. Even when their motives, as expressed in private, demonstrate the importance of collective considerations, the justification for action that is articulated in public is based upon self-centred, instrumentalist arguments. This is because any deviation from this norm is now perceived as "hypocritical" or "irrational". As Jeremy Paxman's scepticism towards "political animals" reflects (2003), attitudes to civic action may increasingly be influenced by similar cultural trends in Britain.

So, whilst approaches in terms of incentives to action shed light upon motives for individual participation, their results remain necessarily limited by their economic premises. Acknowledging the limitations of rational choice approaches, Patrick Seyd and Paul Whiteley have proposed a general incentive model incorporating insights derived from social psychological theory (Seyd and Whiteley, 2002: 51–57). Because few people consciously waste their time and energy if they consider their actions to be pointless, selective and collective feelings of efficacy need to be taken into account. Having conducted several surveys of British party members over a decade, Seyd and Whiteley argue that "there is no clear optimal model that encompasses all the others" which can also satisfactorily explain high intensity participation in British parties (Whiteley and Seyd, 2002: 90). They conclude that, contrary to mainstream rational choice theory, calculations of cost and benefits sometimes take place at the level of the collective rather than the individual (Whiteley and Seyd, 2002: 217). Moreover, "affective variables that focus on the strength of actors' emotional attachment to their parties and the social norms that surround party activism are key factors (...). Such variables provide a solution to the paradox of participation and the free-rider problem" (Whiteley and Seyd, 2002: 218). The problem however is that questionnaires may not be best suited to finding out how these other "motives" work.

Seyd and Whiteley's approach highlights the importance of the two complementary dimensions of identity, labelled "I-we" by Norbert Elias.

As Elias explained, the balance between the two has shifted in advanced industrial societies towards the predominance of the I-identity. Theories of society that exclusively focus on the individual give the impression that *ego* could exist as a *homo clausus* (2001: 256), detached from any social connections. However, we-identity remains a defining aspect of all human life despite the growing uncertainty and fluidity of both dimensions of identity in contemporary western societies (Berger, 1986). At a time when belonging to a particular group defined and constrained one's opportunity for success in society, the individual dimension mattered little. Nowadays, many of the communities (church, town or class) one could identify with are eroded. I-identity is presented as a matter of "choice" manifested through life-styles. Because "personal identity is meshed with group identity" (Strauss, 1959: 175), the need for a we-identity has not disappeared, but follows paths already marked out, despite the insistence on the expression of personal tastes. "A person's identity is not to be found in behaviour, nor (...) in the reactions of others, but in the capacity to keep a particular narrative" about oneself (Giddens, 1991: 54). It is through such narratives that one gets a sense of temporal continuity (Pizzorno, 1991), of individual coherence and thus of ontological security. It is all the more important as identification with a group provides the criteria with which one can assess the value of rewards and incentives. If this is so, then "the process of self-identification will seamlessly motivate the individual and her behaviour in both public and private" (Schuessler, 2000: 51).

Alexander Schuessler suggests a new way to solve the free-riding riddle. He argues that Olson's paradox of collective action "rests on a methodological foundation of outcome orientation that is inappropriate in many instances of large-scale collective behavior" (2000: 5). When trying to overcome the paradox, the solution has often been sought by adding incentives that are based on the same principle of balancing costs and incentives, whether material or not. Schuessler puts forward an approach based on the "logic of expressive choice". First, he assumes that "preferences, values and beliefs all emerge from social practice. They are endogenous to the social context in that they are generated by interaction within that very context" (Schuessler, 2000: 7). Second, he takes into account the increasing role of symbolic expression and identification in "late modernity". Expressive choice serves as a medium of attachment demonstrating not only attachment to the outcome but also to the group of people making the same choice (Schuessler, 2000: 51). In some cases it is precisely the high cost of participation that gives it its value. Both Labour and the Conservative party now have "selective clubs" of donors, where membership is proportional to the level of donation.[44] Members receive silver or gold pins and signed photographs of the leader and are invited to social events such as annual balls and dinners attended by politicians.[45] Clearly the value of being a member of such a Club does not reside in the metal of the pin that one receives but rather in the very act of demonstrating that one belongs to a selective group. It is a way to show to oneself and others that one can afford such membership and that one belongs to the privileged few.

Individuals, Schuessler shows, combine instrumental and expressive types of action, the latter being largely connected to a desire to identify. Identity formation, be it through lifestyle choices (Faucher, 1999a) or specific actions, also plays a crucial role in explaining behaviours that appear "irrational" when viewed in a narrow instrumental frame. Schuessler advocates a combination of the two logics, the addition of an "interpretive, identity-based Being-dimension" to the classic "outcome-oriented Doing-dimension". The act of participation thus becomes both "a source and a signal, to the Self and to others, of *who* the participant *is*". Thus, "the price paid (and seen to be paid) for such participation will in itself determine its value to the participant" (Schuessler, 2000: 27; italics in the text). Because individuals are embedded in social networks that contribute to defining their activities, "who else is (seen or assumed to be) participating in that activity will determine what it means for the individual to be participating in that activity" (Schuessler, 2000: 61).

Conclusion

Party conferences seem to attract increasing numbers of participants at a time in their history when they have apparently taken on less significance as sovereign decision-making bodies. Although they now constitute a minority, party delegates and representatives remain essential actors in these events, if only because they provide the excuse for the meeting. Why do so many people choose to attend, sometimes at considerable cost? Conferences are the largest yearly forum at which party members meet. As a consequence, they concentrate energies and attention. Rather than social glue, they are more like social lubricant since they ease contacts and facilitate the exchange of all sorts of resources. Would-be politicians, party apparatchiks and members with ambition attend in order to make the right impression and meet the right people or simply to know what is going on. All participants also enjoy the sociability of the conference.

An approach solely based on instrumental rationality and self-interest, however, is insufficient to explain why party activists attend conference. Although selective incentives certainly play a role for at least a number of people, such motives do not provide a satisfactory answer to the puzzle of participation in collective action. Assuming that people act in the way that they do because they get something out of it ends up as a self-fulfilling tautology (Green and Shapiro, 1994). Scholars of new social movements have highlighted for instance the need to look at the role played by identity-formation as an alternative paradigm (Melucci, 1989; Pizzorno, 1978). As Schuessler (2000) has argued, it is important to use a variety of lenses and points of view when examining human behaviour in a way that gives more breadth to our understanding of the complexity of social reality than either the "rational choice" or "expressivist" models suggest when applied in isolation. Thus, rather than limit ourselves to a single theoretical approach, I believe that it is more helpful to use various methodological approaches according to how they shed light upon the phenomenon under analysis. Although I do not wish to reject approaches that focus upon the individual agent and his or her self-directed intentions, such approaches tend to isolate the individual from her social context and operate in a circular fashion. Moreover, they inadvertently promote a model of the human being that is at once idealistic (in assuming the rational basis of human action), highly individualistic and insufficiently cognisant of the complexity of human behaviour. Ironically, such explanatory models also reinforce a prevailing consumerist / individualistic trend within the contemporary "crisis of politics" that renders collective identity and agency problematic.

We do not need to "think like a mountain" as Aldo Leopold asked his readers[46] to understand that we sometimes act in ways that appear inexplicable as individuals but make sense if we take into account the groups with which we identify such as our family or our country. If we accept that not all our actions are self-centred or instrumental we can also pay attention to expressive action, which is action that is in itself meaningful to us or that "acts out" for ourselves and others who we claim or aspire to be. To understand the persistence of party conferences we thus need to change focus and look at the collective identities that they contribute to construct. The next chapter analyses the role of conference in the creation and maintenance of party identities conceived as "imagined communities".

3
Imagined Communities

As we have seen in Chapter 2, selective incentives are insufficient to explain high intensity participation such as conference attendance and it is necessary to invoke collective incentives as well. This highlights the need to use varied theoretical approaches to provide a more complicated picture of what goes on. It is surprising, for instance, that the insights provided by research on new social movements is so rarely used when dealing with more established organisations. It is as if collective party identities in such cases are taken as given rather than as constantly worked on and reproduced as is assumed in the case of the Green Party or new social movements. One of the challenges of social analysis is the integration of micro- and macro-perspectives and the articulation of the continuities and discontinuities between the individual level and the social context within which actions take place. The institutionalisation of practices contributes to the construction of social structures that influence in return the ways in which an individual behaves and thinks about the world that she inhabits.

Political parties, like national communities, are not based upon face-to-face contact. In his discussion of the rise of national identities, Benedict Anderson famously coined the phrase "imagined community" to emphasise the role played by the imagination in the creation of feelings of solidarity between people who will never meet all the other members of their community. The reference to imagination here does not imply that these communities are false or unreal, but rather that a sense of common identity and destiny emerges from emotional connections that are projected through time and space. Parties, like nations, are "imagined communities" because in Anderson's sense their members "will never know most of their fellow-members, meet them or even hear of them, yet in the minds of each lives the image of their communion" (Anderson, 1991: 6). The physical absence of "brothers" and "sisters" did not for instance prevent Labour party members believing that they shared with others within the movement similar aspirations and worldviews manifested through symbols such as Clause 4 of the party constitution. Because they are inherently ambiguous and poly- valent, symbols can mean different things to different people[1] and constitute powerful markers of identity across individual boundaries. They create an impression of consensus and therefore facilitate the act of imagining community. "Not only will people always be influenced by their emotions, they also will never be able to make judgements independent of the symbols they use, symbols that can be powerfully conditioned through rites" (Kertzer, 1988: 182). Because many of these symbols operate at an affective level in order to understand the formation of group identities we need to take into account not only their ideologies and values but also their practices and rites of legitimation.

According to Anderson, the birth of nationhood rested on identifi- cation with a territory, a vision of the past and a common language. Parties, like nations, construct boundaries (physical and symbolic) that separate them from their rivals. They thrive on particular interpreta- tions of a collective past. They are characterised by norms of interaction that frame permissible discourse within the group as well as appropriate behaviour. Conferences play an important role in the construction and maintenance of collective identities. "Conferences keep the momentum and the enthusiasm going", explains a senior Conservative, "maybe members cannot come but they know it is happening". According to Anderson, the very imagination of party communion is in itself important. The development of the print press played a crucial role in the process of nation building. Indeed, newspapers (dubbed "morning prayer") allowed readers to become aware that they shared a common present. The media serve a similar role in the case of British political parties, particularly during the conference. Newspapers, TV and radio reports let supporters around the country glimpse the atmosphere and sense that something important is taking place. Many activists follow the annual saga in their favourite newspaper – devotees with time to spare watch BBC2 television or BBC Parliament (a free cable channel) or party websites.[2]

Conferences are not only expensive past times for activists, they are also extremely costly to the parties themselves and it is only recently that such events have become fundraising opportunities (see Chapter 10). However, British parties organise throughout the year a series of such gatherings for which neither fundraising nor publicity can be an explanation. The "only justification for the Spring conference, and an important one for the Autumn one, is the interactions they generate", explains Shirley Matthews of Conservative Conference Organisation (CCO). Conferences produce a privileged social space because many people are in close contact, gathered for the same purpose and therefore open to the possibility of such exchanges and encounters (Lardellier, 2003: 109). They facilitate contacts between strata of the party that do not otherwise meet. They create a *bouillonnement relationnel* that facilitates communication and establishes the group as a collective in communion (Lardellier, 2003: 101). In this fashion, members of large groups can experience the feeling that they belong to a small community.

Physical and symbolic boundaries

A community needs physical and symbolic boundaries. When the two-party system is stronger, conferences caricature the opponent and stress the superiority of one's side. Indeed, beyond their official purpose stated in the party constitution, conferences contribute to the creation of meaningful differences. Thus, despite their increasingly limited role in decision-making, argues Bill Bush a former BBC producer, conferences will continue "because of tribalism".[3] However, when parties compete for the political centre-ground and when confrontational modes of political opposition are obviated, the role of conferences in affirming identities becomes complicated by concerns about image.

There are numerous ways in which boundaries are constructed, dividing insiders from outsiders. The titles of participants provide first clues about what the organisation is trying to say about itself and its place within the political system. Only Labour sends mandated delegates who sit in designated areas on the floor of conference, separated from visitors[4] and from the "Platform". Other parties select "representatives", thus proclaiming their attachment to the Westminster model of government. Beyond voting delegates and representatives, many other participants turn up but colour-coded badges reveal the status of its holder and the zones she can walk into. Party members are thus distinguished from journalists and exhibitors who are barred from seminars and "private party business".

Access to conference used to be easy, with few gate controls protecting the political elite from outsiders[5] but, in 1984, the Irish Republican Army (IRA) attacked the Conservative conference in Brighton, targeting the main hotel and narrowly missing the Prime Minister. Since then, strict security controls have been introduced.[6] This particularly affects the party in government, with the unfortunate consequence of limiting contacts with ministers. By the 1990s, all conference goers had to go through security clearing before they could obtain a pass,[7] then numerous pass checks and electronic screening to enter the conference perimeter. Conferences now create "bubbles" of social identity. Within the cordoned perimeter, participants are protected by the police and security services. They venture outside, not to mix with outsiders but to stroll to the hotels where fringe meetings are held.[8] The closure of conference has enabled parties to increase the symbolic value of attendance and to control the nature of participants, thereby establishing a closer grip on the definition of a collective "we".[9] Indeed, beyond the rules for the selection of representatives or delegates, organisers have the means to refuse entry or facilitate attendance. This is important as the composition of conference influences the atmosphere of the event. Participants bring with them expectations about what is going to happen and dispositions towards action. Thus, their very selection has an indirect effect upon the institutionalisation of behaviours.

Collective memory

A collective identity builds from memories of an idealised past that connect with a wider community. Whilst history is supposed to be an objective account, whose veracity is independent of any particular group, collective memory is precisely linked to a group thinking about its past. It is associated with a particular space-time and favours similarities and continuity at the expense of details and change (Halbwachs, 1997: 140). To an extent, collective memory invents the past (Hobsbawm and Ranger, 1983) as it creates heroes and mythical events that become symbols of the group's identity. It links present members to honoured ancestors or future generations. Ritualisation can be analysed as a situated strategy that distinguishes particular acts in order to accord them a claim to legitimacy through the invocation of the authority of tradition. Such ritualised events affect participants through physical sensations and emotions, sounds and gestures (such as standing ovations, singing, voting). In this way, ritualised practices contribute to the incorporation of norms.

British parties use the opportunity of conference to hand out awards to deserving anonymous activists during ceremonies that are explicitly designed to underline the collective recognition of individual efforts and the historical roots of the organisation. The award ceremony used to be a central element on the conference timetable for the three main parties. It is now increasingly perceived as "private business" and has been re-scheduled not to coincide with live television times. It is interesting to note the strategic use of the ceremony to send a particular message to the membership. In 1995, a few months after the adoption of a revised version of the Clause 4 of the party constitution,[10] Blair took part in the distribution of prizes immediately before his own speech. On this rare occasion, both Tony and Cherie Blair shared the platform with the NEC as well as honoured elderly members, thus demonstrating that the party remained fondly attached to its glorious past and its heroic figures. "New" Labour was thus making claims about its authenticity and respect for tradition to its old members, playing simultaneously on symbols of modernity and tradition.

Victor Turner (1974) distinguished ceremonies and rituals. He considered that whilst the former confirm and legitimise existing social structures, the latter have a transformative power. If we apply Turner's distinction to British party politics we can see that conferences combine traits of both: they legitimise political parties and their leaders; they also, when successfully conducted, lead to the restoration of party unity because they act out a "social drama". Conflict is ultimately resolved through the healing powers of ritual performance. According to Turner, rituals are thus "performative actions". The traditional format for the preparation of conference with the submission of resolutions constructed internal divisions: it highlighted ideological and political divergence, and internal competition. In some cases, pluralism was manufactured (Chapter 5). Conference, however, usually ended with renewed unity, the climax of the ritual being the leader's speech (Chapter 4). In an age of public relations and image management, it is no longer possible to perform the social drama in its full complexity and ambiguity because the differences of opinion expressed in the earlier stages have a tendency to be essentialised as irredeemable divisions. Political parties cannot afford to appear divided at any time and stunts are created to demonstrate unity.[11] As a consequence, conferences have lost a lot of their suspense, unscripted drama and symbolic impact.

As David Kertzer has argued, "a person's identification with an organization is only partly produced by the sharing of beliefs with other organizational members, for belief is a fragile, and not entirely necessary, bond" (1988: 72). Conference participants generally go back to their constituencies with a renewed sense of loyalty to the organisation and the leader.[12] Political arguments matter less than the reactivation of feelings of solidarity. Indeed, British party conferences offer supporters an occasion to be enthusiastic.[13]

Sensory devices of all kinds are used to affect the person's emotional state, from rhythmic chanting to stylised dancing and marching, from powerful singing to the doleful tolling of bells. The most effective rituals have an emotionally compelling quality to them (Kertzer, 1988: 99).

On occasion, emotions are whipped up, with varying success. "Haven't we had a marvellous conference? Let's shout; let's not keep it to ourselves. We've had a conference that was positive, constructive and enjoyable," proclaims the Conservative Conference Chairman at the closing 1998 session.

Sharing emotions fosters bonds. "The creation of an ongoing collective identity that maintains loyalty and commitments of participants is a cultural achievement in its own right, regardless of its contribution to the achievement of political and organizational goals" (Gamson, 1992: 57). Symbolic practices have integrative effects because collective performance is rarely just about shared values and sacred symbols. Such ritual and collective exactments paper over social and cultural divisions. Performing these acts creates the appearance of a common culture without actually needing to create it (Eliasoph, 1998: 112). The collectivity of the performance is what makes the ritual important, not a common set of "beliefs" within it.[14] This is particularly important as one considers the extent to which British parties are broad churches, gathering diverse ideological strands under a single canopy. Thus, collective practice itself is the social glue. To focus on the importance of "group performance" does not negate the existence of collective beliefs but underlines their ambiguous and inter-subjective nature.

Rules of interaction

We have so far distinguished, for the purpose of analysis, boundaries and bonds. Eliasoph and Lichterman also underline the importance of the ways one can express oneself in a group context in a way that emphasises not only physical characteristics but also cultural assumptions.[15] To better understand this influence, the authors offer the concept of "group style". A style consists of "recurrent patterns of interaction that arise from a group's shared assumptions about what constitutes good or adequate participation" (Eliasoph and Lichterman, 2003: 737). Their approach takes into account the influence of settings on the production of meaning and on the interpretation of collective representations. A style is a recurrent and durable pattern of interaction that acts as a filter for understanding the world. These elements of the group's culture are never created from scratch. They are built from the experience of members and the embedded-ness of the group within a wider social framework. Thus, different groups can use the same symbols, stories, vocabularies or codes to different meaningful ends in a variety of settings (Eliasoph and Lichterman, 2003: 782). The concept of group style creates a bridge between macro-social studies and micro-sociology. It can help us understand the diverse ways in which British citizens make sense and justify the ways in which they become, and remain, active in politics. It is also a useful concept for making sense of each party's distinctive culture. Indeed, it allows us to highlight how each party's style combines and recombines traits from other contexts to different ends.

Speech norms are assumptions about what is the appropriate way of talking (Eliasoph and Lichterman, 2003: 739). These norms are group specific and encompass vocabulary and oratorical style as well as what constitutes an acceptable topic. As Murray Edelman pointed out, "syntax and the prevailing sign structure thus implicitly express the ideology of the community, facilitate uncritical acceptance of conventional assumptions, and impede the expression of critical or heretical ideas" (Edelman, 1985: 125). Interactions within a group produce particular definition of a given situation. This does not necessarily imply "symbolic violence" but rather highlights the efforts made by any individual entering a social space to cue herself to the group's style of interaction. Platform oratory is a particular extreme example of the "chronic repetitions of clichés and stale phrases that simply evoke a conditioned uncritical response" and produce sessions that are "mentally restful (...) for their audiences" (1985: 124).

Collective representations are not imposed by social groups upon individuals but are progressively assimilated as part of one's taken-for-granted view of everyday life. These are transformed through routine social interactions (Klandermans, 1992: 83), and through repeated interactions and discussions more than through exceptional circumstances. Affective and cognitive dimensions are tightly intertwined (Newcomb *et al.*, 1965), so that acceptation of a new message is generally linked to an appreciation of its source. Identification with the orator is important if collective representations are to be changed. When interacting with fellow party members, whom she broadly trusts and whose values she assumes she shares, a member is more likely to be influenced into accepting as facts the information she is provided with. Her worldview is strongly tied to the worldview of the group with whom she identifies. Thus, the frames provided by the group are more likely to be accepted, whether they are "true" or "false", as long as they offer effective ways of making sense of the world (Gamson, 1992). Social problems are understood and framed by a process of collective definition, which is produced, and reinforced, through routine interactions. Discussions in which group members voice their opinions, express familiar arguments and articulate new ones contribute to anchoring attitudes in shared representations (Moscovici and Doise, 1992: 266). All party meetings, from the local to the national level, formal as well as informal are important opportunities for members to talk. The imagination of a party community builds on day-to-day exchanges. Face-to-face interactions help reaffirm a sense of collective purpose.

Although speech is the main dimension of communication, we also need to take into account what Goffman called the "rituals of interaction" (1990), that is the non-verbal means used by actors to convey, and reinforce, an impression. Such practices reflect different levels of self-reflexivity and awareness of constraints. Little of what we do in daily life is actually specifically thought through: we act out of habit and we follow routines. When placed in a new situation, we transpose what we have successfully done in the past. We act out of a competence that is embodied rather than discursive. Embodied practices exceed the limits of rational discourse and are not straightforwardly accessible through reflexivity. This does not mean that we are unable to provide *a posteriori* justification, only that calculations about costs and benefits do not bear on these micro-decisions because we are influenced by our *habitus* (Bourdieu, 1974). In a new context, we check out what others do in order to pick up the often implicit norms that structure interactions. Such structural guidelines give institutions their stability and individuals a sense of ontological security. Some of these guidelines are more formal and formalised even though their enforcement largely rests on a tacit decision not to cause a fuss or express dissent. Such ritualised behaviours carry out important ideological work as they patch over contradictions that might otherwise break the system apart. Problems arise, however, when the constructed nature of this collective "common sense" comes into view. The moment one becomes reflexive about a social practice is the moment it becomes denaturalised. This is when collective performances become seen as "empty rituals" and lose their taken-for-granted status but also much of their efficacy.

Large organisations such as political parties – and I include here the much smaller Green Party – are comprised of many different local and regional contexts, each associated with its own styles of interaction.

The intellectual and middle class atmosphere of West Oxford Constituency Labour party (CLP) contrasts with the working-class contexts of the Stirling CLP. Participants bring their personal knowledge and expectations to the national conference but they adapt to these new settings, contributing to the construction of patterns of interaction that then influence the ways they will act back in their local groups. Thus, conference practices not only objectify the continuity of the organisation but they also create seeds of change for a variety of party contexts. Party conferences are one of the key arenas, beyond the local group, in which activists from all horizons get first hand experience of what it means to belong to this community. They can assess the diversity of subgroups through speech or dress codes for instance. These groups are juxtaposed, occasionally overlapping, and also playing out the nuances of encased identities. Face-to-face meetings reproduce established patterns of interaction, thus contributing to the incorporation of social norms and their institutionalisation. Such patterns are not enforced as such but it is striking to witness the caution of "freshers" attending their first conference and careful to avoid blunders (Gellner, 1991). First comers observe the ways more experienced members behave in order to follow implicit and explicit norms. "Doing what the Romans do" is a condition of social integration.

Conferences provide the context in which to observe the interplay of dimensions of group identity and the dynamic construction of a party culture. Performance analogies allow us to focus on what the ritual does, rather than what it means, and to highlight the extent to which such symbolic activities "enable people to appropriate, modify, or reshape cultural values and ideals" (Bell, 1997: 73). Thus, they incorporate the possibility of change because they are less about conforming to immutable rules than they are about the "strategic reshuffling of cultural categories in order to meet the needs of a real situation" (Bell, 1997: 78). Conference is the best place to affect the general culture of the party. First, it is difficult to control what goes on at the local level and the meeting provides an excellent opportunity to address simultaneously activists from all over the country. Second, it is at the level of human interactions that the (re)production of social structures and social integration takes place.[16] Thus, organisers can influence the party culture through changes in formal or informal norms of behaviour. Both are more easily accepted by inexperienced participants who are looking for cues about what to do and how to do it. In this way, new routines are moulded and innovation is more likely to be adopted throughout the organisation. Only the Labour party has fully grasped how conferences are key in the transformation of party culture, although all parties now organise training sessions in order to spread "best practice".[17] In the remaining part of this chapter, we will examine in turn the four parties in order to underline in context the group's style as it is created and disseminated during party conferences.

Conference as communion

Emerging from new social movements and marginalised in the British political scene, the Greens form a small community that aspires to inclusivity and participative democracy. Their objective is to remove barriers to participation. The conference is the sovereign decision-making body. All party members can attend and vote. After reaching 15 per cent of the votes at the 1989 European election, the membership rose to 18,000 members in 1991, prompting disputes over the nature of the party. A new constitution drafted representative procedures. As the membership collapsed, a key argument in favour of a congress subsided[18] and the party resumed holding open conferences in 2000.[19]

In the mid-1980s, after a chaotic and traumatic conference, a number of activists decided to create a working group on Other Ways of Working (OWOW). They drew attention to the importance of sociability as a means of smoothing social interactions and calming tempers flared up by the frustrations of recurring electoral defeats. They pragmatically noted that, as in other parties, many delegates spend much time in the corridors rather than in the hall.[20] "We realised", explains Peter Lang, that people were "unlikely to come back if the conference [was] boring". For a decade, the convenor of OWOW convinced the conference committee to conduct experiments to improve conviviality and increase conference's effectiveness as a decision-making body. The Green Party recognises "that conference is important to create a sense of community"[21] so that members go back to their constituencies energised and ready for months of arduous, and often fruitless, campaigning. Regular breaks were introduced to ensure the best conditions for hard working plenary sessions; a minute of silence[22] to mark the beginning of most Green Party meetings. By 1995, the so-called "attunement" was also used by most local groups. Many Greens noted with some surprise the concrete effect of the ritual on the conduct of meetings: it helps adhere to a schedule, calms heated spirits in cases of disagreements and focuses minds on the objective of consensus. Some of them attribute such success to the fact that it allows participants to visualise the Green ideal of community (Faucher, 1999a).

Parties have their own tradition of conference festive events: the Swedish social democrats organise a disco, the British Conservatives a black-tie Ball, the Liberal Democrats sing along in the Glee Club, the French (whatever their political party) have a banquet. The British Greens organise a Saturday evening "Review" that has become the climax of conference. The show mixes political sketches and parodies with poems, songs and performances by the children from the *crèche*. The dominant note, however, is satire and self-derision. Sketches make fun of dull local meetings or caricature "anoraks" on a canvass tour. Most people turn up[23] – and some would miss it under no circumstances. The Review is therefore a more powerful and important event than its equivalent in other parties and one of the moments when the group becomes conscious of its common culture. Perhaps because it is a comparatively recent organisation, the Green Party does not have an emblematic hymn. However, conferences often close with a farewell song. In 1993 for instance, delegates held hands and sung about "Mother Earth".[24] Such demonstrations are relatively unusual in the party but, after a period of traumatic infighting, which had led to many resignations, the conference had played a cathartic role and healed the wounds of disoriented activists. Moreover, the winning faction included members who were particularly interested in alternative lifestyles and non-conventional forms of action. Holding hands and singing, combined with the anticlimax of the close of conference, created an emotional moment, a strong feeling of communion. Even the activists who normally frown at "irrational" behaviour seemed touched. Conferences provide the context for a fleeting experience of communion during which a deep transformative and fulfilling experience occasionally occurs (Turner, 1989a: 138). Many conference participants spontaneously mentioned the powerful experience of such moments of communion to justify their attachment to the party.

Groups draw boundaries to define a clear sense of identity through language, diets and customs.[25] Symbolic practices help define the limits of the group and create border zones. Moreover, the multiple meanings of individual symbolic practices open the way for a variety of self-definitions within the group. This is all the more important as prescribed identities have been challenged. It is no longer "cool" to belong: parties face a crisis of recruitment. The Green Party's attempts to recruit members are impeded by a reluctance to join, out of a fear that a membership card necessarily entails giving up on one's right to dissent. Card-carrying members are also keen to affirm their individuality.[26] Similar posturing is found in all parties. Moreover, participants are picky about the rituals they take part in because enacting implies that one assents either to its meaning (Connerton, 1989: 44) or to the meaning put forward by ritual masters. Some conference participants come because they feel they belong to the community but they sometimes disagree with a particular definition put forward through the show. Thus, they refuse to attend particular events or ostentatiously make it clear that they object and that they reject a label. British parties are broad churches and the dominant coalition therefore faces a number of more or less vocal groups of dissenters. Some of them will only take part in a few acts of the play, thereby demonstrating how their belonging to the community is conditional. On the other hand, conference socialises activists into internal cleavages because it is through the practical experience/knowledge of those involved that activists learn about internal arguments and disputes. Ideological divisions can be abstract to the isolated member so it is often important to understand how sub-groups interact.

> Malcolm dismisses as "useless and fluffy" the attentive efforts and routine deployed by a conference workshop convenor to make women feel included and valued. He makes a point of avoiding the Review and denigrates it systematically. He reads documents during the minute of silence.[27]

Paul had been a member for some time through the national Peace working group when he attended his first conference in 1992 but he had never properly met Greens from his own constituency. He supported the constitutional reform promoted by the centralising group Green 2000 but claims he had never really reflected on party structures. He thus simultaneously discovered the existence of virulent opposition to the motion he was about to vote for, its critics and their arguments. The experience transformed him. He came back a dedicated local activist. In many ways, joining a faction is similar to joining a movement: ideological proximity or feelings of identification are often activated through personal encounters and networks that provide the needed catalyst.[28]

Merging identities

In 1988, the Liberals and the SDP merged two different political subcultures. The annual conference played a key role in progressively smoothing over the differences and blending between the two groups.

Through interactions, a common identity progressively emerged. Whilst in 1995, speakers referred to "liberals and radicals" thereby demonstrating how they remained attached to older, distinct identities,[29] by 2002 the majority of orators at the rostrum addressed "fellow liberal democrats". The emergence of a Liberal Democrat identity and culture was a slow process that nevertheless unravelled under the sarcastic scrutiny of the media. Unable or unwilling to step out of the two-party system, journalists remain sceptical towards any organisation or political position that does not fit the framework. Therefore, they often dismiss Liberal Democrats as ideologically inconsistent. As a growing third party, the Liberal Democrats have always had to position themselves relative to the two others. In 1995, Ashdown won overwhelming support for the abandonment of the politics of equidistance (Cook, 2002: 230). In the following years, the press constantly questioned the Liberal Democrats' place on the political spectrum to the great frustration of activists. "Paddy's Pact" with Labour was the topic of intense discussions at the 1997 and 1998 conferences. Whilst Ashdown thought about potential power sharing, internal opponents tried to clarify their distance from New Labour. The relative position of the party on the political spectrum will remain a major strategic issue for the Liberal Democrats so long as the political spectrum in Britain is constrained by its "first-past-the-post" electoral system.

The old Liberal party followed an open door policy that was held responsible for chaotic conferences. The Liberal Democrats adopted the rules of the SDP: constituency parties elect representatives for two years. The ballot takes place in November, in time to prepare for the following spring conference. Substitutes can be chosen if the nominee is unable to attend. Representatives, who claim that they are offended when accidentally called "delegates", underline what distinguishes them from Labour: they are not mandated but make up their mind in the light of debates. The Liberal Democrats have inherited from the Liberal party a particular taste for obscure procedural debates and complex argumentations. They hold passionate debates on marginal issues but divisive votes leave few scars. "Having real debates is the expression of a different identity," considers Bill Bush and what could be damaging for a big party has been essential for their survival.[30] Indeed, they sometimes seem to revel in it. They do not (mostly) shy away from contentious issues and the leadership is often anxious about forthcoming debates. There are none of the invectives Labour was famous for in the 1980s but there was in 1996 the feeling that "we can say what we want, nobody's listening to us", as a representative comments. Growing parliamentary success and ambition to confirm the trend has raised the stakes: the party is out of the comfort zone of the political margins. The leadership now seeks to look "professional": socks and sandals are out; the new Liberal Democrat is just as likely to wear a suit as the next Labour activist. The fringe plays a crucial role in helping develop a sense of a community in each party. In a relaxed, holiday-like atmosphere, activists share a glass of something and laugh at the same jokes. Sessions such as the Glee Club[31] are important to build a sense of community, a feeling of shared experience. "I was amazed to see how many representatives were present" at the rally, comments a Liberal Democrat and "[I] quickly got to know what was meant by 'Slaying the Dragon'. Blue dragons are the very nasty Tories, and Red are the dubiously nasty Labour – new as well as old!"

Changing the party culture

When the Labour party was founded in 1900, it followed a model of delegatory democracy whereby delegates from the different components of the party (trade unions, Socialist societies and constituency associations) would be mandated to an annual sovereign conference. Although it placed the Labour party at odds with the Westminster tradition of representative government,[32] this ideal has been instrumental to the party's self-definition as a democratic organisation of the working class. Labour was formed as an indirect organisation and has retained a complex structure. Distinct in-group identities are manifest, be they ideological or social. At conference, constituency and trade union delegates sit close to each other in the hall but their experience of conference differs. The former, particularly novices, take their selection as a matter of pride. In order to fulfil their duty, they tend to be studious, listening to debates and turning up for most votes. Unless they represent strong and tightly knit local groups, they are mostly left to their own devices. On the other hand, union delegates are chaperoned: they receive instructions on how to vote and explanations about what happens. They are given a readily available frame to interpret the event. They hang about in groups and go to unions' fringe meetings. The interactions of such a diverse membership produce a common culture that nevertheless also preserves distinct contexts.

Henry Drucker (1979) has argued that the ideology of a party is composed of a doctrine (intellectual discourse) as well as an ethos, which arises from the life experience of party members. The idea of ethos underlines the importance of the shared values and experiences and how these affect attitudes and behaviours. The ethos arises from the interactions between social agents who possess and are possessed by a set of dispositions and predilections, acquired through (life) experience – Pierre Bourdieu's *habitus* (2000). These are generally neither conscious nor reflexive but are transposable from situation to situation. Thus they affect one's activities and reactions. They are structured and structuring. They embody collective memory and have an impact on the bodies of the participants through shaping their demeanour, sense of confidence or even guiding their choice of clothes. The socio-demographic composition of conference, and thus the prior personal experience of participants contribute to the production of a specific atmosphere that in return influences the norms of behaviours and the expectations of members. Due to the working-class background of its membership,[33] the Labour party combined ambiguity towards leadership and money with a strong sense of comradeship and class solidarity (Drucker, 1979). The expression of *habitus* is affected by localised norms of interaction.[34]

Brighton 1995

Julie is attending her first conference. She is grateful for the opportunity and still a bit surprised by the trust placed in her, so she tries hard to decipher what is going on and what it means. She has come with five other activists from Stroud. Some of them are experienced, even though they are not attending this year as delegates. She is rarely left to herself as she usually finds someone to accompany her to fringe meetings. They all meet up for dinner.

Blackpool 2002

Pete, a postman from London, has taken a week off work. After queuing for three hours, he obtained a visitor ticket that allows him to enter the conference complex, walk around the commercial exhibition and watch the plenary debates on a big screen. He explains over breakfast that he is here to attend antiwar fringe meetings. Every morning he gets up early to hand out leaflets or *Briefing Newsletters* to the delegates entering the Winter Gardens. He is determined not to listen to the Leader's speech on Tuesday.

Tom takes the conference seriously. He attends training sessions, sits through the debates and the votes. He moans at delegates on the row of seats in front of him because they talk too often during

---

(*Continued*)

debates, and constantly wander off for breaks and chats. He applauds when the Chair asks delegates to have their private conversations at the bar and to respect speakers. When the applause for a big speaker dies out, conference halls usually empty. Tom stays.

Sam, a manual worker from Oxford, is a constituency delegate. He introduces himself as "Old" Labour converted to "New" but he feels disempowered and lonely. Ill-at-ease in the white-wine receptions, uneasy in the intellectual chattering fringe meetings of the Left, he spends the evenings on his own.

New Labour is the only party that purposely set out to change the party culture by changing the composition of the conference. The transformation of conference is indeed striking even though it is difficult to pinpoint the precise causal effect. Rules were changed but so did the attitudes of party members. For years, local party elites dominated constituency delegations.[35] They knew the rules and often shared a deep-seated suspicion of the party management and leadership. They opposed what they perceived as manipulations by the platform through points of order or demands for card votes. They also did not shy away from verbal confrontations. These staged arguments gave an image of division and internal warfare that the leadership endeavoured to change in the 1980s. In order to address the root of the problem, reforms were discreetly introduced in the 1990s to change the profile of delegates. Parity and rotation are now compulsory.[36] Women were thought to be more malleable and less confrontational and novices were expected to be more impressionable by displays of grandiose settings and the majesty of governmental power, so their selection was promoted. The leadership hoped that the "humility [of new delegates] could be turned into conformity" (Minkin, 1980: 163) because they would not dare challenge the leadership or would not know how to use the rulebooks to their advantage. The idea that activists are more radical than ordinary members as well as elected representatives and voters is not novel. It was theorised in 1973 by John May in his "law of curvilinear disparity".[37] Nowadays, delegates are elected by members rather than activists. Women have not always proven to be easier audiences and it is generally difficult to assess the reasons for a change of atmosphere because there were at the same time in the late 1990s more women, more first comers, more "New Labour" and more members keen not to damage the party's image. Newcomers have brought their dress codes and their norms of interaction. As a result the *habitus* or group style of the party has been significantly adjusted. The *embourgeoisement* of the Labour conference is visible over the last 15 years, notably through the rise of the "prawn cocktail" tendency. Indeed, an urban professional style increasingly prevails over the traditional working-class atmosphere. In the absence of statistics of the social background of activists, evidence of *embourgeoisement* can only be derived from the transformation of the conference atmosphere, which could simply reflect the evolution of working-class group styles. However, changes in the procedures for the selection of delegates probably reduced resistance to the imposition of new norms of interaction. Both on and off the platform, the general group style has evolved. Changing conference directly affects the party's image; it is a remodelling of the imagined community. This is precisely what the New Labour project was about and the first steps included a number of highly symbolic measures.

> "Tony Blair had an acute understanding of the links between politics, culture and organisation", writes the former General Secretary, [thus he] "chose for his first symbolic leadership challenge not a policy issue, but perhaps Labour's greatest cultural symbol: Clause 4 of the party's constitution.[38] (...) The second major cultural shift in the party originated, not from Tony Blair, but from myself and the NEC. This was called *Partnership in Power*" (Sawyer, 2000: 12).

The strong reaction of the left to the "modernisation project" was somehow "necessary to the drama the leadership hoped to choreograph" because without it, the sense of transformation would have been diminished. "The point of revision was to cause a fuss" (Fielding, 2003: 75). In order to convince party members and affiliated organisations of the necessity of change, New Labour turned to the Manichean rhetoric it has used to depict other aspects of the modernisation of the party and the country. Here as well was

> the past recreated to serve the present's strategic needs. To modernisers, the central problem was the inability of the Party – "Old Labour" – to obtain the trust and confidence of the public. (...) To maximise the public impact of the new name, the contrast with the old had to be as stark as possible (Shaw, 1996: 217).

The policy-making process, "shallow, backward, adversarial", was contrasted with a new way, which is "forward looking, open, democratic, consensual". Old and New Labour were rhetorically opposed but the glorious past of the movement was evoked whenever necessary or convenient.

A sense of the past played a crucial role in Labour's identity and cohesion and it was the vivacity with which it was evoked, rather than its veracity, which was important. A mythic past was partly upheld through the enactment of rituals (Drucker, 1979: 31). Even though any ritual may carry different meaning for different participants, it is a "vehicle for the communication of meaning(s)" (Flood, 2002: 183) and it is particularly apt when it is associated with political myths. In the case of Labour, the conference helps re-enact and remind participants of a number of central "sacred truths" (Flood, 2002: 32) such as intra-party democracy, class solidarity or the mobilisation of the labour movement thanks to the party. Although generally assumed to breed conformism and prevent change, rituals themselves evolve and can be used to trigger change. The decision to transform conference was based on an assessment of the party's electoral situation. The danger was that it perturbed the party's collective memory, that which held the organisation together. "Modernisers" had little respect for conference rituals because they perceived such practices as irrational and without instrumental justification. Thus, they had no qualms about abandoning them. In fact, they actively sought to change the organisation's subculture and uproot some of the traditional activists.[39] The objective was to disorientate both the grassroots and the electorate.

Tom Sawyer, General Secretary of the Labour Party and himself an advocate of change, had actively contributed to the modernisation of what he called "quaint practices" in 1996. When I interviewed him again in 2002, he expressed a different perspective on conference rituals. In particular he regretted the leadership's refusal to sing the *Red Flag* at the end of the celebration of the party's 100th anniversary and the dismissive attitudes of some modernisers towards rituals because he perceived their obsession with destroying them as unnecessarily alienating respectable party veterans. The rejection of so many symbols of Old Labour disconnected modernisers in some emotional and cultural way from a wide group of decent and sensible party members and supporters who saw the rituals and traditions of the past as crucial and important. These were people who saw these traditions as being directly linked to the party's values and a lack of respect and deference to those traditions as a betrayal of values (Sawyer, 2000: 15). Songs are often an end-of-conference tradition that connects present-day singers to previous generations of comrades. "Unisonance" (Anderson, 1991: 145) gives a physical dimension to an imagined community, as if the echo amplified a sense of abandonment to a collective self.[40] The *Red Flag* used to be the Labour farewell but, whilst trying to forge a modern image, the party explored alternatives.[41] This was by no means the first time. Wilson swapped it for *Auld Lang Syne*, then hymns were tried in the 1980s: *Jerusalem* not only sounded too Conservative but it also upset the Scots. In 1991, an un-warned Shadow Cabinet on stage heard a blaring *We are the Champions* at the close of Conference. John Smith reintroduced the *Red Flag* but, from 1996, New Labour used D. Ream's *Things can only get better* as a theme. The problem is that pop songs have a short "shelf life". They do not create the same atmosphere either. After six years in government, there was little risk of associating the contemporary Labour party, even singing the *Red Flag*, with the party of Michael Foot. With growing criticism of the government over Iraq and public sector reform, the leadership is more conscious of the need to preserve its traditional base of support. Thus in 2003, the *Red Flag* was sung at the close of the conference.[42]

"To modernise the party (...) it is important to strike a proper balance between important past traditions and achievements and the modernisation of the party" (Sawyer, 2000: 16). New Labour may have gone too far in its rejection of the Old. Affective ties were loosened because the imagined community itself was being questioned. Loyalty towards the organisation was weakened for those who perceived that their identity was under threat. Over the years, slips in the use of particular phrases hint at deeper cultural changes. In 1995, Labour delegates interacted with "comrades" and female delegates addressed each other as "sisters" on a regular basis. The Chair consistently used the C-word that has since then been virtually eliminated from the vocabulary, except as a tongue-in-cheek reference. The word has been replaced by "colleagues" and "friends". The occurrence of the term "conference" has decreased in all parties but particularly in Labour. Is it because there is less of a sentiment of belonging to such a collective or because the conference has lost some of its importance? At the turn of the 21st century, the Labour party is less of a community or a family and more of a corporation. Interactions are defined in terms of the professionalism they demonstrate. "Modernisation" may have allowed Labour to win but it seems to have been at the expense of the collective identity of the party. How difficult will it be to mobilise individuals in the future?

Rule Britannia!

Until 1998, the National Union (NU) organised an annual conference to which Conservative constituency associations could send up to seven representatives each. Local officers usually attended but the event was so popular that members from large constituencies found ways to obtain a pass. Brian, a retired lawyer from Winchester, whom I met in 1996, wore prominently an anti-European badge. He carried a pass from Tayside because a friend from a Scottish constituency could not fill its contingent for a conference in southern England. In 1998, the new party constitution abolished the National Union. Thus, the annual conference is now organised by the Board of the party. The constitution specifies the procedures for the nomination of voting representatives.[43] Conference is increasingly presented as an "inclusive" event, with its agenda published in the party magazine *Heartland*. All members are now encouraged to attend but it remains convenient to pretend that conference attendance is restricted, if only to increase the subjective value of participation as a privilege enjoyed by a select few.

Conservative 2002, Bournemouth

Peggy is queuing to get into the conference centre. She became an activist when she was seven, following her mother's example. That was more than sixty years ago. Peggy's activism was temporarily interrupted because her husband was in the army but since he has retired, they have both reinvested their energy in the party. Both have been local councillors but he refused to stand as a parliamentary candidate to protect his family life. The couple are attending conference with fellow councillors and friends. The group has stayed amongst themselves because they do not feel part of the "political" wing of the party and they are not, in any case, invited to private parties. A few of them attended the Ball and a fundraising dinner but Peggy and her husband could not afford it.

Chloe comes from a Conservative lineage. Having recently graduated from Oxford, she works for the party as a fundraiser and organiser. At conference, she takes care of the needs of members of big donor Clubs. She has known some of them for many years because they are old friends of her parents.

Boundaries are symbolically drawn through verbal and non-verbal communication, from demeanour and the manipulation of symbols to jargon and ritualised practices. Like the other parties, the Conservatives have a clear group style that, however distinctive to outside observers, is almost invisible to insiders. In 1996, I was struck by the fact that queuing in a perfectly orderly manner seemed to be one of the attractions of the Conservative conference: people queued for refreshment at the champagne and coffee bars, queued to get into some of the debates and, most importantly, queued for hours outside the conference centre and then at the doors of the hall to make sure that they would find a seat to listen to John Major. None of the other parties have mastered the art of queuing so well: Labour and Liberal Democrat activists form in describable packs around bars.[44] Eccentric hats were common in the corridors of the 1996 Conservative conference in Bournemouth and one could lunch on champagne and oysters at one of the many conference bars. It was packed and the exhibition was sprawling into the emptied indoor pool. Anxiety at the thought of the predicted electoral defeat was balanced by the confidence deriving from 18 years of power. The world however is no longer the Tories' oyster. In 2002, the shellfish had gone, along with the hats and blue rinse hairdos. Opposition has brought a different atmosphere: the exhibition is half of what it was six years ago; although the number of seats in the hall has been reduced, there are still empty rows for most debates. Even on the last day, for the leader's speech, the hall is not packed. It is as if many Conservatives had lost faith in themselves.

Conservative conference, Bournemouth 1998

I have just arrived and wander through the mayoral reception at the Pavilion: white-haired men in dark suits and many women who have dressed up for the occasion. "Are you lost?" asks Paul. He is proudly the self-appointed representative of his trade union. He explains at length that he has been a member of both the union and the party for over fifty years. He stands up and out from a group of fellow representatives from Devon. They are sitting around a table sipping wine. They listen to the speeches and hold polite conversations in low voices. Loudly and cheerfully, he introduces me to each of them. They barely look up, probably uninterested. But they also look embarrassed and/or annoyed by his exuberance. A woman though stands up; she is the county councillor. She is "so sorry" that I missed a wonderful day of conference: "You have to get the video, I am sure they sell it. The speeches were great!"

Conservative representatives show high commitment to listening to the debates, maybe because the others do not feel the urge to be present in the hall. Debates present a "synthesis of Conservative points of view", explains John Taylor. The audience is here to listen to them and for the show rather than because conference takes decisions. Laughing at the expense of the "other" is an effective way to make distinctions. Cheap jokes at the expense of the opponent are typical components of conference speech routines. They blend famous English self-deprecating humour[45] with down-to-earth anti-intellectualism.[46] They caricature and they ridicule. The worst puns trigger automatic laughter.[47] "Platitudes are treated as revelations".[48] In interactions with fellow party members, participants follow unwritten rules of deference and politeness, codes representative of an idealised world of "decent" people from a bygone age. With impeccable manners and a politeness verging on the obsequious, the session chairman calls a representative to the rostrum with name and titles. He adds a "personal" touch to explain what makes him/her the perfect speaker on the matter. Very often, the representative directly addresses the Minister/Shadow Minister who is opening or closing the debate as if the meeting were an opportunity not so much to debate but to have views expressed before the decision-maker.[49] Upon leaving the rostrum, the speaker is praised for "his extremely enlightening contribution" or her "superb analysis of a complex situation". In the Tory world, all sessions are invariably "fascinating" and all conferences indubitably "marvellous" and "wonderful".

The embodiment of social hierarchies was particularly striking in 1996 but have persisted in opposition: representatives who line up behind microphones during the Q&A session often adopt a deferential demeanour to address Frontbench MPs: standing straight, hands joined in front of them, and their head slightly tilted. They listen to responses with an air of great attention.

Conservative 1996, Bournemouth

The hall has just opened but James has been queuing for nearly two hours. He eventually finds a seat. He unpacks his newspapers and starts reading. Next to him a woman adjusts the distance on her camera. Another one writes postcards. A Jazz band plays to entertain the audience. The husband of the photographer comes back with little union jacks. On the front row, flags and pom-poms are

(*Continued*)

handed out. After an hour, the platform fills up for an awards ceremony: constituencies with 10 per cent more members this year, with a hundred new members in Scotland, best campaigning in an opposition seat, biggest contribution to the national organisation. A new chair comes in to praise the "charm and competence" of Dame Hazel who chaired the conference this year. She receives her silver bell and thanks everybody from her father to her grandson and her Conservative friends. Lord Parkinson then launches the financial appeal. Whilst he explains "how outstanding this year's conference has been" with "such fine speeches" from Ministers "with enormous talents", conference wardens pass buckets around. Everybody starts searching handbags and pockets. They give coins or write cheques. Tory grandees are then nominally called to the platform, one after the other (the Chairman of the 1922 committee, the treasurer, the chief whip, and the Welsh secretary...The Home secretary is cheered louder than the others...the Vice-chairmen of the National Union...). When the lights come back after a short video, John and Norma Major appear, holding hands. The party Chairman welcomes them and leads the lady to her seat. Keeping his jacket on this time, John Major delivers his speech before an attentive and adoring audience: they laugh at his jokes, cheer at his jibes against Labour, clap every so often. When he stops, they go wild: James has dropped his newspapers and makes a racket with his feet, next to him little ladies in blue rinses wave their flags and throw confetti. Major receives a 10-minute standing, stamping and screaming ovation. His wife joins him on stage. When the chanting starts, the Party Chairman is shaking hands with the Front row. People around me sing *Rule Britannia* at the top of their voice. Then, suddenly, the singing stops, the Majors have disappeared and after a few last hoorays, the audience pack their bags and walk out.

Television and press reports have contributed to reinforcing the image of the Conservative conference as characterised by Christian prayers, deference, pinstripes suits, waving of the Union Jack and hymn singing. The reception of the leader's speech has been ritualised to provide a rousing rally atmosphere in which participants can "lose" themselves and "step out of [their] usual conscious, critical mentality" (Myerhoff,

1984: 173). The event connects members today with those who campaigned a century before them and with an idealised national community. As Kertzer notes, "what makes the emotional side of ritual so interesting and so politically important is frequently its connection to particular cognitive messages. Rituals do not simply excite, they also instruct" (1988: 99). Unashamedly, Conservatives today sing songs lamenting the lost Empire. "For many years Conservative audiences with tears in their eyes would chant the words to 'Land of Hope and Glory,' praying fervently that their country's bounds might be set 'wider still and wider', to the throbbing music of Elgar's march from *Pomp and Circumstance*" (Bulmer-Thomas, 1965: 146). If many members remember these glorious times,[50] the hymn has different connotations and implications for the younger generations. At a time when the legacy of the colonial period is questioned, they define themselves in opposition to a politically correct, global, multicultural world. Similarly, the consistent use of the masculine "Mr Chairman" for all positions in the party becomes surreal when the person thus addressed is a woman (as in the case of Teresa May between 2001 and 2003). Such vocabulary entrenches the Conservatives in a "politically in-correct" world that sets them apart from recent developments of British society. It also emphasises their *décalage*.

After the 1997 electoral debacle, the Conservatives tried to follow the example of New Labour. They endeavoured to demonstrate that they had heard the message and were changing. Hague wanted to draw a line under the image of corruption of the late Major era. Whilst Labour's modernisation was initiated in the 1980s,[51] the Conservative party claimed they would achieve in 10 months what New Labour had done in 10 years. Archie Norman, who had become famous for his success with the chain store ASDA, was entrusted to bring an effective business culture to the organisation. New ways of working and new information technologies were introduced despite the anxiety expressed by (grey-haired) activists when he first presented his plans at a 1998 conference fringe. Much of the success of New Labour had been based on embracing an entrepreneurial culture and the Conservatives, who remained convinced that they were the natural party of business, believed that they could easily apply similar recipes. What they failed to acknowledge though is that the business culture of the late 1990s embraced by New Labour is not quite the deferential "establishment-oriented" approach of the past.

To perfect their new "modern" image, the Conservatives adopted a constitution. The sincerity of this transformation was questioned because, despite new written rules, old practices were preserved from decision-making to established norms of interaction. Organisational and management reforms were not matched by a transformation of decision-making practices. The voluntary organisation did not gain greater influence whilst the leadership obtained firmer control of local organisations. Influential background committees retained their power; conference rituals were re-scheduled but marginally altered,[52] perhaps out of respect for the elderly membership – the only one remaining. The packaging was new but the "product" remained the same.[53] Change was thus largely seen by the electorate as a marketing ploy, focusing on image and public relations. The voluntary and political leadership also showed great hesitation in tackling ideological and symbolic reform in particular in questioning aspects of the Thatcherite legacy. In 1999, a speech by Lilley provoked such outrage from the grassroots that the leadership changed direction and decided to refocus on the mobilisation of core supporters. The party has been unwilling to reinterpret its collective memory and reflect upon its identity in a changing political climate. As a result it has failed both to transform both its image and its internal culture.

Conclusion

In this chapter, I have tried to show how conference not only contributes to the imagining of parties as communities but also sets the scene and frames the interactions between party members. Participants interact within the constraints imposed by structured, and structuring, patterns that they perceive as "appropriate behaviours". In each of the four political parties studied, symbolic practices are chosen in (largely) shared repertoires of action. They draw from the accepted British political repertoires and adapt what they do strategically to, alternatively, demonstrate that they belong to the national community and distinguish themselves from their rivals. All parties draw boundaries between themselves, outsiders and opponents and are constantly reinterpreting their collective past.

Group styles are developed and reproduced in connection with the social experience members bring. However, they reflect contexts of interactions that are specific and to which new members become acculturated. Moreover, they are influenced by the relative position to power: lack of electoral prospect reinforces introspection and a focus on self-definition whilst will to power encourages an instrumental determination to "modernise". As we will see in the following chapters, there is a variety of conference procedures, such as public debates and votes that are ritualised according to each party's own cultural style. Analysed together, these parallel developments demonstrate how these organisations are embedded in a national political culture that provides a framework guiding how legitimate politics is to be conducted.

The two smaller parties devote a lot of their energy to identity-formation and solidarity-building. The marginality of the Greens is comforted by the adoption of non-conventional political behaviours, whilst the Liberal Democrats preserve their libertarian enjoyment of debate because, to a significant extent, "nobody is listening anyway". On the contrary, Labour and the Conservatives are preoccupied by the image they project and are prepared to adapt their "product" (that is themselves) to what they perceive as the electorate's demand.

Media interest in conferences makes the annual gathering a crucial source of free advertising and an opportunity to define what the party "really" is for the benefit of viewers (and for members). Questions of modernity and tradition have been central to these concerns since the mid-1990s. Labour and Conservative group styles show how different attitudes to "tradition" have influenced the evolution of conference practices and party culture. The New Labour "Project" was ostentatiously disrespectful of rituals, perceived as archaic and "tribal". They were seen as being in contradiction with the image of professionalism and pragmatism that the party endeavoured to put forward. Because rituals were non-instrumental, it was felt that one could pragmatically dispose of them. To an extent, this strategy has played an important role in the transformation of Labour party culture but it has also weakened feelings of solidarity and group identity. A few years after challenging rituals, New Labour seems to have understood their importance and has reintroduced them within the organisation. Moreover, the Labour government is also strategically using them for different purposes, such as fostering active citizenship thanks to the creation of a civic *rite de passage* for 18 year-olds![54]

On the other hand, the Tories adopted a distinctively Conservative approach! They re-scheduled offending demonstrations of partisanship and adopted the gimmicks of public relations but they were keen to preserve customs and symbols. They did not really want to change and adopted a few cosmetic reforms that nevertheless allowed them to carry on as before. Despite a rapid succession of leaders (and their staff), they failed to convince the public that the party had changed. Whilst 20th century Conservatives had demonstrated a remarkable ability to adapt and innovate, their heirs seem to think that in a media age, change of image is enough to restore trust. The problem is that they are reproducing rather than renewing a group with whom fewer are prepared to identify. This has been a crucial factor in electoral terms where, as Schuessler has argued, voting patterns are often affected by "expressivist" forms of identification. The successful re-branding of New Labour is linked to the simultaneous transformation of rules, routines and rituals and thus the creation of a new party culture and identity.

4
Constructing Leadership and Authority

According to the British social anthropologist Victor Turner (1989a), there are two opposite models of social organisation. The first, *structure*, is articulated around statuses, roles and offices. It "tends to be pragmatic and this-worldly". The second, *communitas*, often characterises transitional periods of time. Liminality is a period of time, "betwix and between", when hierarchies and norms of behaviour are temporarily suspended. It is a threshold that is characterised by moments of intense, spontaneous and authentic communication between concrete individuals. The *communitas* is emotionally rich and fosters feelings of equality and fraternity. It "is often speculative and generates imagery and philosophical ideas" (Turner, 1989a: 133). *Communitas* is a nearly magical experience of "endless power" in which individuals are collectively empowered as if continuity between participants briefly prevailed (Turner, 1989a: 132). It is, however, often disorderly and therefore an ephemeral and fragile state that soon slips back into structured interactions. According to Turner, societies and groups within them oscillate between these two states of organisation and disorder. In a sense, *structure* and *communitas* are interdependent and intertwined. They reactivate each other. Action within the *structure* can become "arid and mechanical if those involved in it are not periodically immersed in the regenerative abyss of *communitas*" (Turner, 1989a: 139). The chaotic and carnival-like experience of *communitas* renews the legitimacy of the *structure* as the normal way to live in society.

Turner contrasts spontaneous, normative and ideological *communitas* (1989a: 132). Whilst the first is the equivalent of a hippie "happening", normative *communitas* is the product of its institutionalisation into an enduring social system. The third type is a utopian model of society built

71

from experience. It describes the external and visible effects of the inward experience of the spontaneous *communitas* and thereby suggests the social conditions under which such experiences might flourish. This interpretive framework of Turner's is as useful when studying modern western groups as it is when applied to non-western contexts. Democracy holds for instance the promise of *communitas*, which is left unfulfilled by representative government. It represents the utopian horizon that gives many in our societies the dissatisfaction of betrayed ideals and fuels the cynicism with which political institutions are considered. It is also bound up with specific visions of an ideal society, be they socialist or Green.[1] Both Labour and the Greens were originally founded to promote particular visions of politics based on empowerment of the masses and a radical democratic and egalitarian project.[2]

Party conferences create the conditions for the experience of spontaneous *communitas* that regenerates social bonds through shared intense emotions.[3] However, not all party conferences embrace this possibility with the same enthusiasm, partly because they approach power and hierarchies in contrasting ways. Some of the differences between parties on these questions can be traced to their origins. Labour and the Greens grew out of social movements in order to transform the political system for the benefit of the majority[4] and harbour suspicion towards leadership, whilst the Conservatives and the Liberal Democrats embrace it as an effective means to an end (governmental power).

The foundation of both Labour and the Green Party was inspired by the desire to defend the underclass. Labour set out to get representatives of the working class elected to Parliament and defend its interests. The Greens criticise the entrenched power structure that disenfranchises citizens and prevents them from having a say in decisions that concerns them and the planet. Both considered that political elites were too compromised in the economic and political system of the time and therefore committed to the *status quo*. Both parties have, to different degrees, struggled with the "iron law of oligarchy" (Michels, 1962). Michels studied the German SDP's ambition to promote representatives of the working class at the beginning of the 20th century. He concluded that, whatever their democratic ideals, organisations were fatally inclined to develop an internal oligarchy. Leaders, he argued, inevitably become concerned with their durability in power and develop their own interests, distinct from those of their followers. Labour and the Greens share a suspicion towards the personalisation of power and the inevitable betrayal of the partisan elite. The idealisation of political power sheds light on why Labour and the Green Party (Faucher, 1999a: 193–202) have both explored the liminal dimension of conference. Indeed, the festive construction of an imagined community blurs boundaries. At conference, activists and politicians rub shoulders, mingle in the hotel bars and party together. They call each other by their first name and feel they belong to the same "family". A number of practices contribute to an equalisation or an inversion of status.[5] Aware that to control the rules is to control the game, Labour and the Greens adopted detailed sets of written norms defining the powers of the sovereign annual meeting and rules for the accountability of the elites. They have also campaigned for a written British constitution. Indeed, they oppose the argument that customs allow for fluid adaptation to the needs of the time because they consider this as contributing to the reproduction of the domination of established elites who know how the system operates. On the other hand, parties of parliamentary origin do not have the same reservations about hierarchies and leaderships.

Resisting the personalisation of power

The Greens contest the emergence of leadership and regard with suspicion the professionalisation of politics. They are critical of traditional political ways of doing politics. They aspire to the realisation, here and now, of a sustainable society. To them, this means not only environmentally conscious policies but also participative democracy. Because they believe that the means condition the ends, they endeavour to run their organisation in the way they would like society to operate. Although written rules restrain spontaneity, a party constitution was adopted to guarantee equality and prevent the emergence of leaders. "Everybody's got a talent", asserts one activist. Another adds that, as a consequence, all individual members are "expected to do things as leaders, in their own time and according to what they're good at". Moreover, many implicitly share Jill's assumption that "important people at the top are not going to be green", and thus consider that the only way to obtain Green policies is through grassroots mobilisation. Aware of the inherent tendency of organisation to produce leaders, some activists devote a great deal of their energy to preventing such a fate from happening in their own party. They are convinced that the personalisation of politics diverts attention away from "real issues" and discourages citizens from taking their responsibilities seriously.

"I don't see that's it's right to hand my responsibility over to anything else, I'm responsible for my bit. Handing one's responsibility over is one of the very big problems. People don't do their bit because they think somebody else picks up the pieces," explains Jill.

Antipathy to potential leaders has occasionally verged on paranoia and those suspected of having an ambition to represent the party (such as Sara Parkin or Jonathan Porritt) were the object of such relentless attacks that they either left the organisation or withdrew from active involvement.

In the 1980s, as a small party on the margins of the political scene and with little prospect of getting elected, the Green Party could indulge in democratic experimentations. For years, a group of activists reflected on the invention of "Other Ways of Working" that would promote consensus as decision-making, empower activists and preserve the egalitarian atmosphere. The OWOW group exerted direct influence on many practical details of the organisation of conference. They wished to abolish the vertical distinction between the platform and the floor. Hence, the stage was limited to chairing.[6] The number of platform speeches was reduced to quell feelings of superiority that might germinate in the minds of those harbouring ambitions to speak in the name of the party. These innovations echoed the anti-leadership preoccupations of some of the most dedicated activists who fiercely opposed any concessions to public relations. Such intransigence is expressed for instance by Tim Andrewes about what he perceived was the transformation of conference in the late 1980s: "the very concept of a movement without a leader is undermined by the greater emphasis on set-piece speeches in the time-table (...) the membership won't blindly accept changes for the sole benefit of 'presentation'".[7] At the time, the party had no leader but three co-chairs and six speakers. They competed for media attention and got very little of it.

Following the 1989 European election success, a number of activists decided it was time for the party to adapt to the institutional and political environment. They advocated a more effective parliamentary strategy and campaigned for structural reform. In 1992, the party adopted a new constitution[8] to facilitate the co-ordination of campaigns and actions. A small executive was created (Green Party Executive (GPEx)), lead by a Chair whose role was primarily administrative. The number of Speakers was reduced to two. Many activists originally feared that the postal ballots of the membership[9] for the election of party officers would allow people to be elected because of their media profile rather than their sound Green credentials.[10] To prevent such possibilities, hustings have been organised at the annual conference, allowing activists not only to test them but also to hold candidates accountable when they stand again.

To prevent Principal Speakers from becoming *de facto* leaders or from gaining undue influence over decision-making, they were given no voting rights within the GPEx. The idea was to separate charisma and decision-making and thus to confine them to a strictly representational role. Mike Woodin, himself Principal Speaker[11] and "leader" of the Green group on the Oxford City council, considered there was "a strong need" for "leadership":[12] "I don't think a leader is the answer but I do think a recognisable person (or couple of people) for the media to talk to would help a great deal." Bitter disputes died out by 2000 but the party is no more prepared to choose a leader. When the conference discussed the issue again in 2003, the debate exposed similar strong feelings and resistance to the election of a single leader. "My leader is the manifesto", claimed an activist to widespread cheers. In fact, the yearly internal mandates can only be held consecutively for a few years, forcing the party to regularly renew its elite.[13] There are numerous examples of members rising to senior national posts a few months after joining and it is unlikely that the situation would be tolerated if the party was not on the political margins. Nevertheless, a few respected individuals are re-elected after short spells out of office. Moreover, the experience of electoral mandate has given them more confidence in their ability to preserve their originality whilst gaining visibility. Indeed, the party is taking the media increasingly seriously, adapting to some of their constraints and needs in order to get coverage: press releases are professionally handled and there is now a coherent communication strategy; keynote speeches were introduced in 1996 in order to, as an activist put it, "give at last principal speakers a chance to say something"; outside guests are invited to address conference and Caroline Lucas (principal speaker and MEP) even received a standing ovation after her 2004 conference speech.[14]

From written rules to informal arrangements

In the Labour party, "the tradition of intra-party democracy is suspicious of leadership, and there are times when that suspicion appears to be obstructive and critical to the point of paranoia" (Minkin, 1980: 333). These attitudes were manifest from the early days of the party in the reluctance to institutionalise the position of party leader. As a consequence, the post developed through customs outside the remit of the party constitution.[15] This flexibility certainly allowed the parliamentary party to fit within the Westminster parliamentary tradition. The betrayal of the second Labour government in the inter-war period confirmed wariness towards the personalisation of power. On the other hand, the Labour movement's attitude towards leadership was essentially ambivalent as the unionist movement brought in seeds of deference to the leadership. The domination of the leader was embedded in the myth of self-sacrifice and extra-ordinary quality that made the position nearly impossible to challenge (Drucker, 1979: 12). Moreover, the acceptance of conventions with respect to the office of Prime Minister and of Cabinet Government meant that "effective power within the party would be concentrated in the hands of the leadership of the PLP" (McKenzie, 1964: 639). Idealisation of leadership explains both the fear of betrayal (power corrupts) and the means conceived to prevent it, that is a "highly pluralistic, deeply polarised party characterised by the institutionalised dispersal of power and weak central authority" (Shaw, 2000: 133).

Accountability mechanisms were created after 1914 following conference pressure. Since then, National committees and the parliamentary party present annual reports to conference. The efficacy of the controls is relative as potentially contentious issues are raised with great semantic caution. "Reports were handled so as to ensure a minimum of Conference criticism and a diminution of accountability" (Minkin, 1980: 64). From the 1960s, the parliamentary report became increasingly theatrical and delegates were no longer able to ask questions, so much so that conference sovereignty was increasingly exposed as "a myth" at the core of the party identity. The balance of internal power evolved according to the practices of individual leaders. The trade unions played a key pivotal role that ensured close collaboration between the NEC and the leadership. As relations with the unions deteriorated and the party Left strengthened its position in the 1970s, the close collaboration broke down and Labour governments encountered increasing difficulties with the party. After 1979, the party entered a period of division and infighting leading to internal reforms and a shift of power towards constituency activists.[16] However, the pendulum swung back by the end of the 1980s. Kinnock initiated a process of change leading to the emergence of a powerful central authority exercising tight control over all aspects of organisational life, thus moving the party towards what McKenzie thought was the case in the 1960s.[17]

Labour showed a particular reverence for rules,[18] mastery of which became an important resource within the organisation. Nevertheless, many practices (such as voting procedures or "compositing") were defined by customs (Minkin, 1980: 148) and informally passed down over the years. Ways of doing were learnt from experience and explicit information rarely readily provided.[19] As experienced activists are more likely to be aware of the rules, the swell of novice delegates makes conference management much easier as they are more likely to accept as given what is presented to them as the appropriate way to behave.[20] Indeed, even formal rules can be interpreted differently than they have been in the past without raising too many objections.

Interestingly, attitudes to rules have also evolved with an increased interest in informal arrangements. Officially, the objective was to introduce flexibility to promote more efficient ways of working. Under Blair, the dominant view among party managers seemed to be that rules prevent the full blossoming of an entrepreneurial spirit. Moreover, rulebooks have been thoroughly "modernised". Initially most changes were presented as "bringing rules in line with current practices" and they were adopted by conference delegates eager to set the conditions for a long-awaited electoral victory.[21] The idea was to create structures with fewer rules making it more possible to play with grey areas. "We have moved from rules to no rules," explains Meg Russell in reference to the new policy-making procedures. The party used to be "obsessed with rules but it has now become so unfashionable" to think in these terms. The "rules were too strict and stifling but when you take them away, it becomes flabby". New institutions, such as the National Policy Forum (NPF) founded in 1997, are particularly affected. In spite of claims that it would ensure the connection between the national organisation and the grassroots, no formal channels were conceived to allow representatives to report to their constituents. Ann Black, who had many hopes about the possibilities created by the NPF, expresses her disappointment about the failure of the policy process to fully engage members: "they haven't got a clue who you are and you don't even get a chance to talk to them". Moreover, "because members don't turn up at meetings either, you have no idea who are the people you are supposed to represent". Although all those I spoke to insisted that they made every effort to report back to members,[22] the very informality of the process makes it difficult to develop support groups or alternative strategies to those promoted by the leadership. Indeed, the blurring of rules and roles means that the leadership can impose its interpretation as the "normal" way to do things. Isolated individuals with no clear knowledge of definitive norms are more likely to be convinced by those claiming to know what is in the best interest of the organisation.

Leader centred parties

The Conservatives and the Liberal Democrats have less ambiguous attitudes to power. Leadership in these two parties is personalised (Ansell and Fish, 1999). Once elected, the leader benefits from great latitude in matters of policy and strategy. The community-building potential of the conference is thus used, as a regenerative ritual that periodically renews the enthusiasm and the dedication of activists who can thereafter "go back to their constituency to fight" political opponents on the ground. In both parties, the annual conference temporarily levels out differences between participants who sit in the same areas and mingle freely. However, hierarchies are not challenged and social status is on the contrary reinforced. The irreverent Liberal Democrats' Review constitutes no real exception, although party members often mock their leadership in the political satires they act out in these evening gatherings. Remoteness from power makes challenges to the leadership at the annual conference less electorally risky in terms of image. Such border behaviour would probably not be tolerated if the party had any serious pretension to power. Thus, although Liberal Democrat leaders have retained a central role in the organisation, they cannot take the support of the grassroots for granted. Moreover, they often have to struggle to establish a voice of their own as their followers hold them in no unconditional esteem: Ashdown was a charismatic and popular figure but even his conference performances did not seem to trigger demonstrations of adoration similar to what happens in the Conservative party (and increasingly in Labour). Whilst Ashdown commanded natural authority, his successor, Charles Kennedy, had to establish his credentials and demonstrate that he was taking politics seriously.[23] His first conference speech was described as "lacking inspirational political vision" and his second as "vacuous" by the press.[24] The 1999 conference "was supportive of the new leader rather than ecstatic" (Cook, 2002: 254), probably because activists were unhappy that the leader had recently proposed to have the Federal Policy Committee (FPC) elected by the membership rather than conference representatives – a move seen as likely to make it less radical and, more importantly, to limit their influence.[25]

The pre-eminence of the leadership has never been seriously contested in the Conservative party, even by those calling for intra-party democracy (such as Charter). The assumption is that the leader has the right and the expertise to lead and should not be distracted. The membership is not the sovereign of the party, nor is the annual conference. The meeting, which has often been described as a "rally of the faithful rather than a deliberative assembly" (Whiteley, Seyd and Richardson, 1994: 30), has no formal influence on political decisions. However, the considerable powers of the Conservative leader rest in the trust and loyalty of his followers and hence in his/her ability to listen. Although the extent of the sensitivity of the leadership to the moods and opinions expressed is difficult to measure, party leaders put much effort "into persuading the conference of the correctness of a particular policy" (Norton and Aughey, 1981: 207). "The *modus operandi* within the party is the trust invested in the leadership by the membership, a trust based upon an assumption of competence and success" (Kelly, 1989: 6) and that can be evaluated neither through the votes nor through the absence of open criticism of the leadership.

The lack of formal chains of accountability within the Conservative party also stems from the fact that it was until recently composed of three autonomous organisations. The issue of internal democracy thus practically emerged with the unitary 1998 constitution that did not, however, challenge the networks of influence operating through committees. The party remains wary of explicit normative rules that could impose too many constraints on decision-making. The *Handbook for Income Generation for Constituency Associations* details the best strategies to raise funds and advises for instance "Do not elect committees, appoint them." Efficacy and pragmatism thus contribute to explain why the Conservatives have consistently preferred the flexibility of customs and taken their time to settle on a definitive version of the constitution. Notwithstanding the recurrent references to democracy in recent Conservative party documents, which is *de rigueur* in the spirit of the times, the basic equilibrium is the same. Indeed, senior officials admit that most of the changes are "cosmetic". Power remains firmly in the hands of the leader whose position appears to have been strengthened by the new electoral procedures. At the same time, he or she can no more than in the past afford to ignore traditional sensitivities and practices. Duncan Smith, who was the first – and so far only – leader to be elected by members, made the mistake of overlooking traditional modes of operation. Convinced that the membership vote gave him unquestionable legitimacy, he sacked without warning or consultation Frontbench colleagues and senior Central Office staff.[26] Such behaviour might have been tolerated but was an ill-judged decision for a leader whose authority amongst internal elites was limited. Legal-rational legitimacy is never enough to make a strong leader as he realised at his expense when he was forced to resign a few weeks after the 2003 conference. In 2005, OMOV was abandoned.

The leader's speech

Most political parties tend to use the leader's speech as the rallying finale of their conference or congress. In Britain, the tradition dates back to Disraeli's speech at the closure of the 1872 National Union conference. With the apex scheduled at the very end, the conference builds up to its momentum and the press is kept focused through the week.[27] The Liberal Democrats (the Liberals before them) and the Conservatives have followed this pattern for most of their existence but in the 1990s, they occasionally re-scheduled the speech to maximise media attention. The Liberal Democrats tried Tuesday afternoons and the Conservatives Thursdays. The experiments were inconclusive and both parties still prefer to end the annual meeting with a rousing speech. The Labour party is the exception, with a parliamentary report delivered on the Tuesday afternoon.

> This makes it "extremely difficult for the leadership to orientate the occasion to its advantage. The conference continues, organisationally, symbolically and discursively, for 3 more days, thus depriving the leader of the opportunity to present itself as a discursive climax" (Gaffney, 1991: 107).

The objective is to "inspire the party faithful as well as ease the worries of the doubters. It is more like a piece of poetry than prose" (Thatcher, 1993: 369). A good speech manages at the same time to present the leader as a person of vision, to offer a programme for the future and the assurance that past ambitions and promises have been fulfilled. It "cannot just be written in advance; you need to get the feel of the conference in order to achieve the right tone" (Thatcher, 1993: 379). Drafts are thus worked on until the last minute so that events of the previous days are integrated. The speech needs to respond to recent developments within the party conference itself – such as rhetorical challenges by internal competitors – or outside. The "conference speech is torture," remembers Kinnock, "it is a cruel and unnatural form of punishment. All leaders feel the same, only the degree of torture varies." It is also one of the most important opportunities to "assert control, make the case, strike a balance, appeal to the country, get the party to march behind me. All words had to be considered and reconsidered, rehearsed overnight." The words are carefully chosen and the jokes rehearsed *ad nauseam*.[28] Media attention makes the conference speech a crucial occasion. Journalists, such as Michael Cockerel, justify their own interest in the event by the efforts devoted to the event: "Tony Blair really does use the party conference to give his big set speech and an awful lot of work goes into it. The whole of Number 10 is frenzied for over a month." This interesting self-fulfilling prophecy – the Prime Minister sees it as important, therefore it is – legitimises media coverage. Indeed, Alastair Campbell reminded journalists at the debriefing session following Blair's speech in 2002 that the speech was not to be understood as addressing the membership more than the wider public. The difficulty of the exercise, especially when in government, is to do both at the same time and to equally impress them. The event is thus a crucial yet complex test of the incumbent's competence. In the past, Labour leaders had to show that they were not "manipulated by darker forces or incapable of asserting their leadership" (Gaffney, 1991: 9). Since the mid-1990s, Conservative leaders have faced a similar challenge.

There is no space here to analyse leaders' conference speeches in detail but they do share certain characteristics. In 1986, all three speeches "sacralise[d] the people, suggesting that simple people are the wisest (. . .) and that 'wisdom' itself [could] be encapsulated in the persona of a political leader"; they elevated the status of the leader and "involve[d] a high moral tone in the evocation of the leader/people relation"; they tended to be "anti-organisation, anti-state, even anti-party", thus enhancing the notion of an unmediated relationship between leader and people; they suggested "the New Testament themes of the clearing of the Temple, of redemption and of deliverance" (Gaffney, 1991: 194). Contemporary speeches also allow activists to identify with their leader and to believe that their values are transposed into the aspirations and commitments he articulates. Similar references are found in the invocation of "real people" and their "common sense". The rhetoric (and the body language) attempts to resolve the paradox of modern political leaders, caught between the man-in-public-office (the charismatic and extra-ordinary leader) and the private individual (the "ordinary bloke"). John Major and Tony Blair have played these two cards alternatively. In 1996, Major took off his jacket to demonstrate that, despite being Prime Minister, he was unpretentious and relaxed. In 2000, Blair poured with sweat in his blue shirt during his speech – whether the perspiration was caused by the spotlight heat or because he was anxious about his performance and the response from the audience.[29] In both cases, anecdotal events were spun as "real men in action" and as underlining personal traits and style. As Fairclough explains in the case of Blair, leadership style is more than just about words: "it is a matter of his total bodily performance (...) how he sounds, how he looks, the shifting expressions on his face, the way he moves his head and other parts of his body" (Fairclough, 2000: 97). Blair's political persona is clearly crafted, thanks to focus groups (Fairclough, 2000: 118). The power of Blair's style "is his ability to combine formality and informality, ceremony and feeling, publicness and privateness" (Fairclough, 2000: 7). Political identities are carefully constructed in today's media-saturated world, built from work on image and also from the private personality, experience and *habitus*.

Almost as important as the words themselves is the reception of the speech. Expectations about the leader's ability to perform well raise the stakes. The leader's speech is the centrepiece of the conference for the media and a rare occasion where their interests converge with those of the party. The press pays attention to the performance and reactions to it. Journalists keep records of the decibels, nature and length of ovation and also of the number of interruptions during the speech. There has been over the years an inflation in the demonstrations of enthusiasm at the end of speeches. On 30 September 1970, *The Times* commented that "at the end of his speech, Mr Wilson received a standing ovation for a full minute". "If a standing ovation took place, or if it was only half the hall or only for a minute and a half, it would be in all the papers. So you look to raise their vision," explains Neil Kinnock. Much longer ovations are now recorded. In 1995, the *Guardian* reported that Prescott, the deputy leader, received a five-minute ovation. In 2003, Tony Blair, then facing a crisis of confidence, joked that he had probably peaked too early when he started his annual peroration with a standing ovation. That was highly unlikely. The ovation he received at the end of the speech was such that he came back for an *encore*! The competition is getting fiercer now that it is such an important public relations exercise[30] and the media are somehow in connivance with party stage managers because they relish the ostentatious demonstrations of support that so nicely illustrate their reports.

Rituals of legitimation

Parties actively try to project a particular image of themselves that conveys a message of power, competence and legitimacy. The leader's speech is explicitly staged to impress both members and the public.

For this purpose, attention is given to the settings themselves and other ways to manipulate meaning-codes and mass response (Edelman, 1985: 101). The extraordinary atmosphere of the leader's speech is as much a consequence of the leader's authority as a show carefully prepared to create the desired impression of charisma. For better effect, organisers ritualise the event and make the occasion "special". The "leader's speech has to be different from all the others", argues Chris Poole, it needs to "demonstrate the outstanding qualities" of the leader. "Ritual is a vehicle for the construction of relationships of authority and submission" (Bell, 1997: 82) because legal-rational arguments by themselves do not carry the imagination. The three parties use similar strategies to build momentum and create an emotionally receptive atmosphere.

The leader's speech is usually preceded by some ritual waiting that adds value to the experience.[31] Momentum is built and activists entertained with local children's orchestras or choirs. Such warming up numbers also set the session apart from all others. Queues for the leader's speech are famous in the Conservative party and the topic of many conversations the night before. In the days the party was in government, queues were formed outside the conference centre long before the gates opened even though the leader would only appear several hours later to coincide with live television coverage. In the past, Labour delegates did not wait for very long – the parliamentary report is the first item on the Tuesday afternoon schedule – but the situation has worsened. "Attending the leader's speech is one of the highlights of activism," I was told by a queuing Labour delegate. Another confides that it was "so emotional last year" that she cried. It has become difficult to see the speech from the main hall because tickets do not even guarantee entry. It is the only session due to start at 2 pm for which the platform arrives 20 minutes late. In France, François Mitterrand was notoriously late and cultivated the art of keeping people waiting for him. The congress could not start without him and would wait.[32] Tony Blair has learnt this trick and increasingly arrives late. The waiting time must be proportional to status: is not the Prime Minister worthier than the leader of the Opposition? Has the need to be desired grown as his leadership is contested?

There are other means to increase the value of a glimpse of the leader. Precious things are rare. It is not only because he is extremely busy with meetings (or with writing his speech as it is sometimes argued) that his appearances are so few for the many delegates and representatives. Throughout the world, powerful kings and priests consolidate their reputation through isolation. Being seen mingling with activists brings some benefits and Thatcher was the first Conservative leader to show great interest in the event and to attend it in its entirety.[33] Her presence underlined the importance of the conference and, therefore, of members. She used her support amongst the rank-and-file to bolster her position. In 1986 for instance, she was seen as a potential electoral liability but she attended debates

> listening attentively throughout as a leader who had come back from the lonely heights of power to listen and to heed her people (...) before embarking once again on her mission, strong in the confidence of her supporters (Gaffney, 1991: 153).

However, appearing as an ordinary human may diminish the mystery surrounding the person. Only confident leaders take the risk, or those who need to counteract accusations of being "out-of-touch". If the conference potentially eradicates hierarchy, the leader resists this levelling tendency. The distance between the leader and his followers is physically (re)created. At conference, the leader is both close and far away. He is somewhere in town or in the conference complex but he rarely comes down to listen to debates or meet activists on the fringe – and when he does, his presence needs to be interpreted as sending a particular signal.[34]

The backdrop is *"écrin"* (jewel box) and *"écran"* (screen) and symbols are woven according to circumstances and needs. The objective is to impress and to contrast with all other performers. Ritualisation makes power spectacular and thus "different" (Balandier, 1992: 107). In the 1990s, the platform and the rostrum were often especially rearranged for the leader's speech. The steps the leader climbs with a youthful jog, the curtains from which he appears like a *deus ex machina*, the lighting and the settings, all concur to visualise the superiority of the performer. The decorum gives an aura of charisma. In 1995 and 1996, the Liberal Democrats and Labour put up a new lectern for the leader during the lunch break and Labour highlighted how the young (inexperienced) leader was surrounded by a closely knit team. At other times, the leader stands alone in his grandeur (Major in 1996 or Blair in 2000). The media contributes, partly unwittingly, to the construction of authority through the editing, framing and presentation of the speeches: short abstracts are preceded by an expert's analysis that is supposed to highlight most of its content and alternate with clips showing the reaction of the audience,[35] the nodding of colleagues and the standing ovations are highlighted as if underlining the charisma, the wit and the popularity of the speaker. The show in the hall and on the screens constructs the leader as a charismatic character, qualities that the individual leader does not necessarily have. In 2002, Duncan Smith made a fatal mistake: he voluntarily reduced the decorum and placed himself on the level of the crowd, trying to play on the image of the "quiet" man. Unfortunately both the settings and the performance concurred to demonstrate that he did not have the "stuff of heroes".

Do political rituals create followers? Is their role to convince people to obey? Barker (2001) argues that legitimating acts are more important in the eyes of the leaders themselves than for their alleged role in convincing the led to follow. They reassure leaders about the legitimacy of their position, confirm their role in their own eyes and those of their supporters. They also reinforce their privileged position to outsiders and rivals within their party. Legitimating acts highlight what makes leaders "different" and create identities for the groups around the leadership (rulers, "cousins", ruled) whose separate status is legitimised. By allowing rulers to present themselves in the best possible light, rituals help confirm their superiority to others as well as to themselves. Thus, these acts justify positions rather than having a purpose in a rationally instrumental way. Conferences "confer charisma" and construct the internal hierarchy of merit. Although organisers claim that they are organised for the benefit of members and supporters, conferences are also crucially important for leaders, who are thereby comforted about the legitimacy of their position and role. The yearly televised show multiplies the echo of their national stature. Leaders who previously rejected rituals as archaic and empty soon rediscover them as pillars for their legitimacy and means to increase their charismatic standing (Lardellier, 2003: 59).

Rituals construct authority and, as such, are stabilising elements but they can also fail – or open up spaces for resistance (Dirks, 1992). In 1986, a pre-electoral year, several members of the NEC remained seated during the standing ovation and one did not applaud (Gaffney, 1991: 102). It was all the more embarrassing and defiant as it was so public. Ten years later, the party avoided such *faux-pas*: the platform seating has been reduced and the party machine was geared up to ensure a good reception. Besides, party members were eager to win and few dissidents were prepared to risk bearing the cost of defeat. Despite occasional incidents, party members attending the speech are generally keen for the event to go down well and are prepared to help. Audiences in televised shows are warmed up and coached to clap on cue. It is an established theatrical device that has stood the test of time. Conference auditoria rarely need so much work because they *want* to be moved. Stage directions do not mean that activists' cheers are fake, only that their spontaneous expression is augmented. Only conference novices are surprised when they discover that party workers have print outs of the speech with indications of when to clap but those who know this rarely mention it without prompting.

Labour Conference, Blackpool 2002

In the queue for a fringe meeting organised by Young Labour, Jane recalls her days as party staff in 1996. She worked in one of the teams supervised by the Assistant General Secretary to ensure that media events went smoothly. "We had to learn about a vast number of people, what they thought and what they were likely to say if they spoke or to vote if they voted. We made sure that there were friendly people or party workers on the path of the leader after his speech so that he could shake hands on his way out. We isolated people we thought might pose a problem, blocking their way in case they wanted to get close".

Although the event is dramatised as a turning point in the leadership career, most leaders' speeches generally go down well because every effort has been made to ensure that things go according to the plan. There is always the risk that the ritual may fail because someone notices its artificiality, how it is constructed. Journalists are well aware of the practice. They despise the tactic but generally keep quiet about it. In 2003, the stage management of enthusiasm at the end of the Conservative leader speech was exposed for the first time by one of the tabloids:

> Party stooges wearing earpieces, and strategically seated near the platform, kept leaping to their feet on cue. It forced a circle of supporters – including Shadow Cabinet rivals – to follow suit. In parts of the hall, there were clear signs of resentment. Scores of defiant delegates sat on their hands rather than be whipped into a mood of artificial enthusiasm. Some delegates shook their heads and refused to rise to the orchestrated applause (*The Sun*, 10 Oct 2003).

In this instance, the Conservative tabloid was contributing to a long-running campaign undermining Duncan Smith's leadership.[36] The Emperor's new clothes, however, are rarely exposed as they were in this case.

The conference also creates an atmosphere that is propitious to plotting and the co-ordination of resistance. Efforts to use the speech as a demonstration of strength and support can fail dramatically because internal opponents are using the occasion to voice their discontent in a more visible fashion than a refusal to stand up and clap. On one occasion, Major was hissed and booed when he referred to European matters. In 2004, Blair was interrupted twice during his speech despite the efforts of organisers to screen participants.[37] As a consequence, his performance appeared far less impressive than it had been in previous years and the party failed to use the conference as a demonstration of undivided support for its leader. Such demonstrations are rare. The disruptions strikingly contrast with the smooth stage management observers have grown accustomed to seeing but probably reveal the extent of the frustration felt by muted opponents.

Personalisation has become the primary means to instil imagination in politics, particularly in an age of celebrity. Camera work gives an impression of intimacy. One of the objectives of conferences is to demonstrate that power is not remote but is directly associated with famous personalities, somehow heroic characters (Balandier, 1992: 111). Moreover, to a level hitherto unprecedented, audiences can see facial expressions and react emotionally to non-verbal cues. Leaders have always played with this dimension of communication to maintain their dominant status but it is because we tend to over emphasise the rational aspects of democratic legitimacy that we forget the importance of communicating through emotions (Sullivan and Masters, 1993). New communication technologies have played an important role in the privatisation of politics: the conference is home delivered to living rooms (and now computer desks or even mobile phones). The old oratorical style does not suit screens and so more intimate tones have been adopted: brought into people's living room, the politician cannot shout, he converses (McGinniss, 1979: 28). The "sincerity machine" (Paxman, 2003: 152) or "head-up display unit"[38] was introduced at the 1982 Conservative conference (Stanyer, 2001: 30). It allows the politician to look up whilst reading his speech, apparently looking straight into the eyes of those watching him on screens at home or on the giant screens in the hall. "The television screen, presenting a live performance, creates not close contact but a semblance of close contact." Although it presents itself as a cosy discussion, the speech is a "performance [that] concentrates on evocations and impressions, becoming its own justification" (Edelman, 1985: 101).

1996 Labour, Blackpool

Tony Blair gives a visionary speech as the future Prime Minister. When he invokes the example and inspiration given by his father, audiences are treated with a close-up of Cherie Blair holding hands with her father-in-law. A few minutes later, a couple of weeping delegates appear on the screens, fully involved in the emotional communion with their leader.

Settings and acts reinforce each other and define the situation and the appropriate reaction. Little effort is spared in the framing of the leader's speech in order to ensure that it conveys the message of a legitimate and naturally authoritative leader that receives the spontaneous adoration of party activists. Party organisers actively develop the impression of intimacy and closeness. In 2002, the conference set was designed bearing in mind the desire to indicate the proximity of the speaker and his audience.[39] It was cosy and intimate. Tony Blair excels in such a conversational style and it reinforces his image as a friendly, family man who can rise above the crowd. He "naturally" appears personable (Finlayson, 2003: 57–58). He speaks in a direct, no-nonsense, style, exuding frankness and honesty. Blair, argues Finlayson, is the man who "reduces the distance that is the symptom of the illegitimacy of politics" (2003: 54) as if the solution to disengagement and apathy was intimacy (Sennett, 1986). Despite the new conversational tone – a considerable cultural shift from an earlier era of British formality and deference, words uttered by the leader remain as "unchallengeable and unchangeable" as they were before and they carry the same assertion of authority.

Seaside gladiators

Conference is used and experienced differently by participants. Whilst activists tend to emphasise political discussions or the pleasures associated with participation, most MPs I interviewed expressed a more sober appreciation of the event. It is important to be seen but a passing visit is enough to fulfil one's duty. Emma Nicholson considers that attending the conference is "serving the party": meeting representatives to boost their morale and talking to the media. Ruth Kelly concurs. Since her election in 1997, she usually only comes to conference for a couple of days. It is too expensive and too tiring. However, there are also opportunities for MPs to further their own interest. "It is good to show your face", notes Ruth Kelly. As a new MP, she was proud to have been invited to a *Guardian*'s fringe on the economy alongside a Cabinet minister as early as 1998. Another MP explains that his strategy involves delaying as long as possible any firm commitment to any fringe. This allows him eventually to choose the best option for himself: the issues he likes to talk about, the topics that are likely to give him the highest publicity. It is a time to make connections with Non-Governmental Organisations (NGOs) from which one will get support and information on particular issues.

Labour Conference, Brighton 1997

One of the new women MPs attends for the first time in her new capacity. She has given a talk at the Oxfam fringe: "one does not refuse Oxfam!" She walks around with her constituency delegates, who "have worked very hard for [her]". Whilst we talk, a delegate from the union that sponsored her stops by for a word. She gratefully thanks him for the support and asks where his General Secretary is to thank him personally. "Actually, he adds, I have a favour to ask".

The business of Westminster is partly conducted during conference, as ministers are easy to find. Many MPs take the opportunity to talk about constituency business: "I have an appointment with the Home Secretary about insecurity in my constituency. I've written to him but I know civil servants dealt it with. I can achieve something in 15 minutes. It is easier to see him here than in London." All sorts of private audiences are conducted, more or less discreetly. Some ministers deliberately choose not to be at the Imperial or the Highcliff and conduct meetings from their suites in smaller hotels. On the other hand, the accessibility of senior politicians, so much appreciated by the grass-roots, can become trying for ministers who develop strategies not to be constantly hassled by well-meaning supporters. Personal assistants can deter those who might be more daring if the Minister is wandering alone. They also provide escapes, explains one of them, keeping an eye on the schedule or inventing commitments to avoid blunt rejection.

The conference offers different constraints and potential benefits to more senior politicians. "Ministers do not need to have their arms twisted in order to attend", considered Richard Kelly in the case of the Conservatives, either because they take "genuine interest in the morale of party workers" (Kelly, 1989: 181–182) or because they need to bolster their support within the grassroots. "Our role is more diplomatic than it is about speaking" explains Ann Widdecombe, "you address fringes, encourage delegations, you are a cheerleader". Moreover, authority and influence are also at stake. As a frontbencher, conference speeches are "enormously important because it sets the tone for what you intend to do, it is an opportunity to announce your policy. The reception that you get from the party is what makes or breaks the speech. It is very, very important," she adds. A good conference performance is important for anyone harbouring ambitions, would-be politician or minister. Politicians try to innovate and carve out their own style in order to make an impression. Ann Widdecombe found inspiration for her oratory style in the evangelical movement that helped her understand the importance of gripping the audience. She decided to speak without notes for her first big speech in 1998. "I knew that my best speeches were when I could get movement rather than reading out a script, but there was a lot of resistance" from Central Office.[40] Her example has been followed since. She fondly remembers the impact it had on the party. Members were "thoroughly demoralised at the time" and she "gave them something that looked different and was delivered in a different way. I gave them a philosophy, breaking down the Berlin walls between the private and the public sector, they liked it. I've had conference speeches that have gone wrong but that one worked."

It is important to get noticed but success can be dangerous. Conference speeches are gladiatorial performances, often used to remind the audience that alternative leaders are waiting for a chance. One of the best such examples is the 2003 Chancellor's speech. Gordon Brown asserted with talent his strength in a coded challenge to a Prime Minister being criticised from within the party. Ostentatiously avoiding the adjective "new", he offered "Labour" as a vision for the future. This new development in the long running rivalry between the two men was counteracted by an even more impressive speech by the Prime Minister. As Blair's performance the following day re-established the pecking order, the indirect confrontation will only be remembered as another incident between the two rivals. Others are not so lucky. Mo Mowlam's standing ovation during Blair's speech in 1998 may have had the unexpected effect of shortening her political career. Personal success cannot overshadow the leader, let alone the Prime Minister.

Politicians parade on a catwalk that resembles a gladiatorial theatre.[41] They score points for good performances and off each other. Conferences in fact provide excellent opportunities to brief against colleagues because the unpredictable reactions of the audience and the general public can be exploited against the politician. Speech fiascos show weakness and open contests for positions (Bailey, 1969: 36) but an ambush is just as threatening. Two years after the speech that turned her into the "Conference darling", Ann Widdecombe experienced the exact opposite. As a Shadow minister, the outline of the speech had been drafted by Central Office and "trailed" in the previous evening's press. The initiative on possession of illegal drugs was criticised by the Police Federation and by members of the Shadow Cabinet. As the controversy overshadowed the conference, the endorsement of the leadership vanished and the policy was eventually abandoned. "It was particularly nasty because there was a lot of backstabbing by colleagues but it is part and parcel of the political merry-go-round. Undeniably, it had a huge impact on me because it damaged my chances of ever standing for the leadership. But there you go, you live for these things." The audience is almost as ruthless. Even though the Conservative event is described as toothless by some, performers are anxious about the reception they receive. In 1990, Cecil Parkinson's speech at the end of the transport debate was greeted with a chilly silence. He resigned a few weeks later when Major won the leadership. In 1986, Edwina Currie was hissed at Conference, following her comments on the "northern diet". Such jeering of Conservative ministers are rare (see Kelly, 1989: 151) but cool receptions are almost more damaging. Norman Lamont was sacked a fortnight after an unconvincing performance in front of the Scottish Conference in 1993. He had missed a chance to save his portfolio.

Conclusion

Political parties are organisations dedicated to the pursuit of power: they compete in elections to place their leaders in governmental positions. Although parties with extra-parliamentary origins such as the Greens and Labour have been reluctant to admit it, Michels' iron law of oligarchy has been difficult to resist. However much they have tried to be fraternal communities, neither has succeeded in avoiding the question of leadership and authority. The challenge is increased by media attention and the need to put forward a speaker who embodies the movement for the sake of public relations. The closer an organisation is to governmental responsibilities, the more difficult it is to resist the personalisation of power. The Green Party has so far managed to avoid the emergence of professional politicians but their success is not only due to the integrity and the idealism of their elected representatives.

As a (comparatively) young and radical organisation, they remain on the margins of the political system and it is still too early to say whether they will resist the "iron law of institutionalisation". While other parties embrace hierarchies and devote a lot of energy to the legitimisation of leadership, the Greens remain the exception in British politics.

Every politician during the conference week hopes his or her performance will be successful despite the efforts of rivals and unavoidable mishaps because a good show can help fulfil an ambition or severely damage career prospects. These seaside gladiators also know not to count on the mercy of their audience because popularity within the hall is an insufficient condition of future accomplishments. The difficulty is that the audience not only creates the success but also evaluates it and, as in a circus, everybody is waiting for the fall with anticipation.

The leader's speech is on a different scale because it is a crucial event both for himself and for his party. Whilst individual politicians can only really rely on themselves to seduce the crowd when they deliver their set speech, the leader benefits before he/she even reaches the rostrum from the build up of the whole conference. The event is carefully ritualised in order to construct his/her authority and charisma and to make the speech the climax of the week. It is presented as an extraordinary occasion that demonstrates the ability, and therefore the legitimacy, of the leader. The direction and production contributes to the institutionalisation of unequal relationships within the party and it does so not only through scenic techniques (from musical soundtrack to lighting, camera angles and stooges) but also because it physically involves conference participants in the enactment of the legitimising ritual. There is always the danger that the show is seen for what it is, namely an orchestrated and choreographed demonstration of support. In fact, the affirmation of the leader's legitimacy can only be successful if the main characters in the plot – the conference delegates and representatives in the hall, who are shown to be listening – also consent to cheer and applaud for the expected number of minutes. In recent years the major parties appear to have become locked in a spiral of inflation that is bound to be limited eventually by the physical endurance of their activists, or of their stooges. However, excessive and unplanned demonstrations of fervour are also banned because the event is orchestrated for the benefit of the media rather than for the activists who take part.

To be a success the conference speech requires all participants in the ritual to suspend their knowledge of the constructed nature of the event. This is necessary to convince observers (such as the media and the electorate) as well as the delegates/representatives themselves of the authenticity and spontaneity of their performance as an adoring crowd. In this way, the event becomes a key performative rite: it confers legitimacy upon the leadership not only by appealing to the collective memory of the party (and the nation), but also by demanding from its key participants a wilful act of collective forgetting.

5
Setting the Agenda

One of the roles of political parties in a democratic system is the aggregation of interests and the elaboration of policy proposals. National conferences and congresses are generally regarded as the forum where major policy debates take place and where strategic decisions are taken. Parties that claim to be democratic, as social democratic and Green parties do, purport that conferences also allow the grassroots to have an input to the policy process and hold their leaders to account. In most continental European parties, the congress is gathered every two or three years to select the party leadership on the basis of a general programmatic motion. Sometimes, several texts and groups are in competition and a vote decides on the dominant coalition. These general motions do not usually address specific policy details. They state policy goals and political orientations for the next three years. In the German SPD, a draft motion is produced by a special committee including experts, ministers, elected representatives and party officials. It is discussed by local branches who can submit amendments in detail. Ultimately the congress rarely makes substantial changes to the original, so the apex of the meeting is the election of the party president and the executive committee. In the French *Parti Socialiste* (PS), factions that want to assess their strength in the party propose a draft each. The National Council examines the proposals and endeavours to produce a synthetic motion that is submitted to local groups alongside minority positions. Delegates are elected according to the text they support.[1] One of the tasks of the Congress is to produce a single text through negotiations between faction leaders, thus constructing and demonstrating the unity of the party. These discussions are held in backstage rooms whilst plenary debates have little direct impact on their outcome although provocations and dramatisation in the hall raise the stakes. Orators affirm positions from which they cannot retract without losing face. Delegates are expected to approve whatever compromise has been reached not only on the wording of the motion but also on the composition of the new National Council (Faucher-King and Treille, 2003).

All British political parties hold one major annual conference.[2] Although delegates or representatives do not elect the leadership, positions in national committees are at stake. Conference agendas are composed of topical motions and policy papers submitted by local parties or working groups, rather than general documents. These motions open up debates on policy areas. Neither Labour nor the Conservatives need to engage in debates about alliances because the electoral system usually guarantees single-party government but such discussions appear on third parties' agendas. In order to maximise their chances, the Greens and Liberal Democrats have to take into account the constraints of institutions and strategically position themselves in a political system distorted by the strong bias of the "first-past-the-post" electoral rule. In the mid-1990s, the Liberal Democrats for instance claimed to be abandoning a policy of equidistance that had never really existed (Ingle, 2000: 187). At the same time, the Greens were briefly considering refocusing on non-violent direct action rather than exhaust themselves in what seemed like a hopeless parliamentary strategy (Faucher, 1999a) or *ad hoc alliances* with the Liberal Democrats and nationalist parties.[3]

With the exception of the Conservatives, all parties claim that conference decisions play a major role in policy-making thanks to policy motions. Such claims have been criticised as exaggerations or wishful thinking. In his classic study of Labour and the Conservative parties, McKenzie argued that parliamentary groups were largely autonomous, so much so that both organisations were equally dominated by their leadership.[4] He considered that party conferences served merely to confirm party solidarity and to highlight the loyalty and the enthusiasm of the members towards the leader (1964: 189). His thesis was contested for both the Labour party (Minkin, 1980), and the Conservatives (Kelly, 1989; Norton and Aughey, 1981). Minkin demonstrated that the Labour leadership had to negotiate and to work closely with the big unions. Concessions on both sides were necessary to protect party unity. Moreover, the grassroots membership did maintain some influence. Kelly showed that although the Conservative conference has no formal power over policy-making, there are "plenty of occasions when, as a result of intra-party discussion, the policy of the party turned out to be rather different from the one originally envisaged by the leadership" (Kelly, 1989: 20). Overall, if leaderships are not tied to the letter of policies agreed at conferences and benefit from an important degree of initiative, they cannot afford to ignore their followers who find in conference a forum for their views.

Conferences not only provided the grassroots with unique opportunities to push issues on to the party agenda, they also contributed to the development of each party's culture and to the integration of members throughout the country. However, from a practice of communal conferring (debating policy in the old model), they have somehow evolved into "rituals of conferment", conferring legitimacy on decisions made elsewhere.

Conference preparation as a ritual of integration

Until the late 1990s, British parties have followed a very similar pattern in the run up to their annual conference. The preparation of the annual conference kept branches and headquarters busy for several months and it had become a highly routinised activity for all taking part. Consistent with the British tradition of representative government, local communities, rather than ideological affinities were the legitimate bases for representation to the organisation's national forum.[5] Conference organisers sent calls for motions in the spring. Constituent organisations then gathered meetings where members could put forward resolutions on the topic of their choice. Proposals were discussed and weighed by the group because rules stipulated that only one text could be submitted per party unit. Hard choices thus had to be made to decide which topics to put forward. Whatever the length of the motion or its content, discussions on wordings were also difficult. Although there were no restrictions or "instructions", an implicit convention existed in the three parliamentary organisations. In the three parliamentary parties, motions generally followed the same model stating "this conference believes/regrets/suggests or demands".

Submitting a motion to the national conference was an important achievement for members. It could enhance their feeling of efficacy because they could influence internal debates or even party policy. It was also a reasonable objective for those wanting to be noticed because a delegate or representative from their constituency would be called to the rostrum to move their motion to the whole conference.[6] "A carefully worded amendment on a controversial subject appeals to the managers" explains Ann Widdecombe. As an anonymous representative wishing to be noticed, she got an amendment submitted that called for a free vote on death penalty: "the sort of thing they wanted to hear. I was summoned to see somebody who was clearly checking I was not going to be vastly extreme and that's how I was called, I was very pleased about that." Writing a motion flags up a political stance and offers assertive individuals an opportunity to promote an issue they are deeply committed to. There are in all parties, activists who seize any opportunity to promote their own question proposal with the support of their local party. Motions were endorsed by local groups who acted thereby as filters of members' idiosyncrasies but the system remained porous, largely linked to the presence of strong-minded or "big-mouthed" activists in these groups. According to some Labour modernisers, this explains how "unrepresentative points of view" regularly arrived on the conference agenda, pressed on by radical members more determined than others to push their opinion. As these sometimes contentious issues reached the internal party agenda, they also attracted media attention and contributed to tarnishing the image of Labour as a responsible, cohesive governmental party. Whilst the Liberal Democrats and the Greens could flirt with marginality and radicalism, Labour endeavoured to capture the middle ground. Organisational reforms within Labour focused on finding ways to make policies in more private settings.[7]

Motions were reviewed, classified, and then compiled by the conference committee in July, followed by a call for amendment. More meetings were organised locally in order to study the preliminary agenda and submit amendments. The final agenda was published in early September. A last round of meetings was held locally so that delegates could be mandated (in Labour and for a short while in the Green Party) or could get a chance to discuss the matter with fellow members. Area meetings sometimes provided those planning to attend last minute briefings on procedures and tips for a successful trip.[8] The number of meetings held, the attendance and the commitment of participants to engage with the agenda reflected expectations about the purpose of the conference. Mandating implied that collective decisions were taken to provide precise instructions to delegates. In practice however, small Labour delegations sometimes limited the formality of the process to a chat over a beer. Only the bigger unions held a formal meeting before conference to decide their positions (Minkin, 1980: 180). The belief that conference decisions made party policy also raised the stakes. Labour's traditional theory of intra-party democracy purported that resolutions provided an "input from below" that was "debated at the Sovereign Party Conference and then became party policy as a result of the votes of mandated delegates" (Minkin, 1991: 398).

In other parties, representatives are expected to decide how to vote according to their own conscience and many Liberal Democrat activists are very sensitive about this issue. The lack of decision-making power of their conference explains why Conservative representatives were unlikely to spend much time conferring about the implications of the adoption by conference of an amendment demanding the reintroduction of caning in schools. Greens emphasise that politics should be conducted at a local level and have encouraged the development of two levels of membership. Local members focus not only on campaigning for election but also on local policies and changes in lifestyle from transport to waste management. Because the party has no real say in the Westminster political scene, some view policy development at conference as superfluous. Like most Green Party meetings, pre-conference gatherings are open to the public. However, people who do not intend to attend conference rarely turn up. Although most conference participants make up their minds individually rather than through consultation (Rüdig *et al.*, 1991: 48), such meetings are very influential in tightly knit groups, such as the Oxford Green Party, where they lead to the expression of a consensus through a process of careful deliberation.

These preparatory meetings have played an important role in weaving together the different levels and components of the party. They created a tangible link between participants at the local level and the imagined community of the national party organisation. At a time when there were few formal channels of communication between individual members and the national organisation (in particular because local groups were jealous of their prerogative over membership management), the process provided routes for formal communication.[9] The election of delegates, the selection of a motion to put forward and discussions on the agenda fostered feelings of belonging to something bigger than the local political community that is the horizon of most members' activities. Even those who did not attend conference as representatives or delegates could foster the impression that they were directly involved in some of the debates and decisions they would follow through the media. The conference preparation, with its institutional routines as well as the building up of excitement, constituted a process of objectification of the party. It naturalised practices that were culturally specific, from a style of motion to a process of selection and preparation of conference participants. For instance, French socialist activists take for granted the competition between motions for the congress whilst their Labour equivalents find it puzzling, assuming that topical debates are "natural" or in tune with "common sense". Through the very act of participating in activities that appeared to be mandated by the environment, participants contributed to create the reality of their party and to frame the patterns of interactions and of ideas that could be developed.

There is nothing obvious about the way a party should deliberate its policies. Party idiosyncrasies are naturalised through practices that year after year establish what it is to be, say a Green or a Conservative. These structuring practices unconsciously frame ways of understanding the world and behaving within it. In Britain, the preparation of conference served as an integration ritual to be performed every year. It contributed to the strong emotional attachment of members towards their partisan community.[10] "Ritualisation both implies and demonstrates a relatively unified corporate body, often leading participants to assume that there is more consensus than there actually is (...) [and] to mistake the group's reformulation of itself as a straightforward communication and performance of its most traditional values" (Bell, 1992: 210). The ritual of conference preparation also forces members into specific patterns that constructed authority as well as frames of interpretation (Ansell, 1997; Snow and Benford, 1988). It integrates members not only through what was discussed but also through the procedures themselves. What was important was not whether the system is democratic or not but the fact that members behaved "as if" that were the case.[11] The lengthy ritual preparation does not so much reveal a deep-seated commitment to intra-party democracy but rather a determination to work together and pretend this is the case.

Consensus and pluralism

Classic approaches to power tend to focus on decision-makers, key decisions or key issues. However, power is also exercised in situations of covert (rather than overt) conflict where the objective is to influence the very conditions and possibilities of decision-making. Peter Bachrach and Morton Baratz argued for instance that power is involved when "A devotes his energies to creating or reinforcing social and political values and institutional practices that limit the scope of the political process to public consideration of those issues which are comparatively innocuous to A" (1970: 7). Indeed, decision-making can be limited to "relatively non controversial matters by influencing community values and political procedures and rituals, notwithstanding that there are in the community serious but latent political conflicts" (Bachrach and Baratz, 1970: 9). An analysis of "non-decision-making" as Bachrach and

Baratz call it or of the process through which debates are framed (Della Porta and Diani, 1999; Snow and Benford, 1988), that is the ways issues are prevented from being raised or articulated either through self-restriction, threats, cajoling or force, is important if we wish to understand what motions are put forward by local parties and working groups.

The preparation of the conference offers an interesting instance of such practices. At the stage of conference preparation, careful framing of the parameters of debate can effectively prevent the emergence of difficult issues. It contributes to the image of unity and consensus that contemporary parliamentary parties are so keen to project. It is at least as important for parties as deflecting the decision when the vote comes. It is also far less costly than the rejection of resolutions that had already been formulated and submitted – it is also less visible and hence less politically damaging. Any suspicion that the Conference Committee might be obstructing the expression of the grassroots is only likely to provoke complaints. It would also be likely to attract the attention of critical media reports as another proof of stage-management.

Conferences are opportunities for members to "let off steam" about their dissatisfaction with the leadership or its policies. Media scrutiny has challenged this traditional function of conference because parties are not prepared to risk publicising even healthy internal debates that might be presented as divisions. Conference preparation must thus achieve a delicate balance between the expression of loyalty and of dissent. To achieve such goals, the party leadership can stress the advantages of co-operation: participation gives "the illusion of a voice without the voice itself" (Bachrach and Baratz, 1970: 45). No party is exempt from either discrete pressures or internalised constraints and self-imposed censure but these pressures are heightened in the two main parliamentary parties. In the Labour party, weak factional organisation meant that the preliminary agenda was largely spontaneous until the 1970s (Minkin, 1980). However, such spontaneity was framed by dominant values, political myths and institutional practices that always tended to favour the vested interests of individuals and groups who frame debates to reinforce the *status quo* and prevent embarrassing or unwanted decisions. Labour's new rolling policy process, discussed below, perfects the system because it is based on procedures that involve consultation of the grassroots before conference in order to pre-empt the emergence of overt dissensus. Both systems include filters capable of preventing the emergence of proposals that did not fit the group's style. What is new about more recent Labour reforms is that appropriate ways of behaving at conference have evolved from a confrontational style of interactions to one based on consensus.[12]

Until 2000, submitting a motion for the Conservative conference was a staged process with many gatekeepers. Several months before conference, the National Union called for motions to be submitted. After discussion, constituency association chairmen[13] proposed motions to the relevant Area offices who passed them on to the Conference Committee. At each stage, motions were liable to be amended by the body that took the responsibility to submit them. Passing on an ill-judged motion could have consequences for careers as one could be seen as unreliable or labelled a troublemaker thus providing an extra entry in the "little black book" of the conference chairman. The motions published in *Conservative Conference Handbooks*[14] had thus already cleared many hurdles, including the devastating charge, in the polite Conservative jargon, of being "unhelpful". It was impossible to know how many had been withdrawn or rephrased, nor how many had been rejected by various selecting bodies because they articulated views that could bring disapproval to the group (Ball, 1996: 9) or withheld because they did not fit the group style.

Although politics and policies are the *raison d'être* of political parties, not all members aspire to be personally involved in policy-making. "On the ground", many activists are happy to focus their energy on campaigning and its practical management (from fundraising and leaflet production and distribution, to newsletters and local politics). The Conservatives have always acknowledged that members do not all have the confidence, or the inclination, to engage in political debates.[15] Thus, policy discussions and politics have remained separate from the day-to-day business of voluntary groups. The admission of such disinterest in politics is relatively unusual in political parties. It explains, however, how the party thrived on the groundwork of organisations such as the Primrose League and the networks provided by the Clubs.[16]

In contrast, involvement in the policy process provided a sense of personal efficacy that has been an important incentive for participation in Labour[17] as well as in smaller parties such as the Liberal Democrats and the Greens. Alan Sherwell, then Chair of the Liberal Democrat Conference Committee, candidly remarked that "activists want to feel that they are contributing and putting forward policy motions, even though they often do not have the resources to actually propose fully developed documents". Small parties can nurture this drive all the better since they are less concerned about their image and are not involved in permanent campaigning. As the Liberal Democrats improve their representation in Parliament and hope to leapfrog the Conservatives, they are more likely to adopt a prudent approach to their conference agenda. However, they have so far derived their identity from the pivotal role played by conference in the slow and complex policy-making process. Like the Greens, their annual conferences are deliberative forums where each policy paper is examined several times.[18] Both the Liberal Democrats and the Greens have acknowledged for some time the importance of policy groups for the detailed writing of policies.

One explanation for the Greens' passion for policy discussion lies in their political marginality which fosters an inward focus.[19] Another factor is linked to the socio-demographic characteristics of party members. Indeed, the educational background of British party members appears to correlate with the type of motions submitted to conference and the nature of internal policy debate. Surveys conducted in the 1990s, showed that 67 per cent of Green Party members had a university degree (Rüdig *et al.*, 1991: 20). On the other hand, 42 per cent of Liberal Democrats (Seyd and Whiteley, 2005), 30 per cent of Labour (Seyd and Whiteley, 1992: 32) and 19 per cent of Conservatives left full time education at the age of 19 (Whiteley *et al.*, 1994: 43). If we consider these figures to be likely to be relatively stable, it is therefore of little surprise that Green activists feel both competent and argumentative. When grassroots activists drafting motions are themselves experts they are unlikely to accept the idea that the political elite know best.[20] Levels of education are likely to have an impact not only on the motivations of activism but also on the "group style" (Eliasoph and Lichterman, 2003).

Motions reflect not only the nature of members' preoccupations and their ideological orientations but also what is conceivable or "utter-able" in this context and the manner in which ideas can be expressed.[21] Negotiations focus on a turn of phrase and also on the detail of policies. Each conference has its own and unmistakable typical motion. For example, Green Policy papers are comprehensive and often lengthy documents. They provide the philosophical and political rationale for supporting the adoption of the new policy but they are usually an arduous read. All those that have been adopted by conference are integrated into the party programme. Although standing orders stipulate that motions should be written "in plain English", the majority of motions and amendments cannot be understood without prior knowledge of the *Manifesto for a Sustainable Society* (MfSS). For instance, the following type of statement is quite common: "Delete the first sentence of PB [Philosophical Basis section of the MfSS] 10, add 'not' after should and delete the last sentence." Even though the chances of seeing such policies implemented are slim, the visible influence of conference debates on party policies probably contributes to the commitments of members.

Green Conference 2002 *Final Agenda* – Voting Paper "Climate Change"

"Synopsis: This voting paper is mainly a tidying up of GP climate change policy that has accumulated in different parts of MfSS and MOPS over the last ten years. The proposal is to introduce a new section to the MfSS, which is fairly short, gives some background, and focuses on things such as target setting and international negotiations. The bulk of the GP's proposed policies to reduce the UK's contribution to climate change is already appropriately dealt with all over the MfSS, references are given here. It includes a brief section of new policy on attitudes to the current government's Climate Change Levy and its Emissions Trading Scheme. This VP also calls for the deletion of RS137, RS136 and RS127 which are appended to MfSS section PL (Pollution) and of the "Miscellaneous Motions – Climate Change" – which is appended to MfSS section EN (Energy)."

The motion is printed thereafter on seven pages.

By contrast, the Conservative style needs to be understood in the context of the National Union Conference which was "not a meeting for the discussion of Conservative principles, on which we are all agreed, [but] a meeting to consider by what organisation we may make those Conservatives principles effective among the masses" (Bulmer-Thomas, 1965: 111). In fact, the idea that conference could be a place where politics was discussed was so alien that political debates were only introduced a decade after its creation. Moreover, politicians of the time did not hide the scant regard they had for the opinions of the membership: "I have the greatest respect for the Conservative Conference but I would no more consult it on matter of high policy than I would my valet" said Balfour in 1909. Modern politicians may have little more consideration than their predecessors did for their supporters' opinions but they rarely dare to articulate such views. Today, Conservative party members still overwhelmingly trust their parliamentary elite for policy matters and participatory procedures have remained limited to campaigning, with very little input in terms of policy-making. However, headquarters' officials admit that deference is not what it used to be and politicians sometimes face grumbling and resistance.

The Conservative motions submitted until 2000 were very short. They expressed the attitude of the grassroots towards party and government, ranging from enthusiasm to polite praise or chastisement. Coded criticism had become standard practice because the Conservative grassroots shy away from open conflict with the leadership and generally prefer a façade of unity. In 1995, out of nearly 200 motions on the economy, 34 straightforwardly congratulated the government but the majority urged for a return to "true" Conservative principles and policies.[22] Only the boldest of motions jumped straight to criticism without some reverential comment about the "excellent" job the government/leadership was doing. Many praised before "suggesting" that future policy might go in a different direction. These motions had little impact on policy-makers. They were symbolic acts expressing not only policy preferences but also a particular view of *Britannia* and its world-wide influence, an idealised perception of "rural communities" and their "hard working decent families". Kelly (1989) has argued that the autumn gathering is only the culminating point in a process of consultation that operates through a series of national and sub-national conferences. Motions were thus an ultimate opportunity to send a message to the party leadership but one constrained by the, largely accepted, need to "save face". The influence of conferences on policy-making was all the more difficult to interpret[23] as it did not proceed from decisions on the motions tabled.

Conservative Conference Motions

1995 Kingston upon Hull North – "This Conference urges Her Majesty's Government to look again at the Labour inspired taxes of envy, and abolish capital gains tax and inheritance tax."

1995 Surrey Heath – "This Conference congratulates the Government on the steps it is taking to improve the environment and on the leadership it is giving within the European Union. It urges the Government to take further measures to reduce pollution in this country by concentrating on steps to improve air quality."

1998 North Essex – "This Conference wholeheartedly commends HM Opposition on its sensible, logical and total support for those persons living and working in the countryside."

The delegate-democracy enshrined in the 1918 Labour constitution was associated, through the influence of the unions, with a culture of distrust towards intellectuals (Minkin, 1980: 7–8) that partly explains the style of the majority of resolutions. Policy proposals were explicitly and relatively concisely formulated (Bell, 2000: 74); they listed problems and made their policy recommendation. There was little attempt at literary elegance.[24] The stated purpose of Labour conference motions was quite different from the others because decisions were supposed to be "instructions" to the parliamentary party.[25]

Once these voluminous agenda had been produced, how much homework was expected of participants? How much effort did they indeed put into the preparation of conference? The delegates and representatives I interviewed admitted that they selectively read the agenda, focusing on papers that particularly interest them, looking for issues they may wish to speak on. None of the Tory representatives I have spoken to over the years had read the hundreds of motions submitted but some had flicked through the conference booklet. Those who had done so said that they wanted to sense the party mood whilst preparing the conference speech they hoped they would be delivering. Most though had contented themselves with reading the handful selected for the debate. Labour delegates are only slightly more assiduous readers. Most concentrated their efforts on the texts likely to be "composited" with the resolutions they supported in order to make up their mind about what compromise might be acceptable. Because the final agenda would only be available at the opening of the conference, there was little incentive to delve into the details of a thick document that provided only limited clues about what would be effectively debated. Only the Liberal Democrats and the Greens seem to devote more effort to reading the agenda but then both conferences retain important deliberative roles. The average conference-goer in the Green Party spent nearly four hours studying documents with less than 15 per cent of them spending no time at all (Rüdig *et al.*, 1991: 48). Such efforts show how seriously the Greens take conference deliberations.

Initiative from below – all be it at the request from headquarters – was the dominant model for the preparation of the conference agenda for most of the 20th century because input from the rank-and-file was seen as a proof of democracy as well as an effective way for politicians to hear the demands of their electorate. The success of the procedure and the dynamic involvement of the grassroots in conducting, year after year, the required procedures to submit policy motions to the head-quarters led, in all four parties, to the same problems. Hundreds of resolutions were submitted, often redundant, repetitive or contradictory.

Brought together in the conference agenda, they gave outsiders an image of political incoherence and contradiction for the simple reason that they were ideas randomly expressed through the internal channels of policy-deliberation. In 1996, 1415 motions were published by the Conservatives[26] and 575 by Labour[27] in two booklets over a 100-page thick. Neither conference had the time to consider so many individually so only a few motions were effectively looked at. The Conservatives selected a dozen, Labour synthesised those on similar issues into "composites". Because many policy papers are proposed by working groups,[28] the Green and Liberal Democrat agendas have remained within workable proportions.

Such plethora of texts demonstrates that the most important aspect of the conference preparation was the sheer number of resolutions that could be produced and circulated. Their content mattered much less. Despite the wasted energy, the system was preserved precisely because it structured national practices and interactions within each organisation. It is only when it became counter productive that party leaderships, and their communications experts, reconsidered the efficacy of the process. The eagerness to manage to perfection the impression given by the organisation at the time of conference led the two main parties to change their custom, promoting only those issues on which they consider themselves stronger than their rival.

Beyond any question about the risk to the party's professional image potentially created when contentious issues are publicly debated, parties hope to raise the salience of an issue in the public's mind through conference agenda.[29] The risk of the party sending a mixed message to voters is reduced if the conference agenda is "on message". Constant media scrutiny has transformed the nature of the conference agenda. It is no longer about policy deliberation but increasingly about publicising issues, policies and politicians. Labour and the Conservative have now given up on motions submitted by the grassroots, using diverse strategies to legitimate this change. Previously, members of both parties were attached to a procedure that allowed space for voicing concerns and expressing dissent. Resistance was easily overcome though as Labour activists were keen in 1997 to please their new government and unhappy about aspects of the old process. In 2000, Conservative representatives were given the opportunity to discuss the future electoral manifesto. By 2001, new routines had developed. Members have lost their most visible means of influencing the internal political agenda but, practically, their policy input had always been symbolic rather than effective.

Word processing policies

According to the Labour party's constitution and its mythology, the autumn conference is the sovereign decision-making body to which all constituent organisations send delegates. The 1918 constitution created the status of individual members but their influence on the formulation of policy was deliberately restricted (Fielding, 2003: 121). Not only was conference just one amongst several policy-making bodies within the organisation[30] but in practice its role was limited.

The bountiful preliminary agenda of the Labour conference had to be filtered, if only to reduce its size. "Technical" decisions were taken during the summer that allowed the CAC to push off a number of contentious issues because they were reputedly "settled" or addressed by the next NEC report; others fell within the remit of the "three years rule" that prevented an issue from coming up every year. Although the leadership's capacity to prevent discussion was limited because it was assumed that subjects with the most resolutions should be given priority, "in as much as there were significant political exclusions, these were almost invariably to the advantage of the Party leadership" (Minkin, 1980: 83). Special meetings were organised by the CAC on the Saturday before conference. The objective of these meetings was to reduce the number of texts on the agenda by cutting and pasting resolutions into "composites". The final agenda was thus produced over the weekend to be discovered by delegates on the Monday morning. The process prevented any effective mandating of constituency delegates as the motions seen by constituency parties would be quite different from the composites. On the other hand, the trade unions played an important role as "managers" of the various "filters". They dominated the election of the CAC but also had the resources to either steer "compositing meetings" in their direction or plan votes strategically when they had failed to reach the compromise they wanted. "Activists could send as many critical resolutions to Conference as they liked since the general secretaries of the major unions ensured they had no impact," argues Stephen Fielding (2003: 123).

The compositing process was "conventional, rather than constitutional, but institutionalised" (Minkin, 1980: 137). Its opacity gave rise to a number of legends of manipulation by the "Platform" that were passed down the years and those who took part in the process remember the thrill of playing a role in "how it really worked". Most problems with compositing arose from the sheer complexity of a process that "often baffled the lexical ingenuity of all concerned". Every word was important, as it had to be chosen amongst those already used in the resolutions. The only acceptable addition was "and". Party staff remember the whole exercise as a stressful occasion involving scissors and glue, with impossible time constraints and the feeling that something incredibly important was at stake.[31] Compositing involved "long, long battles" and was largely unpredictable because "you didn't have a clue who would turn up, so you couldn't prepare in advance". Resolutions had to be defended by a delegate from the organisation that had submitted it or fall.[32] The outcome thus depended on who would be present to defend their resolution and the mood of the participants.

Considering the constraints, it is no surprise that the composites presented to conference were occasionally such a bizarre "hotchpotch" that they had to be remitted by the NEC. However, champions of the process argued that motions allowed the expression of a plurality of points of view and kept the leadership in check in a way, that could not be replaced. The meetings acted as an "appeals" system for those excluded from the complex system of "soundings" that preceded the elaboration of the agenda. In all parties, actors find strategies to bypass or accommodate normative rules and develop pragmatic ones (Bailey, 1969). They learn to master the process to their advantage. Union delegates usually discovered the pragmatic rules of the game earlier than those from constituencies. Willie Sullivan recalls his first conference as a UNISON delegate: he supported a delegate he knew from another union so that his own positions would be backed. Together, they ensured that the words they wanted appeared in the composite: "it was a bit of a stitch up [but] it was fun".

From 1984, the leadership deployed new instruments of control to circumvent and manipulate traditional policy-making channels. "There was the idea that conference decisions had some form of sanctity. Now that was always rubbish [constitutionally and in practice] but people confused the fiction and the reality and there was a lot of blood spilt", explains Neil Kinnock. Through political and policy advisors, he oversaw the policy process, taking personal initiatives or letting people know what was wanted. "It was a matter of being better organised than the opposition (...) by 1988, towards the end of the Policy Review, I drafted the composite resolutions by March" so that they could be decomposed and spread around the country. In this way, the party leadership used the system to "manufacture" certain key composites simply by being well organised. Although the process remained unpredictable, it became better managed by the leadership. "I remember a session where the Party instructed somebody to put forward a resolution so that it was included in a particular composite", boasts a Scottish delegate. A secret panel of members from regional executives was set up. Its members, unaware of the existence of such an organisation till 1991, could be trusted to mobilise their own networks in the regions as well as in individual constituency parties in order to press a particular angle or wording. "If they didn't like it, they could say no," notes Kinnock: such networking "required a great deal of effort but the more it went on, the easier it got". Towards the end, a five-minute phone call would inform the leadership that the desired wording had been selected. These "building blocks" would then appear in individual resolutions so that vocabulary and phrases could be accepted by the leadership and composited back.

By 1990, there was widespread agreement that the existing system of policy-making was problematic but reform was complicated by members' sentimental attachment to the sovereignty of conference and by the reluctance of the NEC and the trade unions to relinquish their influence.[33] Although the power of conference in Labour party policy-making was primarily symbolic,[34] its alleged sovereignty remained the object of at least rhetoric of reverence for generations (see Chapter 9). Throughout the many years where the "modernisation" of conference procedures were discussed, delegates relentlessly expressed their concern: "Do we really want the sort of conference that the Tories have?" or "Comrades, let us go back to democracy, let us go back to grass root democracy. Let us give more power to CLPs and not to the PLP" (Labour, 1991a: 110). Activists feared that "conference [was] in danger of losing its status as final arbiter of Labour party policy" (1996, resolution 566). No reform of policy-making could be adopted without a commitment to preserve conference's last word on policy. Modernisers acknowledged it was a prerequisite for any successful reform of the organisation.

It was first suggested to hold compositing weekends in London before the conference, so that the final agenda could be published in advance. Proper mandating would have been possible and the conference procedures would have been more transparent to party members and television viewers. Building on a rhetoric of consensus and constructive criticism, an alternative proposition was suggested to eradicate big conference debates that were detrimental to the party's professional image. The 1990 Conference accepted to "set out the basis for the establishment of a rolling programme of policy, the establishment of a National Policy Forum and standing commissions on various policy areas with a two year cycle of policy culminating in Annual Conference" (Labour, 1991b: 76). The decision was not immediately implemented because electoral fever seized the party and all efforts were devoted to campaigning. At that time, the financial situation only allowed the creation of a "provisional" NPF that ran in parallel with the compositing system. After his election as party leader in 1994, Tony Blair put in place a team that was determined to create a process that could give the leadership greater control over policies as well as limit the clashes between a future Labour government and its grassroots. As Meg Russell (2005) highlights, the reform was not imposed on a reluctant membership. The alternative system was debated throughout 1996[35] and adopted by the 1997 conference during the "honeymoon" following Labour's electoral victory. Inclusive politics and the desire to foster a welcoming atmosphere were presented as major arguments in favour of a reform[36] that was supposed to create a "new party culture, at the centre of which would be genuine 'partnership' between different levels of the party". A problem is that the "partners" had divergent interpretations and understanding of their future relationships. From the point of view of "modernisers", this partnership was to be based on members recognising the "fundamental truth" that leaders have "ultimate responsibility for policy-making" and that members could not act as "watchdogs" (Fielding, 2003: 130). Many grassroots supporters of the reform, and some of its architects had a more idealistic and egalitarian perspective on the relative role of each "partner".

Partnership in Power created a permanent NPF whose representatives were elected within months. Since 1998, resolutions and composites have almost disappeared as NPF reports now constitute the main items on the conference agenda. Reluctance to abandon direct submissions to conference was overcome because conference still examines emergency motions that include issues "not substantially addressed by the NPF", either because it arose after the publication of the report or because it has been overlooked throughout the year.[37] Although "conference has always been, and remains, the sovereign body of the party",[38] its work is now strictly controlled by the leadership thanks to the new policy-making process. The NPF normally meets twice a year to produce reports over a two-year cycle. Between meetings, detailed work is carried out by eight policy commissions co-ordinated by Ministers and their departments.[39] In addition, a Joint Policy Committee (JPC), chaired by the Prime Minister and composed of an equal number of ministers and members of the NEC, acts as a steering group to the NPF. Policy reports are discussed twice by the annual conference, once as drafts, then as final policy papers. Thanks to this rolling process, the leadership has obtained an even firmer grasp on the agenda than it had in the past whilst dissenters' options are reduced to submitting emergency resolutions and the referral of NPF reports. Minority positions are a third possibility although such amendments need substantial support amongst NPF representatives to be put forward to the Conference. Thanks to union representatives, the government can avoid such difficulties. Contentious debates do not need to reach conference and can be diffused in private. The genuine democratic potential of the reform has failed to materialise. The new process is essentially a legitimating ritual that grants policies developed by the leadership the seal of democratic consultation. As Eric Shaw puts it, Labour's policy agenda has been "domesticated" (2004: 57).

The reputation of the new process has been tarnished by early day practices. *Partnership* had been presented as a way to create rational and efficient mechanisms for discussions between different spheres of the party. Unfortunately, in the first few years the system operated in a more rigid and strictly controlled fashion than had been envisaged by its promoters. Whilst participants were learning how to use the new procedures, the New Labour machine tightened control at any hint of disagreement. The first NPF representatives were predominantly Blairites elected on slates supported by the government.[40] Moreover, pressure was exerted without hesitation on movers of minority positions, feeding in complaints of "control freakery" (Jones, 2001; Shaw, 2004). The artificial consensus[41] that ensued frustrated the minority but helped the government secure control of the debates and be assured that final policy reports adopted by the conference would be "acceptable". Moreover, NPF plenary meetings have been less frequent than anticipated and members have been disappointed by the little feedback they receive about submissions.

Resistance to *Partnership in Power* focused on the accountability of forum delegates and the difficulty for ordinary members to be informed about the agenda. Albeit imperfect, the old procedure was relatively transparent. Party members knew whether their proposal had been incorporated within a composite discussed at conference or not. Consensus against the previous system of policy-making does not imply uncritical assessment of the new one. With experience, disappointment and frustration have built up. "While compositing procedures [were] flawed, they [were] at least public", complains a conference delegate. It is true that away from journalists' attention, dissent can be voiced without damage to the party's image. This could provide the conditions for frank discussions. However, privacy also makes it easier for party officials to "convince" isolated activists to bow to the leadership's position. Authors of amendments are called for head-to-head negotiations where they find themselves isolated against several members of the commission. They are placed in a subordinated position by the overt demonstration of power and ministerial grandeur. "It can be very intimidating," declares a member who recalls she went "with a friend" to a private discussion with the Minister, members of the Commission and staff from the Policy Unit to discuss the wording. "The first year, the Minister agreed that after all my amendment was not so controversial but the second time, we agreed to disagree," explains Meg Russell.[42]

The policy process is constructed around the uneven distribution of resources within the NPF. Constituency representatives are on their own, whilst those from trade unions can get institutional support. The government and party officials have the expertise and the information. Beyond the space allowed for "genuine, if non confrontational, discussion", explains Matthew Taylor, who played a key role in the conception and the early stages of the reform, there is "the real politics perspective which is that ministers control the proposals and therefore there is consensus". Deliberations are concluded by votes and the amendments accepted by the policy commissions are voted "en bloc". When the author of "unhelpful" amendments has not been convinced to withdraw or rewrite them, individual votes determine those that are to be carried forward to conference as a "minority position". In the first years, efforts were devoted to persuade NPF delegates not to support any minority position. This was the case for instance at the 1999 Durham NPF meeting. After a weekend of intense pressures and backroom negotiations, the amendment on a pension-earnings link failed to get the required 25 per cent of votes. "I felt the amendment should be put through conference even though I was probably not in favour of it. At the end I abstained," explains an NPF member.

The problem, however, was that it projected an image of excessive control that may be at least as damaging as division. It fuelled resentment against a system perceived to be over managed by the party hierarchy even though the NPF was the ultimate resort for the grassroots to be heard and a private forum. Members' scepticism about transparency and about the effectiveness of their participation means that the new policy process fails as an integration ritual. In fact, the process almost threatens the cohesiveness of the party because of the perceived obliteration of pluralism and debate. Loss of faith in the process has meant that representatives are elected unopposed or that positions are left unfilled (Shaw, 2004: 62). More worrying for the party, as Albert Hirschmann showed (1970), when there is no real possibility to voice dissent, supporters are likely to leave the organisation rather than remain loyal. Since 1998, Labour has been haemorrhaging members. Is the new rolling programme a means to paper over disagreements rather than confront them in a private forum? How dedicated to pluralism are the party and the leadership? If the overriding objective is to avoid trouble, it may be tempting to suppress potential disagreement. The danger then is that deviation from the norm is taken as a slap to the government. This happened for instance when conference debated a minority position for the first time in 2000.[43] During the second Labour government, controls within the party were relaxed thanks to a change of General Secretary and a new mood within the higher spheres of the party organisation. Measured dissent was better tolerated in the early 2000s to palliate the public relations disaster of excessive framing[44] and the growing unease of the grassroots. However, the decision to go to war in Iraq has created new sources of tension.

Pretext for debate

In the Conservative party, the process was much simpler if only because until 1998 the organisation never claimed to be democratic.[45] All the motions submitted were published in the Conference magazine in an order presented as arbitrary by National Union officials. Careful decisions were nevertheless taken to place them under specific headings and thus artificially reduce the number of motions in some sections. "Gerrymandering" of motions was of course impossible to prove (Ball, 1996) but a look through conference booklets shows that the first dozen motions of every section were generally positive. Critical ones were hidden in the mass. A dozen of them were then selected by the Conference Committee because their "blandness, vagueness and supportiveness" allowed a "sufficiently broad debate", notes the Secretary of the National Union.

Overall, setting the agenda was a cumbersome and rather pointless exercise at a time when efficient and rationalised management was becoming the new trend in organisations. Through the 1990s, party management worked to eliminate motions altogether. For the first time in 1996, motions were published in a small supplement to the glossy Conference Handbook. The number of motions discussed was progressively and discreetly reduced: 11 in 1996 but 8 the following year because Questions & Answer sessions replaced traditional debates. Conference had been the responsibility of the National Union but the 1998 constitution changed its status. It became the responsibility of the new unitary Conservative Party Board.[46] Decisions that used to be the prerogative of high-ranking members of the voluntary organisation were transferred to a committee composed of party officials, politicians and volunteers. This facilitated the transition to a radically new conference agenda. In 2000, a draft of the general election manifesto replaced motions on the grounds that "every member of the Party must be more involved in the decision-making processes of the Party. (...) All members will have a say in policy-making and every member will have a vote in the election of the Leader of the Party" (Conservative Party, 1997: 38). Although it was supposed to be an *ad hoc* exception to the rule, Headquarters officials privately admitted that motions were unlikely to be reintroduced. The rationale was that the new agenda would be focused on official policies whilst giving grassroots more time and opportunities to comment on precise documents. The decision created a stir because members felt that motions were their only means to voice some measure of public dissent. Motions provided a safety valve for muted internal controversies[47] but rarely went as far as to embarrass the leadership. Rather, they stigmatised the lack of discipline of the parliamentary party, sometimes demanding that the MPs took their lead from the "loyalty of the Party grassroots" or that "disagreements and difficulties [be] constructively [discussed] through the long established usual internal channel".[48] Conservative activists take seriously their contribution to the image of the party and many acknowledge that conference is not the place to hold politicians to account.

In the "new" Conservative party created by William Hague in 1998, the influence of activists on policies remains indirect and rests on the expression of views throughout a "conference system" (Kelly, 1989). However, it would "be quite wrong to argue that in general [Conservative party members] feel powerless and unable to influence the party leadership and Conservative party politics" (Whiteley *et al.*, 1994: 38). Members' perception of their party is closer to Kelly's (1989) than McKenzie's (1964) but the function of motions was never to make policy. They opened debates. Submitting motions allowed constituency activists to express their views on issues that concerned them. Hence their frustration when the process, cumbersome and imprecise as it was, disappeared. It offered in fact discreet but real means of resistance or dissent within the frame of the ritual. As Dirks points out, "rituals often occasion more conflict than consensus" (1992: 220) because relations of power are more vulnerable in these moments. It is a time for the reconstitution and celebration of power and thus the occasion to resist its authority. Although motions were implicitly expected to praise the leadership and give it an occasion to shine, their very obsequiousness reflected a peculiar literary genre and group style. From the leadership's point of view, they were a convoluted and ineffective means to raise attention and they were too general to focus media attention on specific policy proposals. Why not replace them then with texts approved by the leadership? Total control by the parliamentary leadership over the conference agenda was reached through a series of "circumstantial" decisions that eventually left party members with a *fait accompli*. The Conservative party traded members' limited ability to express views in a public (though discreet) way in favour of greater control over the conference agenda and party image. This evolution confirms the shallow nature of the alleged "democratisation" of the party.

A very liberal debate

In the early days, the Liberal Federation claimed its conference was to be the "Liberal Parliament" where policies to be followed by future Liberal administrations would be formulated through open democratic debates. The peak of the Federation's influence was reached in the last few years of the 19th century[49] but the fall of the Liberal government in 1895 was attributed to "its commitment to pledges deriving from the party conference" (Beer, 1982: 58; Ingle, 2000: 14). Thereafter, the parliamentary party refused to be bound by the Assembly's decisions even though the conference was theoretically the source of official party policy. Anarchic debates were tolerated because the party was far from governmental responsibilities and overall the conference had no formal policy-making power.

The Liberal Democrats have not really broken away from this tradition although the SDP probably contributed to bringing greater discipline to conference proceedings. Intense and complex debates on controversial policy initiatives are derided in the press[50] and the leadership remains occasionally apprehensive about debates. In 1994, the conference voted to legalise cannabis (despite the opposition of the MPs) and narrowly escaped calling for a referendum on the monarchy.[51] The adoption of such contentious positions created great media excitement. The following year the conference agenda was "carefully and ruthlessly excised" of any overly radical motion and renewed care has been put to avoid any similar future embarrassment to the parliamentary party. Considering the circumstances of their foundation, it was important that the Liberal Democrats take great care of their most precious resource: members. As a relatively small organisation, the Liberal Democrats rely heavily on a small group of devoted activists who gravitate between a small number of key positions. They become gatekeepers because they develop the structural knowledge and adequate codes that gives them an advantage over potential competitors. The Liberal Democrats are thus comparable to another stratarchical organisation, the Green Party.

Members are so important, considers Alan Sherwell, that the conference is organised twice yearly primarily for their benefit. It is the sovereign body of the party and it has "the power to determine the definitive policy of the party".[52] In practice however, concedes Liz Barker, also Chair of the Conference Committee, conference is "very important but not too powerful". With just over half of their members elected by conference representatives, the Federal Policy and the Federal Conference Committees (FPC and FCC) guarantee the ascendancy of the parliamentary party and its leadership.[53] Motions and amendments are cleared by the relevant committee who can refer some back for further consultation. This procedure is an effective delaying tactic that helps keep contentious issues off the agenda. Most decisions are reached through compromise but disgruntled activists can appeal or demand explanations to the *Commission des refusés*. When motions slip through the net, as in the case of a motion demanding the relaxation of pornography laws in 2002, the leadership eventually succeeded in convincing its movers to defer it for "further consideration".

Liberal Democrats Conference Committee meeting 1995

"I travelled 400 miles and all the amendments have been accepted", moans a participant, "there is no controversy, there is no debate". The committee chair responds that "last year there was too much controversy, this is subjective. Moreover, members have told us they don't want arguments and controversies 18 months before the general election". Another participant complains that his local party has sent many motions but none has ever been discussed. The quality of the proposals is often the problem, and the "Policy Committee offers help to constituencies to draft motions". "Local parties who benefit from the help of parliamentary assistant tend to submit better motions", adds the chair. He concludes that the conference is organised for the public as well as being a climax of the deliberation process, so "it has to look like it is successful", the objective is to "get as much in the press as possible".

The Liberal Democrats acknowledge the fact that policy groups are better equipped to prepare policy proposals than individuals because they can focus their efforts and consult. Indeed, activists generally accept the need to filter motions or to facilitate certain policy papers. Thus policy groups and commissions are important contributors. Liberal Democrats have used a rolling system of policy-making for years that has preserved the role of the national conference as a deliberating forum. The process starts with an exploratory consultative session held at conference (see Chapter 9). A working group then drafts a policy paper. Members can apply to be part of the specialised working group; they can submit written suggestions or attend further consultative sessions. Policy papers approved by the FPC are examined at least twice by conference. On average, it takes a policy proposal a minimum of 18 months before it is officially adopted by the Liberal Democrat conference.[54] Although the process prevents conference from quick responses, it ensures thorough discussions at the various stages of policy formulation. Thus, if members submit motions, many policy papers are in fact submitted by the FPC and the groups it sets up. In 1998, eight commissions worked on a Policy Review, whose conclusions were endorsed by Conference.[55] Every year, several "policy papers prepared by experts" are placed on the conference agenda. Conference decisions become party policy although the FPC is responsible for the electoral manifesto and acts as an ultimate filter. Despite a constitutional framework that seems based on consultation and democracy, a respected leader enjoys considerable influence on policies. "Activists have frequently said somewhat archly that the best way to discover their party's policy on an issue is to listen to Ashdown on the television" (Ingle, 2000: 189).

Amongst parliamentary parties, the Liberal Democrats are the only ones to be really upfront about the fact that their conference agenda is affected by the electoral cycle.[56] "An informal agreement" means that contentious and controversial issues are tackled in the first part of a legislature and less later. Despite "the myth that the Liberal Democrats are undisciplined and do not care about their image", explains Lady Barker, there is a "growing awareness of the importance of public relations".

A "rolling" process of policy-making

The Greens have modelled their organisation on the principles of participatory democracy. They value debate because deliberation leads to consent and improves participants (Teorell, 1999) as well as policies.

They have created structures designed to facilitate the involvement of members. Members are told that "people are best placed to know what is best for them", so making sure that all participate in policy-making is "not only democratic but also the process leading to the best possible policies" (Green Party, 1993: 2). The idea is that when citizens are conscious of their responsibilities and are provided with adequate information, they naturally tend to agree on the best solution. The professionalisation of politics is therefore one of the key problems of contemporary society and the party has adopted restrictive measures to prevent such a trend amongst its own supporters. As a consequence, all members are invited to participate in policy formulation meetings. Before the Labour party imagined policy forums (Chapter 8), the Greens were welcoming non-members to their deliberations.[57] Although the party has had its fair share of bitter internal disputes, the group favours a style of interaction that makes it easy for grassroots members to participate in the elaboration of policies. On the other hand, the dispersion of decision-making power and the forced rotation of internal officers contribute to create a stratarchy in which active members control and dominate the organisation.

The Policy Committee (PolCom) ensures that conference is "provided with the best policy options", explains Malcom Howe: it facilitates the setting up of working groups and "makes sure that work has been done in the area people feel policy should be developed". It commissions policy papers on issues where the party has been found lacking by conference and oversees spontaneous papers. A policy on trade unions was "clearly lacking and there are now some people looking at the industry", confessed the chair of the Committee. The *Standing Orders Committee* (SOC) supervises submissions to the conference agenda in order to reject "incoherent, retroactive or ambiguous motions" or those that contradict the party constitution or its philosophical basis.[58] The final agenda is usually 50 to 80 pages long, printed in small font. "There are always twice as many motions on the agenda than the conference can possibly debate," bemoans Mallen Baker, so prioritising ballots are organised to formalise the timetable.

Green policy documents are normally examined three times by conference. The initial proposal is discussed in a thematic workshop, then referred back for consultation and drafting. A *Draft Voting Paper* is then submitted to conference and discussed in plenaries and workshops. Eventually, the amended document comes back to conference as a *Voting Paper*. Contrary to expectation, the process works reasonably well and it is just as slow as what traditionally happened in other parties. Moreover, issues are thoroughly examined. The difference lies in the fact that Green conferences seem to immoderately enjoy drafting and redrafting to perfection. Although the party structures have remained weak, they have not prevented a systematic approach to policy development. Attention to detail and hard work contrasts with the image of an amateurish single-issue party that is often presented in the media. In a sense, in the 1990s, the Greens developed a more realistic outlook on policy-making than the Labour party did. On the other hand, the process is likely to have favoured a radical drift that has put off the most moderate environmentalists. The Greens insist on the absence of *a priori* and *a posteriori* control over policy-making but then, they have remained largely free from the burden of political office. Their few elected politicians have not watered down the radicalism of their proposals, partly, but not only, because they have no formal influence on internal party procedures and the production of policies (Faucher, 1999a).

Conclusion

Conferences are not primarily the place where policies are elaborated. They are forums where documents proposed by party elites are endorsed and thus legitimised.[59] The long process of conference preparation contributes to feelings of belonging to something important and bigger than oneself. Policies were never really made by the seaside but the fact that it was claimed that they were had an effect on the public perception of conferences as important events. Although the composition of the final agenda is the responsibility of the conference committee, all four parties organise ballots in order to prioritise some motions (*all* in the Green Party) on the conference agenda and to preserve the impression that the grassroots have a say on the conference agenda. Such democratic procedures are almost empty shells: in the Labour party, the ballot is dominated by trade unions, which act as a buffer between the government and unhappy constituency delegates; in 1996, the Conservative conference hall suddenly emptied when the Chair announced the discussion of a motion that had allegedly largely won the ballot[60] raising doubts about the interest of representatives not only for the topic but also for the selection procedure! Although many of the organisational reforms introduced by British parties in the 1990s have been presented as "democratisation", the grassroots have seen their direct influence on policy deliberation further limited.

Balloted emergency resolutions highlight the token role now played by the grassroots in the elaboration of the agenda. Whilst the process used to be presented as a crucial testimony of the democratic nature of policy-making, it has become too important to be left to amateurs and volunteers. All three main parliamentary parties have tightened their control over policy-making as well as over what conference can debate. This evolution was triggered by a growing concern that conferences contributed to setting the public agenda. In fact, setting the internal agenda now comes second to the communication imperatives of the permanent campaign. The conference agenda provides an excuse for senior politicians to address voters on issues that will promote the party's profile and increase its "electability". Issues positively associated with the party are privileged alongside problems about which the party believes it can improve its image. There is increasingly amongst parliamentary parties the conviction that what the media and the public will remember is not the content of debates, nor the details of policy documents, but a series of pledges. The Conservatives have pushed the logic of this argument to its natural conclusion: they no longer bother with motions, nor really with draft manifestos, they simply hold debates on "the economy" or "the arts". The Labour party has, so far, strategically and symbolically maintained the policy-making role of the sovereign conference in order to take members on board for the important succession of organisational reforms. It is likely that future developments will move British mainstream party conferences closer to American conventions, which have all but lost their policy-making functions. Smaller parties in Britain are likely to be spared such a fate because they largely eschew media pressures. What is potentially problematic however in the demise of conference as a genuine forum for debate (rather than as a stage for the glamorous presentation of policies) is that the whole process of conference preparation traditionally served not only to legitimise decisions but also as a key integration ritual for binding together the different levels of the organisation. Are parties weakened because the bonds that once held members together are being loosened? In the next chapter, we shall turn to the ways in which party communication experts and the media conspire to ensure that the leader impresses audiences well beyond the conference hall.

6
Making the News

Over the years, the conference season has provided British political parties with unique opportunities to advertise themselves for free under the cover of "news".[1] Throughout the year parties compete with each other for the attention of the media but every autumn, for about a month, a tacit convention temporarily suspends the normal rules of political balance. Provided that there is no other pressing news to cover, the media focus their attention upon the current conference and do not seek alternative opinions from other parties.[2] What has been the role of the media in the transformation of conferences from semi-private events into public showrooms? To a large extent, most of the changes have been introduced with an eye on the image of the party and a concern for the ways in which the leadership could remain in control of its communication.

In the 1950s, rows of printed press journalists could be seen next to the stage, frantically taking down notes to publish nearly verbatim accounts. From the 1960s to the early 1980s, conference debates were covered in detail though no longer *in extenso*. By the late 1990s, coverage has shrunk in square centimetres and photographs have become a prominent feature. The content also evolved. Whilst broad sheets[3] still devote several pages to conferences, they focus on keynote speeches rather than delegates' interventions. Debates are summarised and political comment has taken on increasing importance alongside nuggets of news about the fringe and the backstage. TV cameras first appeared at party conferences in 1954 and terrestrial channels soon started broadcasting the main conferences live for several hours a day.[4] "Pre-TV blood didn't matter," argues Austin Mitchell. "Indeed, once in the 1950s, secret policy discussion, from which the press had been excluded were broadcast live to a bemused sea front in Eastbourne.

Someone forgot to switch the external speakers off" (Mitchell, 2000: 114). Until the 1970s, exposure did not significantly alter the direction of conferences. By the end of the decade, party leaderships became aware of the need to manage their organisations' image.[5]

In the last decade of the 20th century, the world of media became much more diverse and segmented than before thanks to three factors: the development of new electronic technologies, the deregulation of the telecommunications market and the concentration of media ownership by large corporations. Although private and public broadcasters have co-existed in Britain since the creation of ITV in 1955, the introduction of cable and satellite channels and the launch of Sky Television in 1989 (now BSkyB) has transformed the "media landscape". New technologies have contributed to the multiplication of media outlets (from private television and radio channels to the Internet and a host of specialised magazines and newsletters). Twenty-four-hour news channels and targeted media have notably affected how and how much journalists cover political issues. Both print and audio-visual media are now driven by concerns about market share and are involved in a ferocious competition for audiences. Debates about the transformation of mass media in Britain often revolve around "tabloidisation" of the media and the related marginalisation of political news.[6] Tabloid newspapers have not reduced their political news coverage but have contributed to the personal-isation of politics and the domination of sound-bites. Moreover, there has been a diversification and segmentation of information outlets (Norris, 2000: 70–73). Whilst political parties can potentially reach new and diverse audiences, they have less control over the message they can convey.

Although it is impossible to gauge the direct influence of conference on an individual party's image,[7] political elites grew convinced that conference could be extremely beneficial if well directed or catastrophic if out of control. Moreover, they believed that the media had the power to sway voters' opinions[8] because it could set the public agenda. The conviction that the media plays a crucial role in directing voters' opinion is not new: agenda-setting theory was first proposed in 1972 (McCombs and Shaw, 1972). This argued that the top stories on the mass media news agenda were correlated with those on the public agenda. The implication was that the media could influence what people talked about and thought about, if not necessarily how they thought about it. Because most people in contemporary liberal democracies make sense of politics through the media, the role of communication outlets is probably more important than ever. Moreover, the media can also transfer the salience of specific attributes to issues, events and candidates. As people draw associations between issues and those parties considered most competent and trustworthy to deal with them, the party that is most strongly and positively associated with tackling the problems featuring at the top of the public agenda is likely to gain in salience (and electoral support). In the traditional British context, Labour was likely to benefit from the importance given by British voters to education,[9] whilst before 1992, the Conservatives were mostly associated with economic competence and lowering taxes. The Greens, of course, tend to be positively associated with the environment.[10] Thus, political parties need not only to present their position on a variety of political issues but also to ensure that issues of their choice are debated in front of TV cameras and in newspapers.

The amount of free publicity gained through conferences is of such importance that no party leadership can run the risk of surrendering the interpretation of the event to others. However, the relationships built in London between party elites and Lobby journalists are not only transposed to other settings, they are also complicated by the access gained at this time to alternative party sources that might challenge the elite's version. The fear of appearing divided has proved a powerful incentive to control every aspect of the show. Publicity considerations have long

> played a part in shaping the managerial consensus on what constituted a "good conference". [In the 1950s for instance, i]t was considered important that the evening newspapers be able to report a "speech by a leading speaker on an important subject" (Minkin, 1980: 75).

At the same time, Labour also ensured that the leader's speech was protected from competing interest that could arise from other speeches or debates. However, the 1990s witnessed a significant change of scale. Political parties have become aware of the importance of their media strategy on their general performance and they have also stepped up considerably the resources invested in this dimension of their activities. The shift was particularly flagrant in the case of Labour because it had so often neglected communication imperatives. After 1992 and a fourth successive electoral defeat, many members became convinced that the media was essentially malevolent, seeking to portray the party as chaotic and unable to govern itself. As a consequence, Labour "communicators" endeavoured to prevent "destruction by a hostile press" (Campbell, 2002: 19) and to present the party as a professional, competent and legitimate alternative government. By the late 1990s, Labour had overtaken the Conservatives in terms of communication expertise and triggered the equivalent of an arms race not only between the three main political parties but also between themselves and the media.[11]

How do party "spin doctors" manage conference? How do journalists resist these attempts to manipulate them? The literature on the increasingly tense relationships between New Labour and the media is considerable but comparatively little attention has been paid to conferences. This situation is all the more paradoxical as these events are a rare opportunity for the media to have access to non-official party sources.

Planning the show

For British parliamentary parties, the challenge of the 1990s communication revolution has been to produce what Daniel Dayan and Elihu Katz (1992) call a "media event", that is pre-planned live TV shows involving a sense of ceremony. Ideally, conferences could bring people together in their living room, provide conversation topics and "create an upsurge of fellow feeling, an epidemic of *communitas*" (Dayan and Katz, 1992: 204). Indeed, television brings the illusion that citizens take part in the conference deliberations and celebrations. The simultaneous experience of watching confers an almost historical dimension to the event.

However, this evolution has turned conferences into spectacles. Scripts are carefully drafted and images crafted to give a particular impression to mass audiences. Modern party conferences are manufactured to attract the audio-visual media[12] and for this purpose careful consideration is given to the journalists' own priorities and to the constraints of the media market and of news production (deadlines, sources of reliable information, need for exclusives). Since 1988 the BBC and the three main parties have negotiated coverage and facilities months in advance.[13] Both parties and media producers share an interest in keeping audience figures up and therefore co-operate to broadcast entertaining and informative programmes. Broadcasters push for "more revealing camera positions particularly on the floor of the main hall"[14] and announce time slots for live transmission.

Good conference planning[15] helps to ensure that everything goes smoothly and that the whole party projects a coherent, consistent and positive image. Fewer aspects of the event are left to chance because parties, especially Labour, have developed a heightened awareness of their "corporate image" and the means to enforce it. Conference committees reflexively construct conference, endeavouring to master all aspects of it. They arrange the timetable so that ministers and parliamentarians are broadcast live. They select the order of topical debates so that issues that are favourable to the leadership's position feature prominently whilst potentially difficult debates are scheduled after the cameras have switched off, and preferably on days when the media are likely to be busy with the leader's speech or important policy announcements.[16] They create photo opportunities, arrange interviews or announcements so as to distract attention away from dissonant voices. Party business – such as treasurers' reports and awards ceremonies – is timed so as not to waste precious live transmission. Detailed plans are drafted to ensure that everything is planned and everything goes to plan. Individual performances are rehearsed.[17] Of course, pre-electoral conferences are the object of extra care and attention as they are the last free major communication opportunity before the official campaign.

New Labour's communication offensive in the 1990s first entailed charming and reassuring the Conservative press[18] and their public through a re-branding of Labour. It also led to a more direct and blunt handling of the media, including the bullying of individual journalists and editorial boards and the deployment of strictly "on-message" politicians. Discipline has been tightened to ensure that no individual could "join both the team and the audience" (Goffman, 1990: 50) thereby endangering the impression fostered. In fact, the reason why New Labour's communication strategy has been so finely tuned to the needs and weaknesses of the media is that several members of the leadership team, such as Alastair Campbell himself, were experienced journalists or editors. Other "cross-overs" (Franklin, 2004: 94; Jones, 2001: 68–69) work as communication advisers. They put into practice inside knowledge of their "enemy", teasing competition between individual journalists or newspapers by producing and selectively leaking information in order to maximise effect on the news agenda. Finally, the party moved to a state of "permanent campaign" (Blumenthal, 1982) because "communication [is] not something you tagged on at the end, it is part of what you do".[19] Such views affected the way the Labour party presents itself to the public as well as the government's communication strategy. Proactive (rather than a reactive) news management has been the essential recipe for the transformation of Labour's image.

All three main parties have reflexively adapted to the demands of the media. The transformation was most spectacular and successful in the Labour party but others followed, trying to emulate such an impressive example. Communications professionals produce highly calibrated messages with all the frills (including sound and image) for the benefit of hard-pressed journalists. When necessary they create favourable news items. Press releases are tailored to resonate with the desired impression. In order to maintain control over how their parties are portrayed, directors of communication try to keep ahead of the news, by anticipating events and directing the action. A plot is sometimes constructed to keep the media focused on stories the leadership wishes to promote. Massaging expectations indeed helps as several Labour conference organisers told me: a few months before the conference starts, it is announced that the leadership expects to lose all the votes but as the date nears, the odd victory is predicted. When the leadership wins all the votes, success has turned into triumph.[20]

The press office co-ordinates all requests for interviews. "On-message" politicians are lined up so that journalists' attention is not diverted by politicians talking at cross purposes or from dissenting factions (Stanyer, 2001: 84). Indeed, experience has demonstrated that senior party figures can distract attention at the expense of the party's communication objectives: in 1999, Lady Thatcher speaking at a fringe to support her friend Pinochet attracted more attention than the party leader. The following year, Hague's team asked her to take a lower profile. On other occasions, such diversions are wilfully produced with the complicity of celebrity politicians and their guests. Conference organisers were very proud of what they had planned for the 2003 Labour spring conference in Glasgow. The timetable was devoted to workshops and seminars, with only three plenary sessions, and the rally was staged at the same time as potentially contentious political meetings. As several debates were going on simultaneously in different venues, the media attention was dispersed. The stratagem worked, as there was relatively little coverage of the massive anti-war demonstrations held at the gate of the conference centre or of the heated debates inside the hall.

Photo opportunities are set up to show the leadership in "real life" settings. Visits to local schools and hospitals or the racecourse are constructed. These take a number of journalists and technicians away from the conference centre. The Liberal Democrats altered their schedule in 1995 to improve the image of the conference: they introduced dedicated speaking slots for MPs. Debates on similar issues were brought together to be discussed on the same half day to give outside observers the image of a coherent debate. The leader's speech was moved to the Tuesday afternoon, breaking away from the model of momentum building till the end of the conference. However, the media increasingly focus on the governmental party. In 2002, a parliamentary one day recall in the middle of their conference, led the Liberal Democrats to have Kennedy's speech on the last day in order to force the media to stay (or come back) to Brighton.[21] In 2002, this technique was pushed to an extreme by the Conservatives. The conference timetable was transformed when the party executive manager decided to keep the morning free for photo opportunities outside the hall despite protests from volunteers who felt they were losing control over "their" event. Thanks to orchestrated events in the local community, the party leadership was presented as "in touch" with everyday problems. Party activists were in the meantime left to wander to a few morning fringe meetings or patiently wait for the start of conference sessions. Plenary debates were scheduled from mid-afternoon till early evening, in the hope that they would be covered by the news bulletin. This bold innovation proved disappointing. The Conservatives lost several hours of live coverage without significantly improving its prime time salience in the news. The media commented in the corridors of the Bournemouth conference centre that they could not really make sense of such a decision.

Setting the scene

According to Erving Goffman, "control of the settings is an advantage during interactions (...) [as it] allows the team to introduce strategic devices for determining the information the audience is able to acquire" (1990: 98). Such control also gives a sense of security that can be useful in maintaining a coherent representation. As we have seen, mainstream political parties have endeavoured to produce flattering images of themselves through careful planning of conferences. Settings have been the focus of much attention as communication experts and conference organisers have understood how they can contribute to impressing the audience. This is because "the setting in its widest sense creates the perspective from which mass audiences will view a challenge and thereby defines their response to it and the emotional aura which accompanies the response" (Edelman, 1985: 102). A good set can thus shape a "reality" and present it as a *fait accompli*, through the manipulation of certain symbols. Moreover, argues Murray Edelman, settings "mould the very personalities of the actors" (1985: 108) because they frame interactions, reinforce routines and contribute to the construction of the "ethos" of each party.[22] They also contribute to giving credence to attributes or behaviours that the public will omit to question. Indeed, as

Goffman points out "an audience is able to orient itself in a situation by accepting performed cues on faith, treating these signs as evidence of something greater than or different from the sign vehicles themselves" (1990: 65).

The Conservatives have employed communications professionals since the 1920s, first to run electoral campaigns, then for year-round propaganda. As the conference had no policy-making role and had been set up to publicise Conservative values, it was clearly understood as a platform from which to promote policies and politicians. Indeed, the party used the theatrical dimensions of conference. Although Conservative conference "debates ha[d noticeably] become more professional and more closely argued"[23] as early as 1970, communications experts only started working on party conferences *per se* a decade later. Harvey Thomas, Thatcher's communication adviser, initiated systematic planning of the show and commissioned the first professionally designed set in 1979. In 1994, the Conservatives contracted out their organisation to a private company (CCO) chaired by an experienced Conservative Conference organiser, Shirley Matthews. In line with their faith in the virtues of market competition, they expected an independent company to be in tune with professional conference organisers and keep abreast of the latest staging innovations.

"In 1980, the set tried to say something for the first time" recalls Shirley Matthews, but the most original creations only came once the party became aware of the ability of grandiose settings to impress large audiences. The first step was to clear the stage of the "great and good", who traditionally sat on it throughout the week, "looking down at less deserving activists".[24] The number of platform seats was reduced and those remaining moved to the sides of the platform. "We eventually won the battle of clearing the stage of people, except for the first and last day of conference," she explains. Every year, the Conservatives invest hundreds of thousands of pounds in innovative and impressive sets. By 1996, the National Union was eager to "break away from the long table of seventeen to eighteen people sitting in front of a background of different shades of blue". The chosen design for the set attempted to show that, "after 18 years in power, the Conservatives still had something new to say". John Major spoke from a glass lectern that emphasised both his strength (the Prime Minister) and his vulnerability (the humble man), rejuvenated by the 1995 leadership challenges. In 1998, arrow-shaped screens sought to highlight the party's renewed dynamism.[25] In 2000, the modernisation of the Conservatives was illustrated by futuristic glass construction. Representatives are generally enthusiastic about stage management arrangements. Some of those I interviewed on the matter in 2002 thought the set "showed a new professionalism" and that the party was "modern". It looked much better without "rows of people on the top table looking out at conference", one of them declared approvingly, having not attended for over a decade.

By the end of the 1990s, media pressures had contributed to a homogenisation of conference planning and designing. The three big parties have evicted grandees from the stage so that no one except the conference chair has a guaranteed seat overlooking the audience. As a consequence, seating arrangements have become complicated to organise (Stanyer, 2001: 31–32). The presence of others can be decoded and interpreted. In 1995 and 1996, for instance, the Liberal Democrats devised a rotation allowing "ordinary representatives" to sit behind the platform desks.[26] Such seating arrangements were thought of as a cunning means to demonstrate how democratic and modern the party was compared to its opponents. In 2000, the Liberal Democrats adopted a minimalist approach with hardly anyone on stage. The Conservatives went even further two years later. In 2002, they located the Chair's desk off the platform.[27]

In Labour, the problem was that the conference had been conceived as an internal affair and little attention had been paid to it. Neil Kinnock created the Shadow Communication Agency (SCA) in 1986 to improve the party's image as a competent and responsible party of the rising classes. Conference was singled out as one of the causes of the party's damaged reputation. Initially, many innovations in terms of settings or direction mirrored what was happening in the Conservative party: the parliamentary team gained a more prominent role in debates[28] and party business lost precedence over presentation. The NEC was progressively removed from stage.[29] Transforming the settings also affects the atmosphere of the conference itself and the ways delegates and representatives behave. Apparently innocent innovations were benchmarks for deeper changes. "New Labour" appeared at the 1994 conference. "Putting 'New Labour' in massive letters in front of hundreds of delegates was effectively renaming the party.[30] It was a huge risk," concedes Philip Gould, "but the slogan was used and there was not a murmur from the conference" (1998: 220). The aesthetic transformation of conference, and in particular the choice of platform designs, sparked many critical comments: slogans on a blue background amounted to a betrayal of socialist principles; the set was too expensive; the presence of journalists influenced the political agenda. "Get rid of journalists. It's not their conference, it's ours."

As members became more desperate to win, their attitudes regarding public relations evolved.

Labour Conference 2002, Blackpool

Conference novices are often bemused to have fallen through the looking glass. Miriam is surprised that her experience is more positive than she anticipated. Warned against the excesses of New Labour, she feared "there would be arms twisted" and a lot of tension but she is impressed by the atmosphere, the celebrities and the absence of pressure. Half way through the conference, she is more inclined to reassess her trust in the media than in her party. As Miriam's reaction highlights, press coverage affects the perception of members whose face-to-face interactions are limited. It strongly shapes what can be imagined by members. Because conferences tend to be much more enjoyable to delegates than what they had expected, it is crucial for parties to encourage widespread participation.

"The platform becomes an outward sign of the professionalism of each party, an image which they are keen to convey through the broadcasters to the electorate" (Stanyer, 2001: 32). In all parties, most delegates overall appreciate the transformation of conference from amateurish chaos to hip professionalism although only the Conservatives express no worry that presentation may take precedence over substance. Most, however, do not know how many resources their party is prepared to devote in order to improve the "watch-ability" of its conference. Since the 1990s, Labour and the Conservatives compete for the most innovative sets, prepared in secret and ritually unveiled to the press on the eve of conference. This new type of British political potlatch[31] is fierce and expensive. American political conventions were sources of inspiration. Labour drew from the experience of Clinton's communications team whilst the Conservative looked towards the Republicans and, later to Bush's "compassionate conservatism".[32] In 2002, Labour adopted a new strategy. They publicly played down the efforts they had put into the conception of their set, claiming they were giving up on spin and image management. Privately, those who had conceived the set were extremely proud of their creation. They thought that it emphasised the proximity of the leader and created an almost intimate atmosphere. They also admitted that it was part and parcel of a more general communication strategy devised to help the party shed the image of expert "spinners".[33]

The sets are the jewellery box in which the politicians are shiny diamonds. The main parties parade their heroes on a stage that enhances their performance, highlights how they are more professional, better equipped and better supported than their rivals. The background and the lighting are selected according to how good they look on television. Colours that are easily picked up by cameras are preferred (Stanyer, 2001: 29). Organisers also experiment. Labour tried pistachio green in 1994, "TV white" in 1995 and red and white in 1996. In 1998, the background matched the orator's tie: red for the Deputy Prime Minister, purple for the Prime Minister. However, backdrop, colours and slogans[34] can also distract attention and lead observers to wonder: was the prime ministerial purple trying to appeal to an electorate tradition-ally more attracted to blue? Is Prescott the only Labour politician who can still confidently speak in front of a red background? Whilst in 2002, the Labour delegates could see a predominantly red background, in particular during Blair's speech, the image watched by TV audiences had very little red and was mostly purple. Because settings can be misleading and influence particular readings of a situation, journalists constantly check for signs of inconsistency and for signs of disagreements.

The outcome of these evolutions in the Labour and Conservative parties is incredibly expensive. The beautiful sets contrast with most other European parties where fewer resources are poured into a stage set that few beyond the delegates will see. Smaller parties do not have the means to compete. Nevertheless, some, like Baroness Liz Barker, express satisfac-tion at the party's attempts to behave and appear "more professional". The Liberal Democrats have chosen versatile sets they can re-use for several years: a stylised yellow bird on a light grey background. The main preoccupation, ironically comments a Conference Committee Chair, is to "make sure that the wings of the birds do not appear to give ears to the speakers". For a couple of years, they rearranged the set for the leader's speech and used "friendly" (youthful and diverse) faces to enhance the background. Thus far, the Greens have been the only ones to escape the frenetic search for expensive stage designs. To date, they still adorn their conference stage with a few potted plants. The platform is composed of a foldable background, a simple desk and a lectern and activists bring banners and posters that they hang along the walls.

Spinning out of control

Because they feel they have lost control of what the public hears (Norris *et al.*, 1999: 181), political parties have stepped up their efforts to be portrayed in the most favourable light. So, if political news management is not a new phenomenon, it has nevertheless taken on unprecedented importance in the 1990s. It has also been increasingly professionalised.[35] James Stanyer (2001) produced a fascinating and detailed analysis of the complex interactions between television and parties for the production of political news in the early 1990s that I strongly recommend to readers looking for an alternative to the many journalistic accounts of the rise of political spin doctors.[36] Although, his study stops before New Labour had a chance to extend media management to government itself and thus misses the heyday of spin, he highlights the key directions of subsequent developments and documents the broiling tensions between politicians and journalists. What is the spin doctor's mission?

Communication experts have helped parties become more pro-active and effective in both controlling their image and "spinning" their stories. From their point of view, they are merely ensuring that their employers are "fairly treated" and that press coverage does not misrepresent them or misinterpret news concerning them. Therefore they put forward an interpretation (or spin) that they hope will be picked up. Labour has developed an expertise at "managing for the public consumption the output of conference", explains Shaun Woodward, Labour MP and former Communication Director of the Conservative party. One of the main changes in communication strategy lies in preventing the media from exploring areas of internal dissent, the biggest danger for parties during conference. To make sure journalists interpret things "correctly", political parties multiply briefings of all kind where they offer "objective" – that is highly subjective – readings of what is going on. Moreover, it is crucial to be perceived by journalists as a reliable "interpreter" of news. If Alastair Campbell has proved so effective as Tony Blair's Press Secretary, it is because he could present himself as the confidante of his boss.

Labour Conference 2002, Blackpool

As the audience gets up for the obligatory standing ovation after Blair's speech, journalists quickly withdraw to the media room. They exchange their first impressions and comments, testing ideas with each other. After a few minutes, Alastair Campbell appears, magnetically attracting a crowd around him for a few *impromptu* questions. The pack then moves towards a room where the Prime Minister's adviser launches into a text explanation. He reminds them

(*Continued*)

that the speech is a peculiar exercise, addressing both the party and beyond. He highlights the "message" the Prime Minister was trying to convey. He insists on the vision, the leadership qualities revealed by the outstanding performance. As the journalists try to get the subtext of the message, they ask "Alastair" for clarification. There is a strange atmosphere of complicity. After a dozen questions, Campbell gets up to leave, held up by a few who want a private word with him. The others walk away, commenting on the comment to each other, clearly making up their minds as they talk about the way they will write their piece.

At conference, party communicators hand out to journalists information packs on policy announcements and staged events. The content of speeches is released in advance, and in several stages, in order to tantalise curiosity. Such semi-official leaks have the advantage of responding partly to the constant media demand for fresh news whilst hammering home the same message. Morning newspapers, for instance, want to publish in their early editions what will be announced during the day. The evening ones not only need to publish detailed analysis of the speech but would also like an inkling about what will happen the following day. Senior politicians' full speeches are usually handed out in the press room in the morning.[37] Journalists carefully check against delivery and note unscripted remarks that could make the headline precisely because they play on the surprise effect. A famous example of such a tactic is Tony Blair's first leader's speech in 1994. In his concluding remarks, he announced that

> it is time we had a clear up-to-date statement of the objects and objectives of our party. John Prescott and I, as Leader and Deputy Leader will propose such a statement to the NEC ... And if it is accepted then let it become the objects of our Party for the next election and take its place in our constitution for the next century.

The announcement was so unexpected that many in the hall did not pick up immediately its implications. Rewriting Clause 4[38] was a clear assertion of authority by the young leader. Politically, symbolically but also in terms of communication strategy, it signalled the creation of New Labour.

Conferences are intrinsically "risky" occasions because the "impression of reality fostered by a performance is a delicate, fragile thing that can be shattered by very minor mishaps" (Goffman, 1990: 63). Throughout the week, conference debates and politicians' performances are closely monitored in order to respond to on-going developments. As nothing can be fully controlled and managed, something unexpected or "unhelpful" can happen, from Neil Kinnock tripping on Brighton's beach to internal dissidents or rivals gaining too much attention. Whilst in Westminster, the party leadership controls communication if only because of the privileged relationships developed through the year with Lobby journalists. It is almost impossible at conference to prevent troublemakers from contacting the media and there are no formal ways to prevent embarrassing fringe meetings from taking place. "For the critical claim-makers the news bulletins are open to their views more so than at any other time. These actors, when newsworthy, can therefore overcome any resource disadvantages that exist between themselves and the leadership" (Stanyer, 2001: 156). Disgruntled "old stars" can get publicity (Stanyer, 2001: 121) because journalists are keen to provide their audience with an account of dissenting voices and are prepared to look for them wherever they are.[39]

Party communication experts work tirelessly to limit the gaffes, prevent or debunk them.[40] They discreetly iron out difficulties (Stanyer, 2001: 67), smooth rough edges and deflect discrepant information. They pre-empt and prevent trouble. "Rebuttal units" respond to damaging stories that emerge despite planning efforts. Whilst the Tories have always tried to project the image of indisputable leadership, the Liberal Democrats were slow to professionalise their communication services. Since the devastating coverage of the cannabis debate in 1994, a Director of Strategy and Planning oversees the conference, organising press conferences every morning. These sessions are really opportunities for the major orators of the day to explain the detail of their speeches and answer questions.

The Labour party adopted another tactic to convince delegates to comply. It deliberately fostered a paranoid attitude to the press in order to encourage activists to close ranks against a common enemy (see Chapter 7). When self-discipline was insufficient to tame troublemakers, more ruthless tactics have been employed with the "party machine" gaining the reputation of a bully. Dissenters were threatened that their political careers could be in jeopardy, others were discredited as mavericks or "usual suspects" with little of interest to say.[41] It was as if the party elite not only wanted to be infallible, but also wanted to be seen as such and were prepared to go far to maintain this impression (Goffman, 1990: 52). Moreover, because the performance is supposed to express high standards of morality, it is all the more important to forgo or conceal any action that might be construed as inconsistent with these claims. Because they were convinced that the stakes were high, the Labour party communicators became merciless when efforts to influence the news agenda failed, resorting to attacks on the media that had portrayed them unflatteringly.[42]

The ambivalent role of the media

News coverage of course is not a transparent "window-on-the-world" but a highly selective and constructed interpretation of news items. There is very little direct political communication left of the sort the conference season used to provide at the time when verbatim reports of debates were published and plenary sessions broadcast wall-to-wall. Journalists now perceive their role as interpreting and decoding political messages. As a consequence, political coverage tends to be driven by the media's own agenda rather than by allegiance to a party (Norris, 2000: 175). As we have seen, political parties' communication experts have developed strategies to control the decoding of their performances.[43] On the other hand, the media are not passive victims of the "sultans of spin". Political news is the product of dynamic interactions between actors engaged simultaneously, or alternatively, in co-operative and competitive games. When they converge upon the seaside, politicians and journalists carry experience of each other developed throughout the year in Westminster. Whilst journalists benefit from the information they are provided with,[44] they have become increasingly frustrated with the constant attempts to manipulate them.

The media approaches political coverage from different perspectives. First, a pragmatist view links coverage to its news-value. The outside world is seen as interested in policy announcements rather than debates, in politicians' performance on the platform and in gossip. This attitude predominates in editorial rooms back in London where the primary concern is competition with rival media outlets (Blumler and Gurevitch, 2001). The *Sun*'s editors for instance believe that "people are only interested in stories about people". Thus, they format the stories reported accordingly in their columns. Plenary debates, activists' reactions, fringe discussions are only of interest if they can be presented in a personal, weird or humorous fashion. If that is the case, then the story has some news-value, otherwise it is "a waste of time".[45] However, "no media can afford to ignore what the Prime Minister says". Although the tabloid's approach is extreme, it reflects the attitude many editors have when they decide how much attention to devote to conferences. Thus, party leaderships cannot expect what they do and say to be simply picked up and relayed to the public. Only the most senior politician can benefit from the assumption that what they say is likely to be important, the newsworthiness of everything else has to be demonstrated. News related to dissidents, minorities and sub-national players are treated pragmatically and parties that are either poorly represented in Parliament (such as the Liberal Democrats) or not at all (as in the case of the Greens) are likely to be snubbed, unless they hold debates on controversial issues such as legalising cannabis or banning lottery scratch cards.

A second strand within the media is reverential towards politics though no longer necessarily of politicians. It rests on the conviction that politics is inherently important and thus intrinsically worth covering. BBC political correspondents thus justify conference coverage as part of their "public service mission".[46] However, the transformation of political parties' policy elaboration contributes to the shifting of interest away from conference.[47] So long as the Labour party conference was the place for policy deliberations, it was idealised as a democratic forum. All parliamentary party conferences could, by extension, be considered to be of interest to the general public. But the media are reticent to convey passively what they now perceive as propaganda, explains a BBC producer:

> If it is just ambitious politicians or would be politicians trying to make a name for themselves while standing on the platform, we're not interested in that, it is not public service broadcasting. But any minister or major trade union leader or international guest speaker, we will always take them live.

This approach effectively contributes to exclude third parties in two ways. The electoral system keeps them out of the Commons whilst media ostracism limits their ability to take part in the public debate. This vicious circle feeds the frustration of citizens who do not feel adequately represented by the two main parties and consider that the media conspires with established parties to keep new contenders out of the game by reinforcing the "cartelisation" of party political life (Katz and Mair, 1995).

Journalists' "sacerdotal" duty to cover politics combines with a new self-imposed "democratic mission". New Labour has tightened control over internal debates so much so that members almost appear to sing from a single hymn sheet.[48] Moreover, since the 1997 general election debacle, the Conservatives have been largely unable to counter effectively a triumphant Labour government. In the absence of public debate in the Commons or, apparently, within the parties themselves, some journalists thus perceive themselves as the only real opposition, the counter-weight that can hold politicians accountable. Adam Boulton (*Sky News*) explains his role as self-appointed protector of citizens otherwise the passive victims of devious politicians: "Our job is covering politics. To me that means trying to help people understand what they (our governors) are trying to do to us, the people." Moreover, the shift away from the Westminster model of a centralised state reduces the role of parliamentary political parties to one actor amongst many others. Conferences therefore are less intrinsically interesting. The little entertainment left in the conference season's joust is almost incidental because political parties do not take decisions:

> Government often comes through executive decisions, executive announcements, executive action rather than through straight forward Parliamentary debate, which can often seem not particularly relevant, not particularly focused on what's going on.[49]

However, the threat to leave and stop covering the conferences is void because no one can bypass the conference of the party in government. Whether in Blackpool or Bournemouth, there may be little to cover as everything is increasingly staged managed but the media nevertheless send teams because something "might happen" and if nothing happens dormant conflicts might "sex up" the reports. Although reduced teams can be sent to cover the other conferences, journalists still resent increasingly having to tour the seaside resorts where little happens and they feel they are being duped.

Labour Conference 2002, Blackpool

In the media room, journalists complain that conferences have become useless and boring. They also particularly dislike the tacky Northern resort. Adam Boulton bemoans the fact that conferences are a farce and a "complete waste of time", no longer relevant to the political life of the country. There is "no need to come to Blackpool

(*Continued*)

to meet ministers these days" because "talking to them in the hotel bars and corridors is too obvious", or even counterproductive for those looking for juicy revelations or sniping comments. George Pascoe-Watson (*The Sun*) concurs: the "best way is to contact them on their mobile phones or pagers". A journalist from *The Scotsman* explains to bemused and dismissive colleagues how important the fringe seems to be for delegates: she attended the previous evening women's reception and was struck by an atmosphere of conviviality and solidarity she had never imagined.

Journalists compete but also support each other as team partners in opposition to parties. They share a semi-open plan room where they are granted desks and communication facilities. They receive detailed schedules of what may be of interest to them, lists of people available for interviews, transcripts of the speeches, pre- and post-delivery comments on politicians' contributions. Increasingly, press secretaries and political advisors visit them to "help" decode announcements. Information is brought to them by parties or gathered by those venturing in the main hall, the restaurants and fringe meetings. There, they observe each other and the manoeuvring of politicians and their staff and are alerted by activities in other parts of the room to a news item they had not picked up. Thus, political journalists interview each other as experts: on his way back from a meeting with the Prime Minister where they discussed how the government would respond to the defeat on the private finance initiatives (PFI) document, Trevor Kavanagh (*The Sun*) is interviewed by *Sky News*.[50] Labour's eagerness to ease relationships with his newspaper makes him an important figure on the conference circuit. "We spin between ourselves," admits Jon Snow (quoted by Stanyer, 2001: 58). Because "spin doctors" come to the media room where information sheets are also liberally distributed; journalists hardly have to go in the hall at all anymore. Most make the effort to pop in to "feel the atmosphere" for the leader's speech. They follow most other sessions through internal circuit television screens. For journalists, the tension is often to balance shared information and scoops: what should be shared to ensure reciprocity and collegiality, what is an "exclusive" that can be personally beneficial, what is "public knowledge" and what is an advanced tip-off.[51] There is so much going on that it is vital to maintain good relationships with a variety of potential sources. Walking into the main hotel in Bournemouth, a journalist winks to an MP: "Thanks for the tip. I'll remember I owe you."

Labour Conference 2002, Blackpool

Shortly after the Chancellor's speech, Gordon Brown's political advisor leisurely walks down the media corridor, looking for clues about how the press will report his boss's performance in the next morning's editions. He first approaches the *Sun's* corner for a chat with the editor. Inadvertently, he insists on issues that he would like developed. It is a strange interaction as both actors pretend they do not know the intentions of the other. The anxiety of the political adviser meets the irony of journalists, revelling in the joy of their momentary feeling of omnipotence. Generously, Pascoe-Watson tells him that the story will be favourably covered as the tabloid has decided to support the government on the Private Finance Initiatives (PFI).

The anxiety of politicians and their spinners, their plotting and occasionally their anger comforts journalists as it reminds them that they retain some power over those they have become so dependent upon. The interdependence between the two sets of actors is manifest in their conference confrontation. Rising tensions turn into an "arms race", considers Bill Bush but stop short of open warfare. Excessive "spin" has turned journalists' deference into defiance and disdain. Jeremy Paxman's *Political Animal* (2003) interestingly exposes a condescending, slightly incredulous attitude to anybody invested in politics and particularly party politics[52] that is manifest in journalists' ostentatious reluctance to mix with party members.

The sophistication in controlling what the media can access has provoked resentment and resistance that takes precisely the form that the party communication experts initially sought to overcome. Political correspondents have assumed a more prominent role as they interpret and contextualise, seeing their role as helping the public to see through the propaganda and the public relations gloss. They increasingly frame debates (Stanyer, 2001: 155), explain their policy implications and their ideological background. Debates and policy announcements are framed, dissected, digested by political pundits. Journalists try harder to get behind the scenes, denouncing "manipulation" and spin.[53] Many admit with frustration that party machines "have got better in stage-managing and they are quite astute in what they are prepared to let us see".

If parties are keen to put on a show of inclusive, competent and dynamic organisation rather than self-serving inward looking and divided party hacks, the media also want to be seen as providing cutting-edge professional coverage that is both informed, accountable and entertaining. As they cannot afford to bore their audiences, broadcasters create "infotainment" programmes using the newest technologies. Star presenters and political commentators – such as Boulton, Paxman, Humphreys or Snow – are sent down to the seaside to muster interest thanks to their harsh interviews. For want of anything better, journalists "manufacture" a debate by juxtaposing opinions expressed in different forums (Stanyer, 2001: 137). They interview activists to bolster or balance a particular perspective on an issue (Stanyer, 2001: 153) or to give a "popular touch" to their reports. They try to locate in the context of intra-party disputes. Michael White from the *Guardian* admits that journalists have a tendency to cry "split" at any sign of debate "because it is one way of getting things into print in an adversarial media culture".[54] They also provide comments and analysis in articles and reports for their newspapers or their corporation. Conference coverage is shorter and more reliant on background explanations prepared in London and packaged with analysis and comments from pundits.[55]

Switching off party politics?

Apart from the leaders' speeches, conferences have poor entertainment value for the majority of home TV audiences and, not surprisingly, the number of viewers consistently decreased throughout the 1980s. Between 1992 and 1998, they averaged about 276,000 viewers for the Liberal Democrats, 455,000 for Labour and 557,000 for the Tories (Stanyer, 2001: 165). Commercial networks stopped live coverage in 1985[56] and the BBC live terrestrial coverage peaked in 1986 at 5000 minutes before declining to 2500 in 1998 (Stanyer, 2001: 168). By the turn of the Millennium, wall-to-wall coverage was only available on BBC Parliament to cable and satellite audiences. BBC terrestrial broadcasts less than 2000 minutes for each of the three conferences in 2003.[57] As audiences switched off, both parties and the media have made efforts to rescue the conference season. Parties have tried to create an entertaining political spectacle (Chapter 7) but the era of seaside gladiators seems to have passed. In the competition for shares of audience, media outlets look for newsworthiness and entertainment value. Broadcasters offer more interviews, analysis and "question time". The idea is that rushed "information consumers" now expect pre-packaged analysis and comments rather than unmediated (live and wall-to-wall) coverage.

Paradoxically, the abundance of information outlets has reduced the news content. There is more coverage of the conference but it is fragmented and reduced to a few seconds of sound-bites. There is constant monitoring on the 24-hour news circuit but less coverage. Complex political arguments are necessarily squeezed out in favour of catchy titles. "It has become a niche phenomenon", laments a Labour official, "and we have to make sure we are exciting news to cover." One solution for political parties consists in the targeting of specific audiences so that their position on education or agriculture reaches those concerned. This strategy is of particular importance for the Liberal Democrats who compensate for the lack of interest in the general media by a careful targeting of professional and specialised press. Beyond the TV screens, computer screens can now bring the conference sessions to homes and offices. The Internet has created new opportunities for broad and narrow casting: parties have developed their own online facilities providing live coverage, online chats and access to archives.

To those watching from home however, the event is "flattened", requiring the media and the parties to invent new types of visual attendance (Bell, 1997: 243). Thus, each conference is covered from various points of view that are, most of the time, simply juxtaposed. Interviews of delegates in the corridors alternate with shots of the exhibition area and close-ups of the audience in the hall listening and reacting to speeches. The "15 minutes of fame" are necessary to political organisations when they have to compete with more exciting forms of entertainment – including televised ones. The collective experience of conference, filtered through as a myriad of individual viewpoints, justifies the journalists' role as interpreters and analysts. Participants are asked to express their personal opinion on what they are experiencing in an attempt to personalise the news. As in the coverage of major sporting events, giant screens now also allow live audiences in the hall to see themselves watching, knowing that they may themselves be watched by many more outside the hall. The look of the "spect-actors" transforms activists into actors in a show watched by thousands. As emotions are expected to be less easily manipulated by conference organisers (Sennett, 1986), the reaction of the audience in the hall is often assumed to be an indicator of authentic expression of support for the leadership (see Hochschild, 2003).

Party conferences do not create excitement and this is reflected in the reduction of live coverage and dwindling audiences. They rarely bring people together for festive viewing! The more banal politics becomes, the less it attracts audiences and commercial broadcasters and the more political parties have to make an effort to look attractive. In fact, conferences are increasingly viewed as "irrelevant" and therefore rarely watched, as revealed by a survey commissioned by ePolitix.com in September 2004. According to it, 77 per cent of respondents never or rarely watched conferences whilst 75 per cent declared they were not interested in them. Only 2 per cent found them "very relevant".[58] Whilst the Liberal Democrats claim that, in the words of a Conference Committee Chair, they "want to maintain debate over presentation", Labour delegates generally feel that they have lost important decision-making powers (not that they necessarily had much to lose). Even activists complain that nothing of significance happens or is decided at conference anymore.

If conferences are merely a spectacle, they have to compete with many other forms of entertainment. The exponential development of media outlets provides incredible opportunities to reach a wider audience and shape public opinion. However, this also tends to bring about an information overload. As citizens are constantly bombarded with political images and stories, politics itself has become banal. The ideal modern citizen may be more informed but she is also more bored. Rather than necessarily improve public political awareness, the information society has brought about political overdose.[59]

Conclusion

In the 1980s, conferences were reputed to be an entertaining "seaside blood sport" but, by the beginning of the following century they have become too contrived and predictable to have much news or entertainment value for the media and much suspense for viewers. On the other hand, journalists are increasingly reluctant to report what they see as party propaganda and have taken on the role of analysts and commentators, filtering the news for an information-weary audience. This evolution mirrors what happened to American party conventions two decades before. Until 1952, the Republican and Democratic conventions played a crucial political role: they nominated presidential candidates and agreed electoral platforms. The selection of candidates was then devolved to primaries, but conventions retained a role as civic media events and as get-togethers for activists. However, after 1968, parties grew uneasy with the way they were portrayed by TV networks and endeavoured to improve their image (Karabell, 1998). The two parties began avoiding anything that might give the appearance of internal division. By 1972, the Republican convention was planned and rehearsed minute-by-minute. Stage-management turned the meeting into an insipid but cheerful "infomercial". The conflicts that kept the media and the public interested in the unfolding drama have all but vanished. Whilst after the Second World War, American party conventions were watched by millions of Americans congregating to neighbours' houses, ratings figures dropped dramatically from the 1970s onwards (from 80 per cent of households in 1952 to less than a third in 1996), as did broadcasting time (from 60 hours in 1952 to 10 to 20 hours in the 1980s).

In Britain, decline in the interest for party conferences cannot be blamed on either political parties or the media though both contribute to it. This evolution was the product of interactions between two groups of actors (the politicians and the media) with divergent interests. In order to regain initiative and control over the framing of political news, parties hired communications professionals who contributed to the permanent campaign that justifies their positions. As competitors cannot afford to be wrong footed, they choose perfection in form and rarely stray from the safety of valence issues. To a large degree, this transformation in Britain has been precipitated by the increasing impact of the "public relations" (PR) industry (Miller and Dinan, 2000). The development of this new economic sector was sparked and accelerated by privatisation and deregulation since 1979. By the 1990s, the PR industry was gaining a great deal of influence as the government and the parties themselves seized the opportunity to boost their public image. It has become increasingly difficult to separate "news" from "spin" and self-promotion by highly professionalised party organisations. Political parties now attempt to combine the advertising of their "product" with the selling of a particular version of the news. In a sense, reflexive adaptation to an anticipated future creates its own reality and in this case, a vicious circle of cynicism and suspicion that peaked during New Labour's second term in office. By 2002, New Labour was showing signs that excessive spinning had been more damaging than limiting dissent. "The big age of spin is gone", rejoiced a BBC producer as conference organisers were looking into ways to relinquish some control. But this very attitude inevitably raises questions about spontaneity and authenticity. Are political parties, and Labour in particular, really going to stop worrying about their image? Will it rejuvenate citizen's trust in politicians and their parties? One can doubt whether this is the best means to repair the damage if only because permanent campaigning tends to blur the distinction between politics, as the art of governing, and party politics as the partisan expression of one group's self-interest.

7
The Public Performance

Political debate is the *raison d'être* of party conference. The format of the debate, its style and its structure are largely influenced by the British parliamentary tradition. It follows a fixed motion-centred pattern, inspired by the practice of the House of Commons. Pros and cons are heard, then votes are counted. The British debating tradition is carried on through school and university debating societies.[1] It is reinforced by the adversarial legal system, which puts great emphasis on winning arguments before an audience. It has been more influential precisely because many lawyers have entered politics, including of course Tony Blair and Michael Howard. This traditional style is rigid and contrived. Not only does the contradictory debate often give the impression that the party is divided but it also tend to be of little entertainment value. However, it carries within it the ideal of intellectual rigor leading to a decision.

British political parties have ritualised plenary debates more than any other aspect of conference. These sessions usually follow a fixed pattern that carries "the prestige of tradition and in this prestige lays its power" (Bell, 1992: 120). They are held in grandiose settings that are "unabashedly built up to emphasise a departure from men's daily routine, a special or heroic quality in the proceedings they are to frame" (Edelman, 1985: 96). They are mostly very formal events: participants dress up in sober costumes and adopt a poised demeanour. Speakers use formal language that has little use outside the hall and introduce themselves as "Ms Smith, Derby North CLP, speaking against composite 3". For a moment, representatives and delegates are dissociated from their individual identities as they take on a role. The audience patiently listens to committee reports and an endless succession of speeches. Such formalisation and extra-ordinary circumstances give the public debate a majestic aura.

Participants indulge in the impression that they share a common culture and that they are involved in something crucially important not only for the organisation but also for British democracy. Whilst the solemnity of debates contributed to foster conformism, there remains the possibility of dissent. In fact voicing disagreement was given particular prominence in such formal settings, thereby giving its authors an exceptional importance in influence.

The centrality of policy debate in the constitutional make-up of each organisation as well as in its identity explains the degree to which parties can accept the interference of propaganda imperatives. The Conservatives have always been acutely aware of the performance aspect of conference and have endeavoured for many decades to provide a good showcase for their politicians. As the conference was conceived as a rally, dry debates have never been particularly sought after and the Conservatives have been more innovative than others. Nevertheless they retained motions throughout the 20th century as a token of grass-roots influence on policy discussions. It is only once motions were abandoned as the main item on the conference agenda, that the Conservatives (2000) and Labour (1998) were able to invent new sessions that serve the purpose of promoting policies and politicians. The Liberal Democrats have found sacrificing debates the most difficult. The party leadership would do without the unpredictability of conference decisions if it did not threaten the image activists have of their party. "We have a commitment to debate," explains Liz Barker. In terms of identity, this is more important than the outcome of the votes.[2] Of the fours parties, the Greens are least tied to the adversarial parliamentary tradition. Critical of its effect on the conduct of politics in the UK, they have looked for alternative modes of deliberation based on the search for consensus.

As the media presence at conference has become more intrusive, the atmosphere and the character of the event have been transformed. In an age dominated by 24-hour news channels, control over one's image has become increasingly important. Since the 1980s, acknowledges Neil Kinnock, "conference is a public performance of a drama written elsewhere. It is representational." Delegates and representatives are now part of the cast and are involved in the production of the best performance possible for electoral purposes. Stage-management is not new[3] but it is more systematic and expertly done than in the past. Small parties that attract relatively little media attention have been less affected. This evolution is most striking in the case of Labour, where formerly amateurish and inward looking production has become a professionally directed choreography. Whilst in the mid-1990s Labour and Liberal Democrat officials insisted on the "great opportunity to debate", by the early 2000s conference organisers openly acknowledged stage management and admitted that it was "primarily a media event" for advertising the organisation, its policies and its politicians. In 1996, the Labour officials that I interviewed envied the dynamic of the Conservative conference debates with its supportive and occasionally witty speeches. They had become aware of the need to produce an entertaining and slick performance for participants as well as the wider audience. They believed conference broadcasts a "corporate image" that is decisive in the new electoral market. As the Conservative Chief executive puts it:

> The most important is the television news bulletins as it is through television coverage that the vast majority of people get an impression of conference (...) although feedback from representatives is important, the conference should be organised to achieve the most favourable media coverage.[4]

How have parties adapted the ritual format of a traditional contradictory debate to the demands of a competitive media market? The challenge has been to preserve the impression of spontaneity whilst tightening control on actors and their performance to prevent unchecked improvisation.

The art of chairing

Conferences contribute to the legitimisation of power and of power-holders. They construct hierarchies as they stage the confrontation of these strange seaside gladiators. The conference circus fosters a sense of shared identity as well as respect for the party's champions. Conferences dramatise internal conflicts and rivalries and are occasions of intense, playful and mobilising exchanges (Rivière, 1988: 176). In this context, it is clear that conference directing is a difficult art, complicated by contradictory pressures pulling in different directions. Some of the most complex work is conducted by session chairs, who are constantly manoeuvring between ideals of a conference dominated by the grassroots holding politicians to account and the demands of the leadership for effective public relation management.

Until 1998, the NU was an autonomous organisation. It held an annual conference to which it kindly invited guest speakers. Despite their outsiders' status, politicians have always influenced, directly and indirectly, not only the choice of orators but also the whole event. They have strengthened their grip on the procedures because the Board, which now oversees the "scripting and choreography of the introductory speeches", is in effect dominated by politicians. In 2002, each session involved outside guests, orators from the floor and keynote speeches. Each spoke from a different rostrum. The succession was meant to illustrate the party's message, that "we are listening", explains the Chairman of the Convention. Senior members of the volunteer organisation play a key role in the choice of the cast but this influence is a token of their previous control. However, the selection of speakers is far from anodyne. The party attempts to convey a message about its inclusiveness (ordinary delegates, minorities, gender and regional balance, people with disability), its internal pluralism (not all speakers are supportive of the leadership), its unity and its wealth of expertise (professionally run and informed discussions).

Chairing involves a lot of preparatory work if the objective is to successfully co-ordinate a show that is partly unpredictable. The best *comedia del arte* always follows a canvass. Otherwise, it looks "improvised"! A balance has to be struck between controlling the overall narrative and producing an event that has the authenticity of a genuine discussion. Debates are "orchestrated" thanks to a careful selection of speakers from the floor. Conference chairing is like conducting a musical, explains John Taylor: "speakers provide the words for the music we have chosen [so that] debates provide a synthesis, a point of view". It is important to find potentially good speakers – "people with a story to tell" and a good will to deliver a positive speech. "Between us,[5] we knew hundreds of members and could have an idea of who wanted to speak and what to expect from them." Over the years, orators and contributors are consigned to a little notebook so as to ensure "fairness". A word with the session chair could always be had, provided "it did not disrupt the music". Chairing is about reading the moods of the audience and using this intuition to direct the show.

In the past, Labour and the Conservatives have reserved the right to chair conference sessions to senior officers from the National Union or members of the NEC. From the late 1990s, trustworthy politicians and other personalities were invited to chair to symbolise the new broader role of conference.[6] Surprisingly, the two major organisations leave the quality of conference chairing to chance and personal talent. There is "no specific training", explain several former chairpersons from Labour, it is an art learnt through experience and confidence comes with time. Nevertheless, there is a safety net for this apparent openness. Tom Sawyer admits that "members of the Conference Committee are trained and aids [to the Chair] are always from the Committee because there can be a need to [gather] Intelligence". Conference organisers and party elites know full well that confident chairing can close debates or impose particular readings of procedure without giving delegates time to react or protest. Such arbitrage is sometimes taken in good faith but in others they benefit the leadership. On the other hand, inexperienced chairing can be disastrous if the conference feels it is not treated fairly. The advantage of choosing novice chairs is that they may be more susceptible to officials' advice because they want to have a good session (and to save face in Goffman's terms). Indeed, chairs are keen to do well under the gaze of thousands of people. If one can afford it, independent chairing is a way to assert authority, shows one's integrity whilst the satisfaction of the leadership is a safer strategy.[7] Diana Jeuda recalls

> I used to ask the Grassroots Alliance or others to provide me with a list of speakers they wanted to be called; I wouldn't necessarily call them. I would occasionally take a risk, one cannot know all the delegates.

In the Labour party as well, most speakers are chosen well in advance of the start of a session. Until 1998, the majority of speakers were in effect chosen during compositing meetings. Delegates whose motion had been incorporated into a composite were entitled to defend it. Those determined to be called thus had to make sure that it was the case. Systematic efforts to influence choice of speakers with a "good attitude" had been developed in the mid-1990s, building from the recognition that many considerations have to be taken into account in the "planning of debates and the calling of speakers". Since then, potential speakers are listed to guide the chair's selection. Tom Sawyer explains candidly that there is

> a list of people wishing to speak and had something of interest to tell the conference, like an expert on housing in the relevant debate. So you'd pick somebody from the list, but I'd also choose a few randomly. If you were really nervous you'd stick to the list and look up for councillor X with a red jumper, hoping you would see him

Following a tight script, even novice chairs cannot get it too wrong. Those who have regularly attended may also be familiar with specific conference jargon. Lexical "advice" can also be offered to others. If there is no ban on words such as "comrade" under New Labour, the playful defiance of those who utter it nowadays demonstrates the importance of precise chairing.

"Members need rituals, hierarchies and traditions: it gives meaning to what they are doing," explains John Taylor. As one of the senior members of the National Union and the Convention, he was, for several years, one of the ritual masters of the Conservative Party. He oversaw conference procedures, selecting speakers and also deciding how the conference service should be conducted or who could come and sit on stage. It is tempting to see rituals as a symbolic language that needs to be decoded and reveals deeply held values but conference rituals do not merely express members' attitudes to democracy, participation and power. There is also an *ad hoc* pragmatic dimension to such practices. Far from being immutable, rituals are constantly adapted. It is through this combination of predictability and flexibility that rituals legitimise and naturalise change. Conference organisers constantly adapt what may superficially look like immutable practices in order to fit the *Zeitgeist* as well as to attempt to change perceptions. For instance, the Conservatives have tried over recent years to transform their image of the "nasty party", as Teresa May, then Party Chairman, put it in her 2002 Conference address. To promote a more tolerant image, daring experiments were conducted. Breaking with tradition, the religious service opening the conference was broadened to Christian denominations beyond the Church of England. Then, in 2002 the party held a multi-faith event: clerics representing the three monotheisms led the service. However, criticisms were such that the experiment was not repeated.

If chairing is a difficult task, only the Greens and the Liberal Democrats take it so seriously that they have developed training programmes. Over the years, dozens of activists have been taught how to chair plenary conference sessions while others have had "refresher" sessions. The Liberal Democrats have developed a "good pool of sometimes excellent chairs" and take the opportunity to have a different chair for each session.[8] Future chairs learnt how to handle difficult situations such as rowdy debates or complex clashes of rules. Balancing the debate and ensuring that a wide array of points of view is expressed is widely considered as the objective for any conference chair. "It is important to be worthy of people's trust, so we have a commitment to tell them, for instance, when 80 per cent of the speaker's cards submitted go in the same direction. We train chairs to explain what they are doing", explain the Liberal Democrats. Transparency in chairing is almost as important as an improbable and unworkable perfect balance. "One tries to ignore the media because they are always very negative and only present debates as major splits even though no party can change its policies without internal debate," affirms Alan Sherwell. However, chairs are influenced by image concerns and there has been a pervasive temptation to structure the debate to produce the desired impression.

Choosing the cast

Liberal Democrats and Conservative representatives wishing to speak are asked to fill out speaker's cards. Would-be orators provide all the information that may give them the chance to speak from the rostrum. A couple of hours before their session, chairs select those they will call. Thanks to these cards, chairs can balance the debate and can draw a "representative" sample of the membership.[9] This is all the more important as accusations of geographical and gender biases are commonplace. Scottish constituencies are rarely prepared to accept that someone from a Shire could defend their position. The Liberal Democrats, as a federal organisation, are particularly sensitive to the issue. Because parties try to broadcast a positive image, selecting speakers has become more important. It is crucial to call women to the rostrum even when few put themselves forward. In 2002, 60 per cent of the Conservative conference speakers were male but invited presenters helped to balance genders.[10] Although many sessions have too many volunteers, the opposite also happens. Occasionally, Chairs have to solicit speakers and encourage young representatives, women, ethnic minorities or those with specialist backgrounds to come forward.[11] In over 20 years of conference attendance, John, a Conservative activist from Lincolnshire has spoken twice from the rostrum, each time on an invitation: first as a young Tory, then as an expert on agriculture.

Filling in a speaker's slip is rarely enough though, because there are often more volunteers than time allows. Ann Widdecombe recalls how, as a first timer in the 1970s, she sat through all debates, filing speaker's slips. Unsuccessful and disappointed she asked her MP who suggested that she spoke with her party agent. The following year, she followed the advice and was called to the rostrum.

Conservative Conference Bournemouth 1996

A Tory candidate fails to catch the eye of the chair. After a little while, the person seating next to her gets up and has a word with the chair. A few minutes later, she is called to the microphone. As she concludes, she is congratulated by one of her constituents. She leaves the hall immediately.

"Everything is fabricated, prepared," claims a Conservative parlia-mentary assistant who has helped numerous activists write their speeches. Despite his cynical view, most speakers are genuine but desperate to be called and therefore happy to accept all the help they can get. Gary Meggitt sent a copy of his intended speech to the relevant Shadow Secretary as well as to the Party Secretary. He tells me that "people are not here to contribute to policy-making" and are therefore less both-ered by the process. Conservative representatives not only acknowledge the need for the canalisation of spontaneity for electoral purposes,[12] they also support conference management and stage-management. Early selection of speakers allows organisers to help the performer come up with a stunt or nice illustration. In 1981, Edwina Currie, then a local councillor and a prison visitor, had brought handcuffs to make her point about insecurity in her area. In 1996, Conservative motion movers had their speeches nicely illustrated with appropriate slides projected on giant screens.

At the Green conference, registration with the SOC gives delegates wishing to speak priority over those who raise their hands.[13] People who have attended the relevant preparatory workshop are also placed at the top of the list. The rule was invented to improve the time management of an over-worked conference and to encourage those interested to take part in the relevant small-group discussion. As workshops discuss motions in detail, they are likely to address most questions, which will not need to be brought to the plenary's attention. In the 1980s, OWOW had noted that many points of order were raised because participants did not fully understand the procedures. The SOC thus both filters such procedural objections and collects the names of activists wishing to speak. Peter Lang, who coordinated OWOW considers that "people's right to listen and reflect is thus better preserved even though it restricts other's rights to speak and interrupt".

Consensus is a state of mind and a self-discipline rather than a procedure for decision-making but it also affects the atmosphere of plenary session, where votes are taken. The Green conference audience is silent and studious despite the shuffles of the orators regularly walking to a microphone. Orators introduce themselves and present their point, rarely overrunning the allotted 3 minutes.[14] Occasionally, the Chair asks conference whether to extend the debate by 20 minutes or whether to take an immediate vote. Because they are so keen to encourage all activists to speak during conferences the Greens have considered various ways of making them feel equally valued and listened to. They thus insist on treating all participants strictly equally. National officers have no more time than others to express their views, nor any privilege in being called. Speakers are rarely called by their names so that novices do not feel inhibited to join a tightly knit community of people who know each other well. In 1994, the Chair of the Executive was the "man with the beard and the blue tie".[15] Moreover, the Greens were the first party to put into practice ideas of empowerment inspired by the peace and women's movements. Efforts to facilitate participation from all delegates were stepped up and consensus building appeared as an alternative to the inherently divisive nature of a traditional debate followed by vote.

Managing spontaneity

Labour conference "open debates" last between 5 and 50 minutes, so only a few delegates are normally called for 3-minute long interventions. Apparently, the selection is "random" but this has hardly ever been the case. Experienced delegates have a word with a party worker, sometimes an MP or a member of the NEC, to have their name added to the unofficial list.[16] Efforts to know and control delegates are not new but they are now more systematic. Until a few years ago, delegates were rarely personally known.[17] This was not so important because the trade unions dominated the votes. So long as the leadership could rely on a handful of key unions, individual speakers had little importance. However, constituencies now command 50 per cent of the votes and are more likely to be swayed by debates.

The ritualisation of conference procedures provided some social control over internal disputes but this was increasingly considered insufficient in the hostile media environment of the 1980s and early 1990s. In 1994, New Labour set up a team to screen delegations and smooth debates by flagging out potential troublemakers. They compiled a database of delegates: their political views, how articulate they are, how useful they could be. Before 1998, they attended compositing meetings and pre-selected most of the orators there, providing advice on speech writing and clothing.[18] "You have to know all the delegates to know what they are likely to talk about and what they are likely to say," explains the team co-ordinator. By 2000, members of the team knew all delegates, "who is pro or anti-leadership, who are the non-aligned". They could blacklist some delegates as well as recruit "time-fillers" at short notice. They helped speakers prepare their speech.

Unlike the other parties, Labour cultivates the appearance of spontaneity and improvisation. Delegates are called to the rostrum as "the person with the yellow file" as if they were anonymous. But it is precisely because they are known that they are called. Appearance of randomness preserves the illusion that anybody can be called and that the selection is fair and democratic.[19] Many conference novices believe what they are told and are thus genuinely shocked to discover how this impression is perpetuated. What is also striking is how more experienced delegates first provide this as an explanation for speaker selection and only concede, when pressed on the matter, that there is more to it than meets the eye. They would not spontaneously talk about it nor reflect upon it, unless they themselves intend to be called to the rostrum. It is as if they have chosen to believe their own propaganda because it is consistent with their ideal of a sovereign conference. They are complicitous in perpetuating the illusion of a spontaneous debate.

2002 – Conference has changed Miriam's perception of regional party workers. They are devoted, keen to explain how things work and to help but she has just discovered the other role they play in selecting speakers. "There is a colour coded system for people who will be called to speak," she reports a bit shocked. One of her friends "was told what to wear as well as to wave a yellow piece of paper". She indeed "caught the eye" of the chair and was called to the rostrum.

1997 – Samuel is eager to be called to the rostrum. He has contacted the regional party staff who advised him to submit a draft and announce how he would be dressed. The draft came back "with very helpful comments and advice to wear a blue shirt and a tie". He bought them especially but was not called: "maybe somebody had found a nicer tie", he jokes.

Whilst the Greens call "the man with the blue tie" knowing perfectly well who he is because they want to encourage shy participants to come forward, Labour uses the same technique to stage-manage the image of spontaneity, transparency and democracy. The hypocrisy of the system is acknowledged reluctantly. "It is not completely stitched up", claims a member of the team that selects speakers: "critical but positive contributions will always be welcome because we have to maintain a debate".

Debates have indeed become cleverly orchestrated. Constituency delegates used to be the most critical of the platform but it sometimes seem now as if there is a constant stream of sycophantic speeches.

Supporters of the government are picked from constituency delegations in order to give the impression that government policy is approved by constituency delegates and opposed by trade unions.[20] Critics are only called to the rostrum after televisions have stopped live transmission or when journalists are busy commenting on important speeches.[21] Overall, the general tone has changed. It is "more consensual and constructive", explains Matthew Taylor. From a different viewpoint, it is sweet and bland like vanilla ice cream.

Even though "choosing the cast" has never been left to chance, the tight control now exercised by the party machine has changed the nature of the debate. In the past, contestation was possible and there was a shared recognition of the risk involved. Support was conditional despite efforts to induce conformism. Disagreements and confrontation seemed to demonstrate that the party was indeed a democratic organisation. As speeches from the floor have become a succession of redundant praise of the government, even delegates who consider themselves to be loyal have become suspicious and bored, whilst the media are losing interest in what is little more than a spectacle.

Staying "on-message"

Reluctance towards confrontational debate and efforts to stage "constructive" ones has been primarily motivated in the Labour party by a fear of being presented as divided and unable to govern. An "inclusive" approach was promised: friendly, democratic forums would replace smoke-filled meetings. A less sympathetic reading however is that, as the Labour Co-ordinating Committee itself advocated (1996), conference delegates "become part of an elaborate rubber stamping exercise". The self-restraint now exhibited by New Labour delegates is seen as insincere.[22] Outsiders insinuate that beneath the veneer of consensus, the party delegates are oppressed dissidents. Although potential for rebellion has been stirred up by the war in Iraq and some of the neo-liberal reforms introduced by Blair's government (such as private investment in public services), fear and repression did not quieten conference. The taming of the Labour conference may also be related to the self-control of delegates, as Eric Shaw explains:

> Within the rank and file there developed a greater disposition to acknowledge the functional importance of leadership, a much enhanced sensitivity to the effects of their behaviour on Labour's

image and a greater appreciation of the need (amidst an antagonistic and relentlessly probing press) for Party unity (1996: 220).

This is not schizophrenia. Rather, it reflects a new attitude to the role of the media in the electoral competition. In the 1990s, activists became sensitive to the need to improve the party's image.

Goffman reminds us how everyday interactions are themselves (re-)presentation. Individuals strive to preserve a preferred definition of the situation. They endeavour to convince their audience of the authenticity of their performance and by doing so also end up convincing themselves. "Our conception of our role becomes a second nature and an integral part of our personality."[23] In the 1990s, Labour delegates overall accepted the need to co-operate to improve the image of the party. Many were prepared to restrain their criticism in front of cameras if it might damage the chances of the party to be elected (or re-elected). "The unthinking ease with which performers consistently carry off such standard-maintaining routines does not deny that a performance has occurred, merely that the participants have been aware of if" (Goffman, 1990: 81). The understanding of such role distinctions is comparatively new in Labour, at least in the context of maintaining a positive and united definition of conference.

Following Goffman (1990), we can analytically distinguish the front and the back regions of a public performance. Both regions foster their own patterns of behaviours. Appropriate routines of interaction and demeanour develop. In the front region, actors are under the gaze of the audience even when they are not the primary focus of attention. As a consequence, they control their behaviour and limit communications not directly related to their role. Participant observation and interviews reveal the differences between these regions. Combined, these methods expose how politicians and communication experts maintain front region performance with ease, by mastering the political cant and constantly monitoring what they do and say. Interviewing them is thus often frustrating because it is very difficult to scratch beneath the role. On the other hand, activists, staff, party officials and former employees are generally more forthcoming about discrepancies and role conflicts. They take the mask off and more openly discuss what happens in the back region: how the show is prepared, how the cast feels.[24]

The autumn conference plenary is a front region. In the conference hall, activists diligently perform the role of an engaged and supportive audience. Conservative representatives excel in such decorum (Goffman,

1990: 110). They understood the concept of team representation a long time before Labour and openly explain that loyalty is essential in the presence of outsiders. Once a decision has been reached, it is important to maintain a united front.[25] "It is not enough to do the right thing, one also needs to be *seen* to be doing it", a Conservative activist confided in me. Goffman similarly considers that "dramatising one's work involves more than merely making invisible costs visible" (1990: 42): it is a performance and the efforts put into the acting out of a role are sometimes expanded at the expense of the role's tasks. The corridors and the bars are private settings where actors relax and expect not to be watched.[26] Amongst themselves delegates discuss debates and speeches and exchange information on the production of the show. Some frankly express disgust at efforts to manufacture consent in front of the cameras. Labour activists have learnt to be on their guard and fear looming journalists.[27] Unity is not a front that crumbles in private. Nevertheless back region behaviour is not so structured by expressive norms (Goffman, 1990: 126).

New Labour has created in conference-goers the feeling that staging a united and professional conference is not only a collective effort but also an individual moral obligation towards the party as a whole. In order to control impressions, teams have to prevent *faux pas*, and also ensure that each member plays a role for the collective rather than for himself however small the part he is instructed to play. Self-restriction by delegates and careful planning by public relations teams concur to produce a "positive" debate and a smooth image at all times but particularly so at pre-general election conferences. These events being the last major opportunity for free advertising, they are more tamed and contrived than usual. Well-known dissenters are especially cautious in pre-electoral years and only express conformist views to outsiders who might be a journalist in disguise.

At a time when the most popular television programmes include reality shows like *Big Brother*, conference participants are aware of the importance of the performance they are giving.[28] Activists want to be at their best when they speak from the rostrum and it is all the better if they contribute at the same time to giving a good impression of the organisation they belong to. They speak in their own name but also in the name of the party to the public outside. Addressing a large audience is intimidating. Most speakers experience stage fright but they can be made more confident through relatively simple training. All parties now provide conference participants with advice on how to speak at conference.[29]

Green Party Conference, Hastings 1994

Leaflets are widely available: "speaking without pain," explains how to prepare a speech, how to register to speak and how to face the audience. Training sessions are run during tea breaks where experienced activists show how to use the microphone and give practical advice. Focus on an argument rather than a long list, write down but do not read, be on time for the debate.

Labour Conference, Brighton 1995

In a small theatre at lunchtime, a dozen delegates congregate. The convenor of the meeting is an actress who invites participants to write their speech – if they have not done so already. She gives advice on how to structure it. After a few minutes of work in pairs, volunteers go on stage to give their presentation. She comments on body language, clarity of content and style.[30] Later, I meet Margaret, a first time delegate suspicious of "New" Labour. She had been asked by the regional party worker whether she wanted to speak about her experience as a teacher but has declined. She is weary of the offer to help delegates prepare their speeches and does not want to be "used". Some of her friends were less timid. One of them attended the workshop and was later called to the rostrum.

Liberal Democrats Conference, Brighton 2002

Since 1995 Women Liberal Democrats organise a number of training sessions for representatives. A dozen people turn up, including two men for a session on speaking in public. Most already know which debate they want to intervene in and have come to make sure they do it well. Susan gives a few tips, and then lets participants practice in pairs. Then, everybody has a chance to do a dry run and receives feedback from Susan and other participants. Several attendees are called to the rostrum later in the week – whether or not taking part in training helped them to get called. In any case, they scrupulously follow the advice provided, illustrating their talk with touching personal examples, controlling their body language and focusing on three key ideas.

Training sessions are popular[31] and the effects are noticeable. During the 1999 Labour debate on *21st Century Party*, 9 out of 10 constituency speakers gave well polished speeches, all from the same mould. It is striking to the observer that the style of floor speakers has changed in all parties. Personal experience is used as a justification or as the illustration of a point. To comply with what they perceive as the demands of the media, political parties encourage activists to give personal anecdotes rather than make general and impersonal statements. Communication advisers call to reason but more than ever play with emotions. There is more pathos on stage because it brings a human, down-to-earth dimension to debates. Organisers want us to believe that conferences are a *vox pop* but these "spontaneous" interventions are carefully choreographed to avoid surprises. "Real people" (the female pensioner, the ethnic minority with his turban, the dynamic thirty-something in a suit and the schoolgirl) express support for party policies.[32] The debate is presented as a "reality show" but there is just as much orchestration. Orators are groomed in the same way students on *Star Academy* are trained to improve their performance.

This evolution has followed similar patterns in all four parties, so much so that, beyond the peculiarities of each group style – the resilience of jargon or punctilious procedures for instance – one can talk of a homogenisation of the ways in which speakers address the audience. Recently, Labour's new design for the stage has created an atmosphere of intimacy that has surprised and seduced delegates. "It feels strangely intimate because the speakers are so close to us," remarks a delegate. The intention is that the ordinary man/woman should be able to express his/her position in their own words, rather than translate them into the dominant political language. Unfortunately, the result is "managed emotion". Arlie Russell Hochschild (2003) argues that an increase in "emotion management" in the 1980s explains why spontaneity and authenticity are so valued today. At conference, the more the enthusiasm of the audience is staged and the more standardised and calibrated the speeches and the style of presentation are, the more there is a need for "real people" to express what they feel rather than what they think. Part of the problem here is that sophisticated media audiences at home are less prepared to believe in manufactured emotions and probably more cynical when they suspect that they are being duped. The bitterness and anger often expressed about Tony Blair and New Labour's "lies" is directly related to such personalisation of politics.

Celebrities on stage

Political parties have to struggle to maintain their attractiveness to a choosy TV audience. For this purpose, they have embraced the personalisation of power. There are nowadays more political stars and celebrity guests on stage, more dynamic and innovative sessions and (often) more displays of unity. Conservative conference-goers are up-front about it: they come to listen to ministers/shadow Cabinet members articulate the party position. In other parties, activists tend to put forward other motives for attending plenary debates. Nevertheless, senior politicians' speeches usually attract back to the auditorium those straying in the lounges and the exhibition. Apart from dissenters who make a point of not turning up, participants are keen to listen to big speakers, especially those who have a reputation for being good orators. Heseltine and Prescott, for instance, are on the "must see" list. Giving a platform to politicians is especially important when the team is little known, as were Hague's and Duncan Smith's Shadow Cabinet members.[33]

The domination of Frontbench orators, particularly when in government, is nothing new. McKenzie notes that the ratio of platform domination of the rostrum was about 35 per cent in opposition and 37 per cent in office for Labour and 25 to 37 per cent for the Conservatives (McKenzie, 1964: 498). In the 1970s, members of the Labour executive concluded debates with voting recommendations but senior politicians who were not members of the NEC could not address the conference from the platform. This was progressively remedied under Kinnock: the Frontbench have been given opportunities to address the conference from the platform. Politicians who introduce or conclude debates are usually given about 20 minutes. As Eric Shaw puts it, "the leadership has four bites of the cherry. A Minister introduces the debate in a major set piece speech, the mover and seconder of the report then speak and finally the NEC has the right to wind up the debate" – the leadership now dominates both the NEC and the NPF (2004: 59). It is, of course, difficult for a chair to tell a politician that his time is up and the red light is only flashed at ordinary orators but the constraints imposed by tight scheduling of live broadcasting is an argument even talkative politicians can hear. Party activists complain but understand that pre-electoral conferences are unique opportunities for PPC to raise their profile.

All parties have increased the time dedicated to "platform" speeches. Despite their reputation for not paying attention to their image, the Liberal Democrats have adopted since 1995 a pragmatic approach. Some time is set aside to maximise the use of conference to advertise the party as a whole rather than limit it to an internal talking shop. "MPs and spokesmen need to be able to argue their corner", argues Alan Sherwell, so timetables are "prearranged to suit the press and make sure that they get reported [but] they do not all get a slot each time". The Director of Communication makes "suggestions about who should speak on which issues". As the number of MPs has increased, so has competition to address representatives live on television. Greens and Liberal Democrats do not expect "speakers" to speak for themselves but to express the views of the collective. Clashes occasionally occur. In 2002, the Liberal Democrats' debate on genetically modified organisms (GMO) created a lot of controversy. In the corridors, representatives complained that "some of the MPs reported on it in a biased way" and that it may have influenced the outcome of the debate. Indeed, the vote was very close. Formal questions were submitted to the Federal Policy Committee and Conference Committee (FPC and FCC). However no action was taken[34] because

> Such things happen very rarely. We are unable to stop speakers expressing their views, and the interventions of MPs do not always have such an influence that we can be sure they sway Conference, or in the direction they intend. Conference is able to make its own decisions.[35]

The Chair of the Conference committee played down the incident, insisting that it did not endangered the overall fairness of the conference procedures and debates.[36]

As parties look for new ways to connect with the electorate, they have opened up their conferences. In 2000, a number of senior Conservatives attended the Republican Convention in Philadelphia. They came back with new ideas to improve their own meeting: the Conference Committee searched for people who could contribute and inspire. Symbolically, the platform was opened to outside guests, from pop stars to representatives of charities, whose very diversity was supposed to manifest the new inclusive and diverse Conservative party.[37] In Labour, the floor of conference used to be strictly controlled. Access to the rostrum and the platform was restricted: even Ministers could not speak as they wished. Guest speakers now regularly come to praise the successes of the Labour government. In 1997, the Education Secretary came to the stage with a young boy who had come to testify on the great new Literacy Summer initiative. Since then, head-teachers, nurses and many others are paraded on the autumn conference stages as *faire-valoir*. They bring an illusion of freshness and of "real life" influencing politics. More striking are celebrity endorsements that are further examples of the influence of marketing in politics. In 2004, Bono the rock star was thus invited by Labour to plead for Africa. In 2000, Nelson Mandela was the guest of honour at Brighton. Neither the Conservatives nor of course the Liberal Democrats are at present able to rival Labour's line up of stars.

The politics of entertainment

The traditional formal debate followed a fixed pattern that has now been abandoned. All parties have in the last ten years tried to renew their style. The time allotted to plenary debates has been reduced. Labour devoted 27 hours to plenary sessions in 1996 but 22 hours in 2002.[38] The Conservatives spent 20 hours debating in 1997 but only 13 hours in 2003. The evolution has been less striking in smaller parties because they are less constrained by the demands of the media. Indeed, in 2003, the Liberal Democrats debated for 32 hours and the Greens over 22 hours (their conferences only lasts an extended weekend).

Although parliamentary parties have been hesitant to abandon the format that contributed to granting democratic legitimacy to their conference procedures, they have created alternatives in order to make plenary sessions more entertaining. The Conservatives want to be at the "cutting edge of conference technology". "People are against [any change] at first but, in the end, they enjoy it. The more vocal don't want any change but you have to keep changing", explains Chris Poole. There are "all sorts of things, such as workshops and parallel sessions, that we could try to make conferences more interesting and lively", considers John Taylor, a strong supporter of innovation. Scottish Tories created Question and Answer sessions in 1995 and the British Conservatives used it the following year to liven up their "often tedious Spring Forum". In 1996, John Major took part in a Q&A session to demonstrate that he was listening. On the Tuesday afternoon of the annual conference, he famously took his jacket off for an hour of informal dialogue with the grassroots.[39] Four microphones had been set up and party members were invited to queue up. Party officials thought it was an "interesting innovation" but since then, only members of the Shadow Cabinet team have taken part, probably because the preoccupation for successive Conservative leaders has been to use conference to gain *gravitas* rather than mingle with party activists. "It is more difficult for politicians, admits John Taylor but it gives activists a chance to talk and it is modern and slightly unpredictable." In a sense, it brings a frisson to bored audiences that might otherwise choose to watch something else! After all, many conference goers "zap" the hall and stay on the fringe and the corridors and bars rather than attend debates. As the Conservatives' conference no longer pretends to discuss and amend motions, organisers are freer to use their imagination. Despite timetable alterations, Conservative activists are content with new varied sessions but as we have seen, they are not primarily concerned with policy-making. In 2004, Charles Kennedy was the only party leader to dare face a Q&A session. As the editor of the *Independent* newspaper was brought in to ask questions submitted by activists, there was no risk of a direct and potentially damaging challenge.

Quantity, as well as the cathartic effect of voicing one's concern, is increasingly taken seriously: conferences are about letting activists speak out whilst there is a need to restrain their enthusiasm for lengthy speeches. Audiences are less likely to get bored by droning orators. There are about 40 sessions, devoted to various items on the agenda at a Liberal Democrat conference. They last between 15 minutes and more than an hour. Whilst "policy debates" are open to the public, "party business sessions" (devoted to various reports or awards ceremonies) are in theory private. Conference organisers looked for more attractive formats than set piece speeches and lengthy debates on obscure motions. "We introduced one-minute interventions about 6 to 8 years ago because some people found speaking for 4 minutes too intimidating or they only had one idea. The press really like it," remembers Liz Barker. These new formats are less conducive to policy developments however, so debates now combine traditional 4-minute speeches from the rostrum with 1-minute "interventions", from the two microphones in the hall. Another Chair of the Conference Committee admits that

> it is always a difficult balance between show and debate and between reaffirming policies and developing new ones, depending on when the next general elections are. (. . .) Most activists understand that the media are important and those who disagree with the option taken usually are happy to wait until after the general election to raise again a contentious point.

In 2000, the Conservatives also hoped to increase the number of activists called to the rostrum and liven up dull debates. They thus adopted the model of "snap debate" already used by the Liberal Democrats.

"It encouraged lots of young people to come forward. There was for instance a 16 year old", proudly announces the Secretary of the Board, and the "figures are encouraging": 134 speakers on four topics at the week-end conference in Harrogate in spring 2000.[40] The experiment was extended with suitable caution, he explains:

> 1 minute probably wouldn't work at conference because it lasts four days and there wouldn't be enough people present. That is why we will keep speeches as well as question and answer sessions. It is important to keep the TV audiences interested. It also depends on the subject: we couldn't have 1 minute for Defence or Foreign Affairs but on the Arts and culture that may be OK.

"Serious" topics require a more "serious" (or ritualised!) approach than "snappy comments" allow. After all, the party is keen to maintain the impression that important political debates are held and that grassroots articulate opinions that are taken on board by the leadership. However, in 2004, there were more snap debates and forums with Shadow ministers.

Labour has also looked to America for inspiration. In 1996, the Labour Co-ordination Committee *Interim Report* offered a grim perspective on existing conferences and set the framework for an effective conference:

> with a conference made up of session after session of boring but potentially damaging debates about arcane resolutions, Labour is leaving things to chance. Look at the poll lift, which successful Conventions gave the Republicans and then the Democrats this summer in America. The same opportunity is available for Labour in Britain. Labour takes this with Tony Blair' s speech but misses it with much of the rest of the conference. The Conference should be used to showcase key selected policy themes in Labour' s programme.

The traditional debate of motions entertained the illusion that conference was a sovereign decision-making body. Because such powers were held to be almost sacred by Labour activists, it has been difficult to innovate without being sacrilegious. Implicitly, such caution has further confirmed the centrality of the traditional debate in conference procedures. Nevertheless, a plenary Q&A on public services was organised in 2001. Three ministers sat around a coffee table, answering questions from noticeably tamed delegates.

Unlike the three parliamentary parties, the Greens do not get live coverage of their conference. Moreover, they have been at times so resistant to the demands of the media that party officials in charge of public relations have been suspected of voluntarily undermining the party's self-presentation. On the other hand, they have devoted considerable attention to reflection on ways of working. Aware of fluctuations in the attention span of the majority of individuals, they have shortened their sessions and introduced pauses. Unique amongst party conferences and congresses, the Green timetable takes into account activists' concentration spans.[41] These changes were introduced to make deliberation and decision-making both more pleasant and more effective. Conference now offers varied and carefully timed sessions attended by remarkably attentive and focused audiences. Indeed, plenary debates are mostly free of private conversations and there is very little of the constant to-ing and fro-ing that characterises the Labour conference. A "humane" time schedule is not the only innovation that contributes to the hardworking atmosphere of the Green conference. At the beginning of plenary sessions, the doors are closed for a minute of silence that clearly marks a threshold between serious political debates and socialising.[42] The transformation of the seating space is also unique. In order to create a convivial environment, chairs are placed around tables that can sit about a dozen delegates who can spread their papers. Four microphones are placed in the hall: orators have no intimidating catwalk to walk and can imagine they address a group of friends.[43] This allows a cosier atmosphere that reassures the shyest speakers. When debates become heated, the conference is temporarily split in discussion around tables.[44] The Green conference was never strictly modelled on the parliamentary format and there was little resistance to the invention of new types of sessions. More importantly, none of these changes were introduced with a particular concern about their impact on the party's image.

Conclusion

In the last decade, conference organisers have skilfully transformed the outlook of conference. The annual gathering is no longer a display of passionate ideological oratory. Pressed by public relations experts, political parties now put forward well-rehearsed presentations that fit an age of "reality TV". The idea is to attract viewers through entertainment or news value whilst projecting a slick image of professionalism. Grassroots' interventions give a personal and emotional dimension to a show designed to emphasise the issues the party seeks promoted. The dilemma for mainstream parties lies in the tension between democratic debate and entertainment: serious discussions of policy alternatives on complex issues rarely make for good television but political parties are desperately trying to retain the long hours of broadcasting that provide free advertising every year.

Moreover, efforts have been expanded to control every dimension of the image projected to the electorate throughout the conference week. Although plenary debates remain the centre-piece that justifies media coverage, the traditional format with its set speeches and its in-built confrontation between supporters and opponents of a motion has been progressively replaced by new types of deliberation that emphasise organisational unity and competent managerialism. Is the British debating style doomed to disappear from the Labour and the Conservative conferences as both parties follow the American model of political conventions? This evolution is made possible because the parliamentary debate itself has lost the centrality it once had in the Westminster model. When the government chooses to make policy announcements to the press rather than the Commons, it also contributes to the demise of a style of politics centred around the binary opposition of political parties in Parliament.

There is also a more sinister reading of the disciplining of Labour. Conference was a semi-private event where party members met fellow believers to discuss politics and organisation. The party was a large family of "brothers" and "sisters" with a warm but conflictual atmosphere.[45] The omnipresence of the media has transformed conference and the relations it reinforces. The *panopticon*, argued Foucault, sought to induce particular relationships of individuals to themselves and to instil discipline in self-managing and free citizens (Foucault, 1975: 201–206; Rose, 1999: 242). Conferences have become glasshouses in which party members interact with the unpleasant feeling that they are constantly assessed, measured, and judged. To preserve the electoral chances of their organisation they have had to internalise the discipline. As the phrase goes, "a watched kettle never boils": behaviours have changed because of the risk of beeing seen to diverge from the norm. Nowadays, members do not necessarily need the presence of journalists to constantly follow a front stage demeanour: they are their own public. Constraints have been interiorised and activists are the first convinced by their own spectacle.[46]

Whilst conferences have become more spectacular, they have also lost some of their formalism. Motions and composites are mostly a thing of the past in Labour and the Conservative parties. They have been replaced with NPF reports that use bullet points and address "themes". Orators make sure that they give a personal dimension to their speech and usually invoke autobiographical experience to justify their presence on stage. Procedures have also been livened up, with internal business conducted at times when fewer people are present. Conferences are less solemn than they used to be, no longer a "high mass" and increasingly more like a televised entertainment show. This evolution is significant because it is symptomatic of the reduced importance of the event. However, image management has produced the unexpected side effect of creating a vicious circle of delegitimisation because the very absence of conflict is now perceived as stage management and manipulation. After several years of strict control of the conference floor, following persistent and damaging accusations of spin and "control freakery", the Labour party executive began to release its tight grip on the conference in its second term in office. Unusually sharp debates took place in 2002 on the PFI and the projected war in Iraq. The government nevertheless saved face and reinforced its position as the protector of public interest (Chapter 9). Although too much control and overt management of debates is probably over, no parliamentary party can afford to lose control of its image in a contemporary media age. However, the manner in which such image management is undertaken, and received by the wider audience, is the real issue confronting the future of British parties. There is little thrill and transcendence in the new conference ceremonies.

8
The Discourse of Deliberative Democracy

As in other European liberal democracies, British mainstream parties are criticised as bureaucratic and unrepresentative. Electoral apathy and de-alignment combine with shrinking party memberships to raise concerns about popular support for governmental organisations.[1] Much research has been conducted to try and explain these general trends. It has been argued that high levels of education and economic development have transformed attitudes towards politics. Cognitively mobilised citizens are more critical of traditional sources of authority (including government and political parties) and better informed about specific issues.[2] They are more confident about their competence and effectiveness. As a consequence, they tend to get involved à la carte and focus on directing the political elite rather than responding to their calls. Mobilisation in new movements demonstrates that interest in politics remains high (Topf, 1995) and that problems are related to traditional forms of engagement (Lawson and Merkl, 1988). The alleged crisis reflects the difficulties of institutions in adapting to "critical citizens", who "feel that existing channels for participation fall short of democratic ideals, and who want to improve and reform the institutional mechanisms of representative democracy" (Norris, 1999: 27). New social movements and parties have carried within mainstream politics the idea that "the crisis of democracy comes from its not being democratic enough" (Giddens, 1998: 71).

Bernard Manin argues that representative government has undergone several metamorphoses since its inception in the 18th century. This model, partly invented in Britain, initially developed around the institution of Parliament, conceived as the primary locus of political deliberation. Gradually, political parties gained ascendancy in what was perceived to be the democratisation of a largely aristocratic system of government. During this period of "party government" (1996: 250), disciplined parliamentary groups reflected the state of electoral forces and deliberation took place within parties themselves (1996: 277). Conferences were created and reached their peak during this phase. At the time, they seemed to be the ideal forum for such discussions. Publicity for their semi-private proceedings allowed British citizens to be informed of political debates outside of electoral campaigns. More recently, representative government has entered a phase Bernard Manin labels "democracy of the public", in which public relations constraints make it problematic for parties to appear divided. The public receives political information from the same media sources rather than through partisan channels of communication. Moreover, public opinion is constantly present in political debates through opinion polls (1996: 293–297). Political issues are perceived and debated through consultation between governments and cause and interest groups in informal settings. Politicians moreover tend to present their arguments to voters directly so that deliberation is now public (1996: 298–299). The role of party conferences is thus no longer to deliberate and take decisions that will "instruct" representatives in Parliament but to present ideas to convince voters directly. In today's society, political parties can no longer rely on pre-existing social groups, which they can claim to represent because identities are constantly reshuffled by geographic and social mobility. Instead, they have to demonstrate their responsiveness to the demands of the "people". It is not enough to be in touch with members, parties need to open up to civil society. They need to (be seen to) listen to the electorate. The two main British parliamentary parties systematically invite speakers from "civil society" to address conference or take part in the growing conference fringe (Chapter 10). They have successively launched campaigns such as "Labour Listens" and "Listening to Britain".

Although a phase of debate is taken for granted in the parliamentary tradition, representative government is not based on a belief in the inherent qualities of deliberation.[3] Parliamentary debates aimed at producing consent; they were not the means for decision-making (Manin, 1996: 245). More important as a source of legitimacy was the aggregation of independent wills. Majority decisions were thus satisfactory in a representative regime that evolved from the gradual transformation of a Parliament of equals. However, since the 1970s, new political and social movements have appeared in western representative democracies, expressing, amongst other things, demands for better political participation (Dalton and Kuechler, 1990; Della Porta and Diani, 1999;

Klandermans *et al.*, 1988). In Britain, these movements have been particularly critical of the Westminster model of government that almost fuses legislative, executive and judiciary powers and rests on a strong majoritarian bias. Minority or marginal groups are of course particularly sensitive to the "tyranny of the majority". Excluded by the first-past-the-post electoral system, the Greens have campaigned for institutional and electoral reforms (with the support of the Liberal Democrats and fractions of the Labour party). "New politics" groups have experimented with rotation, recall, internal referendum, postal ballots and general assemblies. They have also explored ways to reach decisions without votes (Polletta, 2002).

At first, the efforts of the critics of representative government focused on "direct democracy" procedures but deliberation now appears as the key element in deepening the democratic potential of representative governments. The decision may not conform to everybody's wishes but it is at least informed by them. As John Stuart Mill argued,

> people feel that the decision is fairer if there is a prior discussion and if they have been at least able to voice their opinion: it does not necessarily mean that they are listened to but they are heard as if those whose opinion is overruled, feel satisfied that it is heard, and set aside not by a mere act of will, but for what are thought superior reasons.[4]

Deliberative democracy has attracted renewed interest amongst political theorists (Elster, 1998) and the

> essence of democracy itself is now widely taken to be deliberation, as opposed to voting, interest aggregation, constitutional rights, or even self-government. The deliberative turn represents a renewed concern with the authenticity of democracy: the degree to which democratic control is substantive rather than symbolic, and engaged by competent citizens (Dryzeck, 2000: 1).

Advocates of deliberation contest the idea that individual wills are predetermined. On the contrary, they highlight the importance of interest formation through a process that engages human qualities of assessing and comparing (Manin, 1987: 352). Thus, they often justify deliberative procedure by its by-product and the fact that it improves individuals – their "eloquence, rhetorical skills, empathy, courtesy, imagination and reasoning ability" (Fearon, 1998: 59–60). The problem with such an idealisation of deliberation is that it overlooks how a final decision is reached. Because of a failure to reach a consensus, deliberations either end up with a concluding vote (Johnson, 1998: 161) or the decision is taken by a body that is informed by the process though not bound by it.

The need for political parties to be internally democratic has been extensively debated (Michels, 1962; Schattschneider, 1942; Schumpeter, 1942). Teorell (1999) renews the argument and claims that deliberative democracy provides the best justification for intra-party democracy. Whilst representative institutions retain their importance for decision-making, they should be complemented with deliberation in the public sphere as well as within political parties. Rather than simply reflect the opinions of the public, he argues, parties should enable issues to be discussed and filtered, so that they can take an informed decision. Teorell conceives deliberative procedures as a means to reinforce the role of parties as linkages between citizens and their governments. Parties would benefit from a wider pool of ideas, thanks to the introduction of internal "deliberative polls"[5] of the entire membership and policy orientations would gain in legitimacy.[6] Although no British party has followed Teorell's suggestion as such, the discourse of deliberative democracy has become fashionable in political parties. Confronted with the challenge posed by new social movements, most mainstream parties have adopted direct and deliberative democracy procedures.[7] From workshops to conference seminars and policy forums, party members – and sympathisers – are consulted. Party leaderships use such deliberative exercises as a justification for their policy choices. These new procedures are in direct competition with conference because they aim to replace the annual meeting as the primary forum for debate.

Consensus building

Although they are often presented as a "single issue" movement, the Greens are strongly committed to a more general understanding of "political ecology" and therefore to alternative party structures (Faucher, 1999c). Their ideal is the creation, *hic et nunc*, of an organisation run according to the principles of the "highest form of democracy", participative democracy.[8] Greens prefer consensus to majority decisions because they believe that "good" politics is the consequence of the "right" procedures (Doherty and De-Geus, 1996). As several Green activists told me, "people know best what is best for them" and if empowered to do so they will do it, they will take the best decisions.

Informed by an individualist and liberal tradition, they do not believe one can force people to behave in a sustainable way. Rather, Green society will emerge when individuals are empowered and responsible for the consequences of their actions.

The Greens developed conference workshops in the 1980s. This creation, explains Peter Lang, was inspired by the conviction that "50 per cent of conference attendees are not familiar with the proceedings and 80 per cent did not really follow plenary debates", either due to lack of interest in a topic or because of the complexity of the discussion. Some debates, on permaculture for instance, are unlikely to raise much passion. Another argument was that the atmosphere influences the quality and nature of the decisions. In a sense, the Greens took on board the idea that the "outcome of deliberation depends heavily upon the sequence in which participants speak and the point at which debate is terminated" (Johnson, 1998: 176). Compared to plenary sessions, small-group discussions not only allow participants to choose topics they are most interested in but also mean that complex issues are discussed by people who are genuinely interested in them. Workshops occupy over 50 per cent of conference time and they are extremely popular. According to a 1990 survey, 84.1 per cent of conference goers had attended one workshop or fringe meeting and 65.7 per cent of them had spoken. On the other hand only 67.4 per cent of conference participants attended most plenary sessions and 16 per cent of them addressed the debate (Rüdig *et al.*, 1991: 42). Activists report enjoying "sitting down to 'hmm' ideas". These intimate sessions provide a space for in-depth yet accessible discussions. It is important to consider that participants "have a right to listen and to make up their mind", explains one of them.

Most approaches to deliberative democracy assume its superiority over votes but at the same time overlook the need to take decisions or assume that aggregative devices will eventually have the last word (Johnson, 1998: 162). Green workshops are an attempt to provide a space where consensus as a means of decision-making can be a reality. In practice, this rarely happens. Conference workshops are tightly scheduled and have to be concluded by indicative shows of hands.[9] However, because participants are focused on the objective of the gathering, it is easier to join in the discussion, express an opinion and feel included in the decision-making process. Efforts to "build consensus" do not lead to unanimity but play a part in creating a space that is congenial to examining every aspects of a debate and to mutual transformation of opinions. "There is a genuine opportunity to say 'I don't like this, I don't like that'", explains an activist, "and you can only do that in a small and more intimate group" in which "people can hear each other". Because of their scale, they allow all participants to speak[10] and a number of activists have been trained to make sure that everybody is given a chance to express his/her point of view.[11] What makes the Green process particularly interesting is that it is not teleologically driven by a leadership with a predetermined agenda. The PolCom offers neither "voting recommendations" nor "advice" on the content of voting papers. At a given conference "Voting papers" are discussed on the same day in one or more workshops and a plenary session. There is no gate-keeper such as headquarters staff to filter the workshops' conclusions before they are synthesised and presented to the plenary session[12] where a final decision is taken. This, of course, does not preclude the existence of factional attempts to steer debates in specific directions but such instances have so far remained few and far between.[13]

"Plenary is an adversarial [format], even [if] you don't get [here] the bitter tactics and manipulation of the microphone and demagoguery you get in other political parties," explains Janet Alty, "and it is often more theatrical". Consensus building, she further argues, requires participants to exchange views and arguments sincerely without attempting to destroy their opponent. If the conditions for communicative action[14] are not met in full conference settings, most Greens consider that workshops provide the context for exchanges largely free of pressure or stratagems. Activists taking part in such meetings seem generally keen to hear all arguments – thereby palliating their limited experience and bounded imagination – in order to reach a consensus. Participation not only allows people to put forward their positions, "it also changes people's ideas, their preoccupations".[15] It helps participants adjust their positions to the new frame, which is jointly being created (Moscovici and Doise, 1992: 247). According to Alty, "the product, when you get consent is usually ten times more powerful and much longer lasting [than majority decision, so] you don't have to go over it again". Although time constraints often require that votes be taken as an expedient measure, deliberation is nevertheless seen as a way to bypass the otherwise flawed process of going straight to the vote (Johnson, 1998: 163). Mutual trust between members plays an important role in the effectiveness of the process. Green workshops, unlike the deliberative polls proposed by Teorell, rely on the self-selection of participants that by definition feel particularly motivated by an issue. As a consequence, they are prepared to spend time discussing it in detail. This certainly does not guarantee that radicalism will be avoided but the Greens are quite keen to be political spurs and hardly run the risk of being marginalised.

Closed conference sessions

Green conference workshops are unique in Britain but there has been a growing interest in small meetings more generally. In fact, they have become common practice from the women's movement to business. Such meetings are the format for many training and motivational sessions in new management methods. They are part of middle class culture where less confrontational and more politically correct attitudes predominate and are seen as a way to improve participants' satisfaction and involvement. Mainstream parties have developed comparable sessions since the 1990s but they do not play a central role in policy-making and merely serve as consultation devices. Whilst Green workshops prepare the decision-making by allowing more detailed debate than is feasible in plenary sessions, Labour and the Liberal Democrats have kept the two processes separate and argue that they want to preserve the sovereignty of the annual conference.[16] Small meetings are part of the process of policy elaboration but are not destined to enlighten decision-making *per se*.

The Liberal Democrats hold "consultative sessions" on draft policy documents prepared by the Federal Policy Commission. These sessions are organised on the eve of the formal opening of the conference and constitute a preliminary "brainstorming" stage. They open to all party members a policy-making process that is otherwise largely dominated by specialised policy groups. Consultative sessions are advertised in the conference documents as forums – "less formal" than plenaries, where representatives can more easily contribute. Despite these claims, they are ritualised in order to mark clear boundaries from ordinary life.[17] The debate is structured, solemn phrases recur. Consultative sessions are hard working and civilised, even though contentious issues occasionally stir up starker disagreements within the audience (such as the GMO debate at the Edinburgh 1999 Spring conference).

Liberal Democrats Conference 1995, Glasgow

When the Consultative session on the reform of constitution starts, the room is packed with well over 50 people, some of them standing at the back. Several official speakers introduce the different sections of the

---

> (*Continued*)
>
> document tabled for discussion. The chair then calls the representatives who have submitted speaker's slips in advance to the session's chair. When cards are exhausted, a more relaxed atmosphere sets in, people raise their hands. The audience is focused and studious; orators speak in a striking silence. Sitting next to the chair, note takers scribble furiously so that the suggestions can be passed on to the policy commission preparing the final version of the document.

"You may have a hundred people talking at conference over the week. This is not participation", complains Tom Sawyer, but thanks to smaller meetings, about 60 more will have a chance. "Private" sessions were thus introduced to the Labour conference to discuss draft policies and canvass ideas. As such, they remain safely consultative. Since 1998, Labour holds policy seminars before the morning sessions of the conference. The innovation was brought in amidst controversy as it was decided to close the meetings to the press and outside observers.[18] Party officials argued that activists were keen to have a space for debate away from the cameras. Opponents derided the fact that Labour wanted to hide delegates determined to criticise politicians.[19] New Labour encouraged their own idea of "constructive" debate and a more congenial party atmosphere. Internal disagreements did not vanish from the organisation but were not expressed in these seminars. Of all those I attended over the years, I have never witnessed anything other than polite exchanges, though tough questions are asked of ministers and direct complaints about policy failings or the slow pace of reform and improvement are expressed. As a former NEC member admitted with regret, they are, if anything, "a bit deferential". Closing some sessions to observers was certainly linked to the paranoia of New Labour regarding the press but it also created the impression that something important was happening. Secrecy is an easy way to tease attention: members felt valued and entrusted with crucial information; the media felt excluded and titillated.

> **Labour Conference 1998, Blackpool – Policy seminars**
>
> Robin Cook, Foreign Secretary, leads one of the first seminars. The Spanish Hall is only half full but there are about a hundred delegates present. As a chair of the experimental policy forum, he is used to the

(Continued)

format but the topic – Europe – enflames no passion. Several microphones are available in the room for delegates who raise their hands. Those selected are rather shy: "What can I answer on door steps to questions about Europe and pensions?" or "Could documents be written in a language that is understandable?" For ninety minutes, Cook "canvasses opinions on the Euro". He responds to anxieties and shares confidences: "there is no journalist, so I can tell you this...". Sitting at the table, someone takes notes so that questions not answered on the spot (too technical or too personal) will receive a written and personal answer.

The following day, the session on Health is held in the Grand Opera House. Despite the chair announcing that "this is a seminar: we want to consult one another and hear your views, although I am sure Frank [Dobson] will be happy to answer", it turns out to be just that. There is no dialogue but a succession of polite questions. It does not feel like a dialogue at all. The chair seems embarrassed that each response from the platform is greeted with applause. Occasionally, the delegate prefaces his/her question with due congratulations of the Minister. After an hour, the chair urges everybody to send suggestions to the NPF.

In 1998, everybody was discovering the new process and norms of interaction were being invented. Most people improvised based on the routine behaviour they knew and what they felt would be appropriate. The atmosphere was clearly influenced by the settings and the context. Labour was still new in government and many delegates seemed intimidated by the prospect of such close encounters with ministers. They asked about governmental policies rather than discuss party policies. Four years later, seminars were slightly less formal but pushed to small rooms, they also attracted much fewer delegates. About 30 participants turned up for a session on Transport and the chair was at pains to encourage oral or written comments that would be integrated within the future document. The majority of delegates seemed to think they had better things to do, whether they were recovering from excesses from the previous night or straying to competing events. The few roaming in the corridors in search of the venue were speculating: "was this a deliberate attempt to discourage them from attending?" If delegates are eager to discuss policies, as it is claimed, then they do not seem to think that conference seminars are the place to do so. Several participants told me that they had little illusion of their influence on policies but were keen to raise personal or local issues.[20] Conference policy seminars may establish "a clear separation between democratic debate within the party and the public disclosure of policy dissensus" (Giddens, 1995: 22) but they raise the question of New Labour's understanding of internal democracy. Does democracy mean interacting with ministers and voicing dissent behind closed doors? Although the appearance of delegatory democracy is preserved (modernisers have always carefully insisted that conference sovereignty was not affected by reforms), the practice has evolved towards a deliberative process in which the government informally listens to suggestions from the grassroots expressed at small meetings held independently of conference. Is this process really all that different from the Conservative "conference system"?

A "system of conferences"

However centralised and bureaucratic major political parties may be and however leadership-dominated their policy-making processes are, all parties need to develop some mechanism to listen or to hear suggestions and feedback from their grassroots. Although "the concept of party democracy is inappropriate in considering the Conservative Party" (Byrd, 1987), observers note the subtlety of Tory ways. Influence is exerted through informal consultations, understatements and hints that have to be decoded. Indeed, if the Conservative conference never had any formal powers on policy or decision-making, there have always been indirect ways to influence policy makers (Norton and Aughey, 1981: 206; Seldon and Ball, 1994: 261). The most detailed and interesting approach was provided by Kelly (1989). In 1986, he followed 8 national conferences and some of the 60 regional ones.[21] This "system of conferences", in which about 20,000 members are thought to take part every year (Tether, 1996: 106), informs the leadership throughout the year of the views of the membership.

Kelly contested the interpretation of the Conservative conference that is usually put forward as lacking influence and power because such readings arise from a "centre-left standpoint" that unduly takes the rowdy Labour conference as the point of reference (1989: 12). The deference of Tory members has been overestimated partly because "politeness, amity and trust seem to be regarded by most authors as inimical to a 'meaningful party conference'" (1989: 21). Even though there may be a stage-management of the autumnal Grand Finale, any attempt to orchestrate and constrain the expression of the grassroots at the sectional conferences would damage their very purpose as sounding boards (1989: 185). Together, conferences form a system that conveys the "mood" of members to be interpreted and acted upon by the leadership. Thus, the absence of criticism in the autumn is to be taken as a sign that the leadership is indeed being responsive, "sensitive and therefore efficient" (1989: 8). In fact, such permanent consultation prevents the necessity of public confrontation. Thus, instances when the annual conference was rowdy (such as in 1950) were cases in which the system failed to work and the membership had to be assertive to be heard. "Senior party figures attend these conferences not only to speak but to listen," claim party activists, because it is essential to maintain close personal contact with members and knowledge of their views. Thus, policy announcements made in October are not new for those who had attended other conferences during the year. For Kelly, this reflects the existence of a deliberative process generally overlooked.

Whilst his study indubitably sheds important light on the existence of informal and "organic" ways that feed the Conservative policy-making, Kelly seems to take at face value representations of harmonious consultation. In 1986, comments made at one conference seemed to find their way into speeches at following meetings: ministers "could be seen vigorously scribbling while speakers from 'the floor' made their contributions – and on most occasions the ministerial reply seemed to encapsulate, and to have been modified in the light of comments and suggestions made by representatives" (Kelly, 1989: 182). It would be strange to imagine that so many interactions have no impact and indeed, "the leadership not only hold consultations, but also make concessions", if only of minor importance (Beer, 1982: 381–382). However, Kelly rather naively concludes that politicians rewrite their speeches according to the debates they are listening to. What happens is more prosaic. There are limits to the number of original contributions anybody can make. Thus, anecdotes, jokes and arguments have been tried and tweaked many times before. They are effectively rehearsed at previous conferences and fringe meetings.[22] Since the 1990s, senior politicians' speeches – prepared and vetoed by Central Office – are distributed to the press in advance[23] but the talented know how to pepper them with the names of representatives.[24] Because they want to get a good reception, politicians adapt their contributions to what they anticipate will be popular with the audience, a senior Conservative told me. Is this what "responsive leadership" means?

Following Kelly, it would appear that the party had an underestimated but efficient two-way communication system. Policies are "the outcome of an organic development": they "emerge" from discussions in a variety of private committees and informal, often social, meetings with powerful figures. At the local level, chairmen and officers hold considerable sway and a sense of fairness translates into a readiness to listen and persuade. "Views evolve within a directed, if informal, democracy" (Tether, 1996: 107). The influence of Conservative conference is "subtle" but real and "politicians must read the mood if they don't want their policies destroyed by the floor. It is rare but it sometimes happens."[25] The grassroots know they have no direct say on policy-making but believe their views are taken on board.[26] "Policy obsessive" members must be able to express their views and it is important for this reason to develop the Spring Forum or the policy forums: "they can get informal feedback from officers that relay the contributions up towards the leadership".

The Conservatives have created their own version of "private" conference sessions. The 1998 constitution meant that the conference was "for the whole organisation". The NU became the Convention, a body that meets in private during the autumn conference. Meetings are closed to observers so that members of the Convention get a sense of their own importance. In an organisation thriving on exclusivity and a hierarchy of private clubs and committees, it is not a negligible incentive. No secret information is debated but as we have seen previously Tories are "timid" when they think they may be overheard. They believe in privacy, discretion and secrecy.[27]

Conservative Conference 1998, Bournemouth

The National Convention holds its first meeting in the Conference auditorium. Doors are closed to journalists and non-members but pass checks are lax. The agenda is dominated by organisational matters, morale boosting and congratulatory speeches. "This is your meeting, do not hesitate to say what you think, we are seeking your views", explains the Chair. The next speaker insists that members have become "stakeholders in a united organisation, you are the people who know if it works, do let us know what you think". A question and answer session follows. Few speakers are enthusiastic about the changes and it is clearly easier for many to express unease or scepticism in private. Some association chairmen raise doubts about new fees, fearing a haemorrhage of members. Others complain that the new constitution leads to further concentration of power. The atmosphere is very different from the conference session. Members of the Convention openly express concern and criticism over the reform.

To extend consultation procedures, a Conservative Policy Forum (CPF) replaced the Conservative Political Centre. The new body's role is to foster political interest and discussions thanks to a series of local meetings focusing on policy issues in synchronicity with the public agenda.[28] Policy documents are circulated to members[29] who express their views during meetings and are also asked sometimes to fill in short question-naires. The results are looked at but only tick boxes tend to be really of any use because, although they are much easier to act upon than quali-tative responses, they remain a very rudimentary way to assess members' opinions. The CPF has no formal role in policy-making but its Director (who belongs to the Conference Committee) can influence the Conference agenda. The CPF's reports are circulated to the Research Department and the Policy Unit.[30] "Members want to feel that they are listened to and that they are consulted" but senior Tories doubt the existence of a real desire for participation amongst the grassroots. Nevertheless, National Union officers hoped that the 1998 Constitution would mean that "the leadership [would] never again be able to ignore" them. Indeed, the Conservative Political Centre could no longer write that to govern was a "specialised 'vocation' requiring a 'habit of mind' that can be acquired only by 'specialised preparatory training' in home and in school".[31] Although Hague also organised ballots to demonstrate his democratic zeal (see Chapter 9), the constitution did not dramatically shift the balance of power within the party. Consultation procedures have been formalised but ultimate power rests with the leader who "determine the political direction of the Party having regard to the views of Party Members and the Conservative Policy Forum".[32] Under Duncan Smith and Howard, the Conservative party has renewed its long held tradition of informal soundings and consultations where members' views, and how strongly they are held, are "sensed".

If the "soundings" process works satisfactorily, how can we explain the crisis faced by the party since the mid-1990s? Did the Conservatives abandon their listening system and did the government lose touch with its grassroots? Or is it because the party listened to an ageing[33] and radi-calised membership that it became unelectable? The very "democratic" nature of the Tories would explain why they are today failing. The short span of Iain Duncan Smith (IDS) as leader of the party seems to corrob-orate such a hypothesis. After two years the first "democratically elected leader" was ousted by a coup. His successor, Michael Howard, "emerged" from the parliamentary party in a comparable way to the procedures used until 1965. If conference representatives are too radical, the party needs to listen to its wider base. In 1996, the party engaged in a large consultation, holding several hundreds meetings in over 400 constituencies. This did not prevent the 1997 general election debacle. The new leader, elected on a platform of change, launched *Listening to Britain* to demonstrate that the party was not arrogant and remote. The objective was to reconnect with the electorate. Seminars were held across the country where politicians were sent to listen. Attendance varied from a dozen to nearly 200 people. Note takers sent reports to Central Office to feed the policy renewal process.[34] Conferences were also opened up to the wider membership. The first experiment was conducted at the 1998 spring forum,[35] then discreetly extended to annual conference.[36] By 1999 though, William Hague refocused its strategy on its core supporters. His two successors have similarly erred in their attempts to reposition the party and both of them have been reluctant to risk alienating their dwindling and radicalised membership for the sake of hypothetical gains in the centre of the electoral spectrum.

Partners in power?

In Labour, interest in study circles appeared in the early 1990s, at a time when the party was looking abroad for inspiration about how to reform its policy-making. Between 1993 and 1997, reflection on policy-making focused on small-scale meetings that could create a line of communication between the party and government.[37] At the same time, the party developed a "political education" programme also based on small-group discussions. Reflections were intensified after 1994 because Tony Blair perceived change within the party itself as necessary, inevitable and desirable. In a context where the party leadership considered that business provided an acceptable model for organising social systems, new management approaches, emphasising quality and accountability, were particularly attractive because they proved effective in helping businesses remain competitive and innovative. In the late 1990s, Labour boasted about embracing innovation, in terms of organisation and practices: "new learning techniques such as study circles [were used] well in advance of any other sister party – including the pioneering Swedish social democrats".[38]

The New Labour team also believed that the party leadership, like business managers, could only succeed if they could rally their supporters. The idea of a "partnership" was promoted as a way to associate the membership with changes in order to avoid the disconnection that had handicapped previous Labour governments. Conviction is the best way to increase productivity and dedication to the party/company's objectives. Thus, changes were gradually introduced through the spread of "best practice" and a committed endeavour to "excellence", participation and democracy. Party staff (and ultimately party members) were expected to adhere to a "mission statement" as well as to various targets. Such rhetoric made the proposed "modernisation" of the party structures and ways of working more difficult to resist. Policies could be developed in "small workshops or study groups, where everyone attending gets the chance to participate, unlike the annual conference where only a tiny minority get the opportunity to speak".[39] How can anyone be against such positively connoted objectives (Salaman, 1997)?

The same framework has been used for all organisational reforms since 1994. In the case of *Partnership in Power*, consultation over several years led to a proposal that was then "sold" to activists at conference fringe meetings and plenary sessions. Modern communication strategies rest on the idea that endless repetition of the message eventually convinces the audience that it is a "fact". This has been systematically applied. For several years, officials and politicians used a Manichean rhetoric emphasising the opposition between good (new) and bad (old). Party members and affiliated organisations were bombarded with a discourse presenting change as a necessity and old practices as utterly terrible. Modernisers voluntarily contrasted a dark picture of the past policy-making process – "shallow, backward, adversarial" with a "forward looking, open, democratic, consensual" way of doing politics. "The past [was] recreated to serve the present's strategic needs. To the modernisers the central problem was the inability of the Party – 'Old Labour' – to obtain the trust and confidence of the public. (...) To maximise the public impact of the new name, the contrast with the old had to be as stark as possible" (Shaw, 1996: 217). Reforms were not imposed on a reluctant membership, they were effectively "sold" to them.

Labour Conference Fringe, 1997

Matthew Taylor, the Assistant General Secretary and architect of the reform, explains how the proposed changes will effectively "empower members" because policy forums would be like "brain-storming" sessions that would serve as permanent sounding boards for government policy. The proposals clearly resonate with patent dissatisfaction with the current system of compositing. The audience is interested and intrigued. Several express anxiety about

---

(*Continued*)

the future role of conference in the system: would it remain the ultimate decision-maker? Women delegates seem particularly open to the prospect: they welcome the proposal because they are convinced that small meetings would "allow members who do not feel very confident to get involved". They have ideas about how to make it work. One even suggests, to a giggling audience, that it would be a good idea to sit in a circle and maybe have a cup of tea.

Partnership in Power was a first stage; further "modernisation" projects followed, touching all aspects of party organisation. Again, the strategy involved convincing everyone that the changes had wide-ranging support from the membership. For this purpose, the preliminary phase of consultation led to the publication of reports that emphasised dissatisfaction with old structures. Unhappy members are abundantly quoted: "women see Labour party politics as being adversarial and not sufficiently focused on practical achievements" (Labour, 1999: 34). "Facts" are used to demonstrate the existence of "a problem" leading to a diagnostic and "logical" solution. The *21st Century Party* report was the long awaited excuse to start the restructuring of local party structures.[40] It described local party meetings as dull, complicated and off-putting and used members' aspirations for more policy discussions as an excuse to challenge established ways of working. Outright condemnation of "outdated", "arcane" and "non democratic" procedures implicitly justified the new, inclusive and outward-looking "open meetings" and "forums".

The NPF was set up in 1998. In the following years, policy forums were held throughout the country with the help of national headquarters. They sent teams to speed up the process and ensure its success.[41] In 1998, about 6000 members took part in policy forums that began to be organised around the country. Progressively, forums were integrated into the party machinery and by 1999, 11 per cent of members had taken part (Whiteley and Seyd, 2002: 215). A typical agenda involves small-group discussions and feedback sessions with senior politicians.[42] The objective was to make them enjoyable and sociable. The "modernisers" progressively disposed of traditional adversarial debates that had, according to them, plagued the relationship between previous Labour governments and the party. "With policy discussions in the forum we spent longer together and we were less confrontational," notes Diana Jeuda, "We tried to explore what united us rather than what divided us." The absence of decision-making powers eases the pressure to convince. Deliberation opens up consultation to outside actors and organisations (such as doctors, nurses and health experts for discussions on the National Health Service (NHS)). Trained facilitators ensure that all participants speak and feel personally involved. According to Eddie Morgan, Assistant General Secretary, participants are given an

> opportunity to hold ministers accountable. If people want to contribute to local and other forums, they can and we are desperately keen for people to get involved. Ministers attend many more party meetings than they used to. (...) In 2002, four times more submissions to the NPF than in 1998 and the aim in 2003 is to get 60 per cent of constituencies involved.

Party officials claim that the reform is a success story despite its difficult beginnings, but do these forums really provide activists with the feeling that they are taking part in policy-making? For those involved, the experience is largely positive. Forums were found interesting, friendly, efficiently run, united and easy to understand. However, reforms have not persuaded members that they have greater influence on policy-making. "Only 32 per cent of participants with experience in a policy forum thought that the forums were influential (36 per cent did not think so)" (Whiteley and Seyd, 2002: 215–216). "The danger to the party is that members will regard them as un-influential talking shops and will have little sense of policy ownership" (Seyd and Whiteley, 2002: 24). Surveys of Labour members show that a stable majority believes that they have "some" influence and that the reforms have not reduced feelings of political efficacy (Seyd and Whiteley, 2001: 88). However, 65 per cent of party members thought in 1997 that the party leadership paid a lot of attention to ordinary party members. They were only 47 per cent in 1999 (Whiteley and Seyd, 2002: 215–216). It is of little surprise that Labour activists feel disempowered by the very policy-making process that was supposed to enfranchise them. Apart from participation in the occasional forum, everything remains out of their sight and beyond their control. Even members of the National Forum feel excluded. The rolling process is "criticised for stopping participants gaining a clear idea of how their own contribution influenced policy" (Fielding, 2003: 135). Indeed, the dissociation between deliberation and decision-making dispels conflict and there are many possibilities to hear and to listen, to take, or not, suggestions into account: "it is about influence rather than a direct role," explains Larry Whitty, who originally initiated the Forum as General Secretary. Like his successor Tom Sawyer, he considers as a good thing that the party policy process has become "organic". As a consequence, the policy process has failed to convince members that they have more of a say over policies and the legitimacy of NPF reports is thus limited. Activists can let off steam by submitting remarks but they merely receive a pre-formatted letter in return assuring them that a Policy Commission is looking at their suggestions. Although more constituencies are holding policy forums, some do not bother sending the results to the party and some feel that "attending local policy forums is pointless, because the big policy decisions are made by the hierarchy of the party and not at a local level".[43] The danger for the Labour party is that a process perceived as "empty of real influence" may accelerate the very spiral of demobilisation it was designed to respond to. As Peter Hain put it, "there is a belief among members that policy forums are intended to neuter rather than empower the membership" (2004: 24).

The deliberation process is not working as efficiently as anticipated because the flow of communication rising from the bottom has been impeded by a belief in the "enlightened" nature of government. Such faith is manifest in Tony Blair's comment in a television broadcast that "it's not rocket science as to what people want or need".[44] Indeed, New Labour's team believed that they could devise the "best" policies, thanks to their awareness of documented social and global trends (Finlayson, 2003). Because they believed the Third Way to be "post-ideological" and based on "facts", they were convinced it also provided indisputable technical solutions.[45] In such an approach, the pluralist ideals of a policy process allowing genuine two-way communication were in direct competition with an equally strong determination to lead. The tension developed within the party organisation, echoing the "double movement of democratisation" advocated by the guru of the Third Way, Anthony Giddens (1998: 72). Devolution of powers to members was combined with a reassertion of authority. Party members were to be set free from the institutional obstacles that prevent innova-tion.[46] Committees and rulebooks were deemed stifling. In theory, the double movement of democratisation should promote a more respon-sive government. In practice, it combines freedom with tighter controls on the ways these new potentials can be used. Participants are expected to reach a consensus on the best possible solution when provided with "pertinent" information. Genuine debate may not have been stamped out but it is freer when it involves issues that are less controversial or is carefully framed by the leadership.[47] In New Labour, consensus building seems to have been used to squash pluralism rather than foster dialogue.

Policy deliberations are essentially about legitimating decisions. "The aim of these reforms has been both to reduce the influence of party members and to re-educate them" (Smith, 2000: 147). Labour developed political education between 1994 and 1997 in parallel with the policy forum and follows the same principles. Small meetings "are good at making people understand the government's position", a key architect of the reform told me, "it is a process of education – or propaganda if you like [because when they are] provided with the same information, people in a small group tend to come to an agreement". Implicit here is the conviction that listening to experts will encourage members to accept/hear the government's point of view. However, the educational objective competes with the drive for innovation because the flux of communication is predominantly top-down. Policy education is thus a way to disseminate ideas and information to members so that they can own them, learn their detail and justification and, through the expression of such views, become more convincing propagandists themselves! "We didn't realise that it would also be very motivational for our members," enthuses a member of the NEC.

Political correctness encourages a non-confrontational/woman and minority friendly approach to politics and attempts to make meetings more inclusive and friendly. It is now rare for participants to come out of small-group discussions without having spoken. What is important is that personal commitment is enhanced by feelings of belonging that are precisely developed in such situations. Invited to defend her position, the participant becomes more involved in the process (Moscovici and Doise, 1992: 272) and is better able to own the decision eventually reached. Thus, the party can hope to consolidate the loyalty of its members and to bind them to the government's policies by fostering a team spirit. As a consequence she is more likely to be prepared to defend the position to other audiences and in particular when canvassing. According to Matthew Taylor, the idea was that "the way you discuss ideas [is] part of the way you win elections (...) the fact that people understood what we were fighting for was giving them confidence to go and fight for them". Intra-party reform thus contributed to the objective of keeping members "on message" so that they would indeed be convincing "ambassadors in the community".[48]

When general elections draw closer, it becomes important to provide candidates with all the media and communication support they may need. Because conference offers unique opportunities to disseminate the latest campaigning techniques, training sessions are organised in ever greater numbers. They offer local parties campaigning tips and strategies, they spread "best practice". At the turn of the Millennium, Labour held about 40 to 50 such sessions each year. The Liberal Democrats and the Greens also take seriously the potential of conference for activist training, though the latter were at first reluctant to organise specific media handling training. Even the Conservatives are now joining the movement. They organised their first session in 2002.

Labour Conference 1998, Blackpool

A training session on "delivering the message" is organised for delegates right after the Prime Minister's speech. Ostensibly, the convenors start by asking whether there are some journalists present because this is a "privileged" debriefing session. "What a good speech that was!" marvels Peter Mandelson, "I told him that was brilliant and well received by the party as well as by the public. The great value and charm of these speeches is that they are written and delivered for the same public. [Now] we can explain to the party so that the party can explain to the people". There are about 20 activists in the room, listening carefully to advice on the dangers of forgetting to communicate when "we" are too busy governing. "We need to sound enthusiastic about conference," he declares with a well rehearsed "spontaneous" smile, "the point of the speech today is our story to tell: something to enthuse people about, it showed the great things we have done in 15 months. We will go to clubs and pubs and the local press, the schools and tell the story: we will do so with sincerity and enthusiasm". The Assistant General Secretary carries on along the same lines: "we shouldn't be afraid of expressing our emotions". It all sounds like a hybrid between the Salvation Army and neuro-linguistic programming. "Campaigning is important and *you* can be part of the change. *You* are this government's team. (...) All the good news announced today needs to be told because the press doesn't do it. You are not part of the audience, you are part of the team. This is not five days by the sea but an opportunity to bring the message back to your constituency". The pep talks are followed by a series of questions. The session ends with Mandelson reminding delegates one last time that "*we* had a privileged position this afternoon: *we* were in the hall where all the country would have liked to be". Referring to the words of the Prime Minister, he concludes with a wink "but with privilege comes responsibility".

Although there is no real support for the old system, there are many critics of the way the new one has been developed. In particular, complaints focus on the ambiguities of policy education: members are told that they can deliberate alternatives while they are in fact most of the time "expected to listen to explanation of policies" and led to "predetermined conclusions".[49] Despite the frustration, most in the party acknowledge that tight financial constraints have limited the potential of the rolling policy process. Because holding regular full NPF meetings over a weekend was too expensive, the party has organised fewer and shorter sessions than anticipated.[50] Moreover, the team in charge of processing grassroots' input was reduced to a handful of over-worked staff. The very success of the system made their task more complicated as they had to deal with an increasing number of submissions. Reports about the new system are invariably upbeat, emphasising how forums "widen the effective franchise and [point to] a new style of political discussion and debate". However, even party officials admit that the forums have not fulfilled all of their promises. The NPF "tries to do too many things", admits Paul Thompson, "people want to influence and the policy forums are not enough". However, even when they recognise the disillusionment brought about by the new process, most Labour officials concur with Tom Sawyer in saying that it is "a great improvement on what went before". Several years after the adoption of *Partnership in Power*, it is certainly true that "no-one wants to go back to compositing", even if the official position put to me by Eddie Morgan – "people now feel that they can contribute" – is an overstatement. Some of the frustration precisely comes from the hype that was deployed to "sell" the reform to party members. The promised partnership has not materialised, perhaps, writes Tom Sawyer, because

> the expectations were too great, and perhaps we tried to achieve too much too soon. It is true that we have a policy making process which is mature and less able to be high-jacked by factions, but it still only involves a small number of party activists, and those who are not involved feel distanced from the process (Sawyer, 2000: 13).

Party officials admit that there is a link between the failure of the consultation process to convince members that their participation is effective and the demobilisation of activists. There are however few signs that indicate a readiness to reverse the trend towards centralisation of decision-making that lies behind a discourse of partnership and stakeholders.

Conclusion

In their efforts to improve their chances of electoral success, governmental parties compete for the median voter. They adapt their "product" (Lees-Marshment, 2001) to meet the concerns of their projected "consumers" and increasingly present themselves as a team of competent managers. The rise of the managerialist model of governance however has tended to reinforce the image of politicians as estranged from the everyday concerns of ordinary citizens. Mainstream parties have thus made great efforts in the 1990s to portray themselves as "listening" to the people. Increasing reliance upon focus groups, the consultation of "experts" and "stakeholders" represent some of the main reactions we have seen to this situation, designed as they are to demonstrate and facilitate a greater responsiveness to public opinion. However, not only do such trends largely exclude party activists but they also remove traditionally important incentives for the mobilisation of members such as participation in policy development.

To counterbalance this growing rift, new procedures have been introduced in the three main British parties that echo the experiments conducted in the 1980s in new social movements and the Green Party. These groups pioneered experimentation with participatory forms of democracy, small-group meetings and decision-making by consensus. "The cognitive mobilisation of Western publics has shifted in favour of participatory democracy" (Scarrow *et al.*, 2000: 132), leading mainstream parties to adopt in the 1990s a discourse of inclusion[51] and a series of organisational reforms. The enthusiastic adoption of a discourse of "deliberative democracy" is symptomatic as in practice it allowed further concentration of power behind a façade of consultation. Clearly, at a time when members were perceived as a source of legitimacy, Labour modernisers envisaged the creation of a "massive but passive" membership that would not interfere with leadership orientations but would nevertheless bring support. In government, New Labour has tried to create a "Schumpeterian state", oriented towards the facilitation of constant innovation in a fast-changing capitalist economic environment (Finlayson, 2003: 190). Internal party reforms sought to create a flexible organisation, free from the constraints imposed by older models of delegatory democracy. In this way, New Labour loosened up party boundaries by opening up local meetings to outsiders and encouraging consultative sessions in the name of inclusivity. Although this development is most striking in the case of Labour, similar changes have occurred in the other parties: from the Greens to the Conservatives, the rhetoric of consensus and openness has been combined with the development of a new format emphasising deliberation over decision-making as the essence of democracy. "Everybody likes being included", argue Conservative officials before they explain that it merely entails members receiving an "annual report", including "an account of the progress from the Leader and a review of Party organisation performance from the Chairman" (Conservative Party, 1998: 25).

Even though political parties may not give their members a determining role in policy-making, they cannot afford to ignore them. To ensure wide legitimacy the decision-making process of a modern democratic party needs to include mechanisms that recognise internal pluralism. The evolution we have considered in this chapter provides the framework for effective two-way communication but this potential can be, and has been, used to very different ends by political parties. The media have considerably influenced the ways each organisation has balanced internal pluralism and the need to appear united. The Greens have endeavoured to practice their ideal democracy. Thus, they have accepted the inconvenience of collective and collegial institutions. They have also imposed on themselves restrictive rules that sometimes appear ineffective or convoluted. The Greens deliberately ignored pressures from the media and set up a slow policy process. The Liberal Democrats have maintained a consultative process that is both open to members and carefully structured. Lack of interest from the media has allowed both parties to explore controversial issues. Moreover, marginality feeds an inward looking approach to policy-making.[52] The Conservatives, on the other hand, have no real tradition of internal democracy. Reforms in this direction under the leadership of Hague have been mainly rhetorical whilst the radicalisation of the membership reinforces the natural prudence of partisan elites who put electoral success above any other priority.

The Labour party has introduced apparently similar procedures through a rolling policy process and small consultative forums open to all members. However, successive reforms of the organisation did not introduce safeguard mechanisms to protect internal pluralism whilst creating an informal process that was expected to breed innovation. The practice has been disappointing to those who hoped it would create a constructive and pluralist atmosphere. Deliberation procedures have been used to force consensus whilst claiming legitimacy through the apparently wide consultation that the discourse of deliberative democracy suggests. The new process also contributed to a concentration rather than a devolution of power. Such a development can be linked to the obsession with image and communication that has guided New Labour's internal reforms as well as its general approach to politics. Concerns about the appearance of division led to the creation of "private" sessions and forums parallel and complementary to conference where dissent could be expressed without risk. However, the early years of the NPF were dominated by the suppression of divergent voices. Overly diligent framing of debates therefore annihilated any hopes that the system would tolerate the expression of dissent. In part, such tight control over procedures was inspired by the conviction that, if properly conducted, the policy process would "naturally" come up with an agreement on the "good" policy conceived by experts. Under such conditions, there is no room for conflict as change is to be managed rather than invented. More worryingly, "modernisers" tend to reject the possibility that disagreements over policy sometimes stem from anything other than unsatisfactory communication as if they believed their own propaganda about objective policies based on indisputable social facts.

Not only does such a development tend to divest conventional politics of much of its traditional excitement, it is also synonymous with the end of politics, which is the art of resolving and negotiating conflicts. The demobilisation of British publics and the growing apathy towards electoral and partisan politics is likely to be linked to the imposition of an apparent consensus and the tight control over the outcome of deliberations. Opening up the policy process to the membership has been accompanied by a strict control over the procedures and the conclusions reached: those consulted are in a sense "free" to agree with the leadership's proposal. Thus, for instance, possibilities of amendments were, during the first few years in particular, firmly restricted to those accepted by the "enlightened" government. Deliberative innovations in Labour conform all too easily to a "consumer-oriented" approach to politics that focuses upon target groups and individuals. This trend is further complemented by voting procedures that "empower" members to choose from a limited range of options put to them by a leadership that increasingly seems to present itself as "omniscient and benevolent". The party has "empowered" members by providing a framework in which to deliberate that also acts as a filter. As we shall see, despite the recent appeal to a discourse of deliberative democracy, it is still felt to be insufficient to legitimate policies, as votes remain the primary symbol of democratic decision-making.

9
Direct Democracy: The Vote as Fetish

In the representative tradition, voting is the procedure by which decisions are taken and legitimised.[1] As a consequence, the authority of conference votes and decisions has tended to be over-estimated.[2] Political parties generally use votes to convince the public (and sometimes themselves) that they are democratic even though their leaderships are reluctant to be bound by them. The Conservative and Liberal Democratic parliamentary parties have never pretended to be receiving instructions from their conference, so the issue of conference sovereignty is really only an issue for Labour and the Greens. Although Clement Atlee wrote that conference "lays down the policy of the party and issues instructions which must be carried out by the Executive, the affiliated organisation, and its representatives in Parliament and on local authorities",[3] there are numerous examples of Labour leaders ignoring resolutions or interpreting them "loosely" because they were "vague and often contradictory" (Punnett, 1987: 104). Despite constitutional claims about the sovereignty of conference, the Labour parliamentary party has maintained, particularly when in power, a margin of interpretation.[4] Robert McKenzie even considered that

> like Bagehot's constitutional monarch, the annual party conference has the right to be consulted, the right to encourage, and the right to warn. But this is not to say that the members of the mass organisation have the right under British parliamentary system to control or direct the actions of their parliamentary leaders (1964: 583).

Nevertheless, the symbolic weight of conference remained sufficiently important for Hugh Gaitskell to go to huge lengths to reverse the conference decision on unilateralism. Dismissing the result as irresponsible

191

he vowed to "fight and fight and fight again" and raised the issue again in 1961. Since the adoption of *Partnership in Power*, the role of conference-as-policy-making has been reduced. However, because these reports can theoretically be referred back, the "myth" of conference sovereignty has been maintained.

Vote as ceremony

Sally Moore has shown that, in the case of the Tanzanian government, ceremonies and public gatherings can be instrumentalised to demonstrate the progress of democracy and popular participation. Similarly, demonstrations of consent are routinely produced at British party conferences. In these occasions, votes are crucial to the elaboration of an official version of the event. The performance of unanimity or consensus manufactures legitimacy because the repetition of dissenting behaviour contributes to the construction of a social reality.

> In order to make social life operable, people must behave as if much that is socially constructed is as non negotiable and as real as something in the natural world. The dramatic format of ceremony is a powerful way to show the existence of a social construct (Moore, 1977: 167).

Although party leaderships are increasingly prepared to override conference decisions openly, thus undermining the instrumentality of votes, the ritual practice of voting continues to give credence to their claims to be democratic organisations. In that sense, votes are not only about expressing consent, they are about instructing and converting.

In all four parties, votes are formal and solemn occasions characterised by a succession of rhetorical formulas and actions that are little open to improvisation. Such ritualisation, whether or not we believe that they reveal how party members approach politics as ominous and sacred, at least demonstrate how organisers endeavour to make the practice stand out. Votes are opportunities to create momentum because internal campaigns mobilise competing factions who then measure their relative strength. The media also contribute by increasing the attention paid to votes because disagreements can easily be dramatised as challenges to the authority of the leadership (see Chapter 6). Conflict, indeed, is newsworthy but the heydays of Labour civil war are gone and the media misses the excitement of debates and ballots that used to provide the main news items. Increasing control of conference proceedings means that platform defeats have become such a rarity[5] that even close results are news.[6] The importance of the event is in the fact that it reveals brewing discontent rather than because of its direct pragmatic consequences.

The importance of ballots can be measured by their ritualisation (Bon, 1991: 175–188). In most cases, votes are expedited through a show of hands.[7] This poses a number of problems when all conference participants are not entitled to vote. Labour and the Liberal Democrats need to differentiate delegates and voting representatives from visitors. In Labour, delegates are cordoned off on the floor of conference and assigned numbered seats. The Liberal Democrats, on the other hand, merely require the displaying of an orange badge to vote.[8]

The symbolic value of the vote explains the compulsive voting in which the Liberal Democrats and the Greens revel.[9] If votes are synonymous with democracy then there can be a temptation to multiply them, skipping debates or shortening them to vote more. A Green complains that "people want to vote as much as possible to achieve as much as possible and sometimes very important motions are voted on after one for and one against". Such Stakhanovism is shared by parties that conceive their conference as a decision-making body rather than a talking shop. "I want to take the votes on the separate votes before the vote on the amendments," announces the Liberal Democrats session chair. Nobody seems troubled by it. To vote or not to vote is an existential question, so counting techniques have been imagined to speed up the procedure. Stewards or Counters are allocated a row of seats or tables (in the Green Party). They count fast, systematically walking up or down their block to minimise errors. They run to the conference committee desk to add up the figures. The result is then carried to the session chair who makes the announcement. During the few years when they held conferences of delegates, the Greens organised a system of daily coloured cards to be shown for each vote. Tellers would go round, counting the number of votes held by each delegate.

The solemnity with which delegates and representatives behave when votes are taken cannot be solely explained by the importance attributed to the outcome of the procedure. Votes trigger passion in Labour, the Liberal Democrats and the Green Party because decisions are legitimised, officers are selected or confirmed, authority is established but the excitement of playing a part in the democratic process rubs off with experience. In the Labour party, constituency delegates have the reputation of being harder workers than those representing unions. First timers are especially keen to be counted, anxious to perform their duty and be worthy of their fellow members' trust. They leave fringes early, rush back to the main hall. They arrive before the beginning of the morning session, check the daily newsletters and the recommendations given by the NEC and/or the Left,[10] read the press and study the agenda. In the three parties, most participants adopt a mixed approach: they play hard and work hard but nearly all of them, when asked, are keen to stress the importance of the vote in the democratic process of their organisation. Experienced conference attendees are not so eager: recovering from the previous night's excesses is also on their personal agenda. They hang around in the corridors, drink tea with old acquaintances, and catch up with old friends. Some hardly bother to enter the main hall to listen to the debates, let alone to vote. They have more realistic expectations about the weight of their vote but participation is a make-believe that maintains their trust in the organisation and the pretence of internal decision-making is what it claims to be. The paradox of the rational voter fails to explain why people carry on voting (Pizzorno, 1991). Similarly, the rational and reflexive activist would be unlikely to take part in internal votes if he was really motivated by the impact of his action on party policy.

Liberal Democrats 2002, Brighton

Ellen is a Liberal Democrat local councillor and a business woman. She has come for the day, as she cannot afford to take the time off to fulfil her representative duties. It is the first time in years she has actually managed to turn up at all but she is "not attending the debates because what is important happens on the fringe or the corridors".

Vote as legitimacy

Votes have implications in terms of image that are increasingly important. Hand votes are the most visible to the observer whilst card votes,[11] in the Labour party, draw considerable attention to the block vote and the weight of the unions.[12] Historically, this procedure provided considerable flexibility for the leadership because it was enough to convince union "barons" to win against more radical constituency activists.[13] Former General Secretary Larry Whitty considers that "80 to 90 per cent of the conference was always predictable". His successor concurs:

> in reality, conference decisions are made elsewhere – in the union delegations, debating and deciding on how block votes are cast and

which resolutions will be carried. The votes are lined up before the first speaker goes to the rostrum.[14]

Whilst trade unions generally delivered conference victory for the leadership, the "undemocratic" block vote could also be blamed when unfavourable conference decisions were adopted.[15] However, the procedure became highly unpopular "not only with the public, the individual members of the Labour Party but also with the trade unions themselves" (Minkin, 1991: 386). Moreover, it considerably contributed to damaging the image of the party because it linked it to organisations that were increasingly perceived as archaic, undemocratic and too influential (Heath *et al.*, 2001). Reducing the role of unions was crucial to making Labour electable again. The unions' share of the vote at conference was reduced to 70 per cent in 1993, then to 50 per cent when direct membership rose above 300,000 members in 1995.[16] These decisions had a primarily symbolic impact because unions remain important players. In fact, they have gained a certain freedom because the leadership is less dependent on them and they do not feel as bound to support it. Moreover, the leadership's excessive anxiety about division has increased their bargaining power all the more as their strength in the NPF puts them in a good negotiating position. They can not only tilt the balance of conference votes but also prevent minority amendments from reaching conference. They can offer to act as buffers in exchange for concessions or threaten to embarrass the government.[17] Nevertheless, the party successfully managed to distance itself from trade unions after 1992 and, in 1997, Tony Blair announced unions could only expect "fairness not favours" from his government (Heath *et al.*, 2001).

Indeed, the importance of the vote does not necessary lie in the content of the proposal that is adopted but in the power struggle between factions who seize the occasion to measure their respective support. Rituals are often associated with order, the restoration of hierarchies, invariance and conformism. However, Nicholas Dirks argues that rituals are potentially subversive. Their performance carries the constant possibility of conflict, fission and paralysis. The compelling, contestable, and dangerous components of the ritual drama raise the stakes (Dirks, 1992: 236). Both the discourse and the practice of the ritual are open to contestation (Dirks, 1992: 229). Moreover, the need to appropriate legitimate accounts and interpretations of what happens increases the importance of the ritual. Conference voting is such an arena of contestation. Even though, as we have seen in Chapters 6 and 7, the leaderships try to control all aspects of the performance, there is always the risk that something may go wrong. The vote may be lost or the procedures questioned. Points of order can be raised, card votes demanded, the distribution of votes interpreted. With the omni-presence of the media, this anxiety is heightened. In the Labour party, conference voting procedures have been strongly formalised (Seyd, 1987: 4) and the object of obsessive attention because it was perceived that the stakes were high. They could be strategically used to promote particular agendas and teams.[18] The primary actors are involved in bargaining and bartering[19] both in private and in public.[20] Pressure is exercised to induce conformism. The successive organisational reforms that have concentrated organisational power have also limited the ability of factions to use votes to mobilise supporters. However, constituency delegates hold 50 per cent of the conference votes and the outcome is less predictable than before. Resistance is not futile as demonstrated by the considerable energy deployed by the leadership to control the conference. Debates have become more important because they may sway constituency delegates. The NEC and factions produce daily newsletters[21] in order to advertise their positions. The leadership consistently puts forward a double argumentation that justifies its proposals but also warns against being divided in front of the media.

Setbacks for the government were rare during the first Labour term of office,[22] leading to recurring complaints about repression of dissent and excessive concern with image. Controls were loosened during the second term as the conference became accustomed again to letting off steam in a managed way. Defeats were "spun" to project the image of a reformist government fighting against the "forces of conservatism". Moreover, the distribution of constituency and union votes has become a precious tool for image management. In 2002, the unions defeated the PFI. The government argued that this deviated from its electoral mandate and contrasted the support of "public spirited constituency delegates" with the unions' narrowly self-interested opposition! Ironically, the same day, the unions prevented another government defeat on the war in Iraq. The media were torn between the two big events of the day and despite relatively rowdy debates and a defeat, the government's position was effectively strengthened. When the leadership lost another vote in 2003 on the creation of Foundation Hospitals, the minister concerned simply acknowledged that the government would "take cognisance of the overall vote at conference".[23] Since constituency delegates had supported the government "2 to 1", he added that "as a party and a government we have a responsibility to (...)

the consumers of health services, not just the providers". This official interpretation was hammered home and generally reported, thereby establishing a consensus on what had happened. Whilst previous Labour governments paid lip service to conference sovereignty, Tony Blair's team takes no such rhetorical precaution but still needs to justify itself in terms of the contemporary lexicon of democratic accountability.

Although they do not take decisions, Conservative conferences vote nearly as much as the others. On these occasions, only "representatives" are entitled to do so though the definition is lax. In 1997 and 1998 for instance, my conference badge indicated that I was the representative for "Conservative Association X".[24] As votes carry no authority, it does not really matter who votes. Until 1998, the Conservative conference booklet described in detail the procedures for voting at conference, asserting that ballots are the "norm" except when there is a clear expression of a majority – which is generally the case![25] The chair announces that the motion is carried "unanimously" or "by an overwhelming majority". Not only is this nearly always the case but they also sometimes appear to contradict the preceding debate. Conservatives vote to express support and the results are generally in favour of the leadership. The lack of suspense reflects the unanimity of the grassroots and their reluctance to show disunity in front of the cameras. Moreover, the motions selected for debate until 2000 were generally so bland that, in many cases, there was little point voting against them. In any case, focusing on the results is misleading: participants vote to demonstrate their belonging, not to obtain a policy outcome (Pizzorno, 1991; Schuessler, 2000). Taking part in the conference vote reaffirms the representative's identity, his/her commitment to a political system where the legitimacy of leaders and their decisions are sanctioned by votes. Many Conservatives do not believe that dissent should be publicly displayed, as a 1995 conference motion reads:

> in a parliamentary democracy, all sections of the Conservative party, including the parliamentary party should have ample opportunities to influence policies in private, but once difficult decisions are taken should place their wholehearted support behind the leader in public.[26]

There are ways other than votes, or overt criticism, for the Conference to indicate its mood, thereby indirectly holding the leadership accountable.

Organisational myths

"New institutionalism" looks at formal and informal rules in shaping social action (March and Olsen, 1989; Powell and DiMaggio, 1991). It highlights the difficulty of deliberate change by emphasising the complex role played by culture in such processes (Newman, 2001: 26–27). In some cases, theories assume that "organisations function according to their formal blueprints: co-ordination is routine, rules and procedures are followed, and actual activities conform to the prescriptions of formal structure" (Meyer and Rowan, 1977: 342). This is rarely the case however and rulebooks can only be taken as one indicator amongst many of the ways in which parties work (Bailey, 1969). Moreover, formal rules may play a symbolic role. Meyer and Rowan explain the "import" of institutions and rules by the need for organisations to justify their practices. Organisations, they write,

> are driven to incorporate the practices and procedures defined by prevailing rationalised concepts of organisational work and institutionalised in society. Organisations that do so increase their legitimacy (1977: 340).

Thereby, such organisations follow public opinion pressure whilst they "increase the commitment of internal participants and external constituents" by "incorporating externally legitimated formal structures" (1977: 349). Some rules are thus adopted not because they improve the efficiency of the organisation but because they bring legitimacy. The existence of these rules demonstrates that the group abides by societal norms. Indeed, "formal structures of many organisations in post-industrial society dramatically reflect the myths of their institutional environment instead of the demands of their work activities" (1977: 341). As organisations try to adapt to their environment's conceptions of "proper, adequate, rational and necessary" ways to behave, they adopt new rules.

Adherence to organisational myths provides an account of activities that prevents the organisation's conduct from being questioned. The proliferation of formal rules of intra-party democracy demonstrates their role as organisational myths rather than their effectiveness in running organisations. When such rules are not in place, accounts of what goes on are open to challenge and organisations become vulnerable to accusations of being negligent, irrational or undemocratic. The influence of rationalised organisational myths has been powerful. Since the

1990s, individual members' ballots have become the criteria to determine whether an organisation is democratic and all four parties have introduced them for at least the election of the leader in the 1990s.[27] Delegatory democracy used to be the organisational principal of the Labour party – an organisation traditionally structured around a sovereign conference. One-member-one-vote (OMOV) proved to be a devastating argument in the internal battle launched by Kinnock against radical activists because they could not oppose it in the name of democracy. It served a similar purpose with regard to the trade unions as resistance could be portrayed as archaic and authoritarian. In 1998, the rhetoric of intra-party democracy spread to Conservative literature and propaganda. The new leader, William Hague, declared his intention to speed up internal change and achieve in a few weeks what had taken years in Labour. The proclaimed objective was to facilitate participation through a variety of new individual rights combining direct membership ballots and new channels for policy deliberation. Was it the reflection of a deep change of heart and a shift in values or a strategic response to Labour reforms and new modes of cultural legitimacy?

Beyond the introduction of rules allegedly inspired by participative democracy, we are now witnessing the rise of business as the new institutionalised myth that shapes organisations from political parties to public services. Government can learn from business "target controls, effective auditing, flexible decision structures and increased employee participation – the last of these being a factor in democratisation" (Giddens, 1998: 74–75). In the mid-1980s, "business culture" became widely accepted as a given facet of British political life (Gaffney, 1991: 152). The market paradigm, presented as both unavoidable and the most effective, has been adopted by Labour and the Conservatives. It was also heralded as reconnecting political parties with public opinion because market research now helps them find out what the electorate wants.[28] Jennifer Lees-Marshment, advocate of political marketing studies in the UK, considers this innovation as progress because, she argues, parties "then design a product, including leader, policy and organisation, that [not only] responds to these demands, but is also one that they can deliver in government, is believable and is adjusted to suit internal views within the organisation" (Lees-Marshment, 2001: 211).

Labour adopted the business model with the arrival of Tony Blair as leader and Tom Sawyer as General Secretary. In the summer of 1995, the NEC attended workshops at the Cranfield School of Management. Sawyer presented the first ever party business plan to the NEC within

10 weeks of being appointed General Secretary (Sawyer, 2000: 8). New ways of working were explored in the 1990s with the objective of making the party more effective once in power. The conclusion drawn was that "what [was] really necessary [was] a 'cultural' change i.e. ways of working, relating and behaving together – which is more difficult to achieve but also more fundamental to the process of change".[29] The objectives included "improving democracy" and "building a healthy party" through the development of a "listening and responsive culture (...) and a review of methods and styles of communications". This initiative was inspired by new management techniques. Party managers discovered quality control and sought new ways to motivate their staff. Party structures were audited, task forces were created to ensure efficient delivery of objectives; "turn around teams" tackled moribund local parties; "best practice" models were spread. Staff were given targets to achieve and went to "team-building away-days", which were organised to "improve communication and provide opportunities to revisit our mission statement".[30] Work atmosphere was also radically transformed with the headquarters moving from Smith House to Millbank (and later Old Queen Street), open plan interior design and new lines of management. All levels of the party were required to produce action plans from 1995. Local and area parties are bound to "performance indicators, which means that staff and parties are required to put on policy forums; policy forums are organised jointly for several constituencies," argues Diana Jeuda. The party also started outsourcing tasks such as membership services. The reforms imposed by New Labour upon its organisation anticipated the wider transformation of British government and society.[31]

A similar inspiration took over the Conservative party. The first "business plan" was produced by the West Midlands Conservative Area. It was immediately promoted as an example to follow at the following Conservative conference whilst the Conservative Policy Centre (CPC) spent most of 1995 writing its own (Conservative Party, 1995: 23). By 1998, such planning was made compulsory in the new party constitution. Constituency organisations are asked to map out their development strategies and justify their practices. New management techniques were imposed by Archie Norman, a businessman famous for his success with the superstore ASDA, who was brought in by William Hague to run Central Office. He had walls pulled down in Central Office and new relationships between departments were encouraged. New information technologies were promoted despite the anxiety of many ageing activists. For Conservatives as well, it is as if customs and traditions were not quite enough anymore to justify a form of organisation.[32]

At a time when trust in conventional politics is challenged like never before (Pharr and Putnam, 2000), parties resort to importing business techniques: auditing has become the new "benchmark for securing the legitimacy of organisational action" (Power, 1999: 10). The new myth of rationalised institutions mobilises a discourse of empowerment and transparency that is increasingly associated with democratic account-ability. It turns party members into stakeholders.[33] However, Michael Power warns, such frenetic passion for auditing probably constitutes little more than a new form of image management rather than a way to empower the "notional publics" it is supposed to help in their assess-ment (1999: 143). It also reflects over-investment in "shallow rituals of verification at the expense of other forms of organisational intelligence" (1999: 123). There is another problem with the import of procedures that may not be adapted to the organisation and that may involve tedious controls. As early as 1977, Meyer and Rowan highlighted how evaluation can itself produce illegitimacy because it is a "public assertion of societal control which violates the assumption that everyone is acting with competence and in good faith". The danger for parties, as well as for other sectors of British society placed under the scrutiny of the audit culture is of a lowering of morale and confidence linked to the undermining of "the ceremonial aspect of organisation" (Meyer and Rowan, 1977: 359).

The individualisation of membership

British parties have for a long time neglected their membership. Communication technology and the nationalisation of electoral campaigns do not require mass memberships that can be considered expensive and difficult to manoeuvre for little return. Recruitment had not been a top priority in the past because of the reluctance of activists to dilute their influence. Trade unions did not want to encourage a rise in direct party membership that would eventually weaken their own position (Fielding, 2003: 122). Indeed, Labour's motivations to boost the membership were precisely to attract and empower a membership base that would prove more supportive of the leadership's perspective.[34] In the 1990s, research on electoral campaigning demonstrated the importance of local mobilisation[35] and British parties re-discovered the benefits of a strong membership base (Scarrow, 1996). Since the work of Olson and with the triumph of economic liberalism, instrumental rationality is seen as the common *idiom* to interpret all human actions. People now have a tendency to justify their actions in terms of outcome even when their motives are expressive (Eliasoph, 1998; Schuessler, 2000: 27). In order to make joining more attractive, British parties endeavoured to lower the cost of joining[36] and to offer selective incentives. National recruitment campaigns targeted potential recruits directly, by-passing traditional routes and activists: national phone numbers were provided, debit and credit card payments were offered, "quick response guaranteed". Membership services were centralised[37] to provide new "membership rights" such as the right to vote in ballots, to attend forums and to receive national newsletters.[38] Thanks to national membership databases, they are now able to send literature by post and email. Labour also puts a great deal of effort into its website.[39] Greater use of mobile phones and "texting" should follow soon as Labour is looking for new ways of promoting "interactive politics". Little thought is devoted to the development of ways to socialise these new members into the organisation.

If we accept that actions can be the expression of an individuals' identity, it makes little sense to evaluate them solely in terms of costs and benefits. Members who identify with the movement do not need any reward or incentive to participate because they demonstrate their belonging to others and themselves through these very actions. Although joining is one such act, it is too discreet to be noticed and therefore hardly expressive. Organisations such as the Conservative party, based on few promises and many symbols, thrived thanks to voluntary labour that expressive members gave without expecting anything back (Ware, 1992). Solidarity thus provided the most important base for activism without the need to satisfy policy or material demands. The ideal situation for a party, claims Alan Ware, is a combination of activists motivated by purposive/material incentives who can mobilise members motivated by solidarity. "Loyalty is weaker today because members do not so much constitute a community as a collection of individuals, and those individuals have less sense of 'letting the side down' if they fail to carry on political tasks for their party" (Ware, 1992: 5–6).

Mobilisation problems are more likely to arise when the membership is both individualised and instrumentalised and thus attracts members who expect influence, promotion, and contacts in exchange for their efforts. There are also consequences on turn-over: studies of members leaving organisations have shown that those who identify with the organisation are less likely to use an *exit* strategy (Hirschmann, 1970; Rüdig *et al.*, 1991: 66–69). In recent years, new members have not proved very loyal and have sometimes left as quickly as they had joined.[40] Indeed, rise in party membership figures was ephemeral. Labour reached nearly 400,000 individual members in the run up to the 1997 general election; a similar campaign by Conservative party started to bear fruit in 1998 but by 2004, the official Labour figure had fallen down to a historic low of 208,000 members whilst the Conservatives claimed around 320,000 members.

Panel surveys allow us to track the evolutions of the Labour membership and the impact of new recruitment techniques (Seyd and Whiteley, 2002). The effort to disentangle membership from local involvement has been a success. New recruits have not been radicalised by local activists and they are less attached to the image and values of the Labour movement than their predecessors.[41] They tend to be "virtual" in the sense of having very little face-to-face contact with other members and research demonstrates that failure to develop affective bonds with the party inhibits socialisation within the organisation and thus future activism (Faucher, 1999a: 115–116; Seyd, 1999: 398). Not only do new members not have the information that would allow them to decide whether or not they would like to become more active (Whiteley and Seyd, 2002: 146) but, because they are isolated, they can neither discuss politics nor impress other members to advance their career. This phenomenon has accelerated the spiral of demobilisation noticed since the 1980s: new members tend to be less active whilst older generations of members are withdrawing from activism.

> While the mobilization strategy was successful in bringing new people into the party, it simultaneously inhibited the participation of these new recruits. Because New Labour members were typically recruited by impersonal means and subsequently had limited contact with the rest of the grass root party, they did not get drawn into party activity. Thus the change [of] mode of recruitment has come with a price, even though it was successful in increasing the size of the membership (Whiteley and Seyd, 2002: 144–145).

The cost of participation has been reduced with new incentives created to make membership more attractive. In the past, personal investment in the organisation and local bureaucracy was rewarded with selection as conference delegates, local candidates or party office. Nowadays, the right to vote in internal ballots is presented as a key membership benefit. The generalisation of OMOV was supposed to give all members an equal say and was advertised as democratisation. With small parliamentary groups, the Liberals and the SDP relied heavily on their membership and had to nurture them. The SDP adopted OMOV for the election of the leader, an innovation passed on to the Liberal Democrats. The objective was to create a direct relationship between the leadership and grassroots that were expected to be malleable. In 2000, the consultative sessions that were held in Bournemouth to reflect on ways to boost participation concluded that it was "necessary to improve communication with members [in order] to empower them". Proposals included broadening OMOV to regional and local levels[42] and new computer systems to improve membership services. Both solutions address the problem at the level of the individual member and overlook social networks and sociability.

It may seem paradoxical that resistance to OMOV has come primarily from parties of the left that claimed to strive for internal democracy. The reaction is less surprising if one considers that the Greens and Labour belonged to traditions placing great emphasis on the collective dimension of emancipation: solidarity and the mobilisation of social networks are central aspects of their world views. Moreover, both parties were dominated by meeting-attending activists whose very influence was threatened by consultation of passive members. Despite the hype about secret and individual ballots being synonymous to democracy, the procedure in effect contributes to a concentration of influence in the hands of those who organise the ballots. Convincing activists to give up their control thus involved talking up the "modernisation" process and the necessary "democratisation of the organisation". The myth of the democratic vote however made the reform difficult to oppose. In the Green Party, empowerment and participation were contrasted with an intermittent right to vote but membership ballots were nevertheless introduced for the election of party officers in 1992. Opponents to the reform regained control over the organisation within a year, largely because the main supporters of Green 2000 decided to withdraw. Although the party constitution was kept, a few amendments were progressively adopted to return to a system of conferences open to all members. Principal speakers are normally elected by postal ballot, except when there is only one candidate. In such an event, the Speakers are chosen by conference.

In Labour, the evolution was slow. Direct membership ballots were for a long time considered incompatible with the party ethos. A first attempt in 1984 was rejected by conference. The new procedure was thus implemented step by step, but eventually came to symbolise democracy against the reactionary influence of trade unions.[43] Ballots were made compulsory for constituency parties for the selection of candidates in 1987.[44] The rule was then extended in the following years to the election of the leader and of the constituency representatives on the NEC. The reforms at first produced the desired outcome: Livingstone, Skinner and Benn lost their seats on the NEC whilst Brown, Blair and Kinnock were elected.[45] In 1993, ballots were also imposed on trade unions for leadership elections[46] and candidate selection. Blair had always been an advocate of ballots but his enthusiasm was confirmed by the success of the campaign for rewriting Clause 4. Confronted with hostility from activists, Blair appealed over their heads directly to party members: they received the new proposal along with ballot papers to return to their local party before the special conference, convened in April 1995:[47] 80 per cent of those who took part in the 1995 consultation supported change. A year later, 95 per cent of individual members and 94 per cent of affiliated members approved the draft document *Road to the Manifesto*.

In 1998, the Conservatives appeared to suddenly convert to direct democracy. Talks of internal reforms had been brewing for some time. In 1996, Hodgson was elected Chairman of the National Union on a platform of reform. Consultations on the party organisation were initiated and, in 1997, the National Union held a secret ballot of 800 key volunteers on the leadership election.[48] Although William Hague was not their favourite, his agenda for change echoed their concerns. However, the constitution he later proposed went in fact much further than they had hoped. Some form of consultation had been discussed but no one could imagine that the membership would get more than a say in an electoral college. No one had envisaged the possibility of internal referendum. The enfranchisement of party members was received as an unexpected "gift". The spirit of these reforms was at odds with party traditions and their practice proved that the imported model was difficult to adapt to. Despite the apparent decentralisation of decision-making through ballots, the referenda organised served to reinforce an already strong leadership. Indeed, ballots preserved the leader's discretionary powers on policy-making grounded on "a general lack of confidence in members and in their ability to take decisions". Senior members of the National Union had initially hoped the experimentation could go as far as setting several questions at the same time but no unnecessary risk was taken. Four internal ballots were organised between 1997 and 2000 to enhance the leader's legitimacy thanks to large anticipated victories. Despite the rhetoric, the bold "cultural revolution" initiated by William Hague remained circumscribed. The new constitution changes little to customary ways of doing and the party elite distrust their grassroots' judgement. This attitude, that had justified the election of the leader by the 1922 Committee, was given new weight by the election of Iain Duncan Smith in 2001. "IDS" only served a short and disappointing mandate as party leader. In 2003, a coup deposed the leader and his successor "emerged" from the parliamentary party to be elected unopposed by the 1922 Committee without the organisation of a membership ballot. The voluntary side of the party and wealthy donors played an important role in the plot. What in 1998 seemed like a reasonable innovation that might improve the party's image now appeared to Conservative grandees as riddled with problems. The experiment was a failure not only because it led to the election of a poor leader but because it was so out of character that it could not convince the public that it was more than a public relations stunt.[49] It is unlikely that policy and electoral strategy reviews will be enough for the Conservatives to recover, so one can expect organisational reforms to resurface but further "individualisation" of the partisan relationships will be insufficient to mobilise the grassroots.

The ideal "massive but passive" membership

All the ballots organised by Labour and the Conservatives have given respective party leaderships massive majorities[50] that were presented as demonstrations that members were being empowered. However, in both parties, democratisation stopped short of giving members a say in the organisation of ballots. Moreover, despite their success, the experiments were short lived. What went wrong since the leaders got the result they were looking for? Low participation severely limited the legitimacy gained by the plebiscites. Tight control of the procedures tended to empty the consultation of its meaning. When nothing is at stake, it is difficult to mobilise voters, even when they are party members. Why vote to confirm a decision that has already been taken and will not be reversed? Why vote if the outcome is so predictable and the act of voting adds little to the expression of a partisan identity manifested through membership?

Conservative party staff claim that membership figures go up before internal ballots,[51] apparently demonstrating a genuine interest in taking part in key party decisions. Referenda have, however, been greatly disappointing: in September 2000, turnout for the referendum *Believing in Britain* was less than 17 per cent! Interestingly, many senior Conservatives believe that participation is "not a particular concern for most members". As Chris Poole put it, "those actively involved in the party were pleasantly surprised by the introduction of OMOV but ordinary members did not care that much". The low level of participation comforted senior Tories in the conviction that the majority of members have neither the competence, nor the desire, to participate in complex policy debates. Moreover, it made the organisation of ballots an expensive means to gain limited legitimacy and little publicity. None have been organised since 1999.

Participation has been equally low in the Labour party with only 27 per cent of the membership taking part in the 1995 consultation[52] despite the publicity it received and the symbolic importance of Clause 4.[53] In 1996, 43 per cent of party members voted against or failed to vote on the draft manifesto. In both cases, the decision to hold an internal referendum was constitutionally dubious as it bypassed the party's normal decision-making process. Some complained that the leadership was introducing major changes in the party through the back door as delegatory democracy was being slowly replaced by plebiscitary democracy but the ubiquitous argument of deepening democracy was relentlessly presented to sceptics. The ballot proved to be a convenient and expedient way to bind party members to the manifesto, thereby allowing the leadership to claim that it had received a mandate from the party to implement these policies.

Has participation in party decision-making been reduced to the occasional introduction of a ballot paper in a box? "Simply giving members the occasional vote, in which they are invited to pass judgement on an issue that has already been effectively decided, is not going to promote widespread grassroots involvement" warn Whiteley and Seyd (2002: 147). It is indeed a somehow strange idea to imagine that the multiplication of ballots could be a cure against apathy! As we know from turnout in general and local elections and from the paradox of the voter, the majority of voters are under no illusion about the influence of their individual contribution to such procedures. For many activists, the new right to vote is at best a symbolic gratification. In fact, despite the appearances, low participation was expected: the Labour Co-ordination Committee has advocated the creation of a "massive but passive" membership that could bring legitimacy to the leadership whilst being more docile in supporting its initiatives. What may not have been anticipated is that low involvement at local level will also translate into low commitment at the national level. Members' reluctance to be used as numbers in a legitimacy competition added to the uncertain benefit of having membership figures dissected and logistical problems in the organisation mocked in the media.[54] These were not isolated instances of low mobilisation:

> many constituencies do not send delegates [to conference], some National Policy Forum representatives are elected by under one-third of eligible constituencies, candidates for the 27 places elected each year have plummeted from 800 in 1997 to 41 in 2000, and turnout in NEC elections has fallen by 50 per cent in three years.[55]

Lack of mobilisation is a general problem in European political parties where most internal ballots get low turn out but the problem might be heightened in Britain because parties tend to privilege postal votes. Although such procedures lower the individual costs of participation,[56] they also contribute to the individualisation of party membership and thus increase the demobilisation of activists.

Aware of the need to socialise new members and include them, the Labour machine has encouraged local parties to "abandon boring matters such as policy and become more fun places" (Fielding, 2003: 141). Indeed, Labour modernisers have called for the transformation of local party structures, arguing that GMCs foster dull meetings. A more cynical interpretation points to the realisation that local groups filter and socialise members, thereby providing the possibility of articulating internal dissent. "The belief that members and their leader should be separated by as few levels of bureaucracy as possible was not simply based on the desire to be rid of the unions and activists" (Fielding, 2003: 131) but on a concerted attempt to short-cut intermediary levels where activists could discuss alternative policies and strategies. Substituting contacts with activists suspected of being dangerously radical with information directly provided by the centre could be an effective way of controlling internal pluralism. Labour "modernisers" thus advocated the convening of open monthly meetings, modelled on policy forums (see Chapter 8). Stripped of their decision-making powers, they could also be formatted and facilitated according to new centrally conceived directives. Such development builds on the tradition of social clubs.[57] "Labour supporters' clubs" have been opened in pioneering constituencies such as Reading West. Labour voters who hesitate to join are enlisted to receive further information and special invitations to political events with the local MP.[58] The objective is to transform the party into a "campaigning organisation" (Farrell and Webb, 2000) that would at the same time grant the leadership a great deal of autonomy and guarantee "foot soldiers" for electoral campaigns (Tether, 1996: 120). The success has been limited, largely because citizens are now provided with a large choice of leisure activities.

What has been the impact of these new practices on the party on the ground? Seyd and Whiteley distinguish "expressive members" whose membership expresses an identification with the movement and "instrumental members", who join in order to obtain selective or collective incentives. Their research also highlights how the former are more likely to be active than the latter (Seyd and Whiteley, 2002: 136). Over the last two decades, Labour has clearly shifted to the right, triggering questions about Blair's Thatcherism (Hay, 1999; Heffernan, 2000). Values traditionally associated with the labour movement have been challenged by reforms in party organisation and policies. Left-wingers, who tended to be more actively involved, are now more likely to be frustrated (Whiteley and Seyd, 2002: 102) and to reduce their activities. Surveys of New Labour members show that active and passive members exhibit different attitudes to party organisation beyond a wide-spread (75 per cent of respondents) dislike for the old model of policy-making through conference. Whilst 37 per cent of respondents want policies formed by the leadership and endorsed by postal vote, 39 per cent prefer policies to be formulated at regional and national forums (Seyd and Whiteley, 2002: 158). Not surprisingly, very active members (who would be the greatest losers in a system by-passing them) show a clear preference for policy forums.[59] The option of forums, if it worked satisfactorily, would give them the most influence. On the contrary, 42 per cent of passive members support plebiscites and only 36 per cent choose forums.

> If the leadership moves in the direction of the plebiscitary model it will not unduly worry the supporters, but it will antagonise the activists. The plebiscitary model appears ideal for a leadership party but it creates real problems for a party seeking to establish a participatory style of decision making that motivates the high intensity participants (Whiteley and Seyd, 2002: 215).

The problem for both Labour and the Conservatives is that they have failed to convince their members that they have the means to influence policies.[60] Thus, rather than mitigate frustration with participation, recent reforms have fed a spiral of inactivity. Could it be because the type of participation on offer has proven not only less attractive than anticipated but also created a vicious circle?

The new member-consumer

The emergence of new social categories of citizens that are more politically and cognitively aware than previous generations is, according to Inglehart (1990), responsible for demands for a new style of politics in which citizens could take a more pro-active role. The "era of pure representative democracy" is drawing to a close because "people want to be more directly involved" wrote Peter Mandelson in 1998, arguing that the solution is in "plebiscites, focus groups, lobbies, 'citizens' movements', and the Internet" (Routledge, 1999: 277–278). The response of the Labour party, imitated a few years later by the Conservatives, was to substitute vertical communication with horizontal links within local or regional parties (Seyd, 1999: 401). Direct communication from the party leadership has been developed with new electronic technologies and all parties now offer weekly email newsletters, but is it more than "preaching to the converted" (Norris, 2003)? "Basically what you get from the party is propaganda", complains an activist. Labour's e-mailings, circulated beyond party members, essentially lists achievements: "there isn't very much politics in terms of what's coming out of Old Queen Street. They don't discuss the movement of issues in policy forums for instance", complains a member.[61] Membership "surveys" maintain the fiction of consultation. In 1998, Labour distributed an "annual survey of supporters' opinion" whose bland questions were designed to highlight support rather than provide feedback (Seyd, 1999: 404 note 22). The Conservatives also circulated small questionnaires in 1998[62] and have explored the possibility of primaries for the selection of party candidates.[63] Despite its promises of interactivity and the fantasy of digital democracy, the Internet remains so far primarily a top-down tool (Farrell and Webb, 2000: 113).

In December 2003, the Labour party launched a "Big Conversation", opened beyond party members to the wider public, thus broadening further the consultative dimension of the policy process.

> Every contribution to the Big Conversation will be heard or read and all contributions will be forwarded to the relevant Labour policy commission to be considered at Labour's spring conference and our spring National Policy Forum. Ideas generated by the big conversation and respondents' priorities will be used to improve your local area and help shape Labour's programme for the next general election. (...) The big conversation is a way of enriching the Labour Party's policymaking process by listening to the British people about their

priorities for the future. We are embarking on it at this stage in our second term in government as people often say that politicians are only interested in what they think during election times. This Big Conversation aims to show that it isn't the case and that we are interested not just at election times but all the time.[64]

This innovation further blurs the boundaries of political parties and it is doubtful that it will contribute to solving the mobilisation crisis. What is the difference between a member and a supporter if both have the same influence on party policy? By the turn of the Millennium, the dominant paradigm within Labour and Conservative headquarters is that members have become consumers.[65] "We want to do this as part of a general approach", explains the Conservative marketing director, Will Harris. "We are looking at voters as consumers; they are the same people who buy sofas or cans of fizzy drink. We are trying to inject a bit of humanity into what we do."[66] So, members are offered "loyalty cards". This radical transformation of British society was initiated by Thatcher who famously claimed that "there is no such thing as society, there are only individual men and women and there are families".[67] It was reinforced by Blair's new Labour government which took the market analogy at face value. In government, New Labour has assumed that politics can operate like Adam Smith's ideal market where individual self-interests compete with each other to reach an equilibrium and that an "invisible hand" operates in politics as well economics. Britain has been turned into a market society. The changes reflect broader international social trends. The argument for popular involvement in politics takes the form of market choice (Finlayson, 2003: 178). This raises particular questions because parties are essential cogs of representative regimes and strive for the production of collective goods and collective identities. Their individualisation therefore produces particular paradoxes, as expressed by Peter Hain:

> One-member-one-vote can't replace the feeling of being directly involved in the party in a collective way. It's all right to be involved in an individualistic way, which is what one-member-one-vote is all about, but being involved in a collective way is what being a member of the party should be about. It shouldn't feel like being a member of the AA or RAC.[68]

When identification with parties weakens, it becomes more difficult to invoke solidarity.

Conclusion

Organisations are mimetic and tend to be influenced by the institutions in which they exist. Historically, British parties have been moulded by the Westminster model of government. As a consequence, they developed throughout the 20th century by incorporating its procedures. In this context, the annual conference gained some of its aura from a comparison with the House of Commons: conference representatives deliberated and took decisions by way of voting. The vote, essential in representative systems, has become the symbol of democracy. Within British parties, the vote of conference representatives has been carefully ritualised as a crucial performative action that grants authority and legitimacy to those who win.[69] For this reason, it has been the focus of internal competition between factions (mainly in Labour and the Green Party) and the means of challenging the leadership in a controlled setting. Even when the decisions taken by conference were not applied by the administrative or the political leadership, the vote remains the symbol of intra-party democracy. As a ritual practice it served the role of expressing support and loyalty towards party and leader, in particular in the case of the Conservative party.

In the 1990s however, there was a shift in dominant social myths that influenced parties as mimetic organisations. First, new social movements contributed to the emergence of demands for renewed forms of democracy (Dalton and Kuechler, 1990). At the same time, a new focus on the individual shifted perceptions of what counts as "democracy" to a model involving individual participation (through voting and focus-group consultation) rather than group representation. OMOV progressively replaced conference voting as the sacred font of legitimate decision-making. This was achieved largely because of the electoral success of New Labour which legitimised a procedure that had been strategically introduced by the dominant faction within the party at that time (the New Labour "modernisers") to ensure its supremacy over its internal opposition.[70] The spread of individual ballots to all parties[71] was by no means inevitable although it fitted well with the spread of social and cultural individualism and a growing "fetishisation" of the ballot as the symbol of democracy. Second, in the wake of the Thatcher cultural and economic revolution and the collapse of the soviet empire, the market has become the dominant paradigm for organisations in British society. Mainstream British parties aspire to imitate the corporate model of the business world as a more effective way of co-ordinating activities within their organisation. Marketing techniques offer the promise of better responsiveness to the expectations of the electorate. Thus, they have incorporated the myths of enterprise, not only outsourcing major party (not to mention state) functions and adapting their "product", but also transforming members into "stakeholders". In this model, the new member has certain rights (to vote, to be consulted and to be informed) but in practice has little influence on the actual decision-making process, thereby allowing a greater concentration of power in the hands of the party leaderships.

The apparent paradox of a double movement of decentralisation (or individualisation) and concentration of power (Mair, 1997, 2000) can be understood if we remember that British political parties are importing a model that derives primarily from the business world. Although keeping stakeholders satisfied is a preoccupation, the organisation is more concerned with corporate branding ("staying on-message") and quick responsiveness to their permanent competition in the electoral "marketplace". The problem with these developments is that, far from solving the spiral of demobilisation (Whiteley and Seyd, 2002), the atomisation and individualisation of the membership has probably exacerbated it. What maintained the strength of parties was their ability to mobilise "expressively driven" members. Treated as consumers or stakeholders, party members increasingly display less loyalty to their organisation. Not only is their membership more likely to lapse, they are also less likely to be active. Moreover, if supporters (rather than members) are consulted on policies, what is the incentive to become a member? Parties are unlikely to find enough selective incentives to distribute in order to maintain the large membership that is both an indicator of popularity and a resource of voluntary work at election time. What is missing in this shift is the "transcendent" dimension (the expressivist identification with the collective) that was worth mobilising for, despite the costs. Such "deep" group identification and engagement becomes severely compromised once one individualises the political process. This would seem to suggest an even greater need for rituals and other mechanisms for constructing and consolidating a sense of collective identity.

10
Fringe Benefits: Dissent vs Commercialisation

Overall, admits Larry Whitty, "conference has always been rather boring and powerless, so most people would come for the fringe" and avoid the hall, except for a couple of important debates. Indeed, self-described "conference junkies" often consider plenary sessions as somewhat peripheral. What matters is socialising, networking and exchanging ideas and all of this happens on the margins of the main hall. The party conference fringe has a long history but it has undergone a deep transformation in the last 20 years of the 20th century. In a development not dissimilar to the famous Edinburgh Festival, the "fringe" has grown exponentially. It attracts performers who use the opportunity of a large and international event to gain attention.

In the 1950s, the Conservatives only held a few political meetings and most fringe meetings were social events. Labour and the Liberals demonstrated their political and intellectual edge through political meetings mostly organised by insider groups ranging from trade unions to ideological groups. Sessions were advertised in leaflets directly handed to participants. Moreover, these groups often had a stall where they offered literature and information on their year-round activities. In order to limit the amount of leafleting and allow representatives to get an overview of the growing range of meetings on offer, the Liberals printed their first conference gazette in 1969.

In the 1980s, the fringe took off as a key dimension of the main conferences. As debates in the main hall were becoming more controlled, controversies and discussions of novel ideas moved to the fringe whilst, at the same time, this new semi-public arena was opened to the actors – public, private and voluntary – involved in various levels of governance. Conferences have *de facto* adapted to the transformation of the Westminster model whereby "policy-making has been transformed from being a state centred and state driven activity to become a complex mix of hierarchies, networks and markets" (Richards and Smith, 2004). Not-for-profit organisations as well as businesses sought to intervene in forums where they could gain access to policy-makers and decision-makers at the national but also sub-national levels. Personal contacts developed on the conference fringe are useful investments for interest groups who, thanks to the resources gathered on the fringe, can influence policy elaboration at the very early stages.[1] Networking thrives in the informal atmosphere of the fringe and a great deal of "conference work" is conducted in corridors, bars and restaurants.[2] The social fringe includes a diversity of events ranging from the Young Conservatives' Ball to fund-raising dinners, Labour's Scottish Night rallies or the Liberal Democrats' Glee Club. The party spirit that predominates is now sometimes tempered because work imperatives prevent some participants from fully relaxing.[3]

Roger, a Welsh councillor, remembers that there was a single stall at the 1954 Liberal conference in Buxton. This was dedicated to fund raising. The Labour party has a long tradition of fringe exhibition as affiliates and insider groups such as trade unions, women's movements or local government's associations took the opportunity to advertise themselves to delegates. The exhibition, however, began to change in the 1980s when the Conservatives developed it commercially in response to businesses' seeking to access government.[4] In 1983, whilst the Tories were experimenting in this direction, the Labour General Secretary categorically refused to accept fee-paying stalls despite lobbyists' insistence that business could substantially help party finances.[5] "Labour clung to a 'politically correct' approach to relationships with business" (Harris and Lock, 2002: 138) until the 1990s but under Tony Blair's leadership, the party on the contrary has endeavoured to demonstrate its positive attitude to business. Labour is no longer ashamed of receiving substantial funds from big business nor seems concerned that such close relationships may contribute to the cynical views that an increasing number of British citizens hold about the honesty and integrity of parties and politicians. This accelerated the commercial expansion of the parliamentary parties' conference fringe.

"Conference matters," argues Lord Norton of Louth, because of the buzz of the fringe meetings that provide a space for public discussion of all sorts of issues.[6] From "Help the Aged" panels to discussions about the future of the railways or fisheries, the fringe offers food and food for thought. Activists attend because "there are exciting debates" and "there is always something of interest": one can discuss the worrying side-effects of aspartame (Greens), learn how to draft a will in favour of the (Conservative) party, consider new legislation granting 16-year olds the right to buy pornographic magazines (Liberal Democrats) or reflect on the "Death of spin: the importance of being honest" (Labour).

Room for dissent

The sub-partisan dimension of British political life is often overlooked in an approach of politics that rests on an anachronistic Westminster model of party competition, which assumes the permanence of a post war "quiescence" (Webb, 2000: 167). British parties are broad churches and they have maintained significant internal debate. Indeed, in a polity where the electoral system strongly limits the formation of autonomous parties, one can expect the coexistence of ideological factions within each party. Despite the tendency to perceive parties as monolithic – a trend reinforced by the assumption that factions are necessarily damaging to the party's electoral fortune, political parties can more accurately be described as coalitions.[7] From the Labour Housing group to the Green Party Animal Rights working group or the Conservative Friends of Israel, all parties foster insider groups, with varying degrees of ideological cohesion[8] and activity, legitimacy and official support.[9]

Whilst in France, factions play a central and constitutive role in most political parties,[10] internal factions have no such recognition in British parties. In Labour, a 1946 constitutional amendment seriously limited organised factionalism (Seyd, 1987: 7). Moreover, until 1970s, fear of "splitters" meant that ideological factionalism was largely confined to the parliamentary party. Factions started to proliferate in the 1960s, driven by the Left.[11] Their organisation remained loose and they were weakened by the urge to unite behind a leader in the 1990s. Nevertheless, they are very active on the fringe: *Tribune* organises every year a rally with prominent speakers, other groups hold more discreet meetings on contentious issues such as the war in Iraq or opposition to the Euro. In the Conservative party, these groups are usually dominated by MPs, even when they involve the wider membership.[12] They range across the political spectrum from the traditionally "progressive" Bow Group to more right wing groups such as the Monday Club or the No Turning Back group. The Charter Movement, created by activists in 1981, has been campaigning for more formal democracy within the party with little support from the elected politicians. It has however been active at conferences, organising critical, if little noticed, fringe meetings. In both parties, Europe has become a major bone of contention and therefore a hot topic for fringe meetings (Gamble, 2003).

In both the Liberal Democrats and the Green Party, groups have benefited from a recognition of their role in structuring internal debate. The SDP regulated its unofficial groups to an extent that impaired the development of healthy internal pluralism (McKee, 1994: 1004) but the Liberal Democrats have adopted a much less restrictive approach. Associated organisations and "specified associated organisations" benefit from an official status that grants them consultation rights in the policy process and, for the latter, an important role in the party machine. Moreover, unofficial organisations have sprung. Single-issue groups benefit from the tacit support of the party establishment but more ideological groups remain marginal. Whilst some maintain a sporadic existence thanks to the conference, others have a national membership, with regular meetings and publications. Nevertheless, only a small proportion of Liberal Democrats are members of such associations because there is a prevalent antipathy towards divisive "politicking" (McKee, 1994: 1020). In the Green Party, the apex of factional activity was in the 1990s when two factions – *Green 2000* and its opposing number *The Way Ahead* co-ordinated slates of candidates to internal elections. Since the defeat of the former and their departure from the party in 1993, internal group activities have focused on recognised working groups who play an active part in policy-making and receive a small budget to run their activities. These groups usually hold fringe meetings at conference and use the occasion to gain new subscribers to their newsletters.

Parties exert little control on the fringe: they co-ordinate room bookings in the main hotel and publish listings[13] but there is a manifest contrast between mainstream events (organised within the secured perimeter) and those that can only be reached after a long walk to a small venue. Marginal groups try to gain legitimacy and audience by inviting senior politicians as respectable "patrons". In the Liberal Democrats, the left leaning Chard group rarely succeeds in finding a parliamentarian or member of the party elite to address its fringe but, unlike many other groups that benefit from official recognition and status, it has preserved its independence. The fringe has traditionally been dominated by insider groups[14] who take the opportunity to promote their views and raise funds.[15] The existence of a space for the expression of divergent points of view that are not endorsed through a discussion in the main hall has established the reputation of the fringe. This is where "ideas that are a bit too embarrassing to be expressed and discussed publicly can be voiced," concedes a Tory. A Green concurs: "there is horrendous stuff sometimes".

Whilst debates in the main hall are constrained by the presence of journalists, the fringe has been a refuge for open political discussions. The evolution has been striking in the case of the Labour party, largely because there has been a conscious effort from the mid-1980s to avoid bitter arguments on the main stage. The fringe thus has been a way to let off steam or air ideas. In the run-up to the 1997 general election, the fringe demonstrated a particular eagerness to discuss issues (such as rail re-nationalisation) that have since disappeared from the agenda. After years in power, delegates comment that they "quickly found the fringe meetings to be the most satisfying aspect of conference where the grass-roots of the Labour party could have their voices heard and their concerns addressed by MPs and Ministers of all Departments".[16] However, because of the nature of the events, there is often more "preaching to the converted" than real debate. There is little mixing: Left fringe meetings do not attract supporters of New Labour. The diversity of the fringe contributes to socialising the grassroots to subtle cleavages within their own organisation.

Conservative Conference 1996, Bournemouth

As Major's policy on European integration provoked the wrath of the radical wing of his party, fringe meetings such as *Save British Fish* gather a large crowd of vocal anti-Europeans. Excited perhaps by the prospect of a free fish supper, they cheer every anti-EU statements, hiss at the mention of Spanish fishermen and boo the "meek" initiatives of the government.

Labour Conference 1997, Bournemouth

The fringe meeting organised by *Save British Fish* is a quiet event chaired by a man with a monocle. The audience listens with great attention to the orator who condemns famine in Africa and makes no mention of the evil European bureaucrats.

Conservative Conference 1998, Bournemouth

The organisers of the fringe on the creation of an English Parliament as a response to devolution have rightly anticipated a large audience.

(Continued)

Representatives and visitors are sitting on the floor and standing at the back. The issue, brought up in many other venues thanks to the diligent questions of a few highly motivated activists, is a general leitmotiv of the conference.

Labour Conference 2002, Blackpool

Whilst the official Labour position on the Euro is supported and discussed in several mainstream fringes hosted by the European Commission, MEPs, Minister for Europe, there are only a few anti-Euro fringes on offer. They were attended by a small group of dedicated activists and MPs.

Conferences are the best chance for minorities to get publicity and they take every opportunity to raise their profile, and therefore their weight within the party through outside visibility. However, "whereas the journalistic orientation towards speeches and debates in the main hall tends to be sacerdotal, their orientation towards the fringe is pragmatic with time and space allocated to it based on a 'strict consideration of news values'" (Stanyer and Scammel, 1996: 17). TV cameras have become part of the *décor* at some of the fringes but they only turn up when a session is likely to be newsworthy. In this context, it is only those events with an edge – dissent, oddity, contentious personalities – or those organised by the media themselves such as BBC Question Time or the *Guardian* Debate that get reported. Because the Greens are themselves on the political fringe, they generally suffer from a lack of coverage for their conference. In 1995, a fringe meeting on "politically correct hugging" that fitted the stereotype of a "weird" party got them to the front pages of the *Independent on Sunday*, the *Times*, the *Telegraph* for the first time in years.[17]

The growth of the political fringe was favoured by the little attention paid to it by the media, so their increased interest in them since the 1990s has contributed to extending image management beyond the hall.[18] If there is more dissent on the fringe, it is carefully circumscribed and largely neutralised. As the fringe is covered as a means to access non-official viewpoints within the organisation, there is the temptation to manage it as well or at least to limit the potential damage. New Labour promotes self-restraint (see Chapter 7). The press converged upon a 1998 Labour conference fringe on social security addressed by the former Minister Frank Field. It was hoped that, after his bitter resignation a few months before, there would be "a bit of sport". The meeting attracted more journalists and delegates than expected but the discussion was both bland and polite. "Ministers who speak at fringe meetings are doing so with knowledge of Downing Street, probably on the order of Downing Street and therefore are only going to be saying what they would say in London", explains Shaun Woodward, a former Conservative Communication Director and MP who joined Labour in 1999. Since 1995 at least Labour politicians and officials tend to preface their fringe speeches with a reference to the presence of the media: "Well of course, we have to watch out for what we say as the media are always trying to whip up some rumour about conflict." Such *mises en garde* have eventually had the effect of taming the fringe. Conference managers also try to divert attention away from potentially damaging meetings by staging an official party event that is likely to attract cameras simultaneously.[19] Another strategy consists in ostensibly denying dissenters any news-worthiness by portraying them as the "usual suspects". Pressure and even bullying can also convince potential trouble-makers to adopt a lower profile.

Activists have an ambivalent relationship to journalists. Many spontaneously express frustration at the picture presented by the media of their party and their conference. They criticise the eagerness of the media to seek out dissenting voices and to present these as evidence of irredeemable division. However, they obtain most of their political information from the same media[20] and are excited to see celebrities or gain their 2 minutes of fame thanks to a rank-and-file interview. The fringe meetings organised by the media are also amongst the best attended.[21]

Radio 4's Fringe Meeting at the 1996 Conservative Conference

"I am not responsible for such a crowd," pleads Steven Norris to a packed audience, "I've just come from a fringe that was absolutely deserted!" Not only was the room packed but the audience was also riotous, whipped up by weeks of media hype about royal scandals and accusations of sleaze. Activists often use the opportunity to complain about the media's political bias, lack of morality, unhealthy interest in division or unpatriotic attitudes. "The media are a danger for democracy," groans the woman sitting next to me, "they condition the public to react in certain ways". "They damage national morality," claims another. "We should privatise the BBC," shouts a man with outrage.

If the BBC is an "institution to boo and hiss" in order "to get the audience properly warmed up" before the Conservative leader's speech (Morris, 1991: 125), the media are generally viewed with a great deal of suspicion in all parties, usually on the grounds of lack of coverage or bias. Frictions for instance surfaced in the run up to the 1997 General election as Liberal Democrat activists criticised the obsession of the press with the party's position on the political spectrum and discussed the "pact" with New Labour. True, most of the media fringe meetings were devoted to the ambiguities of liberal democratic identity, an issue not only irrelevant from the viewpoint of activists but also deeply irritating!

A forum for policy networks

A variety of outsider groups ranging from not-for-profit organisations to think tanks, the media and, increasingly, commercial interests now take part in the fringe. Cause groups take the opportunity to launch reports or campaigns, trying to set the political agenda and to attract support from decision-makers. They provide fringe topics, orators and infrastructure, whether they rely on the help of insider organisations or organise meetings on their own. Often, potential organisers combine strength to maximise the success of the gathering. The range of topics discussed has broadened in all parties between 1986 and 1995 from 44 to 58 in Labour and from 36 to 48 in Tories (Stanyer and Scammel, 1996). Whilst three time slots were necessary to cover what was on offer a few years ago, fringe sessions now succeed each other. Many overlap and some even take place during plenary debates. Official fringe listings are thicker than ever, complemented by persistent leafleting at the gates.

	1994	1995	1996	1997	1998	2000	2001	2002	2003
Labour	112	273	285	279	311	273	**	374	383
Conservative	114	173	175	122	*	137	**	157	174
Liberal Democrats	85	198	241	136	*	*	284	335	249
Greens	39	*	*	*	49	53	60	40	66

* Figures not available
** Conferences were shortened in the aftermath of the terrorist attacks on September 11 and many fringes were cancelled.

Figure 10.1 Number of fringe meetings listed in the Conference magazines.

The topics discussed on the fringe vary according to each party's style. Whilst Labour, the Liberal Democrats and the Greens are policy-oriented, the Conservatives tend to emphasise socialising and rallying the troops. The fringe caters for all tastes within a given party: in Labour, readers of the *Guardian* (35 per cent) and of the *Daily Mirror/ Record* (29 per cent) are looking for different types of entertainment: some go from Radio 4 panels to Institute for Public Policy Research (IPPR) policy discussions. On the other hand, the political fringe of Conservative conference was institutionalised relatively late and only "intellectualised" thanks to the creation of think tanks under the influence of Margaret Thatcher (Morris, 1991). Think tanks, which to an extent are the equivalent of outsourcing policy-making, tend to push up the quality of debate. They are extremely active on the fringe as conferences are crucial for publicising their work.[22] They offer a broad panel of topics as well as expert speakers. In 2002 for instance, the IPPR was present at all three conferences but above all in Blackpool (Labour). They booked a hotel where they organised nineteen fringes: "we've got our whole institute up here – 50 people or so. We left the receptionist in London but that's about it."

There has been very little research on conference fringes, despite its acknowledged importance. One exception is Phil Harris and Andrew Lock's work on the evolution of corporate and pressure group representations that covers the three main parties between 1994 and 1997 (Harris and Lock, 2002). They consider five types of actors (internal organisations, public institutions, unions and professional associations, private companies and not-for-profit organisations) and demonstrate that the growth of the fringe has been linked to private businesses and cause groups.[23] Labour overtook the Conservatives in terms of the number of private businesses using their conference's commercial side when they reached government. Moreover, the interest from not-for-profit-organisations increases as general elections approach as they endeavour to influence the political agenda. This evolution needs to be placed in the context of the transformation of relationships between business and government since the 1970s. As Thatcher's government withdrew from direct ownership and became primarily a regulator, lobbying appeared as the best way to influence political decisions. Thus, "the increasing use of lobbying by major corporations and organisations [was] a means to maintain or gain competitive advantage against increased government regulatory activity" (Harris, 2002a: 239).

The marketisation of British politics was continued by a New Labour government[24] that adhered to the belief in the superior efficacy of market mechanisms. New forms of democratic practice, based on self-government through networks, partnerships and associations in civil society resonate with New Labour's normative discourse of inclusion and democratic renewal.[25] Thus, governance as a narrative of change cohered with an enthusiasm for inclusive networks, and consultation of stakeholders (Newman, 2001). It also reflects a more general transformation of the political arena towards a multi-level led governance in which the state has been somewhat "hollowed out" (Rhodes, 1994). The policy process has become more complex and decentralised through policy networks involving a variety of competing actors such as interest groups, local and national governments and their "semi-detached" agencies.[26]

Conferences are an opportunity for political parties to demonstrate how open they are to wider forces in civil society. However, the evolution in Britain has gone much further. The exhibition has turned annual conferences (this predominantly affects the party in government) into beehives of commercial and business activity. The Labour conference has become so large that lobbying firms produce alternative conference fringe guides (as well as reports) for the benefit of their customers. Moreover, a new perception of politics now prevails. Policy communities are the nexus for policy developments. They extend much beyond political parties but conferences are a forum where they meet. Indeed, think tanks, quangos, local government, business and "other stakeholders" are present at such events. In the 1990s, the "orthodox view was that one had to be present," comments a charity official. Indeed, many of those I spoke to on the fringe were convinced that it was as important to be seen as it was to network. The Falkland Islands Government have had a stall since the mid-1980s and find it "extremely useful to promote their cause". "It is very much worth it", concurs a representative from a children's charity. A representative of the Confederation of British Industry explains that they

> have two press officers and a parliamentary officer here for three days, and the director general for a couple of days. We are not exhibiting, but we have tried for the last few years to do fringe events at party conferences. A lot of our member companies attend party conferences, so it's good for them to see that we're lobbying at the heart of politics. It's about being there because everyone else is.

Lobbying firms send large teams to conferences because they represent several customers at the same time. The objective is to "meet a number of key people in a short period of time" and "promote their clients' goals".[27]

Liberal Democrats Conference 2002, Brighton

Cross Rail sends two teams to each of the three conferences. They share the work and constantly man the stall. They are subsidised by the government and attend to explain and promote the cross London underground rail project.[28] The MP responsible for transport has just left, having agreed on a meeting to present Crossrail to the parliamentary group. Conferences are extremely valuable for a big group like them, explains the team manager: fringes have little interest but a stall means that they can make contact with a large number of people who drop by during the week.

A stall at a highly attended conference is a good promotional strategy that is usefully complemented with topical and well hosted fringe meetings. The British Banking Association promotes its participation to its members:

> Ahead of the Financial Services Authority national strategy White Paper in October, a wide ranging discussion of the options for raising the levels of financial education will be discussed at the BBA fringe event at the Labour Party conference. The BBA panel, including financial secretary Ruth Kelly, will comprise industry, government and consumer stakeholders who will address some of the fundamental issues.[29]

The conference certainly provides good advertisement opportunities for organisations such as BAA as well as a chance to talk directly with members of the government. How useful is it, however, for defending the interests of "consumer stakeholders" if they cannot host a similar event on their own terms?

	1995	1996	1997	1998	2000	2002
Labour	118	123	148	145	188	190
Conservative	86	94	70	58	78	59
Liberal Democrats	91	79	68	*	*	84

* Figures not available

Figure 10.2   Conference stalls and exhibitors.

Commercial participants are attracted by different aspects of conference: whilst some aim at raising their profile with the government, others, such as the Royal Society for the Protection of Birds (RSPB) also relish the opportunity of mixing with local councillors who oversee planning. In this case, whilst both Labour and Liberal Democrat conferences are extremely useful, participation in the Conservative conference is motivated by the need to preserve the Society's non-partisan image.[30] Exhibitors' and lobbyists' interests also vary according to the electoral cycle and proximity of power.[31] Pre-electoral conferences are the most attractive to outside organisations who wish to make contact with future MPs. Even the Liberal Democrats reported a dramatic rise in their income from commercial exhibition in 1996. Being in power, or being about to gain power inevitably raises the stakes for potential fringe participants. Inversely, since 1997, the Conservatives have attracted fewer commercial exhibitors. Luckily internal groups partially fill the gaps.[32]

Competition on the fringe since the mid-1990s has contributed to a new form of arms race: from the quality of material available on stalls, to the slick designs and professional staff. These have become necessities for those aspiring to have an effective participation at conference. The growing number of events on offer makes it increasingly difficult to attract an audience. When they can afford it, sandwiches and drinks make a difference.[33] Organisers also count on crowd pullers to be successful. A number of popular politicians in each party are thus invited to address many fringes in the hope that their presence will boost their image. Ministers and Shadow ministers are, of course, targets for fringe organisers and some are extremely popular: Patricia Hewitt was booked at 13 different meetings in 2003. But there are other conference darlings. Respected outside speakers, from Will Hutton to Jonathon Porritt also bring legitimacy and *gravitas* to fringe meetings. Being invited by a renowned organisation bestows importance to its speakers: rising stars and "exiled" personalities cherish the chance of such platforms. Ann Widdecombe has left the Conservative Frontbench but she is invited to address a dozen meetings every year.

The exponential development of the fringe in the 1990s reflects its new role as a primary forum where policy communities can interact and negotiate.[34] The optimistic idea that all are thus provided with equal access to decision-makers overlooks the consequences of unequal distribution of resources, which prevents market mechanisms from operating transparently. Although all interest groups can participate in the fringe,[35] resources dramatically affect visibility and effectiveness.

Whether they are private companies or not-for-profit, the biggest organisations need to be proactive if they want to maintain their dominant position. This is particularly important as the success of the conference exhibition breeds its own drawbacks: events at the overcrowded Labour conference are often poorly attended[36] by over-stretched delegates who hardly stop in the exhibition. Disparity of resources thus affects success on the fringe. In order to put on a convincing show, a great deal of effort and resources must be invested in the conference season. As business consultants, Harris and Lock thus advise would-be participants to prepare carefully a "campaign" combining "fringe meetings, receptions, adverts and an exhibition stand supported by informal briefings, lobbying and dinner to get over the required message" (2002: 148).

"Those of us who went to the conference felt it was well worth having done it, just this once. It really has raised the profile of Press For Change – and the issues we are standing for – within the Labour Party at the right moment in time" commented a participant at the 1997 conference. Although most exhibitors consider participation useful, changes over the years indicate that the situation is closely monitored. "Competition for attention has become too high," complained both World Wildlife Fund (WWF) and AIDES Fed representatives in 2002. The effectiveness of the strategies are disputed. Realising that they were inherently disadvantaged, a number of not-for-profit organisations have adapted their strategy. Some look for commercial sponsors for their fringe meetings. Others, like the RSPB have cut down their expenses. In 1998, the organisation, whose membership outnumbers by far all British parties taken together, decided not to keep a stall. Instead, they focus their resources on invitation-only receptions with decision-makers and key actors in the sector that concerns them. All of their staff can then ensure that the society's message is heard and that the right issues are pushed on the agenda.

Parties choose whose presence they condone and political choices guide the selection of exhibitors but it looks increasingly as if commercial objectives override their political or ethical positions. Organisers sometimes mischievously locate the stall of arch opponents in the proximity of each other but cohabitation is always peaceful. At the 2003 Labour conference the private mail firm DHL's stand was directly opposite that of the Communication Workers' Union.[37] The Conservatives approached the controversial issue of AIDS and gay rights carefully: in the late 1990s, the problem was circumvented by allowing charities to advertise on health grounds but not on age of consent. The presence of exhibitors proudly listed in conference magazines sends a message about the way parties perceive their relationships with business. The most striking evolution is of course Labour and its enthusiasm for the market, but all the three main parties are affected. "Every year BNFL tries to get in and have a stall but each time we have a discussion and we refuse", claims a Liberal Democrat, momentarily oblivious to the fact that British Nuclear Fuel (BNFL) has been exhibiting for years on the Liberal Democrat fringe, like other controversial groups such as Nestlé. "Whilst we have a policy to boycott Nestlé, they don't have a policy to boycott us!" explains matter-of-factly another Liberal Democrat. Money is odourless indeed but can parties be sure that opening their doors to groups they would otherwise boycott does not contribute to a legitimation of practices and values they condemn? Can parties be assured that activists wandering in the exhibition looking for free pens will respond critically to the justification of activities that these companies will inevitably give rather than assume that issues must have been resolved?

Open for business

State funding was first introduced in Germany in 1959 and is now current practice throughout the European Union. In many countries, the objective was to reduce the dependency of political parties on corporate money. In France, legislation was introduced in the late 1980s after a string of political scandals. Today, French political parties are careful to keep their distance from corporate interests and congresses are no longer "fun fairs".[38] Unlike their European counterparts, British parties cannot count on public funding and are chronically under-funded.[39] They have thus traditionally relied on both individual members and institutional funding.

Members provide an important share of party funds. Smaller parties most dramatically need their members to fund their activities. Seventy per cent of the Liberal Democrats federal party's income can be traced to the membership (Webb, 2000: 237). Ninety-nine per cent of Green Party funds come from individual donations, most of them from members. Big parties cannot overlook members' contributions either. In 1997, Labour drew 40 per cent of its funding from members through monthly subscriptions and regular small donations. Moreover, the Neill Commission report showed that 30 per cent of the party's funds came from the unions, 20 per cent from large donors and 10 per cent from its commercial activities (Neill, 1998: 32). Conferences provide opportunities to tap the generosity of activists. The Conservatives have a prominent stall where members can find advice on how to write a will for the benefit of the party. They also have a plenary session devoted to fund raising. As with the Liberal Democrats, this session used to be organised just before the leader's speech because "this is the one event that the party treasurer can rely on for everyone to be present!" The "Rally" usually involves a senior politician acting like a *batteleur de foire* to whip up excitement and encourage donations. These sessions are nowadays organised at a time when they do not coincide with live television coverage because they project the unflattering image of organisations desperate for money. The Liberal Democrats raised about £24,000 in the 1996 conference appeal alone!

1995 Liberal Democrats Conference, Glasgow

At the end of the awards ceremony, in the growing excitement of a funfair, stewards shake buckets of coins, making an incredible racket whilst the chair shouts: "who is giving £500?, who is giving £250?". Some representatives fill in the special credit card debit forms that have been placed on all seats before the beginning of the session, but most drop coins, notes, cheques and bankcard details in the buckets.

1996 Conservatives Conference, Bournemouth

After the jazz band has gone, the awards ceremony places particular emphasis this year on Conservative Associations whose contributions to central funds have been important or whose campaign organisational skills stand out. Finally, Lord Parkinson leads the financial appeal with a rousing speech attacking the Opposition, praising the Government and gloating about the wonderful week in Bournemouth. "Fill up the buckets", he shouts. Around me, activists search their wallets, purses and pockets and throw coins and notes in as if there is no tomorrow. Many of them wear a badge with flashing red eyes from the "New Labour New Danger" campaign. Sir Cecil and his wife circulate their own bucket, which they then show to the audience. The atmosphere has heated up and, as the buckets are passed up and down the last rows of seats, the Chair calls one after the other those who will sit on the platform for the Leader's speech. All Ministers are greeted with loud clapping and shouts but Portillo's entrance also triggers a frenzied stamping of feet.

In the 1960s, trade unions provided the bulk of Labour funds[40] whilst the Conservatives received up to two thirds of their income from businesses (Webb, 2000: 236). Declining resources from institutions led to the hiring of professional fundraisers. Clubs of big donors were created and new techniques were developed. Dinners, receptions and balls[41] are an established feature of conference but their numbers have increased. Politicians are celebrities whose presence is inherently attractive[42] but they are also good contacts for anyone with a personal ambition or a political agenda. They have become commodities that parties can put forward as guests at fundraising events. Other sources of funding needed to be found. The commercial exhibition took off in the 1990s[43] thanks to new lobbying practices and the opening up of policy networks. Legislation on party funding made the organisation of "commercial events" profitable and a convenient way to attract business support without the strings of strict donation control. Indeed, successive parliamentary committees on standards in public life (Nolan in 1995, Neill in 1998) led to new constraints on donations from individuals and companies. Since 2000, the legislation requires parties to publish quarterly statements of donations above £5,000.[44] Commercial activities do not fall in to the category of donations and therefore escape the legal obligation to declare. In the last ten years, parliamentary parties have diversified and intensified this unexpected dimension of their activities.

Running the conference is itself very expensive, ranging from £150,000 (1999 Liberal Democrats) to about £2 million for the average Tory conference. The costs are transferred to participants who are all charged a fee.[45] There are "no free facilities". Everything is charged, from stall space to security passes. Prices are high and rising. Labour for instance charged £700 to charities in 1996 and £8,000 to commercial exhibitors.[46] In 2000, the Conservatives charged over £7,650 for a commercial stand of 3 meters by 3 meters. It was £8,500 two years later at the Liberal Democrat conference in Brighton. Despite such fees, there is no shortage of candidates: in 1997, stall space was "sold out within three hours of going on sale" (Harris and Lock, 2002: 144). In 2000, there were 190 stalls at the Labour conference and a "bridge" had to be purposely built to connect the exhibition area in the neighbouring hotel to the conference centre. Turned down applicants, such as Liverpool City Council, attended the Liberal Democrat and the Conservative conferences but bemoaned Labour's "two year waiting list". 1996 was the best year for the Conservatives, who since then, usually break even rather than make a profit. Commercial income for the Labour party remained well under a million pounds a year until 1997 (Neill, 1998: 30). In 1996, Labour earned £513,000[47] in commercial activities and £6.2 million in 2002.[48] The Liberal Democrats made over £315,000 at the 1995 Glasgow conference and £465,905 in 1999.

Sponsorship was tested in the late 1990s and expanded rapidly. Business firms are now routinely invited to sponsor everything from private dinners to flower arrangements, the Internet café, *crèche* facilities or stewards' T-shirts. Advertising space is sold in conference newsletters, halls and corridors. Since 2002, Liberal Democrats distribute glossy booklets explaining the importance of the two national conferences, underlying how they represent major policy-making sessions as well as the best place to communicate a message to thousands of party members and workers and the wider policy community. Every advertising opportunity is carefully listed in glossy booklets widely distributed. Labour charges £10,000 to sponsor Question and Answer sessions with senior politicians. Lanyards for carrying conference passes were discreet metallic chains[49] but they now carry advertisements. Many conference participants, in all three parties are unhappy to be treated as walking adverts and refuse to wear them. Others, however, praise the innovative ways that their party has found to raise money. In 1997, lanyards promoted a new online company dedicated to politics.[50] The following year, Labour approached Somerfield for this purpose. The supermarket chain also held a stall in a busy corridor leading to the main hall. They offered passers-by fruit juices and sweets. Attending her first conference ever, the public relations official of the company was, by mid conference both exhausted and sceptical about the effectiveness of this strategy. The company would reassess the strategy after the Conservative conference the following week. McDonald's is a regular sponsor of such party events. For several successive years, they hosted the Liberal Democrats' commercial exhibitors' reception. Party members do not all welcome these evolutions and the resistance is most strongest in Labour. In 2001, delegates discovered that the fast food chain was also sponsoring their party's events. The Chair's reception, with more than 400 guests in the Hilton Metropole's Balmoral suite was charged £15,000, and a fringe on education attended by the education minister £10,000.[51] Labour expected to make more than £2 million profit from conference alone[52] by 2004. The exhibition has become so important that in 2004, Labour changed the entrance in an attempt to force delegates to walk through the exhibition to reach the main hall.[53]

The three main parties take extremely seriously the well-being and satisfaction of their business partners. In 1995–96, several commercial exhibitors complained about the way they were being treated by Labour. Nowadays, organisations and their staff are pampered and invited to private functions.[54] Hospitality thus works both ways: exhibitors are invited to parties whilst their companies sponsor events and facilities.[55] MPs, activists and celebrities (including leaders' wives) comply with a duty to tour the stalls and photo opportunities are set up. The financial impact of conference is such that financial parties cannot afford to take these commercial exchanges for granted and in 2001 the main parties resisted cancelling conference despite the international crisis of 9–11 and the temptation to do so to avoid what had been anticipated to be potentially difficult meetings for both leaderships.

Between pluralism and influence

The development of the commercial side of conference also points to the emergence of a new place to lobby politicians. Good working relationships are established and nurtured. "When MPs have helped us, we owe them a favour", explains one, "so we provide technical support and arguments on issues in their constituencies". Lobbying relies on networks of contacts established over the years and provides considerable resources not only for party members and politicians but also for the nebula of political workers gravitating towards them. Some lobbyists are card carrying party members and political parties benefit financially from the personal support provided by such individuals, and to an extent, by their firms when they take "unpaid leave" during electoral campaigns. Firms benefit from access, and parties gain both funding and "expertise". The career of a number of individuals sheds light on the intricate relationships between corporations and political parties. As Communications Director of the Labour party between 1991 and 1999, David Hill has been close to Tony Blair (Harris, 2002b: 96–97). He became managing director of Good Relations Ltd, a lobbying firm representing Monsanto[56] but was granted a leave of absence to work for Labour during the 2001 general election campaign. He replaced Alastair Campbell at 10 Downing Street in 2003. Moreover, effective lobbying thrives on mutual trust developed through social exchange and interpersonal knowledge.[57] It is based on the provision of reliable information to isolated and hard-pressed politicians, which can then be used for policy development.

Conferences provide cause groups as well as businesses opportunities to meet lots of people in a few days and to promote their image and sell their message. They combine the appearance of transparency with the opacity of informal, personal interactions. Sponsors also gain discreet access. There is only a limited proportion of overt political lobbying going on at conference, most of what happens is difficult to monitor. Private meetings and receptions between politicians and representatives from outside interests are virtually impossible to track in the conference fair. However, the buoyancy of the fringe demonstrates that participants believe that their message reaches public decision-makers.

> The chief executives and chairmen of large corporations relied on their own direct, carefully cultivated personal relationships with senior civil servants and ministers (even the Prime Minister); their interest lay in being at the formative stage of policy-making, before governments had taken public positions from which it could be electorally hard to retreat (Leys, 2001: 56).

This remains un-chartered territory that urgently needs to be explored by political scientists rather than by marketing and business strategy advisers who condone unquestionably the legitimacy and desirability of such practices.

The "risk of cosiness and closed conversation" is privately acknowledged by party officials but publicly denied or dismissed. The promotion of particular interests on the political agenda is now accepted practice. It should come as no surprise that groups campaigning to obtain franchises and public contracts actively lobby decision-makers. Camelot, for instance, turned up at party conferences to help secure the renewal of its license for the national lottery. Few in the Conservative party have qualms about such practices, if only because of the long tradition of business funding for the party, but unease is perceptible on the left, though generally voiced by outsiders or grassroots activists. Friends of the Earth now publishes a review of the government party's commercial fringe:

> These companies are pouring millions of pounds into Labour's emptying coffers. They aren't doing this out of some sense of political altruism. They are trying to buy access and influence. They will use it to try to block any moves to strengthen the law to hold them to account for their activities.[58]

After a few years of almost blissful development, attitudes to the growing interdependence of business and party politics are changing.

Interestingly though, questions about such practices have come from the business world more than from the parliamentary parties. Companies have become more cautious about their sponsorship, worried that their shareholders might complain if they were seen to be contributing to political parties. It is as if politics might corrupt business! To prevent such a fate, political neutrality is allegedly preserved because sponsors equally fund the three big conferences. British Telecom thus explains that they have become selective in the fringe meetings they are sponsoring, keeping clear of political think-thanks in favour of private receptions. Although cause groups are often closer to a particular party, they are also keen to retain an aura of impartiality. Therefore, similar meetings are generally held at the two, or three, main conferences and they feel obliged to be present in some fashion at the three conferences.

A new language of environmentalism, "inclusivity" and business ethics now characterises much of what is on offer (Sklair, 2001). Business sponsors are eager to demonstrate their consideration for the community and New Labour is not the only one spinning a favourable image. The conference organisers are keen to stress that they will make every possible effort to ensure that exhibitors and sponsors get the chance to communicate their message in the best possible light. A politically correct "newspeak" is also spreading. Taking part in conference gives businesses an opportunity to "talk about [their] community-based activities".[59] Who nowadays is prepared to admit that they are defending the interests of polluters or greenhouse gas producers? Exhibitors and sponsors also pay for the insert in the listings of events and stalls and have every opportunity to put their spin on their image.

Labour conference 2003 Exhibition listing insert:

BNFL is changing. Legislation scheduled for this Parliament will create the Nuclear Decommissioning Authority returning responsibility for many nuclear assets and liabilities to the government. To find out more about BNFL's role in the decommissioning and clean up of Britain's nuclear legacy, and its future plans, visit our stall.[60]

By sponsoring fringe events discussing issues related to improving the environment, social issues and human health, corporate sponsors present themselves as ethically and socially responsible and environmentally aware. In 1998, Microsoft sponsored the National Society for the Prevention of Cruelty to Children's promotional material, stall and reception whilst supermarkets supported meetings on sustainable development. In 2002, Shell sponsored a Social Market Foundation fringe meeting on "Doing business or doing good? Is corporate social responsibility the best way to do both?" at the Liberal Democrat conference. A naïve or – if read less sympathetically – cynical approach to inclusivity and political consensus allows large corporations to be seen as supporting good causes and charitable organisations, thereby improving their image and fuelling the myth that big business can act as good Samaritans and disinterested responsible actors invested in the community. New Labour has actively promoted this vision of the business world and of society as a whole.

Conclusion

In the early years of the 21st century, the fringe is often presented as the most exciting development at party conferences. As the centre stage has become stage-managed for the benefit of television cameras, political discussions have moved to other venues. The fringe has always been the place where marginal interests or political minorities could express themselves and mobilise support. This role has been confirmed as the number of political meetings has increased dramatically even though it has not been completely immune to public relations considerations. Communications experts, who exert a growing influence on party campaigning strategies, are concerned that the publicity given to internal debates creates the image of a divided party and a weak leadership. The fringe thus has not failed to become the focus of debate and dissent: it has been transformed into another forum for discussions, lobbying and public relations activities.

Thus, the expansion of the fringe since the 1990s is not due so much to the displacement of dissent but to a combination of two factors: first, we have witnessed the transformation of hierarchical structures of policy-making through the "hollowing out" of the state during the Conservative years and the enthusiasm of their New Labour successors for a new mode of governance pitched in terms of consensus and inclusivity. Second, parliamentary parties have a growing need for cash at a time when the legitimacy of "market forces" and market mechanisms have become increasingly normalised to such an extent in contemporary British politics that no-one with any "common sense" could be seen to dispute them (Finlayson, 2003; Newman, 2001: 50–53). The discovery that political parties could engage in "commercial activities" greatly contributed to the transformation of the fringe from a space where internal factions jousted and plotted into a thriving arena for lobbying and vigorous pursuit of commercial interests.

Whilst this growth has affected all parties including the Greens (though at a very modest level), it is primarily a phenomenon of the party in government. To the uncritical eye, the Labour conference fringe now appears like an ideal marketplace where a plurality of points of views can be expressed, where stakeholders interact, negotiate and contribute to shaping policy orientations (rather than policies as these are decided elsewhere). The beehive atmosphere that is carefully constructed contributes to a reinforcement of the impression that conference is "the place to be", an arena from which one – whether business, agency, institution or cause group – cannot afford to be absent.[61] Organisers proclaim that conference is inclusive and that it gives all participants – individuals or organisations – access to policy networks and decision-makers. However, it is an illusion to believe that such pluralism is "neutral" or "apolitical" because resources considerably influence one's ability to act in this forum and to promote one's cause. When a business sponsors a dinner attended by the Prime Minister, it expects to be treated with the respect due to a big contributor to party finances. It may not in the end be listened to but it is likely to be heard. No such advantage is granted small exhibitors even when senior politicians tour the stalls and stop by for a word and promotional picture. Increasingly, few seem to mind political parties being sponsored by private interests and large corporate donors. This perhaps reflects the wider marketisation of British culture since the 1980s.

The short survey presented here only attempts to highlight this new dimension of the party conference scene that urgently needs to be further explored. There are two reasons why this has been little studied: it is a relatively recent development and it is also particularly opaque. The actors involved are secretive about their practices and their objectives. Interviewees are reticent, cautious, and fluent in the language of public relations. Observation is difficult beyond the public areas of the exhibition and a few receptions.[62] Transparency may well be wishful thinking but it is unlikely that trust in politics can be restored in Britain so long as citizens perceive the disjunction between a moralistic discourse of inclusion and participation and a practice of secret bargaining and compromise. How long will it take before the British understand that public funding for political parties was introduced in most continental European democracies precisely to prevent the sell out of politics or at least to circumvent widespread suspicion of corruption?

Conclusion – Politics in the Age of the Individual

In this book I have used a variety of points of view to try and understand what happens within political parties. Following a dominant theoretical trend within political science that stems from the premise of the rational actor, I explored some of the incentives for conference attendance. However, an approach to party conferences that concentrates only on self-centred, individualist motives is reductionist because most of what goes on there emerges from interactions and relates to broader dimensions of party life and activism. The very peculiar context of the annual seaside gathering is the melting pot where party cultures are formed. I reject the dichotomy that opposes a focus on instrumental rationality that is supposed to drive individual actors (usually taken as isolated entities) and theories that emphasise social context and other dimensions of human activities. I believe we need to go beyond the question of "why" people participate in politics or attend party conferences because the answers, and the behaviours, are too complex to be reduced to post-hoc justifications couched in the idiom of common sense individualism (Fevre, 2000; Schuessler, 2000).

The theories developed for the study of new social movements are rarely applied to traditional political organisations such as mainstream parties despite the insights that they bring to the processes through which members are recruited and socialised (McAdam, 1988). I have explored elsewhere the justifications provided by Greens to explain why and how they joined and became active in their party (Faucher, 1999a: Chapters 3 and 4) and this book focuses on the delicate balance between "I and we-identity" in modern British political parties. As Elias explained, both dimensions of human experience must be taken into account as contemporary cultural shifts increasingly privilege the "I", sometimes leading to what he calls *homo clausus*, an isolated individual whose major suffering comes from the absence of a "we" (2001: 199). The need to belong however remains an essential element of the human condition. As the social trends have consistently moved towards individualisation, we have seen a similar shift in social theories and discourses that emphasise the instrumentally rational individual.

Despite the fact that such theories are presented as neutral tools, they are "part of the very process of societal change they claim to describe and analyse" (Cameron and Palan, 2004: 3) as they influence the ways in which actors interpret the world and frame their action and are themselves influenced by these processes. The paradox of collective action (Olson, 1965) sheds light on the complexity of mobilisation for the provision of public goods but also ultimately and indirectly contributes to the contemporary mistrust in politicians: common sense has it nowadays that individuals only engage if there is "something in it" for them. In the 1990s, political parties have responded to the challenge of "new politics" and to what they perceived as a crisis of their legitimacy through the individualisation of membership at the expense of a contested "we-identity".

Participant observation and interviews conducted over nearly eight years allowed me to immerse myself in four distinct British party cultures that share many contextual aspects but are also extremely different. When trying to make sense of the differences between organisations, the concept of "group style" (Eliasoph and Lichterman, 2003) is useful because it encapsulates the mode of interactions that are viewed as appropriate and largely taken for granted by those involved. We all know from experience that when we enter a group for the first time, we strive at first to get a sense of the rules of behaviour so as to avoid blunders. Throughout my research I have endeavoured to understand how group styles emerge in particular contexts of interaction, how they shape and are shaped by organisations and how they frame ways of seeing and doing politics. Rather than "abstractions" such as values and ideologies, I have explored how consensus within an organisation rests on polysemic symbols that are all the more powerful because they can be diversely interpreted as well as offer implicit norms of behaviours. There are no other ways of approaching the unwritten codes that define what it means to be a Liberal Democrat or a Conservative. Moreover, attention to practices over a long period of time shows how such practices are continually adapted and strategically manipulated by actors. The most striking example of the ambiguous potential for inertia and innovation is the process of ritualisation that takes place in relation to certain conference events. I have argued that conference rituals are not so much of interest because they reveal deep seated values that are shared and enacted by all party members but because they create emotional bonds between those engaged in their performance and thus contribute to the appearance of consensus. In all parties, ritualised practices are used to confer legitimacy, confirm hierarchies and maintain the *status quo* through the naturalisation of contingent experiences. The Greens introduced a minute of silence at the beginning of their conference plenary sessions to foster an atmosphere congenial to convivial and constructive deliberation. The innovation was progressively adopted throughout the organisation and contributed to the development of speech norms that emphasise consensus rather than confrontation. If rituals confer legitimacy because they establish links with the authority of tradition, it is through ritualisation that new practices are legitimised. With Tony Blair as leader, the Labour party endeavoured to present itself to voters as "modern" and therefore jettisoned some of the practices that were associated with "Old Labour". At the rostrum first, then later backstage as well, "comrades" became "colleagues" and emotions and personal anecdotes replaced ideological disputes about working-class predicament. Rituals that connected the membership to previous generations of the working class, such as singing the *Red Flag*, were abandoned. The image of the party has been transformed as well as its group style. Bonds, however, were weakened, contributing to a demobilisation of activists.

Whilst looking at the context of interactions implies an analytical focus on the micro level, it also allows for some inductive generalisations, especially when considering national party conferences. Because these gatherings are the nexus towards which party actors and activities converge, they are the place where many changes either originate or the point at which innovations are diffused throughout the organisation as a whole. "Best practice" (as it started to be called in the late 1990s) can spread when activists share know-how. Changes in the rules for the selection of delegates affect norms of interaction not only because novices arrive at conference with their own background and expectations but also because, deprived of prior experience, they are more susceptible to adopting new practices as appropriate behaviour. This is not necessarily because they are more compliant but because they are "feeling the ground".

Within the shared repertoire of actions available to British political parties, one of the most important is the vote. The practice of voting has become the symbol of democracy to the point of becoming almost like a fetish. It is used in different circumstances and to different ends by all parties and its transformation is always justified in terms of democratisation. In the 1990s, there has been a shift from conference vote to membership ballots in all parties. This evolution mirrors the displacement from a mode of decision-making that emphasised the collective (especially when conference delegates were mandated) to an individualisation of the partisan link (in Britain, parties use postal ballots so that isolated members never have to meet any fellow members). New members recruited through national campaigns rather than through local contacts do not have to be supporters of the leadership line, they are in any case less likely to discuss issues and therefore to be informed and mobilised. Thus, the decentralisation of the party paradoxically leads to a concentration of power in the hands of those who control information and procedures. Because there is usually little real suspense as far as the outcome is concerned (conference "fixers" prepare the decisions and more recent ballots are mere plebiscites), votes are largely rituals of legitimation. However, when the voting delegate or representative raises his hand, he can feel the connection with previous generations of party activists and locate himself within a tradition and a transcendent "we".

Annual conferences are windows into British political parties but the way they have changed also reflects broader changes in British society. All parties have changed as a reaction to pressure from their environment but the adaptation is not merely passive: they proactively innovate in response to internal stimuli such as changes of dominant coalition, they anticipate the evolution of the political competition or they adopt by isomorphism to gain legitimacy. Looking back to the 1990s, it is clear that the most striking changes have happened in the Labour party. After its fourth successive general election defeat in 1992, the party was desperate and ready for radical reforms that could not have been accepted before. Moreover, the new dominant coalition led by Tony Blair was convinced that the party should emulate the business organisational model and constantly adapt to the market in order to maintain leadership in the electoral competition. Building from the reforms introduced under his predecessors and in particular Neil Kinnock, Blair presided over wide ranging changes. The symbolic Clause 4 was rewritten, the weight of unions and activists reduced through changes in voting procedures, decision-making and fundraising and the policy-making process was transformed. Once the symbolic attachment to nationalisation and public services had been removed and the superiority of the market model accepted, policies evolved radically. The strategy involved re-branding the party and an effective public relations strategy centrally devised and monitored through a strict corporate discipline pervasively and progressively extended to all sections of the party through a mixture of authority and cajoling.

The success of New Labour has been an impressive example for other parties to follow. Changes in other parties differ in degree rather than in nature. Whilst the direction of change had sometimes been anticipated (the Conservatives were keen to adopt the business model for their organisation; the Liberal Democrats and the Greens shared convictions about the importance of the individual member and experimented with direct and participative democracy procedures), none had gone as far and as fast as Labour has done during the period I have been studying. One of the reasons for this is that, in the run up to the 1997 general election and in government since then, the Labour party has set the pace of change as well as its frame. It has introduced major constitutional, institutional and practical changes with direct and indirect repercussions on British society and the party system. To an extent, the Conservatives, the Liberal Democrats and the Greens have been forced to react and have lost the initiative. As a consequence, they appear now to have difficulties keeping up with Labour.

For analytic purposes, four dimensions of institutional and cultural change can be isolated though they are intimately intertwined:

- multilevel governance,
- media saturation,
- "marketisation" of new spheres of activity and a corporate branding of political parties,
- individualisation.

The Westminster model of government has been eroded by decentralisation, devolution, European integration and globalisation. Beyond the loss of sovereignty, the powers of Parliament have also been symbolically reduced. Not only has the Parliamentary Labour Party (PLP) posed little challenge to governmental plans – despite growing rebelliousness from backbench MPs (Cowley and Stuart, 2004) but think tanks and policy networks play an increasing role in the elaboration of policies. Moreover, the Labour government has tended to by-pass Parliament to address the electorate directly through the media. Commons debates remain adversarial and partisan but no longer on the old ideological grounds. This reflects New Labour's general acceptance of the Thatcher legacy and the fact that ideological confrontation has been systematically displaced as the government has presented itself as "post-ideological" and inspired by incontrovertible "facts" (Finlayson, 2003). Moreover, the traditional conference debate no longer needs to mirror the Commons and public relations experts have encouraged the adoption of more entertaining and media-friendly plenary sessions for live broadcasting.

In an age saturated by media coverage, all parties have become aware of the importance of public relations and of a concerted and coherent media strategy. Even the Greens have reluctantly yielded and employ communications professionals to supervise relationships with the press and the general public, though they have remained largely unable to use conference as a publicity opportunity. Whilst the Greens were realising that not all media coverage was good, the mainstream parties began to view the autumn conference primarily as free advertising and therefore tightened their control over every aspect of its "production". New information and communication technologies, combined with privatisation, liberalisation and the creation of several 24-hour news channels, have led to fierce competition between a rising number of outlets demanding a steady stream of "news" items to keep the attention of their audience. If coverage has widened, its breadth and depth has been reduced. To maximise the effectiveness of coverage, the mainstream parties' communications experts have asserted control not only over the images and soundbites relayed by the media but also over the interpretations of events articulated by journalists. Resistance to such pressures have led to renewed tensions between politicians and journalists, as illustrated by the rifts between Alastair Campbell and the BBC. Corporate propaganda and advertising have provided useful inspiration for strategies that, especially in the case of Labour, rest on saturation with a carefully calibrated and simple message. The idea is to minimise the diffusion of alternative interpretations.

It is no surprise that the European country in which political parties have readily, and earlier than others, embraced the business model is Britain, where the Thatcher cultural revolution established business as the legitimate and "natural" model for all organisations. As New Labour converted to the ideology of the market and pushed further the "private finance initiatives" created by the Tories, there remains little mainstream opposition to this new consensus. Business culture and new managerialism have transformed British politics. First imported by Margaret Thatcher, they have pervaded the whole of British society. Being professional and business-like is now seen as proof of managerial competence and it is largely on this image that parties compete for election. Political marketing techniques are not limited to campaigning strategies because these now involve year-round supervision and the integration of all aspects of the "product" from conception to sale (Lees-Marshment, 2001). Preoccupation with a corporate image became manifest with Labour's adoption of the rose in 1986. As control over image has become obsessive, it has encompassed all aspects of conference from the planning of agenda and timetable, to settings, the choreography of speakers and post-production (spinning interpretations of what has happened). It also affects the party as a whole, imposing an unprecedented level of centralisation to maintain coherence and consistency throughout the country.

By the turn of the Millennium, British mainstream parties offered nationally homogenised products; they had rationalised their operations and regularly hired consultants. They have centralised decision-making (the 1998 Conservative constitution, Labour's *Partnership in Power* and successive rulebook amendments). They have even outsourced functions that used to be done "in-house" from membership services to conference organisation (the Conservatives' CCO was the first example) or even policy-making (since Thatcher's days, think tanks have become very influential). As political parties compete as brands, they use association of their product (policies, organisation and politicians) with particular images, symbols and lifestyles as a selling point. They treat voters as consumers. "We have a problem with our product, it is not competitive and attractive enough", a Conservative complained to me in November 2004, worried by the prospect of a third electoral defeat.

The strain of the permanent campaign and of the constant need to provide adequate news items for immediate media consumption means that mainstream parties have no time to waste in unmanageable semi-public policy debates. If the Liberal Democrats and the Greens still afford the "luxury" of deliberating conferences it is because, as one Liberal Democrat put it "no one listens to us anyway". More generally, with fewer opportunities to socialise and be socialised into the party culture, members are less likely to develop bonds with fellow members and loyalty to the organisation.[1] Lack of trust in members and the importation of managerial modes of control explain the sudden development of business plans, the setting of targets and the auditing of staff practices. What seemed an oddity in 1995 is now taken for granted in the new regime of *governmentality* (Rose, 1999) where activists internalise organisational modes of conduct. While suspicion regarding the reliability of activists in promoting an electable image of the party is not new,[2] the systematic introduction of evaluation procedures for local parties is. As a new "audit culture" pervades British cultural life (Power,

1999), including parties, an unexpected side effect has been that "public assertion of societal control violates the assumption that everyone is acting with competence and in good faith" and thus lowers morale and confidence (Meyer and Rowan, 1977: 359). If headquarters cannot trust their own members, who can? The importation of the market model into party politics seems ultimately to confirm to the doubting public the illegitimacy of parties!

Thatcher, who famously believed that "there is no such thing as society", initiated and encouraged the development of consumerist approaches in new spheres of life: students, patients and travellers are to be considered as customers and the thrust is towards the "customisation" or "personalisation" of (public and private) services. In a post-Fordist climate, everything is supposed to be tailor-made though much of what we ultimately get is *prêt-à-porter*. Ironically, as political campaigning becomes increasingly expressive in form (Schuessler, 2000), justification for intra-party reform increasingly uses the rhetoric of instrumental rationality and individualism. Individual members' rights have so far failed to stop the long-term haemorrhaging of members in British parties or the spiral of demobilisation (Whiteley and Seyd, 2002) perhaps because members can see that despite the leaderships' claims they have less influence on decision-making than they did in the past.

National databases have allowed the development of new membership services that include the right to vote in internal ballots and the right to receive targeted information on party activities and policies.[3] Members are stakeholders amongst others and their "influence" on decisions is, at best, intangible.[4] Politicians admit that they are accountable to the electorate rather than "self-selected" and unrepresentative conference delegates. In the name of democratisation, the individual member has replaced the activist as a source of legitimacy (through OMOV). A further shift of power from members to supporters (through consultation procedures such as open forums) was justified by the need to be more responsive to voters' demands. New Labour seems to have developed a populist strategy of government that is "partyless" (Mair, 2000). From this perspective, if the government manages the country for the betterment of all rather than on behalf of a particular constituency, the party is superfluous or may even be an obstacle.[5]

Last, but not least, a particular kind of individualism has become the unacknowledged drive for change in British society. The thrust of reforms since 1997 were supposed to create an unmediated relationship between the government and the citizen, the party member and her leader. These changes have conspired to weaken party identity: boundaries between party members and supporters have been blurred; bonds are challenged by the promotion of the individual member and the alleged creation of a direct vertical link. Party identity is linked to branding rather than to community feelings. Victor Turner (1989a) argued that social groups could be understood in relations to two polar models of organisation: *communitas* and structure. The former is characterised by its utopian universalist dimension that emerges through an identification with the lowest groups in society. The appeal of the *communitas* also lies in communion with others and selflessness and it is often a regenerative ideal for the enduring, stable and hierarchical structure. The Labour party no longer stands for the excluded, the unemployed, the working class (Heath *et al.*, 2001)[6] but for "personal prosperity for all".[7] As individualism pervades all spheres of life in late modern societies, where is the *communitas* that gives liberal democracies their "social glue" and an ideal to strive for? Where is the vision that can mobilise citizens for the common good? If all parties reject "ideological warfare" to replace it with a managerial model of politics, it is no wonder that they become perceived as only concerned with their own narrow "self-interest" because they no longer stand for a transcendental vision that differs from the others. Their appeals appear "merely partisan". The Citizen Audit (Pattie *et al.*, 2004) shows that British citizens remain interested in politics but are turned off by party politics. Could it be that citizen-consumers (Needham, 2003) are baffled by the indistinct, austere choices presented to them by modern parliamentary parties? Political domination cannot thrive without imagination and there remains an unacknowledged need for drama that is not satisfied by the bland electoral competition that is increasingly on offer.

The growing influence of public relations experts and business interests on party politics or the "presidentialisation" of the government are sometimes taken as indicators of a hypothetical "Americanisation" of British politics. These trends are manifest in the recent evolution of annual party conferences. However, it seems more interesting to highlight the growing emphasis on the individual and on the language of self-interest, all be it of the "enlightened" kind as Tony Blair likes to put it.[8] As Eliasoph shows, individualism in American culture may be an explanation for the "evaporation of politics" or the reluctance of citizens to see their concerns and their actions as political because they use the "language of motives" that ultimately convinces them that they do, or should, think in terms of their own self-interest (1998: 253–254). If this is indeed the case, then the decline of electoral participation and of trust in politicians is unlikely to be halted by more emphasis on selective incentives. Moreover, the discourse of individualisation and self-interest also acts as a kind of self-fulfilling prophecy of disengagement from the public sphere. When, as political scientists, we exclusively focus on the instrumentally rational citizen, we forget that *homo politicus* may not be equivalent to *homo economicus*, and may end up contributing to the very "crisis of legitimacy" that we are seeking to analyse.

Appendix 1: Quoted Interviews

Conservative Party

Ann Widdecombe	MP	20/6/2002
Chris Poole	National Union Secretary	9/6/1996, 18/5/2000
Gary Meggitt	Secretary of the Bow Group, parliamentary candidate	19/5/2000
John Taylor	President of the National Union, then Chairman of the Convention	23/3/1999, 16/6/1999, 18/5/2000, 24/5/2002
Philip Chambers	Central Office Staff	23/2/2003
Shirley Matthews	CCO	17/5/2000

Labour Party

Tony Benn	MP	19/6/1996
Ann Black	NEC, NPF	22/5/2002
Diana Jeuda	NEC, NPF	1/10/2002
Jon Cruddas	Chief Assistant to General Secretary Number 10, then MP	18/1/1999, 10/2002
Ruth Kelly	MP, Cabinet Minister from 2005	17/5/2000
Neil Kinnock	Party leader	29/9/2002
Eddie Morgan	Assistant General Secretary	23/2/2003
Meg Russell	Political adviser, NPF	15/5/2002
Tom Sawyer	General Secretary, then Peer	6/6/1996, 15/5/2002
William Sullivan	Staff, NPF	15/3/2000, 2/5/1999
Matthew Taylor	Director of Policy, Assistant General Secretary, then IPPR Director	18/1/1999
Paul Thompson	Staff	5/1/1999, 17/6/2000
Richard Taylor	Staff	6/6/1996, 23/2/2003
Frank Wilkinson	CAC	9/1997
Larry Whitty	Former General Secretary, Peer	23/3/1999
Shaun Woodward	MP (former Conservative Communication Director and MP)	30/9/2002

Liberal Democrats

Mallen Baker	Former Green Party Principal Speaker	5/1993, 9/2000
Liz Barker	Conference Committee, then Peer.	24/9/1996, 23/1/2002
Allan Sherwell	Conference Committee	23/9/1996
Diana Maddock	MP	23/9/1996
Penny McCormack	Conference Committee	10/7/1996
Emma Nicholson	MP	23/9/1996
Roger Rogers	Councillor	23/9/1996
Ian Walton	Staff	15/5/2002

Green Party

Janet Alty	Convenor of OWOW	9/1994
Alex Begg	Executive Committee	17/9/1993
Malcom Howe	Chair of Policy Committee	9/1993, 1996
Jenny Jones	Chair of Executive (1994–97), later Deputy Mayor of London	1996
Peter Lang	Convenor of OWOW, Communication officer	1994
Caroline Lucas	Councillor, MEP, Principal Speaker	5/1993
John Norris	Chair of GPEx, Chair of Policy Committee	9/1993, 1996
Mike Woodin	Principal Speaker, Oxford Councillor	5/1993, 6/2001, 12/2003

Media and Lobbyists

Bill Bush	BBC producer, then government political adviser	23/1/2003
Gareth Butler	BBC producer	16/5/2002
Michael Cockerell	BBC journalist	16/5/2002
Nick Jones	BBC journalist	16/5/2002
George Pascoe-Watson	The Sun	30/9/2002
Gary Smith	BBC producer	22/9/2002

I interviewed many others who cannot all be named. Moreover, the names of activists and some informants who requested anonymity have been changed in the text.

Appendix 2: Conferences 1994–2002

	Labour	Liberal Democrats	Conservatives	Greens
1994	Blackpool	Brighton	Blackpool	Hastings
1995	Brighton	Glasgow	Blackpool	Southport
1996	Blackpool	Brighton	Bournemouth	Dover
1997	Bournemouth	Eastbourne	Blackpool	Hastings
1998	Blackpool	Bournemouth	Bournemouth	Weston Super Mare
1999	Bournemouth	Harrogate	Blackpool	Southport
2000	Brighton	Bournemouth	Bournemouth	Weston Super Mare
2001	Brighton	Bournemouth	Blackpool	Salisbury
2002	Blackpool	Brighton	Bournemouth	Lancaster

Appendix 3: Comparative Overview of Change in the Four Parties

	Labour	Liberal Democrats	Conservatives	Greens
First conference	1900	1988 as the Liberal Democrats but 1876 for the Liberal party.	1867	1975
Who votes at conference	Delegates from CLPs, trade unions and socialist societies. Since 1995 every other delegate must be a woman. Constituency delegates are elected by OMOV.	Representatives are elected by local parties for two years.	Representatives are selected by Constituency Associations.	Since 2000, all members can attend conference and vote. It will revert to a conference of delegates if the membership goes beyond 10,000 members.
Attendance	1996 about 6000 passes. Labour claimed 25,000 passes were produced in 2002.	Attendance has risen from about 3000 in the mid-1990s to 4,500 passes in 2002.	In 1996, about 11,000. In 2002, the figure was about 10,000.	About 300 on average throughout the period.

(Continued)

	Labour	Liberal Democrats	Conservatives	Greens
Leadership selection	Since 1981, the Leader and Deputy leader are elected by an electoral college composed of three sections (trade unions, individual members and PLP). Since 1993, OMOV is used in the membership section. The first leader thus elected was Tony Blair in 1994.	The Leader is elected by party members (OMOV). The President of the party is also elected by a ballot of members for one year.	According to the 1998 constitution, the Party Leader is elected by members (OMOV). The procedure was used in 2001 but not in 2003 because M. Howard was unopposed and thus elected by the parliamentary party as had been the case between 1965 and 1997. In 2005, MPs' power of selection was restored, with minimal constituency consultation.	No leader – The 10 members of the collegial Executive are since 1992 elected by a postal ballot of all members unless there are less than 2 candidates. In such cases, election at conference. The same rule applies to the two Principal Speakers (one male and one female) who are non-voting members of the Executive.
Leadership elections 1994–2003	1994 Tony Blair is elected after the death of John Smith (elected in 1992).	1999 Charles Kennedy succeeds Paddy Ashdown.	1995 John Major re-elected by parliamentary party 1997 William Hague elected by parliamentary party 2001 Iain Duncan Smith elected by party members 2003 Michael Howard elected by parliamentary party.	No leader. Annual election of national officers and limits on the number of consecutive mandates for these officers.

Adoption of key organisational changes	1993 OMOV for the selection of candidates and leadership election. 1995 Clause 4 is re-written; the rulebook is "consolidated" with "minor" changes. 1997 Partnership in Power is adopted.	1988 Foundation of the party after merger between Liberal Party and Social Democratic Party.	1998 Adoption of the first party constitution by referendum.	1992 Adoption of the "Green 2000" constitution. 1999 Conference reverts to being opened to all.
What is on the conference agenda?	Since 1998, motions and composites have been replaced by final and intermediary reports of the NPF. A small number of emergency motions are also discussed.	Policy papers are submitted by the FPC or by members.	Policy documents submitted by Party Board replaced motions submitted by Constituency Associations in 2000.	Voting papers are submitted by working groups or groups of members. There is a postal ballot of members to decide to prioritise items tabled for debate.
What is the role of conference in policy-making?	Conference is the sovereign body of the party. It examines and votes on NPF policy reports that then become party policy. It can (theoretically) reject or refer them back.	Conference is the sovereign representative body of the party and determines policy.	None.	Conference is the sovereign body of the party and determines policy. Adopted policy papers are collected in the MfSS.

(Continued)

	Labour	Liberal Democrats	Conservatives	Greens
How binding are conference decisions?	According to a 1905 statement, conference "instructs" the NEC and PLP. In practice, the leadership has been able to interpret these decisions and sometimes to ignore. Tony Blair's government has openly admitted that it was only bound by its electoral mandate and was not accountable to the conference.	Conference decisions constitute party policy but the leadership and parliamentary party can interpret them.	Not at all.	In theory, conference decisions are binding but in practice the party has never been in a position to implement its policies.
What positions are elected at conference?	The General Secretary, the Treasurer, members of the Conference Arrangement Committee and of the National Constitutional Committee, two auditors and the representatives of trade unions and socialist societies on the NEC. Constituency representatives on the NPF are elected by conference delegates.	Liberal Democrats representatives elect "one more member than those listed as ex-officio members of" the Conference Committee, the Policy Committee, and the Federal Executive by postal ballot after conference.	None. The Convention elects officials (in particular a Chairman who is an ex-officio member of the Board, a President, 4 representatives on the Board) and although it sometimes meets at Conference the ballots are not held then.	When there are fewer than two candidates for a position, members of the Executive and the Principal Speakers are elected at conference. 5 members of the SOC, 5 members of the Policy Committee and 5 members of the Conference Committee.

Notes

1 An anthropological approach to "conventional politics"

1. The importance of congresses is often exaggerated as little happens that radically changes the direction of the organisation. Most congresses with a few exceptions such as Epinay in 1971 for the French socialists or Bade Godesberg for the German SPD in 1959 – are quickly forgotten.
2. See Bell's (1992: 27) critique of Geertz and Clifford (1988).
3. Swidler (1986: 281). Swidler's analytic distinction between periods of stability and instability creates an unnecessary opposition where there is frequently an overlap: old forms of action persist whilst new ones emerge filtered through or partly guided by practices and doctrine but people feel freer to experiment and adapt in settled times.
4. Deference was one of the characteristics of British "civic culture", according to Almond and Verba (1963).
5. Labour Coordinating Committee (1996). See also Fairclough (2000: 84–93).
6. In France, political science has developed in the shadow of law and has been more open to the influence of history, sociology and anthropology than in some other countries.
7. I have heard this objection more than once.
8. For a detailed comparison of the French and British Greens, see Faucher (1999a). Field work in French party conferences conducted since 2000 informs the reflections developed in this book (Faucher-King and Treille, 2003).
9. Berry (2002). Moreover, the researcher needs to take into account when and where the interview was conducted as settings influence what is expressed (Eliasoph and Lichterman, 2003: 743).
10. Hobsbawm, Ranger (1983). Bell defines the process as "formal 'modelling' of valued relationships so as to promote legitimisation and internalisation of those relations and their values" (1992: 89).
11. Kay Lawson (1994) argues that "boundaries" frame relationships between leaders and followers. They define the roles attributed and endorsed by different actors in the decision-making process.
12. Labelling a performance a "ritual" is thus a political act in itself.
13. *The Parti Socialiste* (PS) for instance fought against any reference to religion being included in the European Constitution. French politicians are in general discrete about their religious practices because of a consensus on the separation of Church and State and in 2004, Parliament adopted new legislation enforcing *laïcité* in state schools. In Britain, religion is never as remote from politics. Although only the Conservatives open their conference with a religious (Christian) ceremony, attending the service on the Conference Sunday is almost a duty for party leaders.
14. The French Socialists' congress can be read as a social drama in four stages as suggested by Turner (1974). A crisis is opened by the multiplicity of

competing motions and the crisis, here the division of the party between factions, intensifies as a first attempt to produce a "synthesis" fails before the congress. The resolution of the crisis comes with the final re-unification, usually obtained thanks to a general agreement on a single motion. The drama in Rennes in 1991 was amplified by the failure to reach such an outcome without the intervention of the President of the Republic and *de facto* leader of the party, Mitterrand himself. Although no synthesis was reached in 2000 either, the factions nevertheless agreed to share power, thus ending the congress on a note of unity.

15. Voters complain that competing teams are increasingly indistinguishable and interchangeable in terms of the priorities (valence issues such as fighting unemployment or improving security) and solutions (prudent managerial policies) they put forward.

16. This echoes the attitudes of voters (Rose and McAllister, 1986).

17. Political associations were banned in France from the Revolution until 1901 and parties are, to date, still viewed with suspicion because they are seen as divisive (Huard, 1996).

18. Even though conferences are of particular importance when they precede the general election.

19. The season starts with the Trade Union Congress and ends with the Conservatives, the dominant party of the 20th century. Small parties usually hold their conference between the Liberal and Labour conferences. The order only varies exceptionally. In recent years, voices have called for an early recall of Parliament, arguing that there is too much work to afford a long summer recess. Major obstacles to an earlier start are the potential disruption to the conferences and the need to write the Queen's speech on a specially prepared goat skin (as noted somewhat ironically by Robin Cook, then leader of the House of Commons at a conference fringe, September 2002).

20. During the summer, the British media sometimes fill air time with spoof programmes, silly competitions and games, either because their staff are on holiday or because they assume that people on holiday want a break from their normal programmes.

21. Eliade (1965). Party conferences are a highly routinised activity in terms of organisation as well as performance. They are planned years ahead as the conference centres have to be booked as well as accommodation and meeting rooms. The complexity of the exercise has meant that in the early 2000s, the three main parties have increasingly relied on the experience accumulated through years in the job by three people: Richard Taylor (Labour), Penny McCormack (Liberal Democrats) and Shirley Matthews (Conservative). They have been in charge of conferences since 1978, 1993 and 1984 respectively.

22. Despite repeated attempts to eliminate or "modernise" it, the ritual of the opening of Parliament has survived into the 21st century.

23. Whilst the representative regime has embedded in Britain a respect for the opponent, much more radical stances are often taken on the other side of the Channel, where political adversaries are denied legitimacy. French politics is characterised by the overwhelming domination of the State, guarantor of the Common will and ultimate arbiter. Not only have parties and political associations long been perceived as divisive and therefore

illegitimate but political debate is often lived in terms of absolute take over. In 1981 for instance, a socialist *député* famously told his opponents "you are legally wrong because you are politically in the minority".

24. In 1960, the Conservative conference opened with speeches "emphasizing that the Westminster model of parliamentary democracy was the best form of government" (*The Times*, 13 October 1960, p. 4).

25. Many anthropologists refute the idea of a strict separation between a realm of the sacred – the religious – and a secular, political and social realm (Durkheim, 1968; Kertzer, 1988; Rivière, 1988).

26. John Gaffney highlights the importance of the centre/edge dimension of British political culture. The edge can be geographical or social. These edges are perceived as threatening an "imagined and cherished democratic process" (Gaffney, 1991: 4).

27. Baudrillard suggested that Disneyland functions in American culture as an obviously "fantastic" and imaginary world that deflects adults' attention away from the fantastic and imaginary nature of the so called "real world" fed to them by the media (Thompson, 1992). One could argue that conferences, located temporarily away from Westminster, reinforce the primary importance of Westminster (the "real business" of politics). Thus, as multi-level governance limits the centrality of government (Dunleavy, 2002), such emphasis on parliamentary parties appears *décalé*, fuelling media criticism.

28. Due to the sheer increase in size of these gatherings, the number of towns that can host the main conferences has been progressively reduced to Brighton, Bournemouth and Blackpool. When conferences were smaller, they visited other resorts such as Morecambe, Harrogate, Torquay, Margate or Scarborough. Such locations still occasionally host spring conferences or policy forums. Blackpool, the only location in the north of England, has become unattractive because of the degradation of facilities in the Winter Gardens, its unpleasant climate and its remoteness. As conferences have become less important as arenas where policies are made or announced, the media and the political elites have become more reticent to face the awkward train journey to the wind-battered working-class city. Interestingly, for a few years Labour stopped going to Blackpool. The official reason was the poor facilities offered by the Winter Gardens but one could also argue that the town did not fit well with their new entrepreneurial image. On the other hand, the Conservatives insisted throughout that it was of paramount importance to visit the North of England, and thus counter their image as a Southern English party. For some time, the only other city with adequate facilities was Birmingham but there was consensus against it. The modernisation of Manchester in the 2000s makes it a potential alternative for the modern and urban Labour party.

29. The precursors of contemporary organisations can be traced back to the Long Parliament of 1641 (Bulmer-Thomas, 1965).

30. Several bills extended the franchise between 1832 and 1865. Voluntary associations of the early days were often organised by spouses and close supporters who ensured that all voters were properly registered and informed.

31. Seiler argues that the Liberals remained organisationally weaker partly because they developed by diffusion (from the bottom-up or through the coordination of local groups of supporters) whilst the Tories followed a

model of penetration (top-down organisations such as the Primrose League and the National Union) (Seiler, 2003: 292–293).

32. One could also argue that the merger between the SDP and the Liberals first happened on the ground and that the party therefore is not solely of parliamentary origin.

33. These organisations evolved into mass-parties (Seiler, 2003: 287).

34. Founded in 1973 under the name People, it adopted the colour Green and the name Ecology party in 1975. It only developed after the European and general elections of 1979, thanks to publicity gained through party political broadcasts. It became the Green Party in 1985 to benefit from the electoral successes of sister parties on continental Europe and because the scientific connotation of "ecology" was seen as a hindrance.

35. The first Green councillor was elected in 1986. In 2004, they had 2 MEPs, 62 principal authority (GLA, Districts, Counties, Metropolitan and London Boroughs) members, about a hundred parish and town councillors and 1 peer. The Scottish Green Party, an autonomous organisation since 1990, had seven Members of the Scottish Parliament elected in 2003.

36. This model is itself influenced by civil society associations and protestant churches forms of organisation (Morris, 1990).

37. Wales, Scotland and Northern Ireland have developed autonomous and distinct party systems. Thus, despite being British in their scope, national and federal conferences are predominantly English.

38. Leo Amery, quoted in Marquand (2000: 268).

39. Norton and Aughey (1981: 191). One can argue that the party then became increasingly ideological.

40. At the first conference in Birmingham, Chamberlain addressed 25,000 people (Bulmer-Thomas, 1965: 123).

41. They are the recurring theme in Cook's (2002) account and are presented as turning points in the party's history.

42. Four ex-Labour ministers led the break away in reaction to their party's move to the left.

43. With 27.0 per cent of the votes (against 26.4 per cent for the Alliance) Labour returned 209 MPs.

44. A few months after it was created in 1996, the Referendum Party held a national conference. Although very short – it only lasted a day – it helped establish the organisation on the political stage and raise its profile for the coming general elections.

45. Blair uses "change" a lot in his speeches as something that comes from outside and has to be adapted to. He often offers lists that remain unexplained (Fairclough, 2000: 28).

46. The other hollow concept constantly invoked to justify change has been "democratisation".

47. Change is presented as inevitable and linear. See Newman (2001) and Finlayson (2003).

48. Speech at Tübingen University, 30 June 2000.

49. Internal and external stimuli create the conditions for change (Harmel, Janda, 1994).

50. Similarly, New Labour's adoption of economic globalisation has been presented as a *fait accompli* one can only adapt to. This is an example of how

an uncritical acceptance of the inevitability of "globalisation" creates its own reality (Cameron, Palan, 2004).

2 Why do people attend conferences?

1. In continental Europe, party congresses gather a few hundred delegates (400 to 600 in the French, Swedish and German socialist and social-democratic parties). In 2004, the French UMP claims to have gathered 40,000 participants to celebrate the election of its new leader.
2. The BBC dispatched about 500 staff to the Bournemouth Conference (Stanyer, 2001: 39).
3. They also hold at least another national conference in the Spring, which is usually a much smaller affair, with a lighter agenda devoted to policy discussions and little media attention, but is nevertheless expected with similar impatience by activists.
4. 1,500 passes were given to voting and non-voting representatives in 2002, but over 12,000 in 2001 including all staff and technicians (interview with Ian Walton, May 2002).
5. The figure includes all personnel such as security and catering. 527 constituencies sent delegates to the 2002 conference.
6. Whether or not they have taken part in their production, all can enjoy the use of collective goods. Most public policies typically fall in this category, hence the application of the theory to political parties who formulate and implement them.
7. James is a Liberal Democrat representative but he also attends the Labour party conference and his own on behalf of his lobbying firm. So does Andy who works for the Royal Society for the Protection of Birds (RSPB). Many companies take advantage of their employees who are members of political parties as it increases the efficiency of lobbying activities (see Chapter 10).
8. The Conservatives are considering organising weekend conferences, following the example of Continental parties and small British ones.
9. The cost is proportional to the earnings in the Green Party and can go up to nearly £100. Conservative conference goers have to pay about £75. Liberal Democrats and Labour offer student discounts and the Greens discounts for the "un-waged".
10. In fact, high intensity activism in the party can be very costly (see Faucher, 1999a: 118–124; Rüdig *et al.*, 1991: 43).
11. If we assume that 15,000 of the 25,000 passes were Labour members, the Labour conference attracted less than 5 per cent of its 300,000 members in 2002. In 1991, 18 per cent of Green Party members had attended at least one conference (Rüdig *et al.*, 1991: 42).
12. Traditionally, Labour delegations were composed of union officials and local party officers. It is still the case to an extent in the Conservative party as half of each constituency "delegation" is composed of constituency association chairmen and vice chairmen. MPs attend conference *ex-officio*.
13. They are the only delegates fully subsidised.
14. The influence of constituency association chairmen is primarily exerted at the local level through the selection of candidates and local committee

members, and the management of the association. As members of the Convention since 1998, they contribute to the election of members of the Board but they have no formal power on policies nor on the selection of the leader. Only the highest-ranking volunteers have easy access to senior politicians, unless they are also big donors.

15. The other positions listed are "presidents", "directors". The Convention is composed of Constituency Association chairmen and area executives. Its president chairs the Convention and the Chairman of the convention is the Vice-chairman of the Board!

16. Schedule 3 on the National Conservative Convention stipulates that positions as representative or Chairman cannot be held for more than 3 consecutive years or as President for more than a year (article 7). Members of the Convention include "past presidents and past chairmen" of the convention, immediate past Area chairmen and Regional co-ordinating chairmen (Part 5, paragraph 20).

17. One of the few amendments to the party constitution in 1999 precisely dealt with this issue. For instance, John Taylor, former Chairman and President of the National Union and the Convention later moved on to become President of the Conservatives Abroad.

18. Holt and Turner (1968) noted that symbolic incentives such as a place on the Honours list most attracted Conservatives to activism. All senior members of the now defunct National Union had an OBE or CBE. The interest in the organisation is less in political debate than in networking.

19. Passes also have to be provided for spouses even if they do not go on stage themselves.

20. The 2004 Labour Conference gala dinner cost £475 per person. The tradition of such fundraising dinners is long established in the Conservative party but is a more recent development in Labour.

21. New Labour has understood the importance of celebrities and uses them extensively.

22. "There is no power relation without correlative constitution of a field of knowledge, nor any knowledge that does not presuppose and constitute at the same time power relation" (Foucault, 1977: 27).

23. As a regular conference attendee myself, I became acquainted with a number of people on the conference circuit. Over the years, this allowed me to follow their career advancement or development. From activist to candidate, MP and minister or from one cause group to a lobbying firm or from one party to another.

24. The "trade" is not limited to party members but also involves journalists, exhibitors and visitors. Others invent stratagems to get past gatekeepers.

25. One of the most popular fringe events at the Conservative conference is the Saatchi's reception. Champagne flows, the buffet is delicious and most guests are convinced of their own importance (others like me are gate-crashers)!

26. There are sometimes more positions to fill than volunteers prepared to stand.

27. Members of the NEC are assigned to address conference on behalf of the committee. These can be chores or challenges depending on whether the orator is happy with the collective decision that she has to defend.

28. This is not new of course and Minkin documents it (1980: 137).

29. Since the late 1990s, most European party leaders are elected by ballots of the entire membership.

30. A college elects the Labour leader and his Deputy since 1981. Members have to be balloted since 1993 and hold a third of the votes on the college. Both the Liberal Democrats (since 1988) and the Conservatives (since 1998) ballot their members for the election of the leader. The Conservatives only organised a ballot in 2001. In 2003, a vote was avoided because only one candidate stood, thus renewing the old practice of the "emergence" of the leader that had been abandoned in 1965. In 2005, the party reverted to an MP-oriented system.

31. In Labour, there have been five such challenges at conference since 1922, none was successful. Despite their reverence for the leader, the Conservatives are loyal so long as she/he is successful. Major and Thatcher were challenged whilst Duncan Smith was convinced to step down.

32. The vote, taken "on the recommendation of the NEC" (Rule 7), is a formality. The role of General Secretary is primarily organisational; the post of Party Chairman was created in 2001 by the Prime Minister.

33. Until the 1990s, these elections were "so dominated by unions that it is hardly worth mentioning" (Minkin, 1980: 70). Different systems are used for each section of the party: trade unions and socialist delegates vote at conference. Grassroots members and local councillors are consulted via postal ballots.

34. Conference Committee, Policy Committee, Federal Executive and European Delegation. "One more member than those listed as ex-officio members of the relevant committees" (Articles 7.2 and 8.1 of the August 2003 constitution).

35. Constitution (Article 8.1).

36. Since 1998, the Convention elects five members of the Board. The Board "from time to time determines" the composition of the Candidates, Conference and Membership Committees (Conservative Party, 1999: 25).

37. Though not necessarily of the membership (see Chapter 9).

38. NEC elections were considered to be primarily a matter for union leaderships and the membership were rarely consulted. In the 1980s, this meant that the unions could considerably assist the leadership in producing a relatively docile NEC (Minkin, 1991: 334). This helped the leadership progressively assert its control over the executive, limiting its powers as a policy-making body, increasing the influence of the parliamentary party and introducing reforms that helped control the selection of its members.

39. The term was often used by activists and staff to refer to the coherent New Labour team running the party after 1994.

40. Successive reforms have contributed to "domesticate" the NEC. OMOV was introduced for the election of constituency representatives to limit the influence of delegates (suspected of being too radical). MPs can no longer be elected in this section. Mandates have been extended to two years, which reduces the frequency of difficult internal battles for the leadership.

41. The Labour party reformed procedures for the selection of candidates and exerted stronger control for Scottish and European elections from 1999.

42. Thus, before the 2001 general election the Labour government was faced with a small hardcore of 30 regular rebels in a 417 strong parliamentary group. These MPs clearly forfeited prospective careers as is demonstrated by the rapid promotions of those who do not rebel and joined the government (Cowley and Stuart, 2004).

43. The electoral system severely limits their chance of success. The obstacles faced by the party are such that narrow instrumental rationality fails to explain their relentless efforts (Faucher, 1999a: 128–129). Electoral successes have not fundamentally changed the situation. The Greens have had local councillors since 1986 but regular successes in Oxford, Bradford and London for instance date from the late 1990s.
44. Membership of the Front Bench Club is open to people giving over £5,000 annually to the party. Members meet Front Bench parliamentarians and the leader rather than "ordinary" MPs.
45. The higher the donation, the more senior the politicians met. Access to decision-makers is also an important incentive (see Chapter 10).
46. In *A Sand County Almanac* (Oxford: Oxford University Press, 1966), Leopold puts forward a position that is characteristic of "deep ecology", arguing that we need to extend our understanding of the self so as to include the non-human environment.

3   Imagined communities

1. On the multivocality of symbols, see Turner (1989b). Written in 1918, the famous Clause 4 endorsed socialist goals such as nationalisation of the means of production. It was perceived by most in the party as an ideal that did not reflect the objectives or the policies of a Labour government. Despite recurring debates about the outdated content of the clause, attempts to rewrite it failed until 1995. Resistance to change invoked the potency of a symbol that connected the labour community whilst largely irrelevant to understand party policy. Arguments in favour of a new clause insisted on its negative symbolic connotations, whilst rewriting it would send a pertinent signal to the wavering electorate (see Taylor, 1997).
2. Small parties do not get much mainstream media coverage but they hear about conference from those who attended and read about it in internal newsletters. This is enough to bring in to existence a national Green community whose members live through the year in relative isolation in a political environment that is largely hostile to their views.
3. The same applies to all parties, because those with few MPs (or none) need to reinforce group solidarity to motivate their supporters. In a context of limited resources, it is more difficult to provide material selective incentives to compensate members for their activism.
4. There are different "classes" of visitors and some of them have access to the floor.
5. I am referring here not only to elected politicians but also to the activists who are, in many ways, part of a small elite of politically involved citizens.
6. There are regular gaffes when, for instance, security staff refuse to recognise a Minister or demand that they show their badge and be treated like every other conference participant. Only the leader is exempted.
7. Until 1984, a Conservative constituency pass could be shared between several Conservative representatives coming for a couple of days each. Passes then became personalised with pictures. In 1995, whilst I had no difficulty getting into the Labour and Liberal Democrats, I was refused entry to the

Conservative conference. The following year, I received such privilege after a government minister – whom I had met through an Oxford Professor – introduced me to the National Union Secretary.

8. In 2000, Labour had an expensive bridge built to allow participants to wander between the Conference centre and the hotel across the street without having to get out of the security area. It was sponsored by a trade union.

9. Contemporary British parties do not function as clubs one can only join if introduced and sponsored by a member. On the contrary, they now endeavour to recruit through newspaper advertisement and offer credit card payments (see Chapter 9). For an analysis of how and why individuals join the Green Party and become "Greens", see Faucher (1999a).

10. Adopted in 1918 and printed in part on the back of the membership card, the clause expressed aims and values that committed the party in principle to the nationalisation of industries and services.

11. There are numerous examples. Major kissed Lady Thatcher on stage at the 1996 conference (Stanyer, 2001: 25); Gordon Brown and Cherie Blair hugged after the Prime Minister's speech at the 2004 Labour conference despite their well-known antipathy; Thatcher and Heath shared a platform at the 1998 Conservative conference.

12. This is especially important for ambushed leaders: Tony Blair came out stronger of the 2002 and 2003 conferences.

13. Whyte's (1993) analysis of political gatherings in "Cornerville" can be extended to conferences.

14. Moreover, a distanced attitude to ritual may precisely be the competent performance of it if the ritual affirms distance to rules, conventions and traditions (Eliasoph, 1998: 113).

15. Physical settings (such as the centre in which conference takes place, the design of the stage and rostrum) can intimidate participants or on the contrary suggest intimacy.

16. Interactions articulate social and systemic integration (Giddens, 1984).

17. Best practice awards were distributed at the 2004 Labour conference, reflecting the naturalisation of new management approaches within British culture.

18. The party will resume the selection of delegates if the membership rises above 10,000 members for two consecutive years.

19. As Mike Woodin notes, the national organisation "never developed an efficient system for keeping track of the number of voting cards issued to local parties", conference registration (and votes) were complex and lengthy procedures. In fact, conference never ceased to be a "whoever wants to turn up system" because many local parties did not officially elect delegates.

20. Surprisingly, the most studious audience of the four conferences is the Conservative one: although debates have no real influence on decision-making, many representatives sit through all sessions with remarkable patience.

21. Conference is expected to "offer a wide range of activities and attract a wide range of members" (Constitution, article 8.9).

22. A Quaker who thought that it might help everybody focus on the tasks ahead suggested it.

23. In the 1980s 37.6 per cent of conference participants attended the Review (Rüdig *et al.*, 1991: 42) but the figure was probably higher in the 1990s after the secession of Green 2000 as the Review clearly played a cathartic role in healing the wounds. Moreover, the conference had become a smaller family affair with most participants at least watching for a few sketches before or after going out.

24. The Greens have no dedicated anthem and usually choose to sing pagan songs.

25. See for instance Lincoln (1989). I have discussed elsewhere the importance of lifestyles for the Greens (Faucher, 1999a). This also applies to other parties and I exploited these traits for my research. I wore a pin stripe suit at the Conservative conference (and a red one at Labour: how naïve!) and baggy jumpers with the Greens where I also enjoyed healthy whole foods that contrasted with the rubber chicken I had to endure in mainstream parties.

26. Green parties seem to have more than their fair share of strong personalities, eager to preserve their independence and resistant to any party discipline (Faucher, 1999a).

27. See Chapter 4 on reactions to the leader's speech.

28. Mobilisation processes have been studied in detail by researchers on new social movements. Faucher (1999a: 95–98); Klandermans and Oemega (1987); McAdam (1988).

29. Interviewees who belonged to either previous party usually insist on the tension and the originally split identity. Former Liberals in particular are too keen to point out which rules and practices came from their party.

30. Communication imperatives nevertheless tend to tone down some of the most controversial issues at pre-electoral conferences.

31. Participants sing along to old favourite tunes, some of which have had their words rewritten for the occasion. The atmosphere is festive thanks to companionship, humour and beer.

32. Although respecting the mandates remains in theory central to the party's conception of decision-making, such instructions have been open to diverse interpretations (Minkin, 1980: 165). The parliamentary party retained a great deal of autonomy in the interpretation of conference decisions (McKenzie, 1964: 588; Punnett, 1987: 105).

33. The party ethos thus contrasted with Liberal and Conservative middle-classes (Drucker, 1979: 11).

34. One could say that it is translated rather than transposed.

35. Members of General Management Committees (GMC) selected themselves as conference delegates. In 1949, 300 constituency parties also had professional agents representing them (Interview with David Butler, May 2002).

36. Where only one delegate is appointed, this must be a woman at least every other year (*Rulebook*, section 3). In 1996, 80 per cent of delegates were first timers.

37. MPs appear to be more radical than members on a number of issues (Norris, 1995).

38. Clause 4 only appeared on membership cards in 1959 and became a symbol only after Gaitskell's attempt to change it (Fielding, 2003: 67).

39. The French Communists also used changes in congress rituals to demonstrate how their organisation was modernising and democratising.

40. In Sweden, the Social democrats close their congress with delegates singing the *Internationale*. So do the French Communists, holding hands in the air before the chair declares the meeting closed and invites all participants to a closing banquet that evokes the 19th century Republican tradition and resonates with the national obsession with food. The Spanish *Partido Popular* has songs especially written for each congress: words are distributed to participants who sing along at regular intervals as if to maintain a high level of excitement.

41. The *Red Flag* and the word "comrade" were markers of a distinct Labour Left sub-culture that did not mix well with senior civil servants, industrial and financial elites (Seyd, 1987: 15).

42. This was the topic of intense NEC discussions in 2003 but it was decided not to commit the party to reinstating the *Red Flag*. Cameras showed that few members knew the words. *Jerusalem* had centre stage in 2004.

43. Beyond party officers, candidates and elected politicians, the audience is constituted by representatives of local groups (members of the Convention (i.e. chairmen), two deputy chairmen and three others, whose selection procedures are not mentioned) (Schedule 4, pp. 22–23, *Constitution*, July 2002).

44. In the Labour party, some are prepared to elbow their way into the hall to listen to the Prime Minister's speech.

45. For instance, in 1998, Tony Blair started his speech by telling delegates how he ridiculed himself whilst trying to show off his ability to speak French. Instead of expressing his admiration for Prime Minister Lionel Jospin, he said "he desired him in many different positions". By contrast, French Congress speeches remain distinctly pompous. On ritual joking, see Douglas (1999).

46. One of Disraeli's rambling speeches was interrupted with a request to define his terms better – for example, what was the difference between a misfortune and a disaster? "Well, he said, let me elucidate by example. If Mr Gladstone were to fall into the river Thames that would certainly be a misfortune, but if somebody pulled him out again, that would be a disaster." I owe this anecdote to Stephen Ingle.

47. In 2003, Iain Duncan Smith's attacks on his Liberal Democrat opponent were of particular bad taste.

48. Bulmer-Thomas (1953), *The British Party System*, London: Phoenix House, pp. 196–197, quoted by Kelly (1989: 13).

49. This is according to Richard Kelly the purpose of the "conference system" whereby members exert an influence on policy-making not through votes but through a succession of debates (Kelly, 1989).

50. The average age of the Conservative member was 62 in 1992 (Whiteley *et al.*, 1994: 43).

51. The re-branding in 1994 was somehow the cherry on the cake.

52. Singing of *Rule Britannia* and *Land of Hope and Glory*, loud clapping and waving of the Union Jack were banned from the leader's speech from 1998. Agenda and stage management were centralised and given a more modern look.

53. The jargon of marketing is increasingly *en vogue* within British parliamentary parties with senior officials talking about ways to market their product more effectively.

54. "Ritual arguments", *The Guardian*, 20 January 2005.

4   Constructing leadership and authority

1. See for instance William Morris' *News from Nowhere* that inspired the two traditions.
2. The reference is here to the socialist elements at the core of the Labour party's project. One must not, however, forget that Labour wove quite different philosophical and political trends that did not all harbour a utopian horizon. Trade unionism was more concerned with the amelioration of the condition of the working class than with the realisation of a socialist society.
3. The Greens often express suspicion towards the stifling influence of rules and assert their preference for spontaneity and authenticity over institutionalisation. Many local Green parties did not have written constitutions by 1997 (Faucher, 1999a: 194).
4. The working class is expandable to humanity, whilst the Greens extend their promises to future generations of beings (humans and non-humans).
5. Until the 1980s, Labour ministers had no more rights than ordinary delegates to address conference from the platform if they were members of the NEC: in 1976 for instance, the Chancellor, coming back from a meeting with the IMF, was granted four minutes to respond to the economic debate.
6. Dispensing with the stage altogether quickly proved to be impractical.
7. Tim Andrewes (1988), "Sunflower may be ditched shock!", *Green Line*, 67, pp. 12–13.
8. The faction that supported the reform, Green 2000, mobilised passive members and outvoted its opponents at an acrimonious conference. Reformers considered that by-passing self-selected activists could help the party adopt a more moderate political profile and build on the 1989 European elections. But the reform produced a bitter rift that tore the party apart. Activists resented passive members' involvement in the debate and considered that their own devotion to the cause ought to guarantee their exclusive influence on the organisation (see Kitschelt, 1990).
9. Plurality was abandoned after a year to return to single transferable votes, the preferred system of the Greens.
10. They feared that passive members were more likely to elect a celebrity. Their anxiety had been confirmed by the disastrous appointment of David Icke as Principal Speaker. A former sport commentator, he became Principal Speaker but is mainly remembered for his prophecies of ecological disaster. Many years later, activists still shiver at the memory of public ridicule. He was eventually expelled in 1995, after publishing an anti-Zionist pamphlet.
11. Michael Woodin was Principal Speaker for 6 out of 8 years before his premature death in 2004.
12. The question of leadership was directly posed to the Oxford Greens when, in 2000, they held the balance of City council and made an "agreement" with the Liberal Democrats. The local group opted for a rotating responsibility. As the most experienced councillor, Mike Woodin was the first to hold the position.
13. In 1995 for instance, the rules meant that the new party executive was dominated by people with little experience at the national level. Jenny Jones and Darren Johnson, both later London Assembly members, took national responsibilities for the first time.

14. This showed not only that Lucas is highly regarded in her organisation and that her speech was rousing but also that Greens are following norms of behaviour they would have resisted vehemently a few years before.
15. The post of "Chairman and Leader of the PLP" was created in 1922. Its very title illustrates the reluctance to merge the direction of the movement and the direction of its parliamentary representatives. The title changed several times before eventually settling on "Leader of the Labour Party" in 1978. Party rules caught up each time with changes in practices.
16. Such as the mandatory reselection of MPs and new procedures for the election of the party leader in 1981.
17. See also Mair (1997) on the current trend towards the centralisation of party organisation.
18. Drucker (1979) argues that love for rules was linked to the ethos of working-class members who had little experience of them in their ordinary lives and therefore held them in great respect. Interestingly it was combined with pragmatism as in the case of the leadership position.
19. Exceptionally, the *1995 Conference Handbook* stated that card votes should be granted whenever asked. Such useful advice disappeared in the following years.
20. "It would be highly unusual for the Labour party if (...) rules were fully observed" remarked Minkin (1980: 135). In a country with no written constitution, there is, probably more than in other places, a readiness to admit the importance of the informal.
21. Some of the changes were discreetly brought in, such as the extension to two years of NEC members' mandate adopted in the subdued conference atmosphere following the 2001 terrorist attack on New York.
22. Each representative has adopted his/her own *modus operandi*, and some publish their notes on the web.
23. The accusation was made because Kennedy was one of the very few British politicians to appear on TV quiz shows.
24. *The Guardian*, 24 September 1999 and *The Times*, 20 September 2000.
25. All parties have used ballots to limit the power of activists (see Chapter 9).
26. Outrage was such that it leaked to the press, an unusual move in the Conservative tradition where dissent is expressed privately (see *Guardian*, 19 February 2003).
27. Until the 1960s, the Conservative and Liberal leaders only turned up for, or just after, the official close of the conference to give their speech.
28. Like most other politicians, the leader uses fringe meetings to try out expressions and images.
29. The image management of the incident was masterfully conducted, in sharp contrast, for instance, to Nixon's sweating forehead in the 1960 US Presidential debate, which is widely thought to have made him appear nervous and suspicious.
30. The party website boasted that it lasted a record-breaking 7 minutes (http://www.labour.org.uk/conference2003). A week later, the Tories gave their leader a 9-minute ovation.
31. Schuessler takes the example of John Bonaccorso, who attended the Boston festival every year and secured each time a front seat by pitching a tent a week before the event. To recompense his efforts the organisers offered to

book him a seat. He refused as his enjoyment of the concert was heightened by the time he had to wait for it (Schuessler, 2000: 25). On ritual waiting, see Lardellier (2003: 85).

32. François Mitterrand cultivated his delays, walking round the block if necessary to make sure the person he was meeting was waiting: *"Etre en retard, c'était toujours garder de l'avance sur l'autre"*. French party congresses are often left waiting for committee decisions. Communist delegates used to wait several hours before the start of a session but patience was a feature of the old days. In 2000, comrades got tired of listening to a pianist and started clapping rhythmically to encourage the *bureau du congrès* to speed up its discussions.

33. Disraeli initiated the tradition of major speeches by giving the first one in Brighton in 1872.

34. Wives can sometimes be good substitutes: Ffion Hague was often a silent but smiling guest of honour at conference receptions. Cherie Blair performs a similar role. Women are an important constituency for Tony Blair although his experiences have sometimes been bruising. Since 1997, Cherie often replaces him at their conference reception. Paxman describes leaders' wives as "afternoon arm candy" whose role is to look adoringly at their spouse (Paxman, 2003: 152).

35. The Conservatives produce videos of conference sessions. In 1996, an activist noticed that the enthusiastic reception given to Portillo's speech was used to illustrate Mawhinney's, a much quieter affair. This story, which I owe to Stephen Ingle, illustrates the increasing importance of constructing an impression. On the contrary, a 1994 BBC video (*Politics by the Sea*) of great conference moments completely ignores any such presentational editing.

36. Michael Howard was nominated party leader a few weeks later.

37. The first interruption was by pro fox hunting activists, the second by opponents to the war in Iraq.

38. Kinnock did not use them because he rehearsed so many times that the speech was "written on the inside of my eye lids". Despite rehearsals, Duncan Smith never managed to be a convincing performer.

39. Franklin D. Roosevelt began radio broadcasts to the nation from the White House that became known as "fireside chats" in 1933.

40. It was feared that she might deviate too much from the text approved by Central Office. She was allowed to go ahead because journalists are given a script of all major speeches and would easily correct minor errors.

41. Another comparison would be *Star Academy* as politicians perform and are evaluated by the audience who thereby influence their future career.

5   Setting the agenda

1. Since 1993, the influence of factions has been reduced as a consequence of local groups holding secret ballots.

2. There are through the year many other party conferences of lesser importance: regional and sectional ones as well as a Spring national meeting. Continental parties hold a number of small thematic, regional or sectional meetings.

3. Cynog Dafis was for several years the joint MP for the Green Party and the Plaid Cymru in Ceredigion constituency.

4. The situation was then similar in the Liberal Party (Rasmussen, 1965).
5. As is the case in French parties (UMP, PS, Verts) where factions are institutionalised. On representation in Britain, see Judge (1999). Other groups of members are entitled to submit proposals but none are factions: trade unions and socialist societies in the Labour party or various working groups in the Liberal Democrats and the Green Party.
6. Comparatively, French socialist motions are nominally signed and in practice constitute lists of supporters (Faucher-King and Treille, 2003).
7. This strategy was more discreet than the expulsion of the Militant Tendency in 1985.
8. These meetings also help party staff and officers to assess the characteristics of conference delegates (Chapter 7).
9. National databases of the membership and new communication technologies have reduced the importance of such channels of communication which have been replaced by targeted and often informal communication – both regular and *ad hoc*.
10. These processes are particularly important for the few members that have switched allegiance because their efforts to be accepted in their new community generally implies adaptation to new sets of rules and roles.
11. The "as if" quality of play is an aspect of all socialised human interactions (Goffman, 1990).
12. This "shadowy" dimension of power is obfuscated by the focus on conference as a decision-making body.
13. At conference, motions were often attributed to a Prospective Parliamentary Candidate (PPC) so as to give him a chance to be called.
14. Each party produces conference documents (such as the Conservative Handbook, the Liberal Democrat Conference Directory, the Labour Conference Guide) that are distributed to participants containing motions and papers tabled for debate, daily timetables, listings of fringe meetings as well as practical information about the programme, conference centre and city facilities.
15. Intricate networks of clubs and committees contribute behind the scenes to the elaboration of policy (Seldon and Ball, 1994).
16. The British Conservatives and the French Communist Party have prospered as integration parties, building on ancillary organisations that sometimes portrayed themselves as "apolitical". The Primrose League famously organised Conservative women (Campbell, 1987).
17. Holt and Turner (1968), Seyd and Whiteley (1992: 76). "Old" Labour members are more motivated by process incentives than newer recruits (Whiteley and Seyd, 2002: 132).
18. Both parties hold a smaller spring meeting that is devoted to policy discussions.
19. It is an accusation they throw at each other regularly though it is less and less founded as the party is establishing itself in sub-national government.
20. The Green Party draws heavily from the work of their academic or professional members (Faucher, 1999a: 240–242).
21. Conservatives also showed humour in motions such as Swansea East's 1998: "This Conference urges Humphrey the Cat to return to Downing Street to keep the pests under control".
22. The party grew increasingly restless during the Major government.

23. In 1987, Thatcher mistook the enthusiasm of the Conservative Conference regarding the new poll tax for support amongst the electorate (Kavanagh, 1996: 31). Listening to the grassroots has little to do with listening to the voters/the public if one considers that activists represent a small fraction of society and are not representative (May, 1973).

24. This contrasts starkly with French socialist style where pretentiousness led to a motion being published as a novel (Julien Dray *et al.* (2000), *Sept jours dans la vie d'Attika*, Paris: Ramsay).

25. However, this was never really the case (see chapter 9).

26. It was the highest number since 1977. Between 1992 and 1995, the average was 1200 motions (Ball, 1996).

27. There were on average 518 resolutions a year between 1956–69 (Minkin, 1980: 65).

28. In neither party are members fooling themselves in thinking, or claiming, that the grassroots should write policies!

29. Until the 1990s, the Conservatives tended to focus on economic or fiscal issues whilst Labour felt more comfortable on health and education.

30. Labour policy-making has always had a distinctive elitist character. A variety of committees and sub-committees passed policy papers through the NEC. Some were put to conference without formal opportunities to debate and vote. The NEC maintained an independent policy-making role until the 1990s. Not only did the parliamentary party retain crucial freedom of interpretation and of means of implementation (Minkin, 1980: 5), it also became the source of most policy documents, bolstered by a network of informal links and consultative arrangements between unions and the leadership.

31. Interview with party staff, including Arlene Ryan, secretary to the General Secretary until 1998.

32. In 1996, a local party that had sent a male delegate when they should have sent a female also had its resolution dropped.

33. Trade unions were keen to preserve the right to comment on Government decisions. The national executive has become a primarily administrative rather than political authority and the "conference is now the only time when [it] decides party policy, by proposing statements and supporting or opposing resolutions" (see http://www.annblack.com/nec_oct2002.htm). Resistance built on the fear of a hidden agenda of concentration of powers and on the unions' determination not to let the NEC be side-lined (Minkin, 1991: 382).

34. Policy documents adopted by conference had different statuses: the Party programme had received two thirds of the votes; other policy documents require a simple majority.

35. Several reports by Matthew Taylor, then Director of Policy, highlighted the need to acknowledge the existence and role should be in the party rule book as well as promoted in the party and profile raised.

36. Matthew Taylor, former assistant general secretary, an architect of *Partnership*.

37. Emergency motions require in practice the support of the trade unions to be debated by conference.

38. "All policies and party issues are debated in full and no statement becomes party policy without being approved by Conference" (Notes by the CAC, *Delegates report*, 2000, p. 4).

39. To a certain extent, the new process could be compared to a "system of conferences". Although the Conservative conference is deprived of any formal powers, the system of regional, sectional and annual conferences exerts an important influence on the party's policies (Kelly, 1989).

40. The political orientations of NPF representatives may also reflect a more general cultural shift within the party. It is likely that the "significant revision of the core values of traditional socialism [noticed] within the parliamentary party" (Evans and Norris, 1999: 26) also prevails within the membership. Younger MPs' values tend to be further on the right than their elders', irrespective of when they joined Parliament (Evans and Norris, 1999: 40). This generational trend may be linked to the long-term effect of Thatcher's cultural revolution.

41. The dynamic of the group can also lead to "group think", that is the closure of the group to outside ideas in a conviction of its superiority (Nimmo and Combs, 1990: 152–153).

42. A former political advisor to Robin Cook on parliamentary reform, Russell is an academic and author (Russell, 2005), and was unlikely to be intimidated herself.

43. In 1999, the Durham NPF did not support a minority position on the highly contentious issue of the pension-earnings link.

44. Motions on contemporary issues need to be approved by CAC to be discussed by conference but contentious issues can be avoided because they "are already addressed by the report" (such as a 1999 motion on air traffic control privatisation) or thanks to deals with unions in the priority ballots.

45. Outsiders such as journalists often describe conference as a "sham". Since 2000, the party makes no claim about the agenda being democratically produced.

46. In 1998, the National Union was replaced with the Conservative Party Convention, a body of nearly a thousand members, meeting twice yearly. Most of the issues discussed are administrative and organisational and have little impact. The Convention proposes amendments to the Constitutional Committee, discusses the best ways to ensure an effective organisation, receives and oversees reports from the Board and areas and regions, elects representatives to the Board.

47. In 1998, ninety motions were put forward on the new party constitution, expressing broad support. The exception was the strong resistance to the introduction of a minimum membership fee. Motions were published and could thus help trace the membership's moods better than tamed public debates.

48. Conference booklet 1995.

49. The "Birmingham Caucus" proved so powerful that it was the target of Ostrogorski's attacks (1979).

50. In recent years these included topics such as the legalisation of cannabis, the abolition of the monarchy, banning scratch lottery games or selling pornography to 16 year olds.

51. A serious "trimming of the Civil List" was adopted.

52. Liberal Democrats Constitution, Article 6.7.

53. The Policy Committee of the SDP had the last word. According to Russell and Fieldhouse, MPs have virtual veto powers on policies (2005: 65) but the

influential Association of Liberal Democrat Councillors contributes to keeping the grassroots in the mind of the parliamentary party (2005: 61).

54. Both parties hold two national/federal meetings every year. The autumn session examines officers' reports, elects officers to national committees and discusses a small number of policy proposals. The spring conference focuses on policy.
55. *The Times*, 20 February 1999, quoted by Ingle (2000: 194)
56. In 2001, the deadline for sending motions and amendments was merged, as local parties had been too busy with campaigning to devote as much time as usual to conference *per se*.
57. Greens have so far had few problems with "entrism" and have managed to retain their openness.
58. *Standing Orders*, article C9. In 1993, a motion on rights and responsibilities was rejected. Its authors had managed to reach a compromise between two opposite philosophical approaches after two years. Unfortunately, search for consensus led to a self-contradictory policy document.
59. Conference support is no longer enough: Labour in 1996 and the Conservatives in 2000 felt compelled to organise party-wide referendums on a draft electoral manifesto.
60. The debate featured no important politicians and was poorly scheduled.

6   Making the news

1. Although all parties organise other conferences during the year, none has the importance of the autumn show. "Smaller conferences are more insular" and they are less likely to attract the attention of the press: "you achieve the same thing by sending the leader on a tour and at a different cost", explains Shirley Matthews (CCO).
2. To justify this unusual practice, journalists argue that coverage of conference news would be extremely cumbersome if the media had to balance any policy announcements with counter arguments from the opposing party. Of course, this does not imply that competitors do not attempt to disrupt the public relations show of their opponent. Thus, they will try to synchronise the release of "catchy" news with the others' conferences, be it the defection of an MP or the publication of some report for instance.
3. The British print media comprises five "quality" papers providing extensive national and international news coverage, serious commentary and public affairs with a combined sale of about six million copies. The tabloids are the popular end of the market and tend to focus more on popular/populist stories. The *Sun* is the biggest paper in the sector, selling over 3.5 million copies with a readership of about 10 million.
4. Labour only accepted TV cameras in 1955, following the considerable success of the Conservative coverage the previous year. The general election campaign was televised for the first time in 1959 (Rosenbaum, 1997).
5. As a party with two MEPs since 1999 and representation in local/regional government, the Greens have a much tougher time getting any coverage at all. Plaid Cymru and the Scottish National Party are covered by regional media. The SNP conference remained for many years focused on an internal

rather than external agenda with speeches aimed at securing election to the National Party Council rather than to impress voters. With devolution however, the party has gained more prominence and outside considerations are now taken into account.

6. "Tabloidisation" here refers to the distinctive subject of news stories that increasingly focus on scandals, celebrities or disasters.

7. Although a great number of polls track the evolution of political opinions regarding parties and politicians through the year, they do not allow for systematic comparison of pre/post conference fluctuations. Claims that there is such an impact are therefore based on speculations.

8. One of the most striking example was the *Sun*'s coverage of the 1992 general election and its famous front page the following day "It's the Sun wot won it". There is however no evidence that this is the case (Norris *et al.*, 1999: 115–156).

9. When in 1996 Blair announced that his government's priorities would be "education, education, education", he very consciously played on that factor.

10. In the 1989 European election success, the Green Party gained 15 per cent of the votes. At the time, environment featured at the top of the media agenda and these mid-term "secondary" elections provided a good opportunity to send a warning message to Thatcher's government (Rüdig and Franklin, 1992).

11. The Greens have maintained a marginal position regarding these developments even though their initial antagonism to anything related to the media has subsided. Nevertheless, their communication efforts remain on a totally different scale from what goes on in the mainstream.

12. Although the Greens have become more self-conscious about presentation, they do not benefit from the same media attention as the three main parliamentary parties and are thus relatively affected. A fringe meeting on "politically correct hugging" was staged for the benefit of the media, prompting a debate on whether it was damaging for the party's image or whether publicity was good in itself (*Green Link*, 17 March 1995, p. 8).

13. The BBC demands private rooms and insulated booths, access for cameras, transmitters and computer facilities (Gareth Butler). Stanyer (2002: Chapter 2).

14. They also take pictures of the set, the logos and the rostrum that can be used in the reports produced in their London studios during the conference week.

15. The needs of the media are varied and increasing, from Internet access to telephone connections, sound proof television booths or access for live transmission equipment.

16. The tactic is also used in government as epitomised by the revelation that a minister's political adviser had suggested seizing the opportunity of 9/11 to release controversial decisions. *Guardian*, 9/10/2001.

17. In 2002, Iain Duncan Smith took particular care to rehearse his speeches *in situ* to get used to the set.

18. The most important player was of course the *Sun*. Gould (1998: Chapter 8) and Blumler and Gurevitch (2001: 388).

19. Alastair Campbell (House of Commons' Select Committee on Public Administration, June 1998, http://www.publications.parliament.uk/pa/cm199798/cmselect/cmpubadm/770/8062307.htm.

20. See Chapter 3 for discussion of Turner's social drama. Interviews with John Cruddas and Matthew Taylor, formerly Chief Assistant to the General

Secretary and Director of Policy/Assistant General Secretary of the Labour party (1994–97).

21. Previously, most journalists had left just after the speech.

22. It is probably no coincidence that French party congresses, held in exhibition halls purposely furnished and with deplorable acoustics, never manage to either warm up delegates or impress journalists. The Winter Gardens were inconvenient but they gave a particular atmosphere to party conferences.

23. *The Times*, 10/10/1970: 15.

24. The prestige of a seat on the platform was one of the rewards for activism within the voluntary party or generous contributions to party funds.

25. The choice of IKEA furniture rather than traditional desks and chairs then attracted derision.

26. In 1995 they were keen to demonstrate their openness – and probably to have young female faces on stage – I was asked to sit on stage for a while as they had a vacant seat to fill. At the next session, Ashdown arrived and the anonymous faces were invited to leave.

27. Not surprisingly it proved extremely difficult to direct the show! It was as if the conductor of a symphonic orchestra stood where his musicians could hardly see him.

28. Until the 1980s, only NEC members could address conference from stage. Ministers had no more speaking rights than ordinary delegates.

29. Access to the platform was previously restricted to members of the NEC who sat in half-empty rows that would fill up for important speeches.

30. The following year, "New Labour" was imposed on headed paper and all publications alongside a new logo and new colour designs for propaganda.

31. A potlatch is a form of competitive feasting organised by some North American Indian tribes during which huge quantities of gifts and food were ritually destroyed. A set can cost well over £100,000.

32. Senior Tories came back from the 2000 Republican Convention with many ideas that were experimented with in the following years. In 2002, Duncan Smith hired the Republican communications guru John McLaughlin to provide advise on tactics.

33. Interviews with Eddie Morgan and Richard Taylor at the party headquarters in Old Queen Street.

34. "An innovation of the Thatcher years", says Shirley Matthews.

35. Panebianco (1988) highlighted the rise of the professionals in politics.

36. There are many informative and entertaining journalistic references on the matter such as Jones (1999) and (2001) or Rawnsley (2001).

37. This way any announcement can get at least three days of coverage. In continental Europe, party congresses remain semi-private affairs. In 2000, Laurent Fabius, then French Finance Minister, had photocopies of his hand written speech distributed to activists. The chore of his intervention focused not on economic policy but on the need to acknowledge the growing importance of environmental issues. Like all the other speakers at the Congress, he read from his notes, as no "head-up unit" (i.e. autocue) are ever made available.

38. Clause 4, part 4 of the party constitution committed Labour to state ownership and was seen by many members as the benchmark against which any betrayal by a Labour government could be measured.

39. In the case of Labour, "conflicts between the unions and the leadership are seen as particularly newsworthy" (Stanyer, 2001: 70), as are anti-European clashes amongst the Conservatives.
40. Labour's media strategy also followed the "three Rs" of education (reading, writing, and 'rithmetic) but took them as rhetoric, repetition and rebuttal (Franklin, 2004: 90).
41. According to party officials, these practices disappeared progressively during the second Labour mandate, through lack of adequate staffing and backlash against over-bearing control.
42. The BBC was apparently so used to Labour's ways that it failed to pick up the importance of Alastair Campbell's complaint about Gilligan's accusation that the government had "sexed up" the Iraqi's weapons of mass destruction intelligence dossier in 2003. The battle escalated, leading to the suicide of intelligence expert Dr Kelly and the resignation of the head of the BBC.
43. Political parties are affected by their environment but they also play an active role in shaping it (Katz and Mair, 1995).
44. Effective spinning has created a dependency amongst journalists towards sources of ready-made news.
45. Thus, the *Sun*'s "big" story at Labour's 2002 conference was the revelation of an old affair between Tony PM John Major and MP Edwin Currie.
46. This is complicated by the fact that Parliament oversees the corporation's Charter. Moreover, internal competition as well as competition with private corporations tends to promote popular political programmes.
47. Policy proposals are formulated and discussed in private (Chapter 8).
48. The decision to go to war in Iraq has made it more difficult to impose self-discipline.
49. Interview on "people switching off politics", www.epolitix.com.
50. BSkyB, the *Times* and the *Sun* are owned by Rupert Murdoch.
51. In 2002, personal rivalry between two political correspondents ended up with one punching the other over breakfast at the Imperial Hotel in Blackpool. The gossip of the day made it into some tabloids, and also provided topical conversation for those awaiting the Chancellor's speech.
52. "How can anyone be a politician?" seems to ask Paxman, reminding us of Montesquieu's "*Comment peut-on être Persan?*" in *Les Lettres Persannes* (1721). Trust in politicians and the media has dramatically deteriorated but the latter are not themselves the sole origin of the malaise (Norris, 1999, 2000).
53. A number of books develop the media point of view including Jones (1999).
54. 1998 Select Committee on Public Administration, quoted by Shaw (2004: 67).
55. Howard Kurtz, "Perpetual Punditry: Analysis unto Death", *Washington Post*, 19 July 1992, quoted by Karabell (1998: 120).
56. ITV covered conferences live from 1960 (and the Liberal Assembly from 1959) until 1982. Channel Four continued live coverage until 1985, including the SDP (Stanyer, 2000: 174).
57. It amounts to about 11 hours per party.
58. Survey of 1,000 people in September 2004 published on 7 October 2004 on http://www.epolitix.com.
59. Increased opportunities to find information may create a virtuous circle (Norris, 2000) of awareness and mobilisation though in many cases, it may just as well contribute to private pursuits.

7   The public performance

1. Since 1823, the Oxford Union trains students for public speaking. It sends debaters to "competitions across the country and the world".
2. Indeed, the leadership simply ignores the contentious decisions taken by the conference.
3. Auditorium politics was conducted with an eye on its broader consequences and organisers were eager to have a "good" conference. However, from 1986, parliamentary parties stage-managed their conference (Gaffney, 1991: 154). See Balandier (1992).
4. Mark McGregor, Conservative Chief Executive, October 2002.
5. Robin Hodgson was Chairman of the National Union then of the Conservative Convention; John Taylor, then President of the National Union, later Chairman of the Convention. Chris Poole was secretary of the National Union then of the National Convention and Board of the party between 1993 and 2003.
6. The powers of patronage held by the National Union were also passed on to the Party Chairman.
7. This is possible for established politicians, such as Robin Cook who had the reputation of refusing to follow instructions.
8. As some sessions last no more than 15 minutes, the stage is sometimes like a game of musical chairs!
9. Speakers would ideally be drawn from all sections of the party, including those often under-represented within the membership and the activists such as ethnic minorities, women and youngsters. Being "representative" is increasingly seen in terms of being a direct mirror of the represented.
10. Although 49 per cent of Conservative members are women, there are notoriously fewer involved in the "political" activities of the party.
11. Because speaker's slips are distributed in advance, sometimes people are called who are not actually physically present during the debate, thus causing delays.
12. None of the representatives I spoke to over the years ever complained about it and most praised the ability of the party to maintain good presentation without the arm twisting allegedly going on in New Labour. Also mentioned by Kelly (1989: 157).
13. Since 2000, slips are only taken until the start of the debate to allow for more spontaneous debates.
14. In the three main parties, green, amber and red lights inform speakers of the end of their time slot.
15. This contrived way provoked hilarity amongst many activists because of the very efforts deployed by John Norris to meet as many participants as possible. Conferences usually attract about 300 activists twice a year. Many come regularly and most know each other well.
16. The Chair has a seating plan of delegations in front of him. It is therefore easy to choose someone from Scotland (at the back of block D for instance) or from UNISON (in block A) especially if the person is also wearing a pink shirt and waving a yellow folder!
17. This probably explains why so many left activists spoke.
18. Interview with Jon Cruddas and his team at the 1997 conference, at the height of their influence. Regional workers help collate all the necessary information about the past activities of the delegates.

19. Drawing lots is indeed the only formula that gives everybody the same chance. All other procedures are biased in one way or another.
20. Trade Union (TU) speakers are usually arranged by mutual prior agreement.
21. This old technique has become systematic and was used for instance during the 2002 debate on PFI. American conventions have also been largely expunged of debates to become public relations exercises (Karabell, 1998).
22. This is a serious problem for New Labour and has considerably fed criticism of "control freakery" and spin. See Goffman (1990: 77).
23. Robert Ezra Park quoted by Goffman (1990: 30).
24. The information they volunteer has to be checked for memory lapses, personal grudges or self-importance.
25. In 1995, several motions urged Conservative politicians to discuss their disagreements "through the long established usual internal channels" (motion 1042).
26. Similarly, the small conferences observed by Kelly (1989) do not require the same degree of self-discipline.
27. Largely because they have been constantly reminded by their leadership of the malevolent omnipresence of journalists.
28. Even the Greens now keep an eye on their image and try to produce a good impression.
29. Advice was available in 1995 in the Conservative booklet of 1995 (pp. 31–36) as well as on the Liberal Democrats Conference Directory.
30. In the following years, delegates were provided with access to a word-processor and could ask for help to enhance the quality of their speeches.
31. There are also regional half a day training sessions for delegates going to conference. They are a good place to be noticed and get on the approved list of speakers! The Conservatives organised their first conference workshops in 2002.
32. Such "real people" were propped up by New Labour on the steps of campaigning ministers to the extent that in the few instances when an unscripted encounter happened it was seized upon avidly by the media: a woman admonished Tony Blair in front of a hospital, a man threw an egg at John Prescott.
33. It did not seem to make much difference.
34. The question of asking them to talk on behalf of the FPC in the future was raised.
35. http://www.libdems.org.uk/documents/policies/Conference_Motions/2002 Brighton.rtf.
36. The discussion was rather peremptorily closed with a statement intimating that "democracy is guaranteed by the independence of the Conference Committee that organises the agenda and the debate". The role of the committee is to "enable the conference to do whatever it wants effectively".
37. Inviting so many outsiders would have been unthinkable a few years ago.
38. Since 1998, 4 hours are devoted to policy seminars.
39. Party activists used to have to wait until the Friday to see their leader on stage. A growing number of motions submitted in 1995 and 1996 had been demanding that the government listen to party members.
40. There were 52 speakers at the Conservative 2000 Conference and 61 in 2002.
41. Teachers and lecturers are aware of such patterns and tend to adapt the style and rhythm of their teaching to this biological fact. Surprisingly, other

parties tend to adopt a more "protestant" work ethic. The Greens sometimes hold early evening plenary sessions. At the other end of the spectrum, ideal-isation of hard work or of the physical performance pushes the French Greens to hold interminable and uninterrupted sessions in the midst of constant movement and incessant conversations.

42. The "attunement" can be interpreted as a liminal marker separating the sacred time of politics from the profane time of other sessions and interactions (see Faucher, 1999a: 195–196).

43. See Chapter 5.

44. It is only feasible because of the small scale of the conference. French socialist and communist delegates have also traditionally sat behind rows of tables, as if taking notes and spreading documents was vital.

45. Merelman considers that family tensions and conflictual relationships – as they appear in *Eastenders* for instance – reveal a British (predominantly working class) public culture that is receptive to open conflict (1991: 138–149).

46. This evolution is not limited to conferences, as cameras, audits, targets and controls have taken over most of the professional life of Britain.

8   The discourse of deliberative democracy

1. Membership figures have slumped in many traditional parties. Labour used to claim over a million direct members in 1950 (a figure admittedly highly unreliable due to the lack of a central membership system) and 300,000 in the mid-1990s. An active recruitment campaign and pre-electoral enthu-siasm helped the membership soar to 405,000 in 1997 but this has have fallen sharply since then. The concept of a crisis of political parties is problematic (see Gunther *et al.*, 2002). The two main British parties commanded 96.8 per cent of the votes in 1951, with a turnout of 82.5 per cent. These figures have dropped to 72.4 per cent and a turnout of 59.4 per cent in 2001.

2. Over the last 30 years, Inglehart (1990) conducted cross-national surveys to measure the evolution of attitudes. He claims that "postmaterialist" values have become more prevalent in post-industrial liberal societies, giving rise to new issues as well as new political organisations.

3. The idea that deliberation produces truth can be traced to Plato and Aristotle but was developed by Karl Schmitt and Jürgen Habermas. On the other hand, the existence of a deliberative assembly was largely taken for granted in the 18th century. Discussion was seen as the best way to convince others and therefore leads to a decision irrespective of the Truth (Manin, 1996: 236–245).

4. Quoted in Fearon (1998: 57). Participation in this fashion seems to be increasingly important as radio and television increasingly organise programmes where people phone in to give their views (or to vote).

5. Invented by Fishkin in 1990s, these polls gather a representative sample of a constituency for a couple of days where they are provided with information and put in a context of communicative rationality.

6. Teorell builds on May's "law of curvilinear disparity" (1973), which purports that activists are likely to be more radical than any party's voters or than the pragmatic elites of the party. This law has often been taken for granted, although recent studies cast doubt on its validity

(Norris, 1995). Although drawing lots is a more democratic system and was used in Ancient Athens, it was never properly considered by the promoters of representative government in the 18th century who took elections for granted (Manin, 1996: 109).

7. To paraphrase Duverger, it seems like a "contamination from the margins".

8. *MfSS* (PG102). Many Greens believe that "the means will be consistent with the ends". Thus, they intend to mould their organisation on the principles of an ecological society. This is linked to their conviction that real change in society will come with a "cultural revolution" rather than through legislation and constraints (Faucher, 1999a, Chapter 6).

9. Decision-making by consensus works best at the local level, when the local party forms a cohesive community as the Oxford Green Party did in the 1990s.

10. When the Greens transformed their Annual General Meeting in a congress of delegates (1992–99), the biggest bone of contention was the possibility for non-delegates to attend and participate. The reform was seen as a challenge to the ideal of participative democracy though it had relatively little effect on actual participation.

11. Various experiments have been conducted by OWOW in the 1980s to assess the most effective ways to conduct inclusive and friendly debates. For instance, they suggested creating concentric circles of chairs, with one the chairs of the smallest circle always free for the next speaker. Another technique, less complicated, involved the use of a *skeptron*, passed around to the next speaker. The technique has long been abandoned by the party but is occasionally used by the pagan Greens as a means to focus attention and improve listening skills. William Golding describes it in *The Lord of the Flies* (London: Faber and Faber, 1954).

12. Because they consider that qualified and interested delegates will attend the relevant workshops and take part in discussions, the Greens do not consider that plenary sessions should dwell on detailed discussions of the motions.

13. Green 2000 is the main example of a structured, ideologically based faction. It successfully campaigned for the adoption of the 1992 constitution but was dismantled soon after, many of its supporters leaving the party altogether (Faucher, 1999a). It fostered a counter group, The Way Ahead, that survived through the 1990s.

14. Green democracy bears many traits comparable to Habermas' model of communicative action (Dryzeck, 1990).

15. Morrissey and Norris do not consider preferences as given and insist on the contrary on the mind-changing experience of deliberation (1993: 12–13).

16. The responsibility of the decision remains with the plenary conference where votes are taken. This is also the case however with the Greens where workshops do not pre-empt the final decision of conference.

17. This was striking at the 1999 Edinburgh spring conference where consultative sessions were literally opened to passers-by.

18. The Tories were quick to denounce them as typical of the secretive nature of New Labour (*The Guardian*, 30/9/98). The Liberal Democrats advertise their consultative sessions and some plenary party business sessions as "private" but the implication for restricted media access has never seemed to bother anyone.

19. More than anything else, these reactions highlighted visions of Labour as intrinsically divided. These were almost as the image of idyllic harmony New Labour was trying to project.

20. In a sense they belong to the tradition of "audiences" when anybody could hope to gain the attention of the King.

21. These included meetings of the Conservative Policy Centre (CPC), which claimed 700 local groups in 1995. Taking into account national and local meetings, Kelly extrapolates that "one may therefore assume that the Conservatives hold far more conferences than any other political party" (1989: 179). In trying to defend his thesis, Kelly overlooks comparable sectional, educational and local meetings in Labour and other parties.

22. This is of course true in all parties and was particularly striking in the case of Paddy Ashdown and Tony Blair, both of whom I followed in 1995 – though Tony's apparitions were much rarer.

23. These speeches are "embargoed" and need to be "checked against delivery". Journalists follow the script, writing down the inevitable deviations and omissions. The most famous example of omission was the reference to rewriting Clause 4 in Blair's inaugural leader speech in 1994. Communication experts are extremely resistant to politicians who want to speak without notes as Ann Widdecombe and Michael Portillo have done.

24. As some Conservative representatives try to increase their chances of being called to the rostrum by submitting in advance the text of their intervention to Ministers and session chairs, Frontbench speakers may actually know in advance what will be said! The talent of politicians from all sides for name-dropping is also acknowledged with admiration in the Labour party.

25. In the style of Conservative conference, the absence of responses to a speech is almost worse than boos because it reflects strong – if mute – disapproval.

26. The poll tax is an example of conference almost making the policy.

27. Only the British government is more secretive!

28. The CPC selected topics for debate long in advance and with little consideration for topicality. It primarily served to "educate" members and inform them of party orientations (Tether, 1996: 122).

29. The estimated number of Conservative members taking part in CPF meetings is about 5,000.

30. The CPF, think tanks, experts and business views are considered in the early stages of policy-making, claims Tait from the Policy unit.

31. Geoffrey Butler, 1957, "The Tory Tradition", quoted by Beer (1982: 93).

32. Conservative Party, *Constitution*, 1999, paragraph 3.11.

33. The average age of Conservative members is 62 (Whiteley, Seyd and Richardson, 1994: 42).

34. The Conservative party published a report on *Listening to Britain* but the new policies were abandoned in 1999 when Hague decided to refocus his electoral strategy on the core supporters.

35. The Forum replaces the Central Council. The decision was influenced by expectations of low attendance.

36. Opening up of conference to all members helped increase participation and create the image of a popular and attractive party. However, it was important to preserve the impression that participants were privileged.

37. Note to the provisional NPF by the Director of Policy, November 1996.

38. "The CLPs' conference", Lyam Byrne, in *Progress*, 31, Autumn 1996.
39. John Evans, speaking for the NEC on Policy-Making, *1996 Conference Verbatim*, p. 214.
40. General Management Committees that had been the stronghold of "old Labour" activists are described as an obstacle to the "modernisation" and the "democratisation" of the party.
41. They were particularly active in Scotland where there was a lot of initial resistance.
42. Focus groups are also used to similar effect and at much reduced costs: they provide clues for policy-makers wishing to format proposals and manifestos according to popular expectations. However, they have disadvantages. First, they cannot offer party members process and collective incentives for participation (Whiteley and Seyd, 2002). Typically, focus groups by-pass the party grassroots, whilst enhancing the impression of a disjunction between the elite and the base. They thus feed the feeling that membership is an ineffective way to influence policies. Moreover, it alienates members who miss community and solidarity feelings generated through participation.
43. http://www.annblack.com/npf_july2003.htm.
44. 2001 electoral broadcast (http://news.bbc.co.uk/vote2001/hi/english/newsId_1354000/1354375.stm).
45. The Third Way, argues Alan Finlayson, "is conceptually dependent on a repression of the possibility that social change is something to which politics responds by directing rather than ameliorating" (Finlayson 2003: 136).
46. A similar approach was used in government.
47. Difficult policies have often escaped the party's policy process and been imposed by the government on resistant and resentful MPs and members.
48. The expression, used by Scarrow (1996: 43) began to be used by Labour in the mid-1990s. See Martin and Cowley (1999).
49. Ann Black (interview; letter to the General Secretary, 8 November 1995; report on a National Political Education Conference, Reading, 10 June 1995).
50. This has badly affected constituency representatives on the NPF who have to self-fund their participation to the annual conference where they are elected and to which they are accountable.
51. "Inclusivity is understood as the only way to bring security to people in the new society and as part of the logic of the new economy which must draw on all the talents and creativity of people" (Finlayson, 2003: 130).
52. Many activists in either party are convinced that their debates are riveting.

9 Direct democracy: The vote as fetish

1. The vote determines arithmetically the majority. We live in a world dominated by figures, quantities and counting as shown by David Boyle in *The Tyranny of Numbers. Why Counting Can't Make Us Happy*, London: Flamingo, 2001.
2. Conference decisions have been recorded and compiled even though comparison is of little use because Conservative conference decisions are purely informative (Craig, 1982).

3. Clement Atlee (1949), *The Labour Party in Perspective: and Twelve Years Later*, London, p. 93 – quoted by Punnett (1987: 103).
4. In 1968 for instance, Wilson took "note" of conference decisions on prices but refused to accept it as an "instruction".
5. The 1993 vote on OMOV was "probably the last time a vote really mattered in the Labour Party" bemoans the BBC producer Gareth Butler.
6. The little suspense that now characterises these hyped up conference decisions is not particular to Britain: many European congresses and American conventions are even more predictable. Since changes in the nomination process in the 1960s, delegates to the Republican and Democratic Conventions gather to endorse a choice of candidate decided through state primaries. Combined with the pressure exercised by network news, this development brought about the demise of conventions as "meaningful public events" (Karabell, 1998: 4). They are "institutionalising ritual" (Bourdieu, 2001: 175–187).
7. Occasionally, the vocal approval of the hall is enough to satisfy participants, for instance in the case of the approval of the Labour CAC daily reports on proceedings. The proposal has never been defeated.
8. This is an improvement on the chaotic Liberal conference where it was not always clear who was entitled to vote – but the party had no chance of reaching power so it did not really matter.
9. They even vote on whether or not they are going to vote! In the Green Party, activists convinced that consensus was the only sustainable and legitimate way of taking decision have tended to avoid taking part in such a "divisive" procedure. At conference, such activists focus on workshop and fringe meetings and hardly attend plenary sessions.
10. Daily news-sheets are distributed in all parties but most eagerly in Labour and the Liberal Democrats. In both cases they provide opportunities to sum up the previous day's decisions, announce important votes, and publicise fringe meetings.
11. In the Green Party, card votes are not usually called. In 1992 though, the new constitution was adopted through such a procedure as intense canvassing had allowed its advocates to collect proxy votes from a large number of passive members.
12. Card votes were introduced in 1953 to respond to public anxiety about union leaders holding block votes but served to entrench it further, making it the "natural" form of union participation in the Labour party (Minkin, 1991: 286). Each Labour delegate has a booklet of cards that are coded (with number and bar code) and allow scrutinisers to distinguish in the result not only the orientation of the vote but also whether the voter is a constituency, union or socialist delegate and how many votes she represents (union delegates usually represent several hundreds). For the 1981 election NEC, a million votes "disappeared" from the total expected by one of the candidates. Unusually a recount was called and it appeared that the tellers had made a mistake (Minkin, 1991: 330).
13. Apart from these occasions, the role of unions remained overall "discreet and politically constrained", following "unwritten 'rules' and arrangements derived mainly from industrial considerations" (Minkin, 1991: 323).
14. Tom Sawyer, quoted in Taylor (1997: 61).
15. Even then, it was a matter of interpretation and "spin".

16. At the same time, conference votes were to be announced in percentages rather than millions, as it was the custom.

17. In some cases, it may be easier to vote against the government with the knowledge that its position will not be damaged because the vote is won with the support of constituency delegates. See Shaw (2004: 57–58).

18. Different votes carry different weight from composites and constitutional amendments, to the adoption of reports and the approbation of committee decisions. The General Secretary, for instance, is chosen by the leader, elected by the NEC and confirmed by conference.

19. When delegates have a variety of decisions to make it is always possible to negotiate and bargain their support for something they care little about in exchange for concessions on something they care a great deal about (Coleman, 1966). The compositing system was particularly vulnerable: internal groups rivalled to influence delegates' perception of stakes, procedures and content. When preferences are private, it is impossible to distinguish whether the result was reached without manipulation (Mackie, 1998: 74).

20. The NEC traditionally gives a recommendation on how delegates should vote. Although debates are supposed to convince delegates and representatives, they have rarely swung votes.

21. *Campaign Briefing* is published by Labour Left Liaison (which includes Campaign for Labour Party Democracy and the party's Black Section), *Original Briefing* and the Socialist Campaign Group of Labour MPs. Only the official newsletter can be distributed within the conference centre. Others are handed out to delegates as they go in amongst leaflets announcing fringe meetings.

22. Between 1995 and 2000 Blair was undefeated at conference. In 2000, the unions voted against the government on pensions.

23. Online chat with John Reid organised during conference on the party website (http://www.labour.org.uk/ac2003qandaarchive/?chatid=44).

24. This intrigued activists and was a good way to open conversations. Being an ethically responsible researcher I never distorted the results by taking part in the hand votes ...

25. Votes are very rarely counted – it happened most recently in 1992 on a motion on Europe.

26. Conservative Party (1995), motion 1082.

27. 1988 British Liberal Democrats; 1992 for the election of the Chair of the Green Party executive; 1993 for the constituency component of the Labour college and 1998 in the Conservative party.

28. The rapid development of the new sub-discipline of political marketing follows the adoption of marketing techniques by the two main British parties. It also reflects the growing influence of the business model in Western societies.

29. Note by General Secretary on the party in power, 31/1/1996.

30. Labour party (1996), *NEC Report*, p. 9.

31. The British government now also issues reports on delivery of its promises. The first was published in 1998–99 (Labour party, *The Government's Annual Report*, Stationary Office).

32. There were of course other arguments as well in favour of the constitution such as the need to increase co-ordination of the constituency associations,

centralise and organise relationships with members and rationalise finances – Central Office was structurally dependent on rich Constituency Associations reticent to pass on resources.

33. Matt Carter for instance used the phrase on taking up the post of Labour General Secretary in December 2003. See also Chapter 8.

34. New members, isolated from the traditional networks of party socialisation were anticipated to be potentially less radical. Modernisers in the Labour party argued that traditional activists might deter people from joining because of their entrenched ways of working and their radicalism.

35. Studies show that local campaigning is the key to electoral victory in marginal constituencies and this can only be achieved with mobilisation of activists' networks (Seyd and Whiteley, 1992; Whiteley *et al.*, 1994). See also (Denver and Hands, 1997).

36. Such costs encompassed difficulties in finding and joining the local party. Fees remain low in Britain compared to other European countries where they are sometimes indexed on income, though one objection to the reform was that fees might deter people from joining.

37. Until recently, Labour and the Conservatives were dependent on their local branches for any liaison with members. Local parties managed the membership and provided national headquarters with unreliable figures that made them look good. To give the appearance of competent management, a former Conservative association Chairman explains that he announced every year a steady increase of 10 per cent of new members. That was a sensible thing to do and "only an embellishment" of reality. The Greens had similar problems in their early years but the Liberal Democrats immediately set up such a database for the purpose of internal ballots.

38. Thus, when the Conservative party tried in 1998 to justify the centralisation of membership, arguments emphasised the right to vote for the election of the party leader, improved communication with Central Office that would meet their desire to be heard and valued. In spring 2000, Central Office sent out to members the first issue of *Conservative Heartland*, a new magazine providing a link between the leader and the members.

39. Labour went on-line as early as 1996. The Conservatives advertised Conservatives.com at the 1998 conference before it was actually launched!

40. French parties have often been unable to retain membership to the point that they are called "colander parties".

41. There are a variety of indicators showing that the bases for party allegiance were often belonging rather than agreement. Such attitudes explain for instance, the reactions of the party to the 1931 crisis when MacDonald was expelled from the party, carrying over with him a handful of MPs but not a single constituency organisation nor prominent union leader (Beer, 1982: 85–86).

42. See Liberal Democrats, *Federal Executive Report*, 2001: 8.

43. Labour Co-ordinating Committee pamphlet (1982: 31). Trade unions resisted to the introduction of OMOV because they feared a reduction of their influence. The rhetoric of democratisation was crucial for the success of the reform and trade unions eventually yielded because of the perception that they had become the third most important reason for not voting Labour in 1992 (Ludlam, 2001b: 115). To reassure potential voters, Blair

consistently insisted that unions would be treated like other interest groups, with fairness rather than favours (Seyd, 1998).

44. Unions held 40 per cent of the votes in the new electoral college. The system proved cumbersome and open to manipulation.

45. It is probably an over-exaggeration to attribute to the new electoral system the sole responsibility for the demise of the left but it did "reduce the scope for manipulative stratagems" (Shaw, 1994: 119) at various levels of the party.

46. The vote was won thanks to a passionate speech by John Prescott and a last minute change of tactics from one of the major unions. Despite its mandate to oppose, delegates from MSFU decided to abstain. The electoral college for the election of the party leader was adjusted to three equal constituent parts in 1993.

47. Seventy-five percentage of constituency parties balloted their members and only three of them voted against. As often, New Labour used the national media to win an internal battle (Wring, 1998).

48. Turnout was high (80 per cent) but only highly active and motivated party officers were polled.

49. The transformation of the party was perceived as tactical and hypocritical. It also proved a failure as a marketing strategy and was therefore insufficient to help the Tories (Lees-Marshment and Quayle, 2000).

50. Membership surveys do not appear to confirm expectations about docile or deferential members but there were too few ballots to test the assertion. Meeting-attenders do not appear more radical than members that do not attend (Seyd, 1999: 396) except on issues concerning the role of the trade union and the organisation itself. Blair only organised two such ballots: on Clause 4 in 1995 and on the draft manifesto in 1996. In 1998, the leadership tried to ensure the election of a slate of loyal supporters to the newly reorganised NEC (constituency representatives cannot be MPs) but met organised resistance from the Left who won four out of six seats.

51. Philip Chambers.

52. *Tribune*, 31 March 1995.

53. The reform had been attempted by Gaitskell and Kinnock but Blair was successful because he by-passed activists.

54. Unreliable Conservative membership data was exposed for the 2001 leadership election: lapsed members received ballots whilst others were excluded.

55. http://www.annblack.com/nec_nov2000.htm. Turnout for NEC election was 25 per cent in 2000 and 45 per cent of those who voted chose Tony Robinson, an actor best known for his role in the popular *Blackadder* TV series. But by 1997, considering the increase in the membership and the turnover, 40 per cent of eligible voters were new members (Fielding, 2003: 129) probably more likely to be influenced by celebrity factors outside of the party.

56. The cost of such ballots is carried by the parties themselves. Competition between factions can be intense and there are often allegations of "paper members" joining. French parties organise the votes at local meetings and the practice encourages at least minimum contacts between members. Thus, it is easier to control fraud. Levels of activism in the PS are claimed to be quite high. In December 2004, the PS managed to mobilise an exceptionally high number of members for an internal referendum on the

European constitution: 83 per cent of its 120,000 members voted. The leadership won with 56.6 per cent after weeks of intense public debate and great suspense. On the other hand, internal ballots organised in the late 1990s on policy issues had disappointing turnouts: 46 per cent of members voted on Business and on Europe, 35 per cent on *Territories*. In 1998, 71 per cent of members declared regularly attending party meetings and 80 per cent considered themselves to be activists (Boy *et al.*, 2003). The level of fraud in postal ballots is unassessed.

57. Although workers' clubs existed, the tradition is more associated with the Conservatives (Campbell, 1987).

58. Such extended semi-membership has existed in France for some time. There, political parties are inherently suspected of illegitimacy and there is more reluctance to join.

59. Only 15 per cent of them support a plebiscitary party, 50 per cent are in favour of forums.

60. A sense of personal efficacy and ambition are important to motivate members to take part.

61. Quoted in Peter Hain (2004: 15). The danger of email newsletters is that recipients click the delete button as automatically as they would have thrown away leaflets in the past.

62. Although it had the benefit of letting members express their opinions, the study produced more paper than was exploitable by the small policy team. The exercise was not repeated even though tick box questionnaires are occasionally used on specific issues.

63. The Conservatives experimented with primaries in a few pilot schemes such as Warrington where the selecting meeting was open to the public but the procedure has not been generalised. Removing such an important decision from the hands of radicalised members may be an advantage but the consequences on activism could be important as the selection of candidates has traditionally been one of the few means of influence for Conservative members (Norris and Lovenduski, 1995).

64. Launched at the Southport NPF on 28 November 2003, it received contributions by Internet, phone or text messaging until the 2004 Spring Conference (http://www.bigconversation.org.uk/index.php?id = 679).

65. Members are on other occasions called "stakeholders" but their stakes may not amount to much more than those of supporters. The Labour government, moreover, has repeatedly reminded conference delegates that it is only accountable to voters. See note 23 for John Reid's response on Foundation Hospitals.

66. *The Guardian*, 23 March 2004. A "humane" approach to politics now reduces citizens to shoppers!

67. Interview first published by *Woman's Own*, 31 October 1987, pp. 8–10.

68. Peter Hain, quoted in Seyd and Whiteley (2002: 216).

69. Comparatively speaking, European party congresses vote little: the French socialists for instance vote before the congress when they select their delegates who no longer elect the leader but merely ratify the list of candidates for the national council that is prepared in backroom negotiations.

70. The introduction of OMOV was a long battle initiated by Kinnock but won by Smith.

71. It is unlikely that the Conservatives would have thought about it if it had not been apparently so effective in "modernising" the image of the Labour party.

10 Fringe benefits: Dissent vs commercialisation

1. The RSPB for instance provides information on birds' habitats and environmental protection that is used in particular by MPs and local councillors in relation to projects such as the extension of motorways, city bypasses or airport runways.
2. The main hotels are a central focus but many participants prefer more discreet settings in town.
3. A great deal of alcohol is usually consumed and early morning absenteeism at plenary sessions can often be accounted for by looking at the activities on the fringe the night before. Alcohol is a common denominator of all conferences though in 1996 one was likely to get tipsy with white wine at New Labour parties and beer with the Greens. Champagne was a feature of the Conservatives in government, "now you are lucky to get a glass of Lambrusco" complained disgruntled activists to *The Guardian* (7/10/03). The abuse of alcohol on the fringe is occasionally a matter of concern and was for instance discussed by the Conservative Board after the 2002 conference. British sociability often involves large quantities of alcohol (leading successive governments to imagine ways to control consumption through the regulation of opening times for pubs or on-the-spot fines) whilst it tends to focus on equally large quantities of food (and wine) in France. See Chapter 3.
4. This need for access was amplified by the policy of deregulation conducted by Margaret Thatcher's government.
5. Interview with Bill Bush, former lobbyist and BBC producer, then political adviser at the Department of Culture. It could also be seen as easing dependency on trade union funding at a time when these organisations were under attack from the Thatcher government and becoming less popular.
6. Philip Norton (1995), "Yes the Conference really does matter", *The House Magazine*, 689, 9 October.
7. One can distinguish ideological/broad based groups (such as One Nation Tory-ism) from those coalesced around a single-issue (such as the Euro-sceptic Bruges group). Paul Webb distinguishes factions, tendencies and single-issue groups according to levels of ideological coherence, stability, discipline and structure (Webb, 2000: 171–176). The contrast between the Conservatives as "a party of tendencies" and Labour as "a party of factions" is now disputed (Cowley and Stuart, 2004: 17).
8. Ideologically based groups often attract activists in search of a tribune for their views or those aspiring to make the right connections and enhance their career prospects.
9. Religious groups (predominantly Christian) also take the opportunity to gather. Seventy-two per cent of Green Party members declare they are not religious (Faucher, 1999a: 78). They are also the least orthodox, with only 10 per cent declaring affiliation to the Church of England, 5 per cent Quakers and 5 per cent "non Christians" (that includes Buddhists, Wiccas and Pagans).

By contrast, 70 per cent of Conservatives declare being Anglican, against 28 per cent Labour (41 per cent self-declared non-religious) and 45 per cent Liberal Democrats (35 per cent non-religious). Religious gatherings are organised in all parties, usually as a morning Christian service in a local church. French parties are extremely touchy about the influence of religions on public affairs. Such fringe meetings would be unthinkable, if not "anathema", for the *Gauche Plurielle*, who profess a "religious" attachment to *laïcité*. By contrast, the 2000 French socialist congress discussed the inclusion of references to a Christian or even "spiritual" European heritage. In 2004, the French National Assembly (by 494 out of 577 votes) adopted new legislation to reinforce *laïcité* in schools, banning ostentatious religious signs.

10. Their role is enshrined in party constitution since 1971 in the Socialist Party and since 2004 in the newly founded dominant right wing party, the UMP.

11. Groups such as Campaign for Labour Party Democracy or Labour Co-ordinating Committee developed in the 1970s. In 1980, a rule targeting the Militant Tendency forced all internal groups to register and open to all party members. Those who refused were penalised by being removed from the Conference fringe listing or prevented from holding a conference stall (Seyd, 1987: 63).

12. Groups organise slates of candidates to Backbench committees (Norton, 1990).

13. In 2002, the Liberal Democrats charged a fee of £118 to appear in the Conference Directory.

14. Fringe meetings at the French Socialist congresses are limited to general meetings of competing factions where group strategy and the opportunity to form a coalition to take part in the executive are discussed. Single-issue groups and workshops are however organised at summer gatherings such as the *Universités d'été*.

15. They rely on the contributions and fees provided by their members.

16. Tam McFarlane (2002), "Stage managed? I couldn't say...", *FireFighter*, January/February, p. 25.

17. The fringe had been cancelled due to lack of participants but, after journalists' enquiries, it was staged for the sole purpose of providing pictures of elegantly dressed activists greeting each other. This provoked a heated debate in the party. Despite their eagerness to get attention, the set up could be seen as caricaturing the movement and thus bringing bad publicity.

18. Journalists from the *Sun* claim that they do not even bother checking the listings because "there is always enough time to catch up on what happens at the main hotel bar". The leadership's fear of dissent gives dissenters a bargaining argument as they can threaten to make a fuss.

19. This is by no means an original strategy: at the 2003 French Socialist Dijon congress, the arrival of guests from trade unions or allied parties were "miraculously" synchronised with speeches by delegates from minority factions, thus conveniently diverting attention away from the debate.

20. Thanks to centralised membership lists, parties have stepped up the production of conventional and email internal newsletters.

21. *The Guardian, Sky News, The Independent, The Telegraph*, and the BBC organise debates.

22. These organisations are typically a product of the subcontracting or the outsourcing of policy-making by political parties and the British government. They feed on the network approach to governance.
23. The Green Party is not included in their research. They have no commercial exhibitors.
24. Leys (2001) argues that the movement could not be stopped once initiated.
25. See Janet Newman's (2001) enlightening analysis of New Labour's approach to governance. She underlines the intrinsic contradictions of reforms that sought to combine contradictory models of governance and resulted in a superimposition of hierarchical, centralising methods with initiatives based on the development of new policy networks and communities.
26. Quangos were created by Thatcher to advise and administer matters of public concern (from prisons services to education or health) at arms length from government (Jenkins, 1995). Despite its electoral promises, the Labour government has not dismantled them.
27. James O'Shaughnessy, LLM Communications, 17/05/2004.
28. Interestingly, in this way a publicly funded organisation spends a lot of money attending all three party conferences, thereby creating an innovative way to direct state funds to political parties.
29. http://www.bba.org.uk/public/newsroom/pressreleases/149363.
30. Interviews with representatives from the RSPB in 1995, 1996, 2000 and 2003.
31. Parties are particularly keen to raise money in the run up to an election and therefore offer more opportunity for advertising or sponsoring. Harris and Lock report a 175 per cent increase in advertising between 1995 and 1996 Labour conferences (Harris and Lock, 2002: 142). In 1996, the Conservative exhibition extended to the swimming pool of the Bournemouth conference centre.
32. In all parties, a large number of stalls are affiliated organisations.
33. Ninety per cent of Labour fringe meetings offer free refreshments but the quality of the food varies with the expected guests: champagne and canapés, rubber chicken or instant coffee. In this context, sponsorship by institutional and commercial actors is increasingly necessary. In 1996, few Conservative fringes offered free food and drinks as representatives can usually afford to lunch and dine out. The same year, the *Guardian's* buffets at Labour and Liberal Democrat conferences were ravaged before the debate started and the audience was still queuing as the chair introduced the panellists.
34. Even the Greens have now joined in this pattern and have opened their meetings more widely to other groups: in 2004, conference organisers announced on their website: "this autumn conference is also our AGM and will focus on networking with other leading Green and social justice and human rights groups" (http://www.greenparty.org.uk/index.php?nav = nextconference). The expansion of the fringe has transformed the atmosphere. In the mid-1990s, the exhibition retained a village atmosphere. Every year, the same people manned stalls such as the Falkland Islands or Compassionate Farming. The parliamentary staff of cause groups and lobby firms were experienced on the conference circuit. They knew each other well and toured the three cities, for several years. Newcomers on the circuit such as Bloomberg rotate teams on the stall itself every day.

35. Organisers probably assume that granting charities a discount when hiring an exhibition space is sufficient to redress the imbalance and put them on an equal footing to the private businesses that campaign in the same area. Such an attitude reflects a naïve approach to the reality of the markets.

36. In 2000, the Conservatives had no prospect of winning and a small exhibition but those manning the stalls were happy to receive a lot of attention from participants.

37. The Post Office prevented its rival from exhibiting at Labour conferences until 1994 (Harris and Lock, 2002: 139).

38. The exhibition is now limited to sister or ancillary organisations: the PS Congress in Grenoble had stalls for the *Fondation Jean Jaurès* or the *Office Universitaire de Recherche Socialiste* but its commercial dimension was limited to a post office, a bookshop, a newsagent and a stall set up by the tourist bureau to promote local products. Conference participants could taste walnuts, wines and cheeses but could neither purchase them nor obtain retailers' addresses.

39. In 1997, the combined income of the three main parties amounted to 55 per cent of the German SPD 1990 budget (Webb, 2000: 242).

40. Unions gave Labour two thirds of its income in 1992 but only a third in 2003 (*The Guardian*, 1/4/2003).

41. The Conservative party follows here the tradition of balls that is also preserved by Oxford's wealthiest colleges.

42. Diners were charged £1,500 for a table of ten by Labour in 1997 and £500 by the Liberal Democrats in 2003.

43. Less than 1 per cent of the Green Party income comes from conference stalls (though nearly 9 per cent derives from advertising in the party newsletters). Most of the exhibition space is taken up by campaigning groups. Donations to the Green Party are almost exclusively from members (Adam Stacey, administration officer, 13/4/2004).

44. State funding of the parliamentary opposition was nearly tripled in 1999.

45. Even delegates and representatives are charged for participation (see Chapter 2), in contrast with party congresses in continental Europe.

46. Parties offer discounts to internal organisations (such as Arts for Labour) and to charities (such as Compassionate Farming).

47. *NEC Report*, 1997, p. 19.

48. *The Guardian*, 10 September 2002.

49. Wallets containing conference documents were the first to carry the name of sponsors. In 1998, Labour delegates were given plastic wallets with the logo of the Daily Express – it was the Co-operative movement a few years before.

50. ePolitix.com is a free-to-use politics Internet site that aims to improve communication between elected representatives and the public.

51. Estimates quoted by the *Guardian* (30/8/2001).

52. Thanks to the sprawling exhibition area and a gala dinner costing executives up to £475 per plate (*The Guardian*, October 1, 2004).

53. The weather prevented the strategy as that particular entrance was dangerously slippery.

54. The Liberal Democrats' leader usually gives a short speech to thank commercial exhibitors. In other parties, the role is usually devolved to a high-ranking politician.

55. These receptions are generally also sponsored by a business. McDonald's is one of them though they do not have a stall nor an outlet at any of the conferences – yet.
56. David Hill has also acted as a representative for Securicor Custodial Services, a company that bids for government contracts in the prison services.
57. Loss of trust makes it very difficult for an individual or an organisation to operate in policy networks or with government as a lobbyist (Harris, 2002a: 244).
58. www.foe.co.uk/resource/press_releases/big_business_in_bournemouth.html.
59. Quoted in *Guardian*, 30 August 2001.
60. http://www.labour.org.uk/conf2003nameorder/.
61. This self-fulfilling prophecy guarantees a waiting list for the attribution of stalls and the sponsoring of various events to the great benefit of party coffers.
62. Although many "invitation only" meetings can be "crashed" with a (very nice) smile or a bit of strategic planning, academic researchers rarely get funding to attend dinners that cost several hundred pounds. In any case, I did not.

Conclusion – Politics in the age of the individual

1. New Labour re-discovered events organised for the sake of socialising but they are in competition with more attractive alternatives than in the past and have so far failed to create social glue.
2. May (1973). The introduction of OMOV in Labour was largely inspired by such distrust.
3. It is an interesting manoeuvre to grant members new voting rights with the argument that votes are an effective way to take part in decision-making whilst ensuring on the other hand that the outcome of ballots are as predictable as possible. Although parties proclaim that citizens need to be treated as rational voters, they clearly have little faith in their ability to evaluate the real impact of their participation or little qualms about blatant hypocrisy!
4. In fact, their influence on policies is likely to be small compared to others such as party donors, contributors and sponsors who get access to the Frontbench on the conference fringe as well as throughout the year.
5. De Gaulle, who was not seen by everybody as a reliable democrat, had a similar vision of the relationship between the leader and the electorate and open distaste for political parties.
6. Only the Greens have retained a universalist utopian aspiration (Faucher, 1999a) that contrast with the pragmatic, *Real Politik* outlook of mainstream parties.
7. This is the new objective of the Labour government, according to Tony Blair (Speech at Chatham in Kent, 13 January 2005).
8. Speech to the World Economic Forum, 27 January 2005, Davos.

Bibliography

Abélès, Marc (1989), *Jours tranquilles en 89. Ethnologie politique d'un département français*, Paris: Odile Jacob.

Abélès, Marc (1992), *La vie quotidienne au Parlement Européen*, Paris: Hachette.

Abélès, Marc (1999), *Un ethnologue à l'Assemblée*, Paris: Odile Jacob.

Alderman, Keith (1998), "The Conservative Party Leadership Election of 1997", *Parliamentary Affairs*, 50 (1), 1–16.

Almond, Gabriel and Sydney Verba (1963), *Civic Culture*, Boston: The Little Brown Series in Comparative Politics.

Anderson, Benedict (1991), *Imagined Communities. Reflections on the Origins and the Spread of Nationalism*, London: Verso.

Ansell, Christopher K. (1997), "Symbolic Networks: The Realignment of the French Working Class. 1887–1894", *American Journal of Sociology*, 103 (2), 359–390.

Ansell, Christopher K. and Steven Fish (1999), "The Art of Being Indispensable. Noncharismatic Personalism in Contemporary Political Parties", *Comparative Political Studies*, 32 (3), 283–312.

Asad, Talal (1993), *Genealogies of Religion. Discipline and Reasons of Power in Christianity and Islam*, Baltimore: John Hopkins University Press.

Bachrach, Peter and Morton S. Baratz (1970), *Power and Poverty: Theory and Practice*, New York: Oxford University Press.

Badie, Bertrand and Marc Sadoun (eds) (1996), *L'Autre. Etudes réunies pour Alfred Grosser*, Paris: Presses de Sciences Po.

Bailey, F.G. (1969), *Stratagems and Spoils. A Social Anthropology of Politics*, NY: Schocken Books.

Balandier, Georges (1985), *Le détour. Pouvoir et modernité*, Paris: Fayard.

Balandier, Georges (1992), *Le pouvoir sur scènes*, Paris: Balland.

Bale, Tim (2000), "Crimes and Misdemeanours: Managing Dissent in the Twentieth and Twenty-First Century Labour Party", in Brivati and Hefferman, *The Labour Party. A Centenary Party*, Basingstoke: Palgrave Macmillan, pp. 268–291.

Ball, Martin (1996), *The Conservative Conference & Euro-Sceptical Motions 1992– 95*, Bruges Group, http://www.brugesgroup.com/mediacentre/index.live?article=120.

Barker, Rodney (2001), *Legitimating Identities. The Self-Presentation of Rulers and Subjects*, Cambridge: Cambridge University Press.

Barnes, Samuel (1968), "Party Democracy and the Logic of Collective Action", in Crotty (ed.), *Approaches to the Study of Organisation*, Boston: Allyn and Bacon Inc., pp. 105–138.

Barry, Brian (1970), *Sociologists, Economists and Democracy*, London: Collier Macmillan.

Beer, Samuel H. (1982), *Modern British Politics*, London: Faber and Faber.

Bell, Catherine (1992), *Ritual Theory, Ritual Practice*, New York: Oxford University Press.

Bell, Catherine (1997), *Ritual. Perspectives and Dimensions*, New York: Oxford University Press.

Bell, David (2000), "La conference du Labour Party et le Congrès du PS: Un regard britannique croisé", *Recherche Socialiste*, 12, 71–80.

Berger, Peter (1986), *Invitation to Sociology. A Humanistic Perspective*, Harmondsworth: Penguin.

Berger, Peter and Thomas Lückmann (1984), *The Social Construction of Reality. A Treatise in the Sociologie of Knowledge*, London: Penguin Books.

Berry, Jeffrey M. (2002), "Validity and Reliability Issues in Elite Interviewing", *Political Science and Politics*, 35 (4), 679–682.

Blumenthal, S. (1982), *The Permanent Campaign*, New York: Simon and Schuster.

Blumler, Jay and Michael Gurevitch (2001), "Americanization Reconsidered: UK–US Campaign Communication Comparisons Across Time", in Lance Bennet and Robert Entman, *Mediated Politics. Communication in the Future of Democracy*, Cambridge: Cambridge University Press, pp. 380–406.

Bon, Frédéric (1991), *Les discours de la politique*, Paris: Economica.

Bourdieu, Pierre (1974), "Avenir de classe et causalité du probable", *Revue Française de Sociologie*, 15 (1), 3–42.

Bourdieu, Pierre (2000), *Esquisse d'une theorie de la pratique*, Paris: Seuil.

Bourdieu, Pierre (2001), *Language et pouvoir symbolique*, Paris: Fayard.

Boy, Daniel, François Platone, Henri Rey, Françoise Subileau and Colette Ysmal (2003), *C'était la gauche plurielle*, Paris: Presses de Sciences Po.

Brivati, Brian and Richard Heffernan (2000), *The Labour Party. A Centenary History*, London: Macmillan.

Bulmer-Thomas, Ivor (1965), *The Growth of the British Party System*, volume 1: *1640–1923*, volume 2: *1924–1964*, London: John Baker.

Butler, David and Dennis Kavanagh (1997), *The British General Election of 1997*, London: Macmillan.

Byrd, P. (1987), "Parties in a Changing Party System", in A. Ware (ed.), *Political Parties: Electoral Change and Structural Response*, Oxford: Basil Blackwell.

Cameron, Angus and Ronen Palan (2004), *The "Imagined Economies" of Globalisation*, London: Sage.

Campbell, Alastair (2002), "Time to Bury Spin", *British Journalism Review*, 13 (4), 15–23.

Campbell, Beatrix (1987), *The Iron Ladies: Why Do Women Vote Tory?*, London: Virago.

Carty, Kenneth (2004), "Parties as Franchise Systems. The Stratarchical Organisational Imperative", *Party Politics*, 10 (1), 5–24.

Clifford, James (1988), *The Predicament of Culture: Twentieth Century Ethnography, Literature and Art*, Cambridge, MA: Harvard University Press.

Coleman, James (1966), "Foundation for a Theory of Collective Decisions", *American Journal of Sociology*, 71 (6), 615–627.

Connerton, Paul (1989), *How Societies Remember*, Cambridge: Cambridge University Press.

Conservative Party (1995), *Conference Guide*, London: Conservative Central Office.

Conservative Party (1997), *Our Party Blueprint for Change: A Consultation Paper for Reform of the Conservative Party*, London: Conservative Central Office.

Conservative Party (1998), *The Fresh Future The Conservative Party Renewed*, London: Conservative Central Office.

Conservative Party (1999), *Constitution of the Conservative Party*, October.

Cook, Chris (2002), *A Short History of the Liberal Party. 1900–2001*, Basingstoke: Palgrave Macmillan.

Cowley, Philip and Mark Stuart (2004), "When Sheep Bark: The Parliamentary Labour Party since 2001", *British Elections and Parties Review*, http://www.revolts.co.uk/BEPR%20article.pdf.

Cowley, Philip and Philip Norton (1999), "Rebels and Rebellions: Conservative MPs in the 1992 Parliament", *British Journal of Politics and International Relations*, 1 (1), 84–105.

Craig, FWS (1982), *Conservative and Labour Party Conference Decisions 1945–1981*, Chichester: Parliamentary Research Services.

Crewe, Ivor and Anthony King (1995), *SDP. The Birth, Life and Death of the Social Democratic Party*, Oxford: Oxford University Press.

Cronin, James (2004), "Speaking for Whom? From 'old' to 'New Labour'", in Kay Lawson and Thomas Poguntke (eds), *How Political Parties Respond. Interest Aggregation Revisited*, London: Routledge, pp. 15–40.

Crozier, Michel and Erhard Friedberg (1981), *L'acteur et le système*, Paris: Seuil.

Daalder, Hans (2002), "Parties: Denied, Dismissed, or Redundant? A Critique", in Richard Gunther, José Ramón Montero and Juan J. Linz (eds), *Political Parties – Old Concepts and New Challenges*, Oxford: Oxford University Press, pp. 39–57.

Daalder, R.H. and Mair Peter (eds) (1983), *Western European Party System. Continuity and Change*, London: Sage, pp. 405–429.

Dalton, Russell and Martin Kuechler (1990), *Challenging the Political Order. New Social Movements in Western Democracies*, Oxford: Polity.

Dayan, Daniel and Elihu Katz (1992), *Media Events*, Cambridge: Cambridge University Press.

De Certeau, Michel (1990), *L'invention du quotidien*, Paris: Gallimard.

Della, Porta Donatella and Mario Diani (1999), *Social Movements. An Introduction*, Oxford: Blackwell.

Denver, David and Gordon Hands (1997), "Challengers, Incumbents and the Impact of Constituency Campaigning in Britain", *Electoral Studies*, 16 (2), 175–193.

Dirks, Nicholas (1992), "Ritual and Resistance: Subversion as a Social Fact", in Douglas Haynes and Gyan Prakash (eds), *Contesting Power. Resistance and Everyday Social Relations in South Asia*, Berkeley: University of California Press, pp. 213–238.

Doherty, Brian and Markus De-Geus (eds) (1996), *Democracy and Green Political Theory*, Routledge.

Douglas, Mary (1976), *Purity and Danger. An Analysis of Concepts of Pollution and Taboo*, London and Henley: Routledge and Kegan Paul.

Douglas, Mary (1999), "Jokes", *Implicit Meanings. Selected Essays in Anthropology*, London: Routledge, pp. 146–164.

Downs, Anthony (1957), *An Economic Theory of Democracy*, New York: Harper.

Drucker, Henry (1979), *Doctrine and Ethos in the Labour Party*, London: Allen and Unwin.

Dryzeck, John (1990), *Discursive Democracy. Politics, Polity and Political Science*, Cambridge University Press.

Dryzeck, John (2000), *Deliberative Democracy and Beyond*, Oxford: Oxford University Press.

Dunleavy, Patrick, Andrew Gamble, Richard Heffernan and Gillian Peele (eds) (2002), *Developments in British Politics*, Basingstoke: Palgrave Macmillan.

Durkheim, Emile (1968), *Les formes élémentaires de la vie religieuse: le système totémique en Australie*, Paris: Presses Universitaires de France.

Duverger, Maurice (1964), *Political Parties. Their Organisation and Activity in the Modern State*, London: Methuen.

Edelman, Murray (1985), *The Symbolic Uses of Politics*, Urbana: University of Illinois Press.

Eliade, Mircea (1965), *Le sacré et le profane*, Paris: Gallimard.

Elias, Norbert (2001), *The Society of Individuals*, London: Continuum (1st edn 1991).

Eliasoph, Nina (1998), *Avoiding Politics: How Americans Produce Apathy in Everyday Life*, New York: Cambridge University Press.

Eliasoph, Nina and Paul Lichterman (2003), "Culture in Interaction", *American Journal of Sociology*, 108 (4), 735–794.

Elster, Jon (ed.) (1998), *Deliberative Democracy*, Cambridge: Cambridge University Press.

Evans, Geoffrey and Pippa Norris (eds) (1999), *Critical Elections*, London: Sage.

Fairclough, Norman (2000), *New Labour, New Language*, London: Routledge.

Farrell, David and Paul Webb (2000), "Political Parties as Campaign Organizations", in Russell Dalton and Martin Wattenberg (eds), *Parties Without Partisans. Political Change in Advanced Industrial Democracies*, Oxford: Oxford University Press, pp. 102–128.

Faucher, Florence (1999a), *Les habits verts de la politique*, Paris: Presses de Science Po.

Faucher, Florence (1999b), "Is There Room for Democratic Debates at British Labour Party Conferences?", *Political Science Association Annual Conference Paper*, Nottingham.

Faucher, Florence (1999c), "Party Organisation and Democracy. A Comparison of Les Verts and the British Green Party", *GeoJournal*, 47 (3), 487–496.

Faucher, Florence (2000), "Le système électoral britannique", in Pascal Delwitt and Jean-Michel De Waele (eds), *Le mode de scrutin fait-il l'élection?*, Bruxelles: Editions de l'Université de Bruxelles, pp. 51–71.

Faucher, Florence (2003), "Brève passion ou engagement durable? La démocratie interne et le parti conservateur britannique", Pascal Perrineau (dir.), *La démocratie en mouvement*, Paris: Editions de l'Aube, pp. 149–174.

Faucher-King, Florence and Eric Treille (2003), "Managing Intra-Party Democracy: Comparing the French Socialist and British Labour Party Conferences", *French Politics*, 1 (1), 61–82.

Fearon, James D. (1998) "Deliberation as Discussion", in Jon Elster (ed.), *Deliberative Democracy*, Cambridge: Cambridge University Press, pp. 44–68.

Fevre, R.W. (2000), *The Demoralization of Western Culture. Social Theory and the Dilemmas of Modern Living*, London: Continuum.

Fielding, Stephen (2003), *The Labour Party. Continuity and Change in the Making of "New" Labour*, Basingstoke: Palgrave Macmillan.

Finlayson, Alan (2003), *Making Sense of New Labour*, London: Lawrence and Wishart.

Flood, Christopher G. (2002), *Political Myth*, London: Routledge.

Foucault, Michel (1975), *Surveiller et Punir*, Paris: Gallimard (1977, *Discipline and Punish. The Birth of Prison*, London: Allen Lane).

Foucault, Michel (1984), "Le Pouvoir, comment s'exerce-t-il?", in Hubert Dreyfus and Paul Rabinow, *Michel Foucault. Un Parcours Philosophique*, Paris: Gallimard.

Franklin, Bob (2001), "The Hands of History: New Labour, News Management and Governance", in Steve Ludlam and Martin J. Smith (eds), *New Labour in Government*, London: Macmillan, pp. 130–144.

Franklin, Bob (2004), "A Damascene Conversion? New Labour and Media Relations", in Steve Ludlam and Martin J. Smith (eds), *Governing as New Labour. Policy and Politics under Blair*, Basingstoke: Palgrave Macmillan, pp. 88–105.

Gaffney, John (1991), *The Language of Political Leadership in Contemporary Britain*, London: Macmillan.

Gamble, Andrew (2003), *Between Europe and America. The Future of British Politics*, Basingstoke: Palgrave Macmillan.

Gamson, William (1992), "The Social Psychology of Collective Action", in Alan Morris and Carol McClurg-Mueller (eds), *Frontiers in Social Movement Theory*, New Haven: Yale University Press, pp. 53–76.

Gaxie, Daniel (1977), "Economie des partis et rétributions du militantisme", *Revue Française de Science Politique*, 27 (1), 123–154.

Geertz, Clifford (1993), *The Interpretation of Cultures*, London: Fontana.

Gellner, Ernest (1991), "L'animal qui évite les gaffes, ou un faisceau d'hypothèses", in P. Birnbaum and J. Leca (eds), *Sur l'individualisme*, Paris: Presses de Sciences Po, pp. 27–44.

Giddens, Anthony (1984), *La Constitution de la société. Eléments de la théorie de la structuration*, Paris: Presses Universitaires de France.

Giddens, Anthony (1991), *Modernity and Self-Identity. Self and Society in the Late Modern Age*, Cambridge: Polity Press.

Giddens, Anthony (1995), "What's He Up To?", *New Statesman and Society*, 24 February.

Giddens, Anthony (1998), *The Third Way. The Renewal of Social Democracy*, Cambridge: Polity Press.

Goffman, Erving (1990), *The Presentation of Self in Everyday Life*, London: Penguin.

Goody, Jack (1977), "Against Ritual. Loosely Structured Thoughts on a Loosely Defined Topic", in Sally, Moore and Barbara Myerhoff (eds), *Secular Ritual*, Assen/Amsterdam: Van Gorcum and Comp, pp. 25–35.

Gould, Philip (1998), *The Unfinished Revolution. How the Modernisers Saved the Labour Party*, London: Abacus.

Green, Donald and Ian Shapiro (1994), *Pathologies of Rational Choice Theory. A Critique of Applications in Political Science*, New Haven: Yale University Press.

Green Party (1993), *Making Policy. A Handbook for Green Party Members*, Green Party.

Gunther, Richard, José Ramón Montero and Juan J. Linz (eds) (2002), *Political Parties – Old Concepts and New Challenges*, Oxford: Oxford University Press.

Hague, William (1997), "A Fresh Future for the Conservative Party", Speech at Central Office, 23.07.97. Available on line at http://www.conservative-party.org.uk/freshsta.txt ref.: 1108/97.

Hain, Peter (2004), *The Future Party*, London: Catalyst.

Halbwachs, Maurice (1997), *La mémoire collective*, Paris: Albin Michel.

Harmel, Robert and Kenneth Janda (1994), "An Integrated Theory of Party Goals and Party Change", *Journal of Theoretical Politics*, 6 (3), 259–287.

Harris, Phil (2002a), "Strategic Corporate Lobbying. The Evolution of Strategic Political Lobbying in the UK and the Psychological Network Underpinning Machiavellian Marketing", *Journal of Political Marketing*, 1 (1), 237–249.

Harris, Phil (2002b), "Who Pays the Piper? The Funding of Political Campaigning in the UK, US and The Consequences for Political Marketing and Public Affairs", *Journal of Political Marketing*, 1 (2/3), 89–107.

Harris, Phil and Andrew Lock (2002), "Sleaze or Clear Blue Water: The Evolution of Corporate and Pressure Group Representation at the Major UK Party Conferences", *Journal of Public Affairs*, 2 (3), 136–151.

Hay, Colin (1999), *The Political Economy of New Labour*, Manchester: Manchester University Press.

Heath Anthony, Roger Jowell and John Curtice (2001), *The Rise of New Labour*, Oxford: Oxford University Press.

Heffernan, Richard (2000), *New Labour and Thatcherism. Political Change in Britain*, London: Macmillan.

Hirschmann, Albert O. (1970), *Exit, Voice, and Loyalty. Responses to Decline in Firms, Organizations, and States*, Cambridge, MA: Harvard, University Press.

Hirschmann, Albert O. (2002), *Shifting Involvements. Private Interests and Public Action*, Princeton: Princeton University Press (1st edn. 1982).

Hobsbawm, Eric and Terence Ranger (1983), *The Invention of Tradition*, Cambridge: Cambridge University Press.

Hochschild, Arlie Russell (2003), *The Managed Heart. Commercialization of Human Feeling*, Berkeley and Los Angeles: University of California Press (1st edn. 1983).

Holli, A. Semetko (1991), *The Formation of Campaign Agendas: A Comparative Analysis of Party and Media Roles in Recent American and British Elections*, Hove: Erlbaum.

Holt, Robert and John Turner (1968), *Political Parties in Action. The Battle of Barons Court*, London: Collier Macmillan.

Huard, Raymond (1996), *La naissance du parti politique en France*, Paris: Presses de Sciences Po.

Ingle, Stephen (2000), *The British Party System*, London: Pinter.

Inglehart, Ronald (1990), *Culture Shift in Advanced Societies*, Princeton: Princeton University Press.

Jenkins, Simon (1995), *Accountable to None. The Tory Nationalization of Britain*, London: Hamish Hamilton.

Johnson, James (1998), "Arguing for Deliberation", in Jon Elster (ed.), *Deliberative Democracy*, Cambridge: Cambridge University Press, pp. 161–184.

Jones, Nicholas (1999), *Sultans of Spin*, London: Orion.

Jones, Nicholas (2001), *The Control Freaks. How New Labour Gets its Own Way*, London: Politico's.

Judge, David (1999), *Representation Theory and Practice in Britain*, London: Routledge.

Karabell, Zachary (1998), *The Rise and Fall of the Televised Political Convention*, Joan Shorenstein Center discussion paper D 33, Cambridge: Harvard University.

Katz, Richard and Peter Mair (1995), "Changing Models of Party Organization and Party Democracy: The Emergence of the Cartel Party", *Party Politics*, 1 (1), 5–28.

Kavanagh, Dennis (1996), "British Party Conferences and the Political Rhetoric of the 1990s", *Government and Opposition*, 31 (1), 27–44.

Kelly, Richard (1989), *Conservative Party Conferences: The Hidden System*, Manchester: Manchester University Press.

Kelly, Richard (1994), "The Party Conferences", in Anthony Seldon and Stuart Ball (eds), *Conservative Century. The Conservative Party since 1900*, Oxford: Oxford University Press, pp. 221–260.

Kelly, Richard (1999), "Party Activity and the Making of Party Policy an Overview", in R. Kelly (ed.), *Changing Party Policy in Britain An Introduction*, London: Blackwell.

Kenny, Michael and Martin Smith (1997), "(Mis)understanding Blair", *The Political Quarterly*, 68 (3), 220–230.

Kertzer, David (1988), *Ritual Politics and Power*, New Haven: Yale University Press.

Kertzer, David (1996), *Politics and Symbols. The Italian Communist Party and the Fall of Communism*, New Haven: Yale University Press.

King, Richard (1999), *Orientalism and Religion. Postcolonial Theory, India and "The Mystic East"*, London: Routledge.

Kirchheimer, Otto (1966), "The Transformation of Western European Party Systems", in J. La Polambara and M. Weiner (eds), *Political Parties and Political Development*, Princeton, NJ: Princeton University Press, pp. 177–200.

Kitschelt, Herbert (1990), "New Social Movements and the Decline of Party Organization", in Dalton and Kuechler (eds), *Challenging the Political Order. New Social Movements in Western Democracies*, Oxford: Polity, pp. 179–208.

Klandermans, Bert (1992), "The Social Construction of Protest and Multiorganizational Fields", in Alan Morris and Carol McClurg-Mueller (eds), *Frontiers in Social Movement Theory*, New Haven, Co: Yale University Press, pp. 77–103.

Klandermans, Bert and Dirk Oemega (1987), "Potentials, Networks, Motivations, and Barriers: Steps Towards Participation in Social Movements", *American Sociological Review*, 52, 519–531.

Klandermans, Bert, Hans Kriesi and Sydney Tarrow (eds) (1988), *From Structure to Action*, Greewich, CT: JAI Press.

Kuper, Adam (1999), *Culture: The Anthropologists' Account*, Cambridge MA: Harvard University Press.

Labour Coordinating Committee (1982), *Pamphlet*.

Labour Coordinating Committee (1996), *New Labour: A Stakeholders' Party. The Interim Report of the Labour Co-ordinating Committee's Commission on Party Democracy*.

Labour Party (1991a), *Conference Verbatim*.

Labour Party (1991b), *National Executive Committee Conference Report*.

Labour Party (1996), *National Executive Committee Report*, London: Labour Party.

Labour Party (1997), *Partnership in Power*.

Labour Party (1999), *21st Century Party. Members – The Key to Our Future*.

Lardellier, Pascal (2003), *Théorie du lien rituel. Anthropologie et communication*, Paris: L'Harmattan.

Lawson, Kay (ed.) (1994), *How Political Parties Work. Perspective from Within*, London: Praeger.

Lawson, Kay and Peter Merkl (eds) (1988), *When Parties Fail*, Princeton: Princeton University Press.

Lees-Marshment Jennifer (2001), *Political Marketing & British Political Parties*, Manchester: Manchester University Press.

Lees-Marshment, Jennifer and Darren Lilleker (2001), "Political Marketing and Traditional Values: Old Labour for New Times", *Contemporary Politics*, 7 (3), 205–216.

Lees-Marshment, Jennifer and Stuart Quayle (2000), "Spinning the Party or Empowering the Members? The Conservative Party Reforms of 1998", *Political Studies Association Annual Conference Paper*.

Le Galès, Patrick (2004), "Contrôle et surveillance: Les instruments de la restructuration de l'Etat en Grande-Bretagne", in Le Galès Patrick and Pierre Lascoume (eds), *Les instruments de l'action publique*, Paris: Presses de Sciences Po, pp. 253–272.

Leys, Colin (2001), *Market Driven Politics. Neoliberal Democracy and the Public Interest*, London: Verso.

Liberal Democrats (2001), *Federal Executive Report*, London: Liberal Democrats.

Lincoln, Bruce (1989), *Discourse and the Construction of Society. Comparative Myth, Ritual and Classification*, Oxford and New York: Oxford University Press.

Ludlam, Steve (2001a), "The Making of New Labour", in Steve Ludlam and Martin J. Smith (eds), *New Labour in Government*, London: Macmillan, pp. 1–31.

Ludlam, Steve (2001b), "New Labour and the Unions: The End of the Contentious Alliance", in Steve Ludlam and Martin J. Smith (eds), *New Labour in Government*, London: Macmillan, pp. 111–129.

Lukes, Stephen (1975), "Political Ritual and Social Integration", *Sociology. Journal of the British Sociological Association*, 9 (2), 289–308.

Mackie, Gerry (1998), "All Men Are Liars. Is Democracy Meaningless?", in John Elster (ed.), *Deliberative Democracy*, Cambridge: Cambridge University Press, pp. 69–96.

Mair, Peter (ed.) (1990), *The West European Party System*, Oxford: Oxford University Press.

Mair, Peter (1994), "Party Organisations: From Civil Society to the State", in Richard Katz and Peter Mair (eds), *How Parties Organize*, London: Sage.

Mair, Peter (1997), *Party System Change*, Oxford: Clarendon Press.

Mair, Peter (2000), "Partyless Democracy: Solving the Paradox of New Labour?", *New Left Review*, 2 (2), 21–35.

Manin, Bernard (1987), "On Legitimacy and Political Deliberation", *Political Theory*, 15 (3), 338–368.

Manin, Bernard (1996), *Principes du gouvernement représentatif*, Paris: Flammarion.

March, James and J. Olsen (1989), *Rediscovering Institutions: The Organizational Basis of Politics*, New York: Free Press.

Marquand, David (2000), "Democracy in Britain", *Political Quarterly*, 71 (2).

Martin, Alan and Philip Cowley (1999), "Ambassadors in the Community? Labour Party Members in Society", *Politics*, 19 (2) 89–96.

May, John D. (1973), "Opinion Structure of Political Parties: The Special Law of Curvilinear Disparity", *Political Studies*, 21 (2), 135–151.

McAdam, Doug (1988), *Freedom Summer*, New York: Oxford University Press.

McCombs, Maxwell and Donald Shaw (1972), "The Agenda Setting Function of the Mass Media", *Public Opinion Quarterly*, 36, 176–185.

McGinniss, Joe (1979), *The Selling of the President*, London: Penguin.

McKee, Vincent (1994), "British Liberal Democrats: Structures and Groups on the Inside", *Political Studies Association*, http://www.psa.ac.uk/cps/1994/mckee. pdf.

McKenzie, Robert (1964), *British Political Parties. The Distribution of Power Within the Conservative and Labour Parties*, London: Heinemann.

Melucci, Alberto (1989), *Nomads of the Present. Social Movements and the Individual Needs in Contemporary Society*, London: Hutchinson radius, p. 288.

Merelman, Richard (1991), *Partial Visions. Culture and Politics in Britain, Canada and the United States*, Madison: University of Wisconsin Press.

Meyer, John and Brian Rowan (1977), "Institutionalized Organizations: Formal Structure as Myth and Ceremony", *American Journal of Sociology*, 83 (2), 340–363.

Michels, Robert (1962), *Political Parties: A Sociological Study of the Oligarchic Tendencies of Modern Democracies*, New York: The Free Press (1st edn 1911).

Miller, David and William Dinan (2000), "The Rise of the PR Industry in Britain, 1979–98", *European Journal of Communication*, 15 (1), 5–35.

Minkin, Lewis (1980), *The Labour Party Conference. A Study in the Politics of Intra-Party Democracy*, Manchester: Manchester University Press.

Minkin, Lewis (1991), *The Contentious Alliance. Trade Unions and the Labour party*, Edinburgh: Edinburgh University Press.

Mitchell, Austin (2000), "Making of a Minister", *The House Magazine*, 913 (25), 114–116.

Moore, Sally F. (1977), "Political Meetings and the Simulation of Unanimity: Kilimanjaro 1973", in Sally Moore and Barabar Myerhoff (eds), *Secular Rituals*, Amsterdam: Van Gorcum, pp. 151–172.

Morris, R.J. (1990), "Clubs, Societies and Associations", in F.M.L. Thompson (ed.), *The Cambridge Social History of Britain. 1750–1950. Vol. 3 Social Agencies and Institutions*, Cambridge: Cambridge University Press, pp. 395–443.

Morris, Rupert (1991), *Tories. From Village Hall to Westminster: A Political Sketch*, London: Mainstream Publishing.

Morrissey, John and John Norris (1993), *A New Direction*, pamphlet.

Moscovici, Serge and Willem Doise (1992), *Dissensions et consensus. Une théorie générale des décisions collectives*, Paris: Presses Universitaires de France.

Myerhoff, Barbara (1984), "A Death in Due Time: Construction of Self and Culture in Ritual Drama", in John McAloon (ed.), *Rite, Drama, Festival, Spectacle. Rehearsals Towards a Theory of Cultural Performance*, Philadelphia: ISHI Publication, pp. 149–178.

Needham, Catherine (2003), *Citizen-consumers. New Labour Marketplace Democracy*, London: The Catalyst Forum working paper.

Neill, Lord (1998), *Report of the Committee on Standards in Public Life on the Finding of Political Parties in the UK*, vol. 1, CM4057-1, London: Stationery Office.

Newcomb, Theodore, Ralph Turner and Philip Converse (1965), *Social Psychology: The Study of Human Interaction*, New York: Holt, Rinehart and Winston.

Newman, Janet (2001), *Modernising Governance. New Labour, Policy and Society*, London: Sage.

Nimmo, Dan and James E. Combs (1990), *Mediated Political Realities*, NY, London: Longman.

Norris, Pippa (1995), "May's Law of Curvilinear Disparity Revisited: Leaders, Officers, Members and Voters in British Political Parties", *Party Politics*, 1 (1), 29–48.

Norris, Pippa (ed.) (1999), *Critical Citizens. Global Support for Democratic Governance*, Oxford: Oxford University Press.

Norris, Pippa (2000), *A Virtuous Circle. Political Communications in Postindustrial Societies*, Cambridge: Cambridge University Press.

Norris, Pippa (2003), "Preaching to the Converted? Pluralism, Participation and Party Websites", *Party Politics*, 9 (1), 21–45.

Norris, Pippa, John Curtice, David Sanders, Maggie Scammell and Holli Semetko (1999), *On Message. Communicating the Campaign*, London: Sage.

Norris, Pippa and Joni Lovenduski (1995), *Political Recruitment. Gender, Race and Class in the British Parliament*, Cambridge: Cambridge University Press.

Norton, Philip (1990), "The Lady's Not for Turning but What About the Rest? Margaret Thatcher and the Conservative Party 1979–1989", *Parliamentary Affairs*, 43, 41–58.

Norton, Philip and Arthur Aughey (1981), *Conservatives and Conservatism*, London: Temple Smith.

Olson, Mancur (1965), *The Logic of Collective Action: Public Goods and the Theory of Groups*, Cambridge, MA: Harvard University Press.

Ostrogorski, Moisei (1979), *La démocratie et les partis politiques*, Paris: Seuil (1st edn 1902).

Panebianco, Angelo (1988), *Political Parties: Organization and Power*, Cambridge: Cambridge University Press.

Parkin, Sara (1989), *Green Parties. An International Guide*, London: Heretic Books.

Pattie, Charles, Patrick Seyd and Paul Whiteley (2004), *Citizenship in Britian. Values, Participation and Democracy*, Cambridge: Cambridge University Press.

Paxman, Jeremy (2003), *The Political Animal*, London: Penguin.

Peele, Gillian (1997), "Towards 'New Conservatives'? Organisational Reform and the Conservative Party", *The Political Quarterly*, 69 (2), 141–147.

Pharr, Susan and Robert Putnam (2000), *Disaffected Democracies. What's Troubling the Trilateral Countries?*, Princeton: Princeton University Press.

Pizzorno, Alessandro (1978), "Political Exchange and Collective Identity in Industrial Conflict", Colin Crouch and Alessandro Pizzorno (eds), *The Resurgence of Class Conflict in Western Europe*, New York: Holmes and Meier.

Pizzorno, Alessandro (1986), "Some Other Kinds of Otherness: A Critique of 'Rational Choice' Theories", in Alejandro Foxley, Michael McPherson and Guillermo O'Donnel (eds), *Development, Democracy and the Art of Trespassing. Essays in Honor of A. O. Hirschman*, Notre Dame, Indiana: University of Notre Dame Press, pp. 355–373.

Pizzorno, Alessandro (1991), "La rationalité du choix démocratique", in Pierre Birnbaum and Jean Leca, *Sur l'individualisme*, Paris: Presses de Sciences Po, pp. 330–369.

Polletta, Francesca (2002), *Freedom Is an Endless Meeting: Democracy in American Social Movements*, Chicago: Chicago University Press.

Powell, W.W. and P.J. DiMaggio (eds) (1991), *The New Institutionalism in Organizational Analysis*, Chicago: University of Chicago Press.

Power, Michael (1999), *The Audit Society. Rituals of Verification*, Oxford: Oxford University Press.

Punnett, Robert Malcolm (1992), *Selecting the Party Leader. Britain in Comparative Perspective*, London: Harvester Wheatsheaf.

Punnett, Robert Malcolm (1987), *British Government and Politics*, Aldershot: Dartmouth.

Rasmussen, Jorgen (1965), *The Liberal Party. A Study of Retrenchment and Revival*, London: Constable.

Rawnsley, Andrew (2001), *Servants of the People*, London: Penguin.

Rhodes, R.A.W. (1994), "The Hollowing Out of the State", *Political Quarterly*, 65.

Richards, David and Martin J. Smith (2004), "The 'Hybrid' State: Labour's Response to the Challenge of Governance", in Steve Ludlam and Martin J. Smith (eds), *Governing as New Labour. Policy and Politics under Blair*, Basingstoke: Palgrave Macmillan, pp. 106–125.

Rivière, Claude (1988), *Les liturgies politiques*, Paris: Presses Universitaires de France.

Rose, Nikolas (1999), *Powers of Freedom. Reframing Political Thought*, Cambridge: Cambridge University Press.

Rosenbaum, M. (1997), *From Soapbox to Soundbite: Party Political Campaigning in Britain since 1945*, Basingstoke: Macmillan.

Rose, Richard and Ian McAllister (1986), *Voters Begin to Choose: From Closed-Class to Open Elections in Britain*, London: Sage.

Routledge, Paul (1999), *Mandy. The Unauthorised Biography of Peter Mandelson*, London: Simon and Schuster.

Rüdig, Wolfgang and Mark Franklin (1992), "The Green Voter in the 1989 European Elections", *Environmental Politics*, 1 (4), 129–159.

Rüdig, Wolfgang, Lynn G. Bennie and Mark N. Franklin (1991), *Green Party Members. A Profile*, Glasgow: Delta Publications.

Russell, Andrew and Edward Fieldhouse (2005), *Neither Left nor Right? The Liberal Democrats and the Electorate*, Manchester: Manchester University Press.

Russell, Meg (2005), *Building New Labour. The Politics of Party Organisation*, Basingstoke: Palgrave Macmillan.

Salaman, Graeme (1997), "Culturing Production", in Paul Du Gay (ed.), *Production of Culture/Cultures of Production*, London: Sage, pp. 236–268.

Sartori, Giovanni (1976), *Parties and Party Systems: A Framework for Analysis*, Cambridge: Cambridge University Press.

Sawyer, Tom (2000), *The Politics of Leadership*, London: Progress.

Scammell, Margaret (1995), *Designer Politics: How Elections are Won*, Basingstoke: Macmillan.

Scarrow, Susan (1996), *Parties and Their Members*, Oxford: Oxford University Press.

Scarrow, Susan (1999), "Parties and the Expansion of Direct Democracy: Who Benefits?", in *Party Politics*, 5 (3), 341–362.

Scarrow, Susan, Paul Webb and David Farrell (2000), "From Social Integration to Electoral Contestation: The Changing Distribution of Power Within Political Parties", in Russell Dalton and Martin Wattenberg (eds), *Parties Without Partisans. Political Change in Advanced Industrial Democracies*, Oxford: Oxford University Press, pp. 129–153.

Schattschneider, Elmer E. (1942), *Party Government*, New York: Rinehart.

Schlesinger, Joseph (1994), *Political Parties and the Winning of Office*, Ann Arbor: University of Michigan.

Schuessler, Alexander (2000), *A Logic of Expressive Choice*, Princeton: Princeton University Press.

Schumpeter, Joseph (1942), *Capitalism, Socialism and Democracy*, London: Allen and Unwin.

Scott, Andrew (2000), *Running on Empty. Modernising the British and Australian Labour Parties*, Annandale: Pluto Press.

Scott, David (2003), "Culture in Political Theory", *Political Theory*, 31 (1), 92–115.

Seiler, Daniel-Louis (2003), *Les partis politiques en Occident. Sociologie historique du phénomène partisan*, Paris: Ellipse.

Seldon, Anthony (1996), "When Tory Governments Fail", in A. Seldon (ed.), *How Tory Governments Fail: The Tory Party in Power since 1873*, London: HarperCollins.

Seldon, Anthony and Stuart Ball (eds) (1994), *Conservative Century. The Conservative Party since 1900*, Oxford: Oxford University Press.

Sennett, Richard (1986), *The Fall of Public Man*, London: Faber and Faber.

Seyd, Patrick (1987), *The Rise and Fall of the Labour Left*, London: Macmillan.

Seyd, Patrick (1998), "Tony Blair and New Labour", in Anthony King, David Denver, Iain McLean, Pippa Norris, Phillip Norton, David Sanders and Patrick Seyd (eds), *New Labour Triumphs: Britain at the Polls*, Chatham, NJ: Chatham House, pp. 49–73.

Seyd, Patrick (1999), "New Parties/New Politics? A Case Study of the British Labour Party", *Party Politics*, 5 (3), 383–405.

Seyd, Patrick and Whiteley Paul (1992), *Labour's Grass Roots. The Politics of Party Membership*, Oxford: Clarendon Press.

Seyd, Patrick and Whiteley Paul (2001), "Conservative Grassroots: An Overview", in Steve Ludlam and Martin Smith (eds), *New Labour in Government*, London: Macmillan, pp. 73–85.

Seyd, Patrick and Paul Whiteley (2002), *New Labour's Grassroots. The Transformation of the Labour Party Membership*, Basingstoke: Palgrave Macmillan.

Seyd, Patrick and Paul Whiteley (2005), *Third Force Politics: Liberal Democrats at the Grassroots*, Oxford: Oxford University Press.

Shaw, Eric (1994), *The Labour Party since 1979. Crisis and Transformation*, London: Routledge.

Shaw, Eric (1996), *The Labour Party since 1945. Old Labour: New Labour*, Oxford: Blackwell.

Shaw, Eric (2000), "The Wilderness Years, 1979–1994", in Brian Brivati and Richard Heffernan (eds), *The Labour Party. A Centenary History*, London: Macmillan, pp. 112–142.

Shaw, Eric (2004), "The Control Freaks? New Labour and the Party", in Steve Ludlam and Martin J. Smith (eds), *Governing as New Labour. Policy and Politics under Blair*, Basingstoke: Palgrave Macmillan, pp. 52–69.

Sklair, Leslie (2001), *The Transnational Capitalist Class*, Oxford: Blackwell.

Smith, Martin (2000), "From Old to New Labour, 1994–2000," in Brian Brivati and Richard Heffernan (eds), *The Labour Party. A Centenary History*, London: Macmillan, pp. 143–162.

Smith, Philip (2001), *Cultural Theory. An Introduction*, Oxford: Blackwell.

Snow, David A. and Robert D. Benford (1988), "Ideology, Frame Resonance, and Participative Mobilization", in Bert Klandermans, Hans Kriesi and Sydney Tarrow (eds), *From Structure to Action*, Greewich, CT: JAI Press, pp. 197–218.

Stanyer, James (1997), "The 1996 British Party Conferences as News Events: Assessing the Contribution of the Broadcasters to Conference News Agendas", *Contemporary Political Studies*, Volume 1, Oxford: Blackwell, pp. 53–61.

Stanyer, James (2001), *The Creation of Political News. Television and British Party Political Conferences*, Brighton: Sussex Academic Press.

Stanyer, James and Maggie Scammel (1996), "On the Fringe: The Changing Nature of the Party Conference Fringe and its Coverage by the Media", *Political Studies Association Annual Conference Paper*.

Strauss, Anselm (1959), *Mirrors and Masks. The Search for Identity*, New Brunswick and London: Transaction Publishers.

Sullivan, Denis G. and Roger D. Masters (1993), "Nonverbal Behavior, Emotions, and Democratic Leadership", in George E. Marcus and Russell L. Hanson (eds), *Reconsidering the Democratic Public*, University Park: Pennsylvania State University Press, pp. 307–332.

Swidler, Ann (1986), "Culture in Action: Symbols and Strategies", *American Sociological Review*, 51, 273–286.

Taylor, Gerald (1997), *Labour's Renewal? The Policy Review and Beyond*, Basingstoke: Palgrave Macmillan.

Teorell, Jan (1999), "A Deliberative Defence of Intra-party Democracy", *Party Politics*, 5 (3), 363–382.

Thatcher, Margaret (1993), *The Downing Street Years*, London: Harper and Collins.

Tether, Philip (1996), "The Party in the Country: Development and Influence" and "The Party in the Country: Members and Organisation", P. Norton (ed.), *The Conservative Party*, London: Prentice Hall, pp. 97–126.

Thompson, Kenneth (1992), "Social Pluralism and Post-Modernity", in Stuart Hall, David Held and Tony McGrew (eds), *Modernity and Its Futures*, Cambridge: Polity Press.

Topf, Richard (1995), "Beyond Electoral Participation", in Klingemann Hans-Dieter and Dieter Fuchs (dir.) (1995), *Citizens and the State. Beliefs in Government*, Oxford: Oxford University Press, pp. 52–91.

Turner, Victor (1974), *Dramas, Fields, and Metaphors. Symbolic Action in Human Society*, Ithaca and London: Cornell University Press.

Turner, Victor (1982), *From Ritual to Theatre. The Human Seriousness of Play*, NY: Performing Arts Journal Publication.

Turner, Victor (1989a), *The Ritual Process. Structure and Anti-Structure*, Ithaca: Cornell University Press.

Turner, Victor (1989b), *The Forest of Symbols. Aspects of Ndembu Rituals*, Ithaca: Cornell University Press.

Ware, Alan (1992), "Activist-Leader Relations and the Structure of Political Parties: Exchange Models and Vote Seeking Behaviour in Parties", *British Journal of Political Science*, 22 (1), 71–92.

Ware, Alan (1996), *Political Parties and Party Systems*, Oxford: Oxford University Press.

Webb, Paul (1994), "Party Organizational Change in Britain: The Iron Law of Centralization?", in Richard Katz and Peter Mair (eds), *How Parties Organize*, London: Sage, pp. 109–133.

Webb, Paul (2000), *The Modern British Party System*, London: Sage.

Webb, Paul (2002), "Political Parties in Britain. Secular Decline or Adaptative Resilience?", in Paul Webb, David Farrell and Ian Holliday (eds), *Political Parties in Advanced Industrial Democracies*, Oxford: Oxford University Press.

Webb, Paul and J. Fisher (1999), "The Changing British Party System: Two Party Equilibrium or the Emergence of Moderate Pluralism?", in D. Broughton and M. Donavon (eds), *Changing Party Systems in Western Europe*, London: Pinter.

Wedeen, Lisa (1998), "Acting 'As If': Symbolic Politics and Social Control in Syria", *Society for Comparative Study of Society and History*, 40 (3), 503–523.

Wedeen, Lisa (2002), "Conceptualizing Culture: Possibilities for Political Science", *American Political Science Review*, 96 (4), 713–727.

Welch, Stephen (1993), *The Concept of Political Culture*, New York: St Martin's Press.

Whiteley, Paul F. and Patrick Seyd (2002), *High Intensity Participation. The Dynamics of Party Activism in Britain*, Ann Arbor: University of Michigan Press.

Whiteley, Paul, Patrick Seyd and Jeremy Richardson (1994), *True Blues. The Politics of Conservative Party Membership*, Oxford: Clarendon Press.

Whyte, William F. (1993), *Street Corner Society. The Social Structures of an Italian Slum*, Chicago: University of Chicago Press, pp. 232–235.

Willetts, David (1998), "Conservative Renewal", *The Political Quaterly*, 69 (2), 110–117.

Wilson, David (2004), "New Patterns of Central-Local Government Relations", Stoker Gerry and David Wilson (eds), *British Local Government into the 21st Century*, Basingstoke: Palgrave Macmillan.

Wilson, Frank (1994), "The Sources of Party Change: The Social Democratic Parties of Britain, France, Germany and Spain", in Lawson Kay (ed.), *How Political Parties Work. Perspective from Within*, London: Praeger, pp. 263–284.

Wolinetz, Steven (2002), "Beyond the Catch-all Party: Approaches to the Study of Parties and Party Organization, Contemporary Democracies", in Gunther Richard, José Ramón Montero and Juan J. Linz (eds), *Political Parties – Old Concepts and New Challenges*, Oxford: Oxford University Press, pp. 136–165.

Wring, Dominic (1998), "The Media and Intra-Party Democracy: 'New' Labour and the Clause Four Debate in Britain", *Democratization*, 5 (2), 42–61.

Index